THE NEW MAINSTREAM

THE NEW MAINSTREAM

How the Multicultural Consumer
Is Transforming American Business

GUY GARCIA

An Imprint of HarperCollinsPublishers

HarperCollins books may be purchased for educational, business, or sales promotional use. For information, please write: Special Markets Department, HarperCollins Publishers Inc., 10 East 53rd Street, New York, NY 10022.

FIRST EDITION

Designed by Kate Nichols

Printed on acid-free paper

Library of Congress Cataloging-in-Publication Data is available upon request.

ISBN 0-06-058465-3

04 05 06 07 08   DIX/RRD   10 9 8 7 6 5 4 3

If we carefully examine the social and political state of America, after having studied its history, we shall remain perfectly convinced that not an opinion, not a custom, not a law, I may even say not an event is upon record which the origin of that people will not explain. —ALEXIS DE TOCQUEVILLE

Would it not be true to say that North Americans prefer to use reality rather than to know it? —OCTAVIO PAZ

You know the world's gone crazy when the world's greatest rapper is white and the world's greatest golfer is black. —CHRIS ROCK

Contents

Introduction

When Christopher Columbus set foot on the shores of the New World, one of his first recorded impressions was of the natives, whom he described as "young . . . well made with fine shapes and faces. . . . Some paint themselves with black, which makes them appear like those of the Canaries, neither black nor white; others with white, others with red, and others with such colors as they can find."[1] Columbus could hardly have guessed that more than five hundred years later his description of Americans as a youthful, multicolored tribe enhancing and inventing their identity from a palette of countless hues would ring uncannily true.

America is a nation transformed by the fulfillment of its own ideals. Never has its population and culture been more vibrant and diverse, never has it been more reflective of—and connected to—the rest of the world. The new America is taking root in major cities, suburbs, and towns. The new America exists at the lowest rungs of the socioeconomic ladder and is striving for a better foothold at the top. The new America is defining—and defined by—the urban lifestyle, but it is also moving to the suburbs and smaller rural towns. The new America is transforming life at the office, where managers seek to increase productivity by diversifying their workforce; at the beauty parlor, where Anglo socialites use hair relaxers created for African Americans; and on the Internet, where online communities for Hispanics, Asians, African Americans, and other groups are competing with major portals for eyeballs and cybercash. It is changing how we look and what we drive, what we eat and why we eat it. Most of all, it is changing how people make money and spend it, where it comes from and where it is going.

Today, the 80 million blacks, Hispanics, and Asians living in the United States make up more than one-fourth of the country and spend over $1.2 trillion a year. By 2050, non-Anglos will have grown to 47.2 percent of the population. Hispanics, blacks, and Asians are already outpacing the rest of the United States in terms of population and income growth. The buying power of Latinos alone is growing at a compound rate of 8.7 percent, almost double that of non-Hispanics, and is projected to reach $926 billion by 2007.[2] As a group, the nation's non-Anglo minorities purchase more consumer goods than the general population, are more brand loyal, and collectively represent other important new social patterns, influencing everything from images in advertising to attitudes about religion, family, education, and the afterlife.

Led by the growing statistical clout and buying power of Hispanics, blacks, Asians, and other so-called minorities, the New Mainstream is a loose but sweeping coalition of groups that for myriad reasons have been forced to forge an identity outside the Old Mainstream. Yet the New Mainstream consumes media, products, and services at a greater rate than the general population.

In an effort to tap the lucrative new markets of the multicultural masses, corporations are changing their image to reflect the ethnically savvy sensibilities of the new American consumer. Even politicians—reading the writing on the wall and noticing it's not necessarily in English—are asking for your vote, *arigato, obrigado, por favor*. The continuing influx and confluence of new people, nationalities, and ideas is not only reshaping and invigorating the American economy and ensuring growth and prosperity for years to come, it is redefining and reaffirming the very essence of what it means to be an American.

Not since the original thirteen colonies declared their independence from the British crown has the Latin phrase inscribed on the one-dollar bill, *Novus Ordo Seclorum*—words that announced "a New Order of the Ages," an era of opportunity, community, and justice not just for America, but for all of mankind—been more palpably true. The future, as Rainer Maria Rilke observed, "enters into us, in order to transform itself in us, long before it happens."

That future is upon us, and the transformation of the mainstream has long since begun. But transformation into what?

To be sure, most Americans, to one degree or another, are aware that something important is happening. We know that if present demographic trends continue, European non-Hispanic whites will eventually be outnumbered, that Hispanics have overtaken African Americans as the country's largest minority, that foreign-born immigrants—both legal and undocumented—are changing the flavor, texture, and look of American neighborhoods, schools, and churches. We know that these newcomers are from many different countries, are of every race, and speak many languages, though often not English. We might also know that salsa long ago replaced ketchup as the country's most popular condiment, that Oprah can make or break a book, that gays have better taste than straights, and that women and people of color can—and do—run major corporations.

But what most Americans might not realize is that the culturally charged images they see on TV and in the streets are just the visible tip of a deeper, more fundamental change. It is a change that cuts across corporations, institutions, and organizations and is putting a transnational spin on the increasingly global realms of business, politics, and media. Most Americans might also be surprised to find out that this same demographic and social shift—a "New Mainstream" of foreigners, trendsetters, outsiders, and iconoclasts—which some regard as a threat to the American way of life, is in fact its most likely salvation. The New Mainstream is the latest chapter in a story that reaches back to the birth of the Republic, and has roots in the formative milestones of Manifest Destiny and the closing of the American frontier. It is the story of who Americans have been, and who they are becoming.

Creative Currents

Wider than a movement and deeper than a trend, the New Mainstream is an unprecedented intersection of demographic, cultural, and economic forces that are remolding the rhythms and textures of American society. The Old Mainstream—and the Eurocentric, agroindustrial values that go with it—is shrinking even as a new cultural movement rides the crest of a major demographic wave. As population trends and the profit-driven interests of corporations converge, they are being joined by a potent third force: the rise of the so-called knowledge workers, or the "creative class." Young, affluent, and highly educated, the creative class creates and maintains the infrastructures, systems, and content for the information age. Members of this group, often referred to as "explorers," "first adopters," or "tastemakers," tend not only to be tolerant of communities and cultures that are not their own, but are more likely to find value in—and actively seek out—experiences and customs that add flavor, variety, and diversity to their lives.

This attitude is the antithesis of ethnocentric nativism (think Old Mainstream) and synchs perfectly with the increasingly multicultural dimensions of today's international youth and entertainment industries. The cultural shift is evident all around us. From the sudden respectability—and soaring value—of African American "outsider art" and Australian aboriginal paintings to the Afro-Asian tinge of Broadway's The Lion King and megahit movies like Spy Kids and The Matrix, the cumulative impact of this simultaneous massing and fragmentation of the population is the principal engine behind the New Mainstream.

The convergence of America's creative and multicultural classes is the driving force behind the postethnic economy—a consumer-driven market in which race and ethnicity are blended into the buying habits and behaviors that drive two-thirds of the U.S. gross domestic product (GDP). In his book The Rise of the Creative Class, Richard Florida, an economist at Carnegie Mellon University, defines members of the creative class as those "who [use] creativity as a key factor" in their work—for instance, engineers, architects, designers, writers, artists, and musicians. In his analysis of U.S. census data, Florida detected a "tectonic shift in the U.S. class structure" during the last two decades of the twentieth century as both the creative and service class sectors grew larger than the declining blue-collar working class. He estimates that by 2000 there were 38 million members of the creative class, or 30 percent of the U.S. workforce, versus 33 million working-class workers. The largest group was the service class, with 55.2 million workers, or 43 percent of the U.S. workforce.[3]

Because of its association with—and thirst for—the bold, the new, and the hip in business, media, and the arts, the creative class tends to influence and lead the way for other social groups. But in the multicultural Milieu of the New Mainstream, the opposite is also true. This blurring effect increases as age decreases and spills over into the more progressive elements of the working and service classes. Despite the disparity in average salary between the creative and service-class worker (about $50,000 a year versus $22,000, respectively, in 1999),[4] there is a significant overlap between the two groups in terms of social values, attitudes, and aspirations. The college-educated nanny in New Haven, Connecticut, who quit her full-time job to watch the children of an Irish American urban housing architect while she tries her hand as a playwright just might share her employer's desire for flexible hours and work that aims to improve people's lives, not to mention a fondness for Audi automobiles and Thai cooking. Meanwhile, the architect's Puerto Rican cleaning lady shares his Catholic faith and a determination to build a better life through hard work and self-improvement.

The symbiotic relationship between the creative and service classes—which together constitute three-fourths of the total American workforce—has other, less obvious dimensions. Members of the creative class regard food, music, and art from other cultures as an avenue for personal enlightenment and growth. Exposure to people and ideas from around the world is something they take for granted and complements their feelings about social responsibility, protecting the environment, civil and women's rights, and other socially progressive values that characterize their outlook. Thus the relationship between the architect and his cleaning lady goes well beyond a financial transaction. As she straightens up his living room, her hands brush past a dog-eared copy of *One Hundred Years of Solitude* by Gabriel García Márquez and CDs by Jennifer Lopez, Marc Anthony, and Eminem. On the next shelf, not far from the framed photos of his back-packing trip to Nepal, are DVD copies of *Y Tu Mamá También*, a Mexican film that features an all Latino cast and English subtitles, and *Monsoon Wedding*, an Indian film set in New Delhi that the architect bought on realgoodmovies.com. "Creative-minded people enjoy a mix of influences," writes Florida. "They want to hear different kinds of music and try different kinds of food. They want to meet and socialize with people unlike themselves, to trade views and spar over issues. A person's circle of closest friends may not resemble the Rainbow Coalition—in fact it usually does not—but he or she wants the rainbow to be available."[5]

This notion that cultural diversity is a basic element of a rich and fulfilling life is not just affecting how many Americans work, but also determining where they live. Florida discovered that the creative class tended to gravitate to cities, or "creative centers," that met their expectations for a diverse cultural lifestyle—and that the corporations that depended on the creative class for its workforce tended to follow them there. When Florida graded the nation's largest forty-nine metropolitan areas in terms of employment opportunities, concentrations of high-tech and innovative industries, population growth, and general economic vitality and cross-indexed them with a "composite diversity index" or CDI—which combined higher than average concentrations of immigrants, gays, and artists—he discovered a high correlation between cultural diversity and economic progress. Simply put, diversity breeds money.

The economic value of social diversity is even greater if one considers the ripple effects of putting a premium on the value of art and entertainment. In New York City, where the two leading industries are tourism and Wall Street, businessman-turned-mayor Michael Bloomberg has wisely put an emphasis on boosting the city's reputation as a cultural mecca. By attracting tourists and financial executives to its eclectic mix of museums, restaurants, theaters, and teeming public spaces, New York's cultural diversity buoys the municipal economy, reinforcing the perception of New York as the world's number one tourist and business destination, which creates more jobs, which in turn draws more immigrants and artists. It's a self-perpetuating cycle. If New York were ever to lose its creative edge, that cycle would sooner or later begin to reverse, draining the city of energy, people, and money. From that perspective, cultural diversity is the true foundation of New York's fiscal health and the key to its economic future.

The same dynamic, to one extent or another, applies to every city and town in America and every industry and institution, raising questions that affect each and every one of us. Corporations, for example, need to understand how the New Mainstream is changing not just the marketing of and advertising of products, but the conception and development of the product itself. Why is cultural diversity key to boosting the bottom line of any and every business, no matter where it is or what it sells? How does the New Mainstream embody and reinforce the core values that always have—and still do—make America great? Why are history, nationality and identity critical to understanding the modern consumer—and the economic future of our country? In what ways is the New Mainstream altering how Americans look at themselves and the world—and how the world looks back at us? Why is the one dollar bill the ultimate New Mainstream document? What happens when the minorities become the majority, and consumer economics become the principle driver of social change? Finally, what lies beyond the New Mainstream, and who is the post-ethnic consumer?

As the demographic and economic currents of the New Mainstream converge and swell, the redefinition and affirmation of democratic principles—the universal right to life, liberty, and the pursuit of happiness—is being advanced simultaneously on multiple fronts: the aspirations of immigrants and minorities seeking to realize their version of the American dream, the balance sheet aspirations of corporations eager to tap the ballooning influence and buying power of the nation's ethnic minorities, and the financial windfall being enjoyed by cities and towns whose cultural riches are a magnet for the diversity-loving legions of the creative class. The blending of these powerful interests, and how they are transforming every aspect of American life, is the driving force behind the New Mainstream. Diversity and dollars have become symbiotic and intrinsically linked. The new color of money is black, brown, red, yellow, and white, male and female, gay and straight. When the mix is right, we all win.

PART I

Terra Incognita

1. Ethnicity Inc.

I t's a balmy summer day at New York City's historic South Street Seaport. Outside, tourists in T-shirts and shorts stroll the cobblestone avenues that surround the Fulton Fish Market and gape at nineteenth-century sailing ships that conjure a bygone era. A few yards away, in an air-conditioned loft with panoramic views of the East River and the Brooklyn Bridge, a hundred or so men and women in business attire are staring at a PowerPoint projection screen, trying to peer into the future. They have come to the historic Bridgewaters complex to attend the tenth annual Multicultural Equity Conference, sponsored by the Strategic Research Institute (SRI), a privately owned company that caters to the information and networking needs of executives and human resource officers in finance, technology, marketing, media, and other industries. For the better part of two days, the SRI attendees will be listening to a parade of distinguished speakers telling them everything they need to know about the multicultural economy and why they need to know it. Omar Wasow, an Internet entrepreneur and TV technology commentator who is serving as master of ceremonies, keeps things moving at a brisk talk show tempo, pacing the room with a wireless microphone and pausing occasionally for a well-timed quip. The attendees chuckle at Wasow's jokes and then continue taking notes as if their jobs depend on it, which to a certain extent they do. In a consumer environment where white non-Latinos will make up only 50 percent of the population in 2050, understanding the New Mainstream has become critical for business survival. Those who thrive in the multicultural marketplace will do so not just because of their ability to anticipate what's to come, but because they've absorbed the degree to which things have already changed.

Part data download, part meet and greet, part born-again revivalist meeting, the SRI Multicultural Equity Conference is predicated on the notion that the multicultural market is growing and that the people in the room are in the right place at exactly the right time to capitalize on it. As the conference breaks for lunch, the attendees cluster in the corridors and trade business cards. "It's gotten bigger every year," notes Rupa Ranganathan, a senior vice president of ethnic strategy for SRI who has been organizing ethnic marketing conferences for the firm since 1998. "The demographic is achieving critical mass. The mainstream is going multicultural. That is the trend. And we are at a very exciting crossroads. Because it's like when you plant a garden, and now is just the time when you see it's beginning to bloom. Earlier you had to fight for it, but now you don't have to make too much of a case for multicultural marketing, because who in their right mind is not aware of this growth?"

Ranganathan has noticed an evolution in the interests and attitudes of ethnic marketers, who are increasingly focused on the business case for diversity, which includes tracking return on investment as well as internal staffing and representation. "There are more and more sophisticated discussions at these conferences, simply because the practice is evolving very rapidly," she says. "Every year we see new topics, new buzzwords, new issues, new challenges. The next phase we are all headed to right now is how to do it right, how to do it more effectively, how to be creative. Because it's not enough to say, 'Okay, I've said it in a different language,' or 'I've used a few important cultural cues.' It's going beyond language, to where you're really empathizing and making a cultural connection." Ranganathan, who was born in India and worked in the advertising industry there before coming to the United States, sees parallels in marketing trends between America and her native country, which has long been a multiethnic, polyglot democracy. "Fifty years from now, you may not really need a South Asian or a Latino to effectively market to that segment, because hopefully there is going to be such a cross-pollination of ideas and understanding of culture and behavior issues that by that time everyone will be a global, multicultural citizen," she says. "It's all going to be mixed up. So you might find a Chinese writer coming up with an excellent creative for a Latino ad. That's something way ahead, but I see it coming."

Back in the main conference room, the mood is expectant, even conspiratorial, like that among a group of revolutionaries who know that what they are hearing will change everything, even if most people don't realize it yet. The speakers range from Ray Celaya, an assistant vice president of emerging markets at Allstate Insurance Company, to Miriam Muley, an executive director of diversity growth markets for General Motors. AT&T Wireless, Lehman Bros., Fannie Mae, and more than a dozen other major U.S. companies are also represented. Some of the speakers have come to build their brands, some have come to raise their profile or plug their new book, but every one of them is there to spread the multicultural gospel. The message of the entire conference, and others just like it in Miami, Los Angeles, Chicago, and other cities across the country, is crystallized at one point in a single sentence by Jeffrey Humphreys, an economic forecaster at the Simon Selig Center for Economic Growth at the University of Georgia: "We are witnessing a shift in economic power that will reshape the economic, political, and cultural landscape of America."

Humphreys has the numbers to back up his claim. The Selig Center projects that by 2008, the combined buying power of African Americans, Asians, and Native Americans will account for 14.3 percent of the nation's total, or $10.6 trillion, up from 10.7 percent in 1990.[1] Latino buying power, or total income after taxes, will rise from $653 billion in 2003 to $1,014.2 billion, outpacing the buying power of African Americans, which will rise over the same period from $688 billion to $921 billion. Those numbers translate into an increase of 315 percent for Hispanics, 287 percent for Asians, and 170 percent for African Americans, compared with a projected growth of 112 percent for whites. According to the Selig study, "The Multicultural Economy: Minority Buying Power in the New Century," the numbers represent a doubling of Hispanic buying power in eighteen years to 10 percent of the U.S. total, up from 5 percent in 1990. Asian American buying power, $344 billion in 2003, will reach $526 billion by 2008; and Native American buying power will reach $63.1 billion.[2] The buying power of the gay and lesbian community is also growing. According to a report by Witeck-Combs Communications, a New York–based marketing research firm, the buying power of gays, lesbians, and bisexuals will climb from $451 billion in 2002 to $608 billion by 2007.[3]

The steep rise in the buying power of U.S. ethnic and minority groups, Humphreys argues, besides making them a bigger piece of the overall consumer marketplace, will make it cheaper on a per capita basis to market to those groups. That means that companies that are already spending to reach multicultural consumers will spend more, and those that are considering it are more likely to jump in. Ford, Pepsico, and Diageo's Johnnie Walker are just a few of the brands that are pumping up ad budgets targeting Hispanics and other groups. Media Economics Group reports that ad dollars in Hispanic magazines grew by 24 percent between 2002 and 2003, versus a growth rate of 8.6 percent for the general market over the same period. General Motors, for example, raised its spending on Latino-targeted magazines $7.7 million, a 166 percent jump over the previous year. Procter & Gamble, for its part, raised spending on Latino magazines by a third in 2003, to $11.2 million.

The fastest growth is coming from Hispanics and Asians, whose cultural impact is widespread, highly visible, and very different from that of African Americans, who in many ways paved the way for the myriad groups that are making their own contributions to the New Mainstream. It doesn't hurt that the data indicates ethnic consumer spending will continue to increase into the foreseeable future. U.S. Hispanic population growth rates and purchasing power are both rising faster than those of the general population. And because U.S. Hispanics are younger as a group than the rest of America, their prime wage-earning years are still ahead of them, suggesting the current projections could be conservative. Adding to the ethnic upswing is the fact that Hispanics and African Americans are starting businesses at a rate four times faster than that of the overall population. Statistics like these, according to the Selig Center, can be used to "measure the relative vitality of geographic markets; help judge business opportunities for start-ups or expansions; gauge a business's annual sales growth against potential market increases; indicate the market potential of new and existing products; and guide targeted advertising campaigns."[4]

As Hispanic buying power overtakes the buying power of African Americans, differences in spending patterns between the two groups will have implications for entire industries. A Consumer Expenditure Survey conducted in 2003 by the U.S. Department of Commerce shows that Hispanics and African Americans differ considerably in how they spend across a number of consumer categories. For example, African Americans significantly outspend Hispanics on books, contributions, education, health care, household furnishings, housing, insurance, and media, while Hispanics spend more on alcoholic beverages, consumer electronics, housewares, sports, and toys.[5]

The path to new markets being forged by African Americans, Latinos, and Asians is not limited to people of color, or even groups that have traditionally been viewed as minorities. The New Mainstream includes people like Kenneth Willardt, a Danish immigrant who moved to the U.S. in the early 1980s and built a career as a world-class photographer before becoming a U.S. citizen, and Givi Topchishvili, the Russian-born founder of Global Advertising Strategies (Global), a New York–based multicultural marketing consultancy that focuses on Central and Eastern European Americans, or CEEAs. According to Global, CEEAs constitute the third largest U.S. ethnic market, commanding more than $400 billion in spending power. Like their better-known ethnic precursors, the 20 million Russians, Poles, and other Eastern Europeans living in the United States have distinct cultural needs and habits that determine what and how they buy. Just like Latinos and Asians, many are non-English-speaking immigrants and their economic growth rate is outpacing the general population, yet because of their largely Caucasian makeup they have so far remained largely invisible to U.S. advertisers. Topchishvili, who came to New York City in 1999 and founded Global the same year, points to recent efforts by Western Union, AT&T, Citibank, Verizon, and MetLife to reach Eastern Europeans as evidence that CEEAs are finally starting to get the attention they deserve.

"The CEEA market is part of a revolution in marketing that goes beyond any single race or nationality, and can no longer be overlooked or taken for granted," Topchishvili asserts. "The lesson here is that race is merely one indicator of the cultural differences—ranging from language to psychographics and a shared history—that truly creates a distinct ethnic group. In today's multicultural economy, a failure to understand the importance of ethnic identity is a failure to understand the American consumer."

But while the growing economic clout of ethnic and minority groups and their increasingly critical role in the growth and bottom line of the nation's largest companies are clear, the best and most efficient way to reach them can be murky. Like a photographic image made of millions of individual pixels, the more one zooms in on the multicultural market, the more fragmented and blurry the picture gets. U.S. Latinos, for example, are not a single monolithic group, but a plethora of different nationalities and ethnic extractions. Some of them, especially those who are born in the United States, are mainly English speaking and take their cultural cues from the general mass media. Others, particularly immigrants, are more likely to speak Spanish and not much English, if any. Yet even among Spanish-speaking immigrants, the cultural disparity between, say, a Mexican immigrant from Puebla and an Argentine from Buenos Aires can be huge. Even countries from the same region of Latin America are likely to have different national and historical references and an abiding sense of national pride that is a key part of their personal identity. There is also a sizable percentage of U.S. Hispanics who are bilingual and bicultural. These Latinos are equally at home with their Latino identity and the habits, attitudes, and institutions of the general culture. These post- or pan-ethnic Latinos are likely to see themselves as a blend of races and cultures or even as belonging to more than one race or ethnic tradition at the same time.

Among African Americans, the market is split between middle-class professionals and urban youth. Likewise, the term *Asian American* typically lumps together dozens of culturally distinct groups, including Chinese, Japanese, Indian, Pakistani, and Vietnamese, who practice religious traditions ranging from Buddhism to Hinduism to Islam. Mass merchandisers, mindful that between 1990 and 2000 the percentage of Americans who classify themselves as Christian dropped from 86 percent to 76.5 percent, are adding ethnic overtones to their holiday blessings. JCPenney and the U.S. Post Office are making sure that their season's greetings include images of Kwanzaa, Hanukkah, and Ramadan. Sears even produced an ad that featured an Asian Santa Claus.[6]

As the New Mainstream expands and grows, corporations and organizations of virtually every stripe need to understand not only what is happening, but how they should be responding to it. This means going beyond halfhearted efforts like translating an ad into Spanish or hiring an African American sales manager. At SRI's Multicultural Equity Conference, one of the terms that comes up repeatedly in the presentations is "in culture" marketing and advertising. "In culture" means speaking to customers in their native language or the language they respond to the most when making a buying decision. "In culture" means being sensitive to ethnic and nationalist sensitivities and not making cultural gaffes, like the one Buick committed in Canada when the company called its new vehicle the LaCrosse, a name that in local slang refers to masturbation. It means that when selling life insurance to ethnic Hindus, anything other than an indirect advertising campaign will backfire by triggering cultural taboos about discussing death in public. "In culture" means understanding that Spanish-dominant U.S. Latinos tend to be hyperaware of cultural differences and may be ambivalent or suspicious of assimilation, whereas English-dominant Latinos take assimilation for granted and tend to ignore ethnic distinctions. "In culture" means reaching out to social organizations and civic leaders to make sure that your marketing campaign or editorial slant won't trigger a boycott by disgruntled community activists, something *Details* magazine learned after a tongue-in-cheek feature titled "Gay or Asian" failed to amuse Asian readers or the Asian American

Journalists Association. But most of all it means hiring a multicultural marketing expert to make sure that you know what is "in culture" and what is not.

The multimillion-dollar industry of research firms, consultants, and other companies that help corporations navigate the mysterious waters of the ethnic market is openly questioned on the second day of the SRI conference when a tall black man named Leon E. Wynter stands in front of the group and makes the heretical assertion that multicultural experts are a dying breed. Wynter, a former *Wall Street Journal* columnist and author of *American Skin: Pop Culture, Big Business, and the End of White America*, seems to take a mischievous enjoyment in telling his audience that if they are truly successful at integrating ethnic marketing consciousness into the corporate mainstream, ethnic marketers, as such, will no longer be necessary.[7] The battle to convince corporate America that minorities have joined the consumer mainstream, Wynter argues, has already been won. The blurring of races and cultures in America is well under way, and the Anglocentric culture that once characterized the mainstream no longer exists. Hispanic Americans, who represent all races and are intermarrying and merging into the mainstream with demographic inevitability, Wynter says, "are the cutting edge against the throat of race in America" and have therefore made racial and ethnic considerations all but obsolete. But ethnic marketers, rather than acknowledging their irrelevance, Wynter tells his visibly nonplussed audience, have a vested interest in perpetuating the status quo and "the myth of racial particularity" that is their bread and butter and raison d'être. When Wynter is done, there a smattering of polite applause and a few innocuous questions.

Though the issue he raised is never openly discussed at the conference again, Wynter's utopian, postethnic vision of America has given the attendees a glimpse of a society where "in culture" and "in America" are synonymous. Never mind the fact that racism, or intraethnic "colorism," will probably never disappear completely or that the ongoing influx of immigrants from Latin America is constantly feeding the ranks of marginalized and socially isolated Spanish speakers who aren't ready to be absorbed into the New Mainstream. But the gradual blurring and melding of races and ethnicities into something new, a distinctly American fabric woven out of innumerable ethnic threads and bound together by shared aspirations and a multiculturalized mass media, is undeniable, and the only real question is how long it will take and how far it will go.

Ethnic marketers will no doubt take some comfort in the fact that Wynter is only half-right or, at the very least, ahead of his time. In a generation, maybe two, marketing executives at Coke and Nike won't need to calibrate their product launches for ethnic market segments because pan-ethnicity will be the norm, and the likes and dislikes of Hispanics, African Americans, and Asians will be built into the products and services being offered to them—because they will be the ones developing and selling them. But for the near future, at least, the pressure for instant profits and the still perceptible gap between sellers and increasingly diverse buyers will continue to drive market segmentation by age, race, ethnicity, and gender. And most corporations will need somebody to help them figure out a way to do it. As long as companies are motivated by financial self-interest to pay for that expertise, multicultural marketers will be happy to sell it to them.

Not that defining and measuring the multicultural marketplace is easy. Conflicting conclusions, contradictory data, and inconsistent strategies abound. Like the allegorical blind men who arrive at completely different descriptions of the same elephant because their impressions are determined by the parts they touch, marketers tend to define Hispanic consumers through the filters of their own business assumptions. Companies that poll their own customers will get different answers from those who use a national sample. Surveys in English will skew the findings away from Spanish. And the pollsters themselves tend to interpret data through the lens of their own personal experiences and expectations. The task is made trickier still by the fact that Hispanics may shift languages and attitudes depending on the circumstances in which they find themselves. A study by Daniel Lund of MUND Americas and Sammy Papert of Belden Associates found that Hispanics prefer Spanish when seeking a service, such as an Internet provider or a travel agency. But when buying a product, like a car or a cell phone, they prefer English, a language they associate with rational decisions. To put it another way, Latinos use Spanish for emotional transactions, while English is the tongue of calculation and dispassionate choice. Of course some purchases, like buying a home, can be both.

Dream Machines

In the United States, home ownership is regarded as more than just a good investment; it is a psychological stake in the future and a source of social empowerment. It signifies stability, security, and permanence. For Hispanics, who value family and community above all else, home ownership is a material validation of self-worth and a literal stake in the national future. In that sense, for many minorities and immigrants, owning a home is a turning point in their own identity and the terra firma of their aspirations.

It's no coincidence that home ownership is the single most important generator of personal wealth in the United States. Real estate, in terms of both the housing market and the consumer confidence home ownership inspires, is a key driver of the national economy. Even for foreign-born immigrants, the dream of owning a home is as strong as—or stronger than—it is for ethnic natives. A 2003 report by the U.S. Census Bureau found that foreign-born U.S. citizens are more likely to own their own homes than native-born members of the same ethnic groups. Hispanics, blacks, Asians, and Pacific Islanders who are naturalized citizens have higher home ownership rates than their U.S.-born counterparts, reflecting the degree to which immigrants associate owning a home with being an American. Home ownership provides social and economic legitimacy, a sense of belonging and security. The report "Moving to America—Moving to Home Ownership," found that the rate for foreign-born U.S. citizens (67 percent) was about the same as for persons born in the United States, but foreign-born citizens of Hispanic origin were more likely to own a home than native-born Hispanics by a margin of 63 percent to 54 percent.

The home ownership gap was even wider between naturalized Asians (70 percent) and native-born Asians (57 percent). Home ownership for the United States overall, despite a lackluster economy, remained at record levels in 2002 for the entire U.S. population at 67.9 percent. Overall home owner rates were also at record levels for non-Latino whites (74.5 percent),

Asian Americans (54.7 percent), and Latinos (48.2 percent).[8] Home ownership is also growing in areas with large ethnic populations. In El Paso, Texas, where 78.2 percent of the population is Hispanic, home ownership grew by 27.7 percent between 1990 and 2000.[9]

During the mid-1990s, when Fannie Mae, the federally sponsored mortgage company, realized that home ownership among white families in the United States had reached almost 75 percent, it began looking for new markets. With home ownership for minorities and young families of color still below 50 percent, it announced a trillion-dollar "American Dream Commitment" to increase ownership in the multicultural market. By insuring second mortgages made available through the Native American Housing and Self-Determination Act, Fannie Mae was able to extend ownership to Native Americans through the Housing Authority of the Muscogee Nation of Oklahoma. The company also co-underwrote the development of eight hundred public housing units in Boston's Mission Main district and helped underwrite affordable home mortgages for immigrants from Africa, Asia, and Latin America.

Fannie Mae executives, who describe themselves as being in the "American dream business," instituted a multitiered strategy for the U.S. Hispanic market in California and several other states where Latinos constitute a high percentage of the population. They started by identifying the business opportunity, which began with a national home ownership gap between Hispanics and non-Hispanics of nearly 20 percent. Initial efforts focused on California. Besides having one of the largest Hispanic populations in the country, with 12 million Latinos out of a statewide total of 35 million, California has the fifth largest economy in the world, exceeding the gross national product of France. They also noticed that of the top surnames of California home buyers, three of the first four were Hispanic, as were five of the top ten.

1. Garcia
2. Smith
3. Lopez
4. Rodriguez
5. Nguyen

6. Martinez
7. Lee
8. Johnson
9. Gonzales
10. Williams

In a 2002 survey conducted by Fannie Mae, 78 percent of the Hispanic respondents saw home ownership as the best possible investment, and 73 percent felt that "now is a good time" to purchase a home. Fannie Mae knew that Latinos valued personal relationships and that recognition of their language and culture was a key to connecting the brand to the Hispanic consumer. The company worked with Univision.com, the leading Spanish-language Internet portal, to create Casa ("House"), a co-branded online area with Spanish content on how to buy or refinance a home, as well as tips on renting, decorating, gardening, and house repair. The company also tailored its products to the Hispanic market, which meant accepting nontraditional down payment sources, including cash, providing low or no down payment loans, making financing available for nonresident immigrants, allowing broader income to be considered in underwriting, and incorporating community programs into financing structures. The company also aligned itself with the aims and priorities of local and national community leaders who had a stake in improving the lives of their constituents. Fannie Mae partnered with the Southern California members of the U.S. Congressional Hispanic Caucus to bring educational support, on-site mortgage approval, and home buyer counseling to six congressional districts in the state. In Atlanta, Fannie Mae created a series of Latino-lending Leadership Forums, which generated support and credibility from sixty local Hispanic leaders. Fannie Mae's bottom-up approach helped it generate record growth for the period and solidified its links to ethnic communities. And by giving immigrants and minorities an anchor in the community, it fostered links with political representatives and accelerated the assimilation process by giving new home owners a foothold in the general economic and social infrastructure.[10]

Allstate Insurance Co., after reaching out successfully to Hispanics and African Americans, launched a campaign targeted at the Chinese community in New York City, which has one of the highest concentrations of Asian Americans in the country. By translating its slogan, "You're in good hands with Allstate," into Mandarin and Cantonese, the company hoped to pitch a sense of security to Chinese foreign-born immigrants, who make up 65 percent of the U.S. Chinese population. Like Fannie Mae, Allstate used local community partnerships, ethnic media advertising, and in-language promotions and materials to educate potential customers on the psychological and economic benefits of insurance. After investing $60 million on marketing to Latinos in the late 1990s, the Northbrook, Illinois–based insurer saw its business among Hispanics increase from $1 billion to more than $2 billion.[11]

Aetna Inc., in a move that it says is aimed at addressing disparities in the quality of medical care of minority patients, began collecting data on the racial and ethnic backgrounds of its 14 million health plan members.[12] The gap in medical care between whites and other population groups has triggered an outcry from health care professionals like Carmen Green, a pain management specialist at the University of Michigan, who told *USA Today:* "African Americans and Hispanics are more likely to experience pain, and less likely to receive relief for it, even when under a doctor's care." In early 2003, Senate majority leader Bill Frist vowed to reduce disparities in health care between minority and nonminority Americans. He criticized lower than average life expectancy rates for African Americans and suggested that ethnic sensitivity training at medical schools was insufficient to meet minority patient needs. Senator Frist's remarks, coming just days after he was chosen to replace Senator Trent Lott, who was forced to resign for making racially insensitive remarks, were widely regarded as a dose of political placebo, and in fact the Bush administration quickly moved on to other priorities.[13] Aetna's commitment was more convincing, if only because it was presented by its CEO as a business imperative that would ultimately contribute to the bottom line. Aetna said it planned to use the data it gathered to better understand the reasons behind the health care gap and develop prevention, education, and treatment programs to address it. But in remarks to *The Wall Street Journal,* John W. Rowe, Aetna's chairman and chief executive, also said that meeting the needs of minority patients would help the company compete. "Responding to the needs of these different populations is an important part of our growth strategy," he said. "Establishing programs that are effective in the area of disparities will be good business as well as good medicine."[14]

Dollars and Centavos

For Bank of America, the key to protecting its bottom line meant understanding the relationship between U.S. Hispanics and their friends and relatives in Mexico. When Mexicans cross the Rio Grande in search of work and a better life, somebody is always left behind—a wife and family, a mother or father, or possibly a constellation of relatives and their dependents that make up a typical extended Latino family. Like immigrants from China and Italy and Ireland before them, Mexican workers will take double shifts and share a room with six other men to make sure there's money left over from their paycheck to send home. The river of dollars flowing south from the United States into Mexico is a multibillion-dollar lifeline for the Mexican economy and a tantalizing market for financial institutions hoping to get their share of the resulting $1 billion in bank transfer fees. Like Fannie Mae, Bank of America had done the math and understood that tapping the U.S. Hispanic market was a key to future growth. Of the 38 million Hispanics in the United States, 21.8 million (or 60 percent) were unbanked, yet 11.8 million (or 33 percent) were sending money to Mexico. The dollar value of remittances from the United States to Mexico was $12 billion to $14 billion in 2002 alone. What's more, the electronic money transfers between the United States and Mexico were expected to grow at a rate of 30 percent through 2005.[15] Those projections, plus the fact that Bank of America's footprint in California and the American Southwest overlapped with the bulk of the U.S. Hispanic population with roots in Mexico, made Bank of America determined to get its share of the remittance pie. The number of people living in the United States with roots in Mexico is estimated to be at least 21 million, a number that grew by 53 percent during the 1990s. Some 16 percent of them are concentrated in the southwestern United States, in states such as California, Texas, Arizona, Nevada, and New Mexico.

"We had mixed feelings about the 2000 census report," says Jeffrey Bierer, Bank of America's senior vice president of multicultural debt and international remittance. "The census confirmed what we knew, but it also brought a lot of competition. We wanted to be first." That meant understanding how and why Mexicans in the United States moved money to Mexico and creating a seamless financial link between sender and recipient.[16]

Once Bank of America decided to go after the U.S.-Mexico remittance market, it moved quickly and simultaneously on several coordinated fronts, including the 2002 $1.6 billion acquisition of Grupo Financiero Santander Serfin, the most profitable bank in Mexico. The move followed the purchase of Banamex by Citigroup, one of Bank of America's top competitors for U.S.-Mexico remittances, eighteen months earlier. The consumer keystone of Bank of America's strategy was an entirely new product—called SafeSend—an electronic fund transfer system leveraging the Internet and thousands of existing ATMs in the United States and Mexico. Bank of America knew that U.S. Hispanics were looking for a safe and secure way to move funds that was also convenient and fast. Bank of America's solution also needed to be nondependent on its existing customer base. In fact, SafeSend was seen as a way to lure new customers to the bank's other services, making it a win-win proposition. Bank of America also made sure that SafeSend accounts could be set up over the telephone, on the Web, or in person at a local Bank of America branch office. And by leveraging the network of twenty-thousand-plus ATMs available in most Mexican cities, the prospect of sending instant cash from an ordinary credit card to any ATM in Mexico gave SafeSend a much-needed degree of differentiation in a competitive market.

Meanwhile, Bank of America's brand marketing group began testing SafeSend's appeal with potential users in the United States and Mexico. They conducted focus groups in both countries to determine the optimal colors, design, and tone of the SafeSend marketing materials and produced a series of Spanish, English, and bilingual print, radio, and TV ads that reassured prospective customers with the tag line *"Creemos en ti"* ("We believe in you"). The media campaign was supported by a community outreach program that emphasized SafeSend as a service that, by enabling relatives and loved ones in Mexico to get cash whenever they needed it, would enhance the well-being of U.S.-based Hispanics.

SafeSend's marketing and public relations campaign supported and echoed the strategic business opportunity, which was solidly supported by the highest level of management and empowered with the staffing and resources to deliver quantifiable results. By previewing SafeSend to the local press in major Hispanic markets, Bank of America was able to generate favorable media coverage for its launch. Similar events at the Mexican consulates in key cities spilled over into favorable media coverage in Mexico. And by actively enlisting the blessing and support of Mexican and local U.S. Hispanic politicians and community leaders, the bank made sure that SafeSend was endorsed by members of the U.S. Congressional Hispanic Caucus, the National Council of La Raza, and the Mexican government.

Like Fannie Mae, Bank of America, rather than making a halfhearted attempt to capitalize on a short-term gain, took a longer strategic view that would build its business for decades. Instead of cobbling together a patchwork of matrixed resources, Bank of America mobilized and staffed an entirely new subdivision dedicated to the task and created a new product that spoke to a practical and emotional need in the U.S. Hispanic population and its Mexican counterpart. The supervising managers all had extensive experience with the U.S. Hispanic community and/or the international remittance market, and whenever possible the potential customers themselves were invited into the process as partners. Instead of looking for confirmation of its existing business model, Bank of America was willing to redefine itself by listening carefully to its employees and customers. A sense of trust and commitment was fostered inside and outside the company, and a dialogue with the Hispanic community was not treated as a marketing afterthought. Most important, Bank of America's initiative had the unqualified support of upper management, who made sure that the bank's strategic interests were aligned with its operational goals and that managers at the customer level were empowered to get the job done. As a result, Bank of America's SafeSend division has already "exceeded expectations."

Other financial institutions are waking up to the growing reservoir of ethnic dollars. Brokers are looking at ways to increase the percentage of

African Americans who invest in the stock market, which has stalled for the past few years at around 57 percent, compared with 79 percent for whites.[17] And Citibank is vying with Bank of America for the U.S.-Mexico remittance market with a program called Citibank Global Transfers, which charges a $5 transaction fee for moving money between the United States and Mexico, compared with $10 charged by most U.S. banks.[18] Merrill Lynch, meanwhile, is focusing on the most affluent segment of U.S. Hispanics. The company notes that the number of Hispanic households earning more than $100,000 a year grew 125 percent between 1991 and 2000.[19] As U.S. financial institutions pursue the new ethnic money markets, products like SafeSend and other culturally customized products and services will become indispensable for banks and financial institutions hoping to capture the cash flow of the New Mainstream.

The Human Factor

Once upon a time, the CEO of a large media company had a serious problem. Despite strong revenues and a huge customer base, the company's growth was projected to level off in the near future. Already the perception that its domestic market might be close to the saturation point was battering the stock and creating a looming sense of crisis among the company's shareholders and top managers. An emergency strategy team was assembled and tasked to find some solutions, which were presented to the executive a few days later. A survey of potential growth areas had produced some eye-opening statistics: In the coming five years, nearly 30 percent of the company's potential new customers would be minorities, with the lion's share to be derived from the U.S. Hispanic population. After all, research had shown that Hispanics—who numbered about 37 million, or 13.6 percent of the U.S. population—were growing at a faster rate than the general public and that their annual purchasing power had reached $630 billion and was still climbing. The buying power of African Americans and Asians was also climbing. If the company could tap into this growth, the minority market was worth millions of dollars to its bottom line.

The good news was that a large percentage of U.S. Hispanics, African Americans, and Asians were already customers. Even better, a small bilingual content area for U.S. Hispanics had already been launched on the company's Web site the year before, and an in-house customer survey had shown that most of them preferred their content in English. The marketing department had already translated a few ads into Spanish and was buying space in a leading magazine for African Americans. This merely confirmed what the CEO already knew when it came to media services and content: minorities were looking for pretty much the same things as everybody else. The executive approved the hiring of a few more sales managers to capture the incremental business, handed the project over to its existing programming group, and turned to more pressing matters, confident that the company's share of the burgeoning minority market would help it get back on a fast-growth track.

A year later, it was painfully clear that the CEO could hardly have been more wrong. The now departed executive had glimpsed the importance of the New Mainstream yet had failed successfully to grasp it. The company's ethnic market strategy was in complete disarray, and the dismal subscriber and revenue gains against what everyone agreed was a lucrative and desirable opportunity had sparked a frenzy of finger-pointing among various divisions. The bilingual Web content programmers, who were being supervised by non-Latino managers with little or no experience in the Hispanic community, felt unappreciated and understaffed. The marketing group was frustrated by a lack of reliable research and an inability to raise brand recognition in local ethnic communities. The sales team, for its part, quickly discovered that the company had no credibility with the Latino community, which was a critical factor for advertisers looking to tap that market. Meanwhile, the product development group, besieged by mixed signals and a lack of focused input, had yet to deliver a single title or service that spoke directly to the ethnic audience. "The market was ours to lose," lamented a senior manager close to the project. "But no one was willing to take responsibility, so nothing ever got done. It was a complete train wreck."

But this story has a happy ending. Before long, a new management team that included ethnic minorities in key positions was in place, and the

Latino initiative was put on a priority fast track. Management of the initiative was consolidated under a new general manager, and the group was given the resources and budget to hire a dedicated staff that reported to the new general manager. New research on Latino customers had revealed the existence of at least three separate markets: English-dominant, Spanish-dominant, and bilingual youths. Different products for each segment were in the development pipeline, and initial focus group feedback was positive. An integrated marketing and sales force was preparing a marketing campaign that could be calibrated for different cities and states, and a multicultural PR specialist was hired to arrange meetings with community leaders and to spread the word through tiered media buys that included local ethnic TV, radio, and print.

The media company is apocryphal, but the scenario is not. As American companies reach out to the markets of the New Mainstream, they are being forced to reevaluate not only what they make and how they sell it, but also their internal values and human resource initiatives for recruitment, training, and employee motivation. Corporations are learning that without a diverse workforce they will not only be at a disadvantage when it comes to hiring the best possible candidates, but they will also lack a cultural link to an increasingly critical part of their market. U.S. corporations are realizing that diversity in their workplace can help them

- increase profits and cut costs.
- improve morale and boost productivity.
- expand market share and develop new products and services.
- cultivate new markets and position their brands for continued growth.
- recruit and retain top talent.

The dramatic rise in minority population and buying power has forced many corporations to rethink their long-term growth strategies and even the structure of their businesses. Unlike the affirmative action programs of the 1960s and 1970s, which were seen primarily as a way to redress the effects of past discrimination, the overriding incentive for the new wave of change is financial. Companies that have aggressively courted minority

customers are seeing concrete returns on their investments. Allstate Insurance, which spent $60 million advertising to Latinos between 1996
and 2001, has seen its business with Hispanics grow from $1 bil-
lion in 1995 to $2.1 billion in 2002. Since the Ford Motor Company began
advertising and partnering with Latino communities in the mid-1990s,
overall sales to Hispanics have risen by 50 percent. According to Ford executives, Ford vehicles registered to Latinos have increased 74.2 percent
since 1996.[20]

U.S. Hispanics are projected to make up 25 percent of the population
by the middle of the century, and population growth by African Americans
and Asians will also outpace the rest of the nation. U.S. market share for
non-Hispanic whites is expected to decline from 87.4 percent in 1990 to
80.1 percent in 2007, according to Selig Center data. Over the same period, market share for ethnic groups is projected to rise—from 7.4 percent
to 8.6 percent for African Americans, from 5.2 percent to 9.4 percent for
Hispanics, and from 2.7 percent to 4.7 percent for Asians. With so much
at stake, companies are realizing that simply marketing to Latinos is not
enough.

"An ethnic program is not marketing, it's an investment," Andrew
Nuttney, a partner of the Research Advisory Group, said to insurance and
financial services executives who had gathered in New York City for a conference on multicultural strategies and best practices in their industries.
Tariq Khan, a vice president of marketing at MetLife, was among those
who pointed out that companies that waited for the fruits of a diversified
workforce to become apparent would be left behind by those who had
acted with foresight. For now, the bar for entry to ethnic markets for large
companies is relatively low, but that is sure to change. "The longer you
wait, the more it will cost you money," Khan told the attendees. "It's on
sale now."

In *DiversityInc* magazine's 2003 list of the "Top 50 Companies for
Diversity," Ford was ranked number one. The magazine's criteria included
an understanding of the "diversity-to-profit ratio," focus on inclusion in
areas of vendor procurement, employee and executive recruitment, marketing advertising, and business development. "Ford has developed a
diversity initiative that ensures the 'rubber meets the road,' as Ford execu-

tives say, meaning there are proven financial results," explained *Diversity-Inc.* "Realizing a return on a diversity investment has kept Ford executives vigilant—always seeking methods to extend their outreach so they can continue to boost the company's bottom line." Other corporations that topped *DiversityInc*'s list were Fannie Mae, American Express, Verizon, and IBM.[21]

Forging relationships with minority-owned suppliers and business partners creates links to ethnic communities and builds brand integrity. At the same time, top talents gravitate to companies with diverse employee populations because they see them as places where they will have a chance to advance and build their careers. For the same reason, it's critical that diversity be reflected in upper-management levels as well as the rank-and-file. Companies that fail to diversify have higher attrition rates and are vulnerable to having some of their best employees lured away by companies that can show a commitment to minority employment and recruitment. Tyco International, a global manufacturing and services company that operates in more than one hundred countries and had fiscal 2003 revenues of approximately $37 billion, recently announced a three-year $300,000 partnership with the Lagrant Foundation to "cultivate high-potential students of color for careers in advertising, marketing, and public relations" for its various operations. The program, which amounts to a small step in the right direction, calls for guidance, career advice, and mentoring for interns, with the goal of placing at least ten interns a year within Tyco's U.S. marketing and communications departments. "A diverse workforce offers a competitive business advantage, especially for global companies like Tyco that must effectively manage diversity in products, businesses, customers, and markets to achieve business results," said Charles Young, a Tyco senior vice president.[22]

But even as more Fortune 500 companies are acknowledging the importance of diversity to their bottom line, ethnic representation at the senior executive and boardroom levels continues to lag. According to Microquest, a company that tracks minority executives and directors, between 1999 and 2002, African American representation on corporate boards rose by 4 percent, while Hispanic representation actually fell by 9 percent.[23] According to the Hispanic Association on Corporate Responsibility (HACR), a Washington, D.C.–based minority advocacy group, while Hispanics make up 13 percent of the U.S. population, their representation on the boards of the Fortune 1,000 companies is a mere 1.83 percent. HACR runs a database with the names of about one thousand potential Hispanic candidates for board positions. The Executive Leadership Council, which counts American Express CEO Ken Chenault and Time Warner chairman and CEO Richard Parsons as members, sponsors director seminars and board certification seminars on corporate governance for promising African American and other minority executives. And the New America Alliance, a business advocacy organization cofounded by National Council of La Raza president Raul Yzaguirre and former U.S. secretary of housing and urban development Henry Cisneros, holds an annual Wall Street summit with the aim of expanding American Latino presence on corporate boards, increasing access to capital for Latino businesses, and investing in education and mentoring for American Latino students and entrepreneurs.[24]

Hoping to add a political stick to diversity's economic carrot, Hispanic political organizations are trying to pressure corporations to accelerate their diversity efforts. The U.S. Congressional Hispanic Caucus in 2004 created a Corporate America Task Force, headed by George Herrera, a former president of the U.S. Hispanic Chamber of Commerce (USHCC).[25] In a statement announcing the formation of the task force, Herrera said it "sends a clear and powerful message to corporate America—act now to make your boardrooms reflect the diversity of the nation and level the playing field for procurement opportunities for Hispanic-owned businesses."[26] The USHCC, representing the interests of more than 1.2 million Hispanic-owned businesses in the United States and Puerto Rico, which together earn more than $200 billion annually, also serves as an umbrella for more than 130 local Hispanic chambers nationwide. The task force, which is partnering with the HACR, the New America Alliance, and other Hispanic advocacy groups, is also looking to increase commitments from U.S. corporations for Hispanic student outreach and scholarship programs. "For those companies that don't get it," Herrera said, "we'll just let our constituency know that they're not interested."[27]

For Stephen Baum, CEO of Sempra Energy, a San Diego–based company with two African Americans, a Hispanic, and an Asian American on its thirteen-member board of directors, diversity has a pragmatic value that goes beyond good public relations. "It provides a diversity of opinions and a different perspective," Baum told *USA Today*. "It causes us to think a little more. The quality of our decision making is better. If we were all right-wing Republicans, we might miss opportunities."[28]

As a result, the business case for diversity will only become stronger in coming years and decades. Inevitably, more minority men and women find their seats in executive suites and corporate boardrooms. As they do, they will join other members of the New Mainstream elite, an amorphous but powerful group of racially and culturally diverse innovators and leaders in entertainment, media, business, advertising, politics, technology, and other fields, who are setting the style, mood, and direction of what America is and what it will become as it leads the way into the twenty-first century.

2. The Tiger Effect

Midway through the 2003 MTV Video Awards, after a performance by the African American rapper 50 Cent, Chris Rock, who was hosting the show, noted that it also happened to be the fortieth anniversary of Martin Luther King, Jr.'s "I Have a Dream" speech. "Isn't it nice to see that his dream really came true?" Rock mused in an apparent reference to the mainstream acceptance of an orphan from Jamaica, Queens, who was shot nine times by his rivals yet went on to become one of the nation's biggest acts. Or perhaps he was alluding to the multicultural complexion of the performers and awardees who had been parading across the stage at New York's Radio City Music Hall all evening. But the most convincing evidence that something in America had changed since King's historic speech came during the commercial break that immediately followed Rock's comment. In every one of the ads, whites, blacks, and Latinos appeared together without the slightest hint of racial self-consciousness or tension. One ad, which showed a multiethnic gang of young people piling onto a sun-drenched beach to gorge on soda and chips, was entirely in Spanish, *without subtitles*. The most striking thing about the 2003 MTV Video Awards was not the overhyped—and shamelessly contrived—kiss between Britney Spears, Christina Aguilera, and Madonna, but the seamless convergence of multicultural consciousness and capitalist consumption that was happening around the show.

The increasing visibility—and commercial cache—of ethnic celebrities and public figures in advertising is one of the most visible manifestations of the multicultural economy. The videos that MTV was celebrating were themselves ads designed to sell more records by artists like Christina Aguilera and 50 Cent. And 50 Cent's appeal as a role model to young people who hope to escape their circumstances and achieve a more fulfilling, glamorous life is hardly limited to urban African Americans. So the rapper was undoubtedly sincere in his response when *Murder Dog* magazine asked him if his hit album *Get Rich or Die Trying* was autobiographical. "It's universal," 50 Cent said. "It's the hustle. When you say it with the aura that's around me, it feels negative—get rich or die trying. But if a working-class person tells you they're gonna get rich or they're gonna die trying, it just means they're determined."

Determination, perhaps, to join the ranks of rapper-producer Sean "P. Diddy" Combs, who struck a deal with Lincoln to produce a special edition of its Navigator SUV. The "Sean Jean" limited edition of one hundred sells for $85,000 and includes such must-haves as a Pioneer Premiere audio system with satellite radio, three DVD players, and six TV monitors, a PlayStation 2, logo-embossed leather seats, suede-covered center consoles, and black wood paneling.[1] The hip-hop term *bling-bling*, which was popularized by rappers the BG (Baby Rappers) to express hip-hoppers' ostentatious obsession with diamonds, designer clothes, and Mercedes-Benz cars, was recently added to the online edition of *The Oxford English Dictionary*.[2] In the conspicuously cash-conscious world of rap, living well is not just the best revenge, it's the only acceptable option.

So it makes perfect sense that the ads sold to sponsor a show about ads designed to sell records would be designed to reflect the material aspirations and ethnic and racial diversity of its audience. The 2003 MTV Video Awards show and the ads that made it possible are just one example of how Madison Avenue, in its unquenchable thirst to identify new markets and sell products to them, not only reflects the social and demographic changes of the New Mainstream, but often helps to advance them. From Michael Jordan and Gatorade to Jackie Chan and Hanes, from Enrique Iglesias and Doritos to James Earl Jones and Verizon, advertisers and the marketers who help them sell their wares have forever seen only one color: green. During the 2004 Super Bowl, a survey conducted in sports bars found that sports fans were most likely to take advice about buying a car from rapper P. Diddy, followed by 50 Cent, Shaquille O'Neal, and Derek Jeter.[3] Snack food aficionados were more likely to be swayed by Oprah Winfrey, followed by Jennifer Lopez, Dr. Phil, and Martha Stewart. And because a growing percentage of the consumer market is anything other than white, Madison Avenue has necessarily become a powerful force, however inadvert, in legitimizing a multicultural vision of America. Advertising contributes to the breakdown of outdated stereotypes and promotes tolerance because projecting a positive image for a brand is a prerequisite for selling its products, and the positive images it projects contributes to the mainstreaming of minority groups, which in turn boosts their ability to buy more products.

Nowhere is the symbiosis between advertising and celebrity more apparent—or lucrative—than in the field of professional athletics. And there is no better example of the multiethnic sports superstar than Tiger Woods. Since upending the pro golf world by becoming the youngest winner of the Masters Tournament in 1996 at age twenty-one, Woods has dominated a sport once associated with middle-age white men. Even more than Michael Jordan, arguably the most famous athlete in the world until Tiger came along, Eldrick Woods embodies the global, transcultural nature of the New Mainstream. A practicing Buddhist and a mix of African, Thai, Chinese, Native American, and European bloodlines, he is the son of Earl Woods, a U.S. Army lieutenant colonel and former Green Beret, and Kultida (Tida) Punsawad, a Thai. The nickname "Tiger" came from his father, who gave him the moniker in honor of his South Vietnamese combat buddy, Nguyen Phong, who saved his life during the Vietnam War.[4] A pro golf legend while still in his twenties, Woods, whose endorsement deals include a $40 million contract with Nike and a $30 million contract with American Express, has provided a sense of unlimited possibility for a new generation of Americans of every race and ethnic stripe. In its list of the 101 most influential minorities in sports, *Sports Illustrated* magazine listed Woods second, after Charlotte NBA team owner and Black Entertainment Television network founder Robert Johnson and ahead of tennis player Serena Williams (third) and Michael Jordan (fourth). "After years of battling for fair opportunities," proclaimed *Sports Illustrated* online's editors, "people of color are finally running the show (in some places) and driving the economics in sports."[5] Also on *Sports Illustrated*'s list were Chinese-born Houston Rockets center Yao Ming, who is credited with raising team attendance by 17 percent and who has cut endorsement deals with Apple computers and Visa. Among the Hispanics mentioned are baseball player Alex ("A-Rod") Rodriguez, who made headlines when he signed a $252 million contract with the Texas Rangers and went on to join the New York Yankees, and Mexican-American boxer Oscar De La Hoya, who "has become the most marketable non-heavyweight in boxing" and was the first Latino to own a national boxing promotional firm.[6]

Among the legions of sports star sponsors, Oregon-based Nike has been particularly aggressive in footing the bill for celebrity endorsements. It completed a high-profile $90 million deal in 2003 with then eighteen-year-old basketball prodigy LeBron James, who, like Jordan and Woods, will be given his own sub-brand of sports products, including signature basketball shoes. Nike was the winner of an intense bidding war with Adidas and Reebok for James, who was the number one pick in the NBA draft.[7] Nike also offered an endorsement deal last year to then fourteen-year-old major league soccer player Freddy Adu, who became the youngest to play professionally in the sport when he joined D.C. United for the spring 2004 season. A native of Ghana, Adu immigrated to the United States at the age of eight when his parents won a visa lottery. Adu, who also has signed a major endorsement deal with Pepsi, is seen as a potentially bigger asset than either Michael Jordan or Tiger Woods because of soccer's worldwide appeal. "Participating on a global stage allows him and those brands and products that he's affiliated with to speak to a global audience," explained Rein Patton, president of Mastermind Group, a New

York–based brand strategy and talent firm that also represents Venus and Serena Williams and LeBron James. "He has the ability to transcend not just race but also culture; he's going to be able to bridge cultures between the United States and the globe."[8]

The sports superstars of the future will be rewarded not just for their athletic prowess, but for their ability to connect with an increasingly diverse and global fan base. The crowds will cheer them on not just for breaking barriers of race and ethnicity, but for merging and melding them into the excellence of their game. In the arenas and stadiums of the New Mainstream, the championship will be determined not just by winning, but by who you are when you play the game.

Cuervo Nation

When Taco Bell shows a young white man at a party pretending he made the fajitas "from an old family recipe," the not-so-subtle message is that being Latino (and eating Mexican food) is not just okay—*it's a plus*. By reflecting and connecting with the self-image of the consumer, ads modify the individual's perception of the world around him. Subtle but powerful signals concerning social status and cultural relevance are conveyed by the context and content of the most generic advertisements. As people of color and other minorities are increasingly portrayed in the media as home owners, car buyers, and everyday shoppers, the message to all consumers is that once marginal groups have joined non-Hispanic whites in the economic and cultural mainstream. In turn, those companies and organizations that establish themselves as protagonists of diversity will reap the benefits of leading rather than following the new economic wave.

U.S. companies are gradually waking up to the long-term benefits of advertising to the New Mainstream, but they still have a long way to go. The Association of Hispanic Advertising Agencies (AHAA) reports that the percentage of ad budgets devoted to Spanish and bilingual markets has grown by 17 percent between 1997 and 2002. But while Hispanics represent about 13 percent of the U.S. population, American advertisers as a group allocated only 2.4 percent of their total media budget to the segment between 2001 and 2004. AHAA contends that in order to be effective, companies should allocate at least 8 percent of their budgets to Hispanics. Among the industries that AHAA has found lagging are pharmaceuticals, U.S. government agencies, automotive, travel and entertainment, software, computer makers, security and financial services, and retail. AHAA has set even higher ad spending targets of 10–25 percent for categories in which Latinos are overrepresented as buyers, including baby products, personal electronics, and cosmetics. For these industries to understand why change is in their best interests, they need consider only the demographic trend represented by Hispanic teens, who command $19 billion in spending power and who will grow by 62 percent over the next sixteen years, compared with 10 percent growth in the number of teens overall.[9]

As advertisers gain experience and confidence in New Mainstream markets, new marketing strategies are changing the nature and future of the industry. Commercials targeted at Hispanics, which once consisted mainly of English ads translated into Spanish, have in some cases achieved a kind of reverse crossover. An ad for Crest toothpaste that aired during the 2003 Grammys was in Spanish but ended with the English tag line "White teeth and fresh breath—in any language." And a Spanish McDonald's ad showing a father taking his son to the fast-food outlet for "the talk" was eventually converted into an English ad. Similarly, a Miller Lite ad created by LatinWorks, an Austin, Texas–based U.S. Hispanic agency, was so well received that it was turned into an English version and aired for the general market. The commercial, which debuted during the 2003 NBA finals, shows a man being chased by bulls through the streets of a Spanish town much like Pamplona before halting in front of a butcher shop. The ad then cuts to the man recounting his tale of a close encounter with a bull's horns to friend at a barbecue. "It's a big win for us, to be able to have a general market ad," LatinWorks Alejandro Ruelas told the *Austin American-Statesman*. "It had a Hispanic angle, but it's becoming more and more prevalent that the general market is influenced by the Hispanic market. You can show Hispanic situations to the general market in ways that are very effective."[10]

Or it just might be that as Hispanics join the New Mainstream, the two markets are simply merging and becoming interchangeable. Messages that capture the multicultural zeitgeist can have universal appeal and build long-term equity for the brand even as it sells more products. Within the advertising industry, the trend is sparking consolidations between Hispanic and African American specialty shops and driving large advertisers to partner with one or several different agencies to get the right mix for a particular campaign. A bilingual Coca-Cola commercial aimed at both Hispanic and non-Hispanic consumers showed Mexican-born actress Salma Hayek sneaking into the kitchen of a swanky restaurant for a taco and a Coke as she chats in Spanish with the Latino kitchen staff. Her craving for authentic fare satisfied, she returns to the dining room and, speaking in English, waves away a plate of nouvelle cuisine with the excuse that she's watching her figure.[11]

As ethnic elements merge with mainstream marketing, agencies aimed at minorities are being forced to alter their approach. One of the things that makes the Hispanic market so amorphous is the fact that several generations of people speaking different mixes of English and Spanish and with overlapping but distinct media habits can be found in a single household. To cover the increasingly wide spectrum of cultural possibilities, the New York–based Hispanic youth agency Ruido Group is launching a new holding company, Latin Vox Communications, that will include Conoscenti Publicidad, which *Advertising Age* has called "the first agency aimed specifically at affluent Latinos"; C/I Hispana, a public relations shop; and ID3 Publicidad, a more traditional Hispanic ad agency.[12] The new entity is configured to reach more traditional Hispanics as well as younger ones who are experiencing "retro-acculturation."[13] HBO Latino, a cable network for U.S. Hispanics that launched in 2000, faced the problem head-on with a series of promotional ads that showed a wide cross section of Latinos—from older Spanish speakers to recent immigrants and members of acculturated second and third generations—delivering speeches, poetry, comedy bits, and rap while mixing English and Spanish the same way a modern Latino family would.[14]

Still, for the majority of those who measure, track, and sell to the U.S. Hispanic population, language remains a kind of Mason-Dixon line that divides two opposing statistical and ideological camps. On one side are the pro-Spanish dominants, who maintain that anywhere from half to three-fourths of the U.S. Latino market prefer to speak and read in Spanish. This group includes media companies like Univision and multicultural marketers that specialize in helping corporations and other organizations translate and market their message for the Spanish-speaking population. Their core rationale is that English media advertising and marketing efforts do not reach these people and that even bilingual Hispanics respond more positively to messages in their native tongue. On the opposite side are the pro-English dominants, who point to data and studies showing that anywhere from half to three-fourths of the U.S. Latino market speak English or are bilingual. This camp includes people like Jeff Valdez, the writer-producer behind Nickelodeon's Latino family series *The Brothers Garcia* and the founder of Sí TV, a cable channel aimed at the English and bilingual Latino markets. Their main argument is not only that this group is growing faster than the Spanish dominants, but that Latinos who lean toward English tend to be more educated and affluent and are therefore a more attractive marketing target. These people will usually also point out that U.S. Latinos under eighteen tend to be bicultural, biracial, and bilingual and live in large urban centers, making them de facto representatives of a new cultural phenomenon that is unlike anything America has seen before and which has its own pan-global, multiracial style of thinking, eating, dressing, and shopping.

There are also those in the second group who accuse the first group of perpetrating a self-serving misinformation campaign designed to convince advertisers that the majority of U.S. Latinos are a world apart that will respond only to the "in culture" marketing techniques that only they can deliver. In her book *Latinos, Inc: The Marketing and Making of a People,* Arlene Davila explains how Spanish-language marketers can paint themselves into a linguistic corner. "Convinced that Latinos who are English-dominant or bilingual are already being reached through mainstream media, corporations almost always approach Hispanic marketing agencies having already decided to limit their marketing efforts to Latino customers who are Spanish speaking," she argues.[15]

So is Spanish the true lingua franca and emotionally resonant tongue of all Latinos, regardless of age or socioeconomic status? Or is English the

inevitable and preferable bridge to a better life, the voice of the Latino future? Or is there something in between, a linguistic DMZ that is Spanglish
blended with hip-hop slang and the street-smart banter of urban youth?
The vexing, confusing, and ultimately illuminating answer is, of course, all
of the above. There is without a doubt a bona fide—and growing—market
for Latinos who prefer their media in Spanish and who identify more with
their country of origin than with the United States. And there is also a large
and expanding group of Latinos who have assimilated in a traditional
immigrant pattern and belong to the middle and professional classes,
send their kids to college, speak excellent English, but possibly not much
Spanish, and have no problem calling themselves Americans while continuing to feel a strong kinship with their Latino roots. The children of both
groups, depending on their socioeconomic circumstances, geographic
location, and other factors, will fall somewhere along this spectrum, although their postethnic, transcultural fusions tend to both incorporate
and transcend the first two groups.

In the typical twenty-first-century Latino household, it's completely
natural for *Abuelita* to be watching her favorite novella from Mexico on
Univision, while her daughter whips up grill-smoked salmon with chipotle
mayonnaise she watched Zarela Martinez make on a television cooking
show, and her teenage grandson surfs the Web on his laptop for Latin-
techno mp3 music downloads and the latest *Matrix* screensaver. After dinner, the whole family might gather around their wide-screen TV to watch a
DVD of *Spy Kids 3* or *George Lopez* on ABC. Unlike Spanish networks Univision and Telemundo, which get most of their programming from Mexico,
Venezuela, and other countries in Latin America, Sí TV is committed to li-
censing and developing original programming for a U.S. Hispanic audience. Cofounded by Valdez and investor Bill Bishop, the network has hired
former Argyle Television executive Bob Owen as its CEO and Leo Perez,
from SonyPictures Entertainment, as its chief operating officer. Sí TV will
be carried on the EchoStar satellite network, as well as cable franchises
owned by Time Warner and Cox Communications, giving it access to
more than 18 million U.S. households. On its Web site, Sí TV describes itself as "an English-language, Latino network featuring culturally relevant
programming targeting the growing young Latino and multi-cultural TV

audience." The network plans to launch with an eight-hour block of original and rerun specials, sitcoms, and movies aimed at Latinos and a multicultural audience. Among the programs slated for the channel's 2004
launch were *Fly Paper: Fashion That Sticks*, an edgy urban Latino fashion
show; *Urban Latino*, a youth-oriented lifestyle show that spotlights Latino
fashion, music, and food; and *Malcolm & Eddie*, a sitcom starring Mal-
colm-Jamal Warner and Eddie Griffin that originally aired on broadcast
TV from 1996 to 2000. Sí TV's movie offerings will include Cheech
Marin's *Born in East L.A.*, Robert Redford's *The Milagro Beanfield War*,
and the film version of Luis Valdez's play *Zoot Suit*, starring Edward James
Olmos.[16]

If Sí TV succeeds, it could prove Jeff Valdez's contention that Latinos
want to see themselves in English-language, culturally relevant programs
that are not available in Spanish. That in turn could open the door to
a new wave of media programming made specifically by and for South
Asians, Chinese, Koreans, Japanese, and other growing ethnic communities in the United States, just as the Black Entertainment Network and
other media entities cater to the sensibilities of African Americans.

Some advertisers are hedging their bets by adding ethnic flavors to
general market messages and linking their ad campaigns to cross-media
promotions. Chrysler used the cast of *Chasing Papi* in its ad for Jeep. The
film's three female stars chase a Jeep thinking the driver is the Romeo
they all lust after, intentionally mimicking the movie's plot line. Other
advertisers are happy to aim for the top tier of their target demographic
and then fine-tune their message for local markets.[17] Cognizant of the
fact that the most affluent Latinos tend to be English speaking or bilingual, Absolut vodka spiced up its first foray into the Latino market with
"Absolut Ritmos," an English-language campaign that uses Latin *ritmos*,
or rhythms, to give its brand a cool, multicultural edge. The ads, which
were supported by Spanish print campaigns, were accompanied in select
cities by a series of nightclub salsa and merengue events that featured
Absolut *mojitos*, a vodka-infused version of the classic Cuban rum
cooler.[18]

Mickey Mouse jumped on the Latino bandwagon for Fiesta Latina at
Disneyland, a September festival offering Latin food, dance, arts and

crafts, and Cinco de Mayo, which only a few years ago was a minor Hispanic holiday celebrated mainly by Mexican Americans in the southwest
United States but has since mushroomed into a national event that is ea-
gerly promoted by the makers of beer, salsa, and chips. Never mind that
contrary to popular misconception, the fifth of May is not Mexico's Independence Day but actually the date of a Mexican peasant victory over the
French army during the battle of Puebla in 1862. Hardly observed in Mexico, Cinco de Mayo has caught on in the United States as a kind of Latino
pride fiesta fueled by beer, tequila, and jalapeño nachos. For Corona,
made by the Mexican beer company Modelo Group, which also produces
Modelo Especial and Pacífico, the holiday is the foundation of a $5 million
advertising campaign that generates sales of an estimated 100 million bot-
tles.[19] Other brands that spend heavily on Cinco de Mayo promotions
include Frito-Lay and Pepsi. A recent Corona television ad, playing off
Cinco de Mayo's emerging status as a kind of Latino St. Patrick's Day,
showed an Irish man walking into a pub where the locals "celebrate their
favorite holiday" only to discover that a Cinco de Mayo party has taken
over the joint.[20]

In communities like Fresno, California, where Latinos make up 44
percent of the population, the Latinization of U.S. culture—and the New
Mainstreaming of Latino culture—is a foregone conclusion. At Sequoia
Brewing, a bar in Fresno's Tower district, Cinco de Mayo festivities
boost sales by at least 25 percent. In response, Sequoia has introduced a
Mexican-style light ale called Del Oro, which appeals to the beer tastes of
Latinos as well as non-Latinos who have already developed a taste for
Mexican beers like Corona. On Thursday nights, an ethically diverse
crowd congregates at the Starline, where salsa dance instructors give tips
on how to swing to the mambo and other Afro-Cuban rhythms.[21]

To capitalize on America's growing thirst for tequila, Jose Cuervo has
created its own mythical country, an on-line island paradise where tanned
and toned "citizens" can get a Cuervo Nation "passport" and download
movies from "global outposts."[22] The tongue-in-cheek tone of Jose
Cuervo's margarita manifesto contains a serious psychographic message:
All people, regardless of ethnicity or nationality, are united by a desire to
enjoy life, and that desire supersedes differences and binds us together.

Like MTV's egalitarian video utopia, Cuervo Nation is an equal opportunity paradise, where race and ethnicity are ignored as irrelevant or celebrated as trendy accoutrements of creativity and style.

Even premium ice cream is discovering the New Mainstream. Häagen-Dazs introduced its Dulce de Leche flavor in 1997 and added an ice-cream bar in 2000. "The original intent was to appeal to the Hispanic palate," explained a Häagen-Dazs spokesperson. "But it became bigger than that. It's a great flavor. It flew off the shelves." [23]

Penalty Zones

Pitching to the New Mainstream is not without its pitfalls, however, and ethnically targeted ad campaigns can backfire when cultural sensitivities are overlooked or ruffled. As advertising executives are well aware, a cultural gaffe can turn a multimillion-dollar marketing campaign into a public relations disaster. In the mid-1990s, Taco Bell launched a $500 million ad campaign that featured a precocious Chihuahua named "Dinky" who uttered "Yo quiero Taco Bell" ("I want Taco Bell").[24] The popular TV spots drew flak from Mexican Americans who regarded the dog as a demeaning stand-in for Spanglish-speaking Chicanos. Yet not all Hispanics were offended by the ads, and some even took the use of Spanglish in a national media campaign as a sign of social progress.

Sometimes the offense lies within the product itself. When Stella D'Oro, the Bronx, New York–based maker of Italian cookies and breadsticks, changed the recipe of its Swiss Fudge cookies as a cost-saving measure, Kraft Foods, which owns Stella D'Oro, was besieged by complaints from the Union of Orthodox Jewish Congregations of America.[25] The Stella D'Oro Biscuit Company was founded by Italian immigrants in 1932, but in a classic case of New York cultural symbiosis, the cookies have been a staple of the Jewish Orthodox community for decades. Jews love Stella D'Oro's Swiss Fudge cookies because they are one of the few widely available brands of cookies made without milk or butter and are thus acceptable to be eaten immediately after meat by those who adhere to Orthodox Jewish dietary laws. The uproar was triggered when Kraft began reabeling the cookies as OU-D, for Orthodox Union dairy, as opposed to OU-P, for Orthodox Union pareve, which the company said it did to warn consumers that it was planning to start making the cookies with a less expensive, milk-infused chocolate. Kraft quickly reversed itself, saying that plans to change the Swiss Fudge recipe had been put indefinitely "on hold." But according to members of the New York–area Jewish community, the real reason was that the company had been besieged by its distributors, who were losing money as Stella D'Oro cookies languished on shelves owing to a de facto boycott. Starbucks Corporation, the Seattle-based boutique coffee chain, narrowly avoided a national boycott by Jewish Americans after an e-mail chain letter suggested the company was leaving Israel because it had joined the Arab campaign against U.S. businesses in the Middle East. Starbucks executives moved quickly to quash the rumor by contacting the Anti-Defamation League and other Jewish leaders to explain that the store closings were strictly business related and that the company had plans to return to Israel as soon as possible.

Most of the time, though, the threat of economic pressure from disgruntled ethnic advocates is anything but inadvertent. Pepsi dropped Ludacris as a corporate spokesperson in 2002, after conservative FOX TV commentator Bill O'Reilly questioned the rapper's suitability as a role model for youngsters and called him "a thug rapper" who "espouses violence, intoxication, and violence toward women."[26] The Afro-coiffed singer fired back by calling for fans to rally against anti-hip-hop politics and announced the formation of a campaign called "It's Got to Be Ludacris." In a statement aimed at both O'Reilly and Pepsi, the rapper defended his music, saying that his "message represents an ideology and a way of life that is true to me and the new generation to an extent that corporate and political forces can't touch. At one time, I helped Pepsi to navigate their product through inner-city communities that are vital to their sales." Ludacris added that over the past few days, he had "rethought my approach as to how I do business and retained a team to take the power back for the good of the hip-hop community." At the time, several media observers pointed out that Pepsi's moral standards apparently did not extend to Papa Roach, a white, hard rock band that retained its Pepsi endorsement status despite their own questionable behavior, which included appearing in the film *Backstage Sluts* 3 and reportedly urinating onstage into an empty bottle of Gatorade, a Pepsi Co. subsidiary.

Several months after the initial Ludacris flap, Pepsi became the target of a boycott led by the Hip-Hop Summit Action Network (HSAN), which accused the soda maker of "cultural disrespect."[27] HSAN, which was founded by rap mogul Russell Simmons, called on the hip-hop community to "massively join" its national "Campaign for Respect" and urged consumers to avoid all Pepsi products. HSAN also proposed a three-point plan to end the boycott: reinstate the commercial Ludacris made for Pepsi; issue a public apology to Ludacris and the hip-hop community; and contribute $5 million to the Ludacris Foundation, a nonprofit organization set up by the rapper to help inner-city youth.

HSAN's boycott was ostensibly triggered by a new Pepsi Super Bowl ad featuring Jack, Kelly, and Ozzy Osbourne, the notoriously profane Black Sabbath front man and his family. But even those who agreed that Pepsi's standards were hypocritical, to say the least, questioned HSAN's willingness to send a message "that moral indignation has a price tag." Pepsi, for its part, responded to the HSAN boycott, which was subsequently settled for about $3 million, by saying that "the entire Ludacris situation was unfortunate for all concerned. We learned from it and we moved on. We completely understand and respect Russell Simmons' passion for promoting hip-hop and we are working with him and others to do just that."

While Pepsi's Ludacris episode may indeed quickly fade into marketing history, the prickly issues that it raised will not. In the multicultural marketplace, social responsibility and brand identity can become indistinguishable. When corporations like Pepsi use rappers like Ludacris, or rockers like Ozzy Osbourne and Papa Roach, for that matter, to conjure an aura of creative relevance and authenticity for their products, they must be willing to stand up for their spokespersons' right to artistic expression, no matter how unsavory their message might be to people outside the target demographic. As Pepsi learned, a failure to do so can instantly turn a potentially beneficial brand association into a public relations liability.

At the same time, those who use their celebrity as a platform to vent ethnically divisive polemics may find themselves crossing the invisible foul line of New Mainstream economics. When conservative commentator

Rush Limbaugh observed on ESPN that Philadelphia Eagles quarterback Donovan McNabb was overrated because the (liberal) media is so anxious to see a black quarterback succeed that it is willing to lower the bar of achievement for black athletes, he wasn't saying anything he wouldn't have said on his popular radio show. When the resulting brouhaha got him fired from his job as an ESPN commentator, Limbaugh seemed more surprised than contrite. His real mistake, of course, was failing to realize that the demographics of a national TV sports network are very different from those of his conservative radio audience. Whether Limbaugh's comment was merely tasteless or racist or both, his punishment came not from suggesting that McNabb was getting extra points from the media for being black, but from doing it on a prime-time network show where so many of the viewers that ESPN's sponsors were trying to reach are also African Americans.[28] Television networks like ESPN are in the business of consolidating audiences, not dividing them, and sponsors are in the business of paying to reach as many potential customers as possible, including the people of color who were offended by Limbaugh's remarks.

Jan Stephenson, an Australian golfer on the Ladies Professional Golf Association (LPGA) Champions Tour, also took some heat for alluding to perceived quotas, except in her case she was suggesting that they be used to limit the number of South Koreans on future LPGA tours.[29] In the November 2003 issue of *Golf Digest*, Stephenson criticized the Asian women players hurting the sport by dominating the playing field, not projecting enough sex appeal, and generally failing to promote the tour in the American media, even though many of them spoke at least some English. *Golf* magazine quoted her saying that "Asians are killing our tour" and that if she were an LPGA commissioner, "I would have a quota on Asian players. . . . I'm an Australian, an international player, but I say America has to come first. Sixty percent of the tour should be American, 40 percent international." Stephenson, one of the world's best-known women golfers, once posed seminude in a bathtub of golf balls for a promotional golf calendar. Of the top nine players on the LPGA's 2003 top earners' list, four are Asians. Overall, the tour included a record eighteen South Koreans, as well as six from Japan, two from Taiwan, and one apiece from Malaysia, India, and the Philippines. The upswing in Asian female golfers is attributed to strong support and training in their home countries, especially South Korea, where the LPGA games are televised. In response to the Stephenson controversy, a spokesperson for Bloomington, Illinois–based State Farm Insurance, which is an LPGA sponsor, said that State Farm understood "the power of female buying power" and that the company stood behind its support for "the LPGA and diversity—for our employees and our customers." Stephenson later apologized for making remarks and begged the LPGA for forgiveness. "To all Asian Americans, the Asian community, the fans of the LPGA, and to anyone else who has been offended by these statements, I am genuinely sorry to you as well, and ask you to accept my apology," she said in a statement. "As an Australian residing in another country I have experienced what it is like to be singled out, and I was not sensitive to that feeling of yours."[30]

Rush Limbaugh and Jan Stephenson could hardly be more dissimilar, and their comments were prompted by entirely different situations and motives, yet their stories do overlap in at least one significant way: they both underestimated the consolidated clout of diversity, which has become a corporate imperative not out of some newfound sense of social responsibility, but because of its indispensable contribution to the bottom line.

3. Eye of the Beholder

When African American actress Halle Berry made the cover of *Cosmopolitan* magazine in 2002, *The New York Times* hailed it as a cultural milestone, noting that Berry was "evidently one of a cadre of nonwhite celebrities who are deemed to have enough crossover appeal to appear on the cover of mass consumer magazines."[1] But as racial boundaries continue to blur and ethnic beauty increasingly characterizes the multiracial look of the New Mainstream, it may be blondes who are the ones "crossing over" to reach the masses. Ethnic inroads into the worlds of television, film, theater, and comedy are changing not just what we see, but also how we see it. On Broadway, the transformation is evident in New Mainstream crowd-pleasers like *The Lion King*, *Rent*, and *Russell Simmons' Def Poetry Jam on Broadway*, as well as *Take Me Out*, a play that examines homosexuality in the context of the all-American pastime. *Bombay Dreams*, a $14 million Bollywoodesque extravaganza that opened on Broadway in 2004, was aimed at not just selling tickets to some of the five hundred thousand South Asians living in the New York area, but also expanding Broadway's cultural vocabulary in a time of demographic change. International film franchises like *The X-Men*, *The Matrix*, and *Spy Kids* are reflecting their global audiences and projecting ethnically blurred images of peoples, cultures, and even extra-terrestrial worlds.

Multicultural chic is showing up on the streets of suburbia and in the effete salons of cutting-edge couture. With the British-born Chinese Jamaican Naomi Campbell entering her second decade as a "supermodel," it's no longer a question of whether black is beautiful, but merely to what extent new colors and shapes will alter the spectrum of the physical ideal. Berry was only the fifth black woman to appear on the cover of *Cosmo* since the magazine began using color cover photographs in 1964, and the first since Naomi Campbell in 1990, but there's also no question that a new generation of beauties of every shade and ethnic mix are becoming increasingly visible on the newsstand and behind the scenes in the media and fashion industries.

A *New York Times* survey of 471 covers from thirty-one magazines published in 2002 found that about one in five, or 20 percent, depicted a minority on the cover. Five years earlier, the figure was only 12.7 percent. The *Times* also found that over the same period, fashion magazines had almost doubled their use of nonwhite cover models. Between 1998 and 2003, blondes featured on the cover of *Allure* magazine went from an overwhelming majority to a rarity, and mixed race models have been recruited for high-profile ad campaigns by Louis Vuitton, YSL, and H&M.[2]

The blended look is particularly chic among younger Americans. On the 2000 census, respondents under eighteen were twice as likely as adults to identify themselves as multiracial. Brown has become the new white, especially to the MTV generation, which was reared on the ethnically and sexually diverse images of music videos and shows like *Road Rules* and *The Real World*. The trend is jump-starting the careers of models and actors who have exotic, pan-ethnic features. Miles Thompson, a fourteen-year-old of Jamaican, Native American, and Eastern European extraction, has already appeared on TV's *Third Watch* and was hired to pose in ads for Microsoft's X-Box game player. Other icons of ambiguity include Jennifer Lopez, Beyonce Knowles, Vin Diesel, Jessica Alba, and Christina Aguilera. In 2002, almost half of the women featured on the cover of *Maxim*, a lifestyle magazine aimed at hip young men, were nonwhite. Publications aimed at teenagers such as *CosmoGirl, Seventeen, Teen People,* and *YM* had almost twice as many minority cover subjects as their grown-up counterparts.[3]

In 2003, Susie Castillo, a brunette model and actress whose background is Dominican and Puerto Rican, won the fifty-second Miss USA Pageant in San Antonio, Texas; the same year, Ericka Dunlap, an African American from Orlando, Florida, was crowned Miss America. Dunlap, who is the eighth African American to be crowned Miss America since Vanessa Williams became the first in 1984, chose to make building awareness of the business benefits of corporate diversity the platform, or thematic message, of her reign. "Inclusion simply makes good business sense and impacts the bottom line," Dunlap wrote in her platform statement. "Once CEOs realize their diversity outreach without, as well as within, their business they will be able to realize greater product quality, greater profit margin and greater pride in their companies."[4]

Even dummies are getting an ethnic makeover. "Cityscape," a new line of fashion mannequins by the New York–based Ralph Pucci company, feature vaguely Asian and Hispanic features and skin tones ranging from eggplant and ivory to nutmeg and pink. "They are sort of the way you see people look in downtown New York," said Robert Clyde Anderson, who designed the mannequins. "You can't tell what their ethnicity is."[5]

Evolving notions of beauty have begun to affect industries devoted to helping ordinary women look more beautiful, including hair care products and cosmetic plastic surgery. Not only are women of color more likely than ever to request such procedures, but their aesthetic goals have also changed. Reversing the historical trend of minorities trying to hide their ethnicity, doctors report a growing number of African American and Asian patients who specifically request that their nose and eye alterations not make them look *too Caucasian.* According to the American Society for Aesthetic Plastic Surgery, the number of cosmetic procedures performed on minority women quadrupled between 1997 and 2002 to about 1.3 million, outpacing the national average by about a third. Minorities now make up nearly 20 percent of all plastic surgery procedures performed in the United States.

Doctors report that for African American women, the old technique of narrowing the nose and adding a pointy tip has given way to a broader, flatter profile that preserves the shape of the nostrils. The new approach for Asian eye lifts leaves more tissue near the lower lid to prevent the eye from looking too round. The trend away from facial alterations that attempt to ape Anglo beauty is due to several reasons, surgeons say, including a growing conviction that ethnic beauty is as—or even more—attractive than the traditional Anglo standard. Another factor fueling the trend is a growing recognition by doctors and patients alike that appending Anglo features to ethnic faces can be counterproductive, since the whole point is to make woman look younger and more attractive without leaving indiscreet clues.

At the same time, the "divafication" of ethnic celebrities like Jennifer Lopez has given previously shunned body features a new cachet among nonminority women. Salt Lake City plastic surgeon Renato Saltz, for example, has noticed a rise in buttock implants among his female patients. For Nely Galán, a Cuban-born TV producer who immigrated to the United States with her parents, the shift is dramatic. "When I was growing up, I felt like, How come the idea of beauty isn't me?" she recalls. "And now when you watch *Dateline* on NBC, they're saying that the most popular form of plastic surgery is a butt implant because of Jennifer Lopez. Well, I think that says it all. When I was growing up, having a butt was a bad thing."[6]

The aesthetic evolution from white to darker shades is also cropping up in the realm of hair care products. Companies that sell products designed for the hair of African American women are beginning to broaden their focus to include Hispanics, Asians, and whites. In 2003, SoftSheen-Carson, the African American division of France's L'Oréal, SA, launched a multiethnic campaign for Wave Nouveau Coiffure, a professional salon line originally designed and marketed for the hair needs of blacks. The company is now developing a range of hair care products formulated to appeal to women of all races and ethnic backgrounds with special hair needs. While manufacturers continue to target certain products exclusively to African Americans, the newer product lines illustrate a growing recognition that female consumers increasingly fall across a spectrum of racial and ethnic identities rather than fitting into a single niche market.[7]

Meanwhile, magazines like *Latina* and Oprah Winfrey's *O* are willing to portray a new, confident, and spiritually empowered image of women that appeals to whites and nonwhites alike. "The image of beauty has evolved," notes Christy Haubegger, a Hollywood film producer and former founding publisher of *Latina*. "What Latinas have brought to this country is a more forgiving sense of beauty. It has something to do with the image of larger hips and breasts—the symbols of fertility that are now at the core of feminine power and Hispanic culture. It's acceptable now to be full-figured. And, also because of Latinas, it's more okay to be successful and sexy. There was a time when succeeding as a woman meant that you had to be more like a man. The androgynous look in media and fashion was a reflection of that. But now things are changing again."

And not just for women. Even though minority men are even more underrepresented than women when it comes to magazine covers and fashion spreads, the boundaries of what constitutes masculine style are morphing along with the multicultural market. Ethnic males are following the lead of punk rockers and more adventurous men who are willing to highlight their hair with a touch of color or even dye it completely blond. NBA maverick Dennis Rodman, who is black, and Ricky Martin, who is Puerto Rican, are just a couple of the high-profile ethnic males who aren't afraid to have more fun. Aging male baby boomers seeking to keep their youthful looks, and twenty- and thirty-something men who don't mind testing the traditional boundaries of masculine behavior are showing up at beauty spas for facials and manicures and exhibiting a discerning interest in designer clothing and trendy grooming products once considered the exclusive territory of women and homosexuals.

The phenomenon of heterosexual men who are willing to embrace their feminine sides—and the beauty accoutrements and activities that go with it—has inspired a flurry of macho-sounding new beauty products, including Axe, a full-body cologne by Unilever, and a *Maxim* magazine-branded hair-coloring line. In fact, a term often used to describe such men, "metrosexuals," was coined by Mark Simpson, a gay journalist, to lampoon the shamelessly consumerist aspect of the trend, which he suggested was actually an invention by marketing executives designed to get schlubby guys to open their wallets. And while the blurring of straight and gay lifestyles goes back to the days of glam rock, there's a newfound assurance in the way young straight men flaunt their feminine sides. British soccer star David Beckham, the metrosexual role model of the moment, is a once improbable blend of macho athlete and fussy fashion aesthete. In Europe, where he is a major celebrity, the press dote on his latest outfit and hairstyle almost more than on those of his wife, Victoria, a former Spice Girl who doesn't seem at all to mind her husband's fashion icon status. In 2003, the metrosexual movement reached a kind of apogee with the surprise success of the cable TV program *Queer Eye for the Straight Guy.* The show chronicles the good-natured exploits of a superherolike "Fab Five" of gay lifestyle experts who descend like a merry pack of fairy godfathers on a not quite hopelessly grubby guy and give him a metrosexual makeover, usually to the purring approval of the fellow's female mate. *Queer Eye* was one of the highest-rated programs in the history of the Bravo channel and a hairy-chest-pounding victory for metrosexual marketers. The slyly subversive premise that gays and women are conspiring to turn heterosexual men into metrosexual pinups is the show's unspoken punch line, and while the program's fluffy bonhomie is a tad too seamless to be fully convincing, there was never any doubt that the Fab Five would trounce the forces of bad taste—and open vast new markets for products aimed at suddenly style-conscious guys.

Phat Cats

In the increasingly fluid cultural channels of the New Mainstream, gays are not the only formerly fringe group to inform—and transform—the fashion world. Just as gay men in the media are shorthand for trendy sophistication and style, the ubiquitous beat of hip-hop and rap reverberates with youthful rebellion and urban authenticity. Primed by the music and video's of superstars like P. Diddy, Jay Z, and Snoop Doggy Dog, and embraced by a multiracial generation of baggy jean–wearing youths, hip-hop fashion has become a $1 billion-a-year business. Retailers like d.e.m.o.

and Jimmy Jazz have sprung up to satisfy the swelling demand for hip-hop clothing in the suburbs, where 70 percent of their customers are white.

In the two decades since rap music blasted its way to the top of the music charts, hip-hop styles are the fastest-growing category in the clothing industry. But the same things that make hip-hop cool—an outsider sensibility and a restless need to oppose the establishment—make it a restless, fast-moving target for anyone who's trying to cash in on the next dope thing. The New York–born 50 Cent, who momentarily replaced his mentor and friend Eminem as the world's hottest rapper, is perhaps the biggest star so far to sport hip-hop's latest must-have item: the "doo rag." A kind of nylon skullcap that first hit the fashion radar in the 1990s, when NFL players like Deion Sanders started wearing them under their helmets (doo rags have since been banned by the league for safety reasons), the doo rag is the latest ghetto staple to take on fashion cachet. Traditionally used by black men to cover an unkempt Afro or protect a snazzy hairstyle, the doo rag has become a transracial badge of hip-hop cool (Bentleys sold separately), as is the style one uses to knot the tie strings that hold the doo together from the back. Costing less than $5 but difficult to find outside black communities, it has already spawned an upscale cousin: the Dew-Rag, an extraabsorbent, easy-to-fasten version produced and marketed by James Evanow of Medford, Oregon.[8]

Evanow, who is white, may soon find himself competing with Russell Simmons, who is not. Simmons, forty-five, is a one-man cultural phenomenon who, besides cofounding Def Jam Recordings, and producing the *Def Jam Comedy* series on HBO, is the president and principal shareholder of Rush Communications. Rush is a multicultural media empire that includes projects and franchised partnerships devoted to records, film, television, advertising, promotion, publishing, philanthropy, soda pop, banking, and clothing. Simmons's clothing line, called Phat Fashions, comprises $300 million worth of goods sporting his brand, including nylon basketball jerseys, zebra-print bustiers, and baby clothes. Simmons, who is trying to sell his company to a larger retailer with the aim of expanding his distribution and promotional reach, says Phat Fashions' sales have risen by 30 percent in 2003 to about $30 million. Simmons is planning to remodel his retail outlet, the Phat Farm store in New York's SoHo district, and launch a new department store line called Def Jam University, which is targeted to the college market. Baby Phat is a women's and baby clothing line run by his wife, Kimora Lee, a former model with a Japanese American mother and an African American father.[9]

Simmons's full-service vision includes the ultimate fashion accessory: a charge card. The Rush card, a prepaid variation of Visa, is a joint venture between Rush Communications and Unifund, a buyer and seller of distressed debt. For a onetime $19.95 enrollment charge and a monthly fee, consumers whose credit rating prevents them from owning a regular credit card can use the Rush card to buy more Rush clothing.[10]

On the West Coast, Hispanic entrepreneurs are putting a Latino spin on the Phat formula. Rodney Rodriguez, Doug Williams, and Chris Hoy are part of a new breed of marketers who are cashing in on the cachet of T-shirts, tank tops, and baseball caps emblazoned with Spanish phrases and images of religious icons that get their street cred from East Los Angeles barrio boys. Rodriguez founded his West Los Angeles–based company, Vato (barrio slang for "homeboy"), in 2002 on $500. In the beginning, he was literally giving away his black tank tops with the word *Mamacita* ("Hot Mama") printed across the front in white Old English or Gothic lettering. Now Vato clothing is carried by some of the hippest stores in Hollywood, Tokyo, and New York. Williams and Hoy, co-proprietors of Teenage Millionaire, also based in Los Angeles, have a more pious take on barrio chic. Their best-selling shirt features a tattoo-inspired drawing of Jesus Christ and the words *Jesus Is My Homeboy.* Pop stars like Jennifer Lopez, Christina Aguilera, and Pink have been spotted snapping up *Mamacita* shirts, and Teenage Millionaire's wares have sold briskly at Urban Outfitters.[11]

Variations of the *cholo* look—a mix of hop-hop and Latin styles that includes oversize T-shirts, bandannas, low-slung chinos, and religious tattoos—have seeped into the urban mainstream, appearing on college students, middle-age hipsters, and delivery boys and other workers who identify with its antiestablishment edge. The look has roots in the L.A. barrio–based "zoot suit" era of the 1940s and 1950s, but the updated concept of *chingaso*—a Latin gangster term that means "ready to fight"—has been broadened to imply that life itself is a struggle and that even affluent suburbanites need to stand up for their beliefs. The religious imagery that's part of the look can be intended as ironic or displayed as a sincere expression of personal spirituality, an ambiguity that only adds to the *cholo* allure.[12]

In New York City, Rafael Jimenez, a Domincian American who grew up in Washington Heights, has built a thriving fashion business producing Latin-themed T-shirts, hats, and accessories that he sells through Bloomingdale's and at his SoHo shop, República Trading Company. It all started in 1995 when he got the idea to make a variation of Banana Republic T-shirts by replacing "Banana" with "Dominican." Since then, his fashion line has expanded and refined its Hispanic message for a multicultural audience. Featured in his 2004 collection are several new T-shirts, including one with roosters meant to evoke rural Latin America and one featuring the masked visage of Mil Máscaras ("A Thousand Masks"), a *"lucha libre"* pro wrestler and cult figure in Mexico and the U.S. Hispanic community. Others are marked with the word *Freedom, Culture,* or *Peace* in English and Spanish, and one shows the word *Revolución* superimposed on a tank with a quote from John F. Kennedy: "Those who make peaceful revolution impossible will make violent revolution inevitable."[13]

Some major retailers, citing the notoriously fickle winds of fashion, have expressed skepticism about the longevity of the trend. That argument, not incidentally, is one that Russell Simmons also encountered when trying to find a buyer for his Phat franchise, and there's no doubt that the numbers of young, multiethnic urban shoppers will continue to rise. Not that the minority entrepreneurs who are making millions by blending irony and ethnic pride seem very worried. More interesting, though not much more convincing, is the claim, coming from inside the Chicano community itself, that barrio-based couture somehow debases Mexican American culture by making it available to—and wearable by—nonminorities. But just imagine where Giorgio Armani would be today if he had tried to limit the buyers of his suits to Italians or if Russell Simmons had decided to limit his hip-hop clothing to blacks. More likely, *cholo* fashion will continue its journey from the inner-city fringe to becoming just one more way to dress like an American.

Barbies and Homies

Cholo consciousness is also the creative force behind a new breed of American icon. It's almost impossible to walk down the streets of any major city, for instance, without running into Bobby Loco. He's a bouncer at a local dance club called Homie Hot Spot. Bobby loves professional wrestling and drives a vintage 1957 Chevy, which he customized by lowering the suspension so that the car cruises inches above the ground in classic lowrider style. His friend Hollywood has slicked back 1970s-style hair, wears a baggy zoot suit, and has connections in the film industry. One of his clients is Papi Chulo, a good-looking Cuban American actor who moved to Los Angeles to become a star. Then there's Wino, a former dot.com millionaire who hit hard times and now relies on his friends to buy him cheap wine. There are girls, too: Shy Girl, FlyGirl, and Lady Joker, to name just a few. Every now and then, La Muerte ("Death") comes along and takes someone away.[14]

These colorful characters, or "Homies," and nearly two hundred more like them are familiar to millions of children and adults across the United States. Only two inches tall, Homies are detailed plastic dolls, usually sold for fifty cents apiece at sidewalk vending machines, grocery stores, and flea markets and via the Internet. The Homies are the brainchild of David Gonzales, a Mexican American illustrator and cartoonist who in the 1970s and 1980s started drawing characters based on people he knew growing up in Oakland and San Jose, California, for a comic strip in *Lowrider* magazine. Before long, the Homies started showing up on T-shirts. In 1999, he produced his first batch of toy Homies. The distributors Gonzales approached initially turned him down, arguing that the urban toy market was still too small to matter. A fanciful combination of collectible and empowering barrio symbol, the Homies filled a need that no one else in the toy industry even knew existed, and by 2003 more than 100 million had been sold. Since 1999, they have generated more than $50 million in sales revenues and Gonzales has become a star in the flagging toy market.[15] Gonzales's Homie empire has expanded to include other characters: Mijos, the baby-faced school-age offspring of the Homies, and the Palermos, a family of former Italian gangsters who quit the Cosa Nostra to run a pizza parlor. Showing a deference to elders that typifies his cultural roots, Gonzales has also released a group of larger, bendable Homies "for the ol' school *vatos* who remember Gumby."

Much like *La Cucaracha (The Cockroach)*, a nationally syndicated Latino-themed comic strip that tackles thorny topics with unvarnished zeal, the Homies are anything but politically correct. They don't just walk; they slouch and strut. They drink, they chase girls, "lots and lots of girls," and they drive souped-up '57 Chevys, the lowrider status chariot. With their tattoos, baggy chinos, miniskirts, and gold chains, they could be mistaken for miniature hoodlums. So it's not surprising that Bobby Loco and his crew have taken fire from upstanding citizens who question the image they project to younger Latinos. The Los Angeles Police Department tried for a while to get stores to drop them. But some of the heat has come from inside the Chicano community itself. Critics say that the Homies set a bad example for the youth and perpetuate negative stereotypes. Gonzales's answer has been that the Homies are not an exploitation of Mexican American archetypes, but simply a reflection of what he saw growing up in Latino neighborhoods. Community leaders and law enforcement authorities have gradually begun to agree. Psychologists and youth outreach counselors see positive benefits in giving kids toys that provide an authentic reflection of themselves and the people they know. Others consider them no different from—or more dangerous than—satiric cartoon characters like those in *The Simpsons*. Nevertheless, there are signs that the Homies are growing up; more recent additions to the crew include lawyers, doctors, college students, and other professionals. Willie G, a goateed Homie who wears a gold chain with a cross and sits in a wheelchair, is described in his profile as "an ex-gangster that has turned his life around and is now a handicap youth counselor. Paralyzed from the waist down, Willie counsels the young Homies about the possible consequences of living 'La Vida Loca.' "

On his "Official Homesite of the Homies" Web site, Gonzales describes his creations as a group of "tightly knit Chicano buddies who grew up together in the Mexican-American barrio (neighborhood) of 'Quién Sabe' (who knows) located in East Los Angeles. The four main characters are Hollywood, Smiley, Pelon, and Bobby Loco. Their separate and distinct personalities and characteristics together make up a single composite entity that is 'HOMIES.' In an inner-city world plagued by poverty, oppression, violence, and drugs, the Homies have formed a strong and binding cultural support system that enables them to overcome the surrounding negativity and allows for laughter and good times as an antidote for reality." If that sounds like a TV sitcom, it may well turn out to be one. Gonzales is in negotiation to produce a Fat Albert and Cosby Kid–style TV show based on his characters, and Scholastic Books has signed him to write and illustrate a series of children's books based on the Mijos.[16] And in early 2004, Wal-Mart and Kmart invited the Homies and Mijos into the heartland by featuring them in thousands of their stores across the country. They won't be lonely. LEGO and G.I. are also rolling out multiethnic versions of their popular action figures.

If Mijos and their plastic buddies could grow up and get jobs, they'd probably dream of dating somebody like Tika, a twenty-five-centimeter-tall, caramel-skinned beauty with vaguely Latina-Asian features and a taste for two-toned hair, short skirts, denim jackets, and platinum jewelry. Her friend Kiyoni has chocolate brown skin and blond-tinted long hair and carries a boom box to listen to the latest hip-hop tunes. Both girls come in graffiti-decorated packages and are part of Mattel's new "Flavas" doll line. The Flavas were created to compete with the Bratz, a brassy, sassy line of dolls that were more in line with—and physically representative of—shifting racial and cultural trends than the WASPy Barbie doll, who is also made by Mattel. The Bratz dolls are the brainchild of Isaac Larian, an immigrant from Iran, who founded his company, MGA Entertainment Inc., in California in the late 1970s. Barbie, who still dominates the fashion doll market for girls aged three to seven and posted $1.7 billion in sales last year, has been losing touch with the "tween" set, or girls between the ages of eight and twelve. The Bratz started moving in on Barbie's turf in 2001, a year in which sales for Barbie dolls in the United States slipped by 12 percent. The Bratz have also eaten into Barbie's market share, which dropped from 85 percent to 70 percent between 2001 and 2003.[17] After My Scene Barbie, a Barbie iteration with a bigger head and feet and fuller lips, was beaten by the Bratz in 2002, Mattel decided to take the hip-hop phenomenon head-on by rushing the Flavas into production. There are six Mattel Flavas, four girls and two boys. When the boxes are arranged together, the graffiti mural they create spells out "FA SIZZLE," a play on the hip-hop expression *Fa' shizzle,* which means "for sure." The fact that Mattel read the graffiti writing on the wall and was forced to launch a separate line to defend itself from Bratz is seen by some as proof that the fashion doll world has changed forever, and for the better. Not that Barbie, who is pushing fifty, has remained totally clueless. Yet another mod makeover of the buxom blonde is under way. Meanwhile, her latest boy toy is "Fashion Insider Ken," a metrosexual male who helps Barbie shop and has just about every trendy accessory a happening guy could want, except, of course, a penis.[18]

Switching Channels

Hispanics have long bemoaned the dearth of Latino faces and recognizably Latino characters on TV. They watched with frustration and envy as African Americans became a permanent presence on network comedies and dramas and personalities like Bill Cosby, Oprah Winfrey, and the Wayans brothers became entertainment icons with long-running hit shows. Latinos had to think back to Desi Arnaz and *I Love Lucy* in the 1950s to remember what it was like to have a Hispanic star on a major television show. Even *Zorro,* a popular series from the same era about a dashing masked Robin Hood–like character set in colonial Mexico, was played by a non-Hispanic. Some Latinos found the lack of Hispanics on TV especially grating since studies had shown that they watched the tube 7 percent more than the general population. Then came the 2003 television season. Almost overnight, it seemed that Hispanics had found a way to "finally break the TV barrier."[19] A study by Initiative Media Services noted the number of Hispanic actors on network TV had grown fivefold since 1990 and that the proportion of Latino actors on TV had grown from 4 percent to 7 percent in just two years.[20]

FOX and ABC led the way, with Hispanic actors making up 11 percent of their prime-time totals, up from 4 percent and 3 percent three years ago, respectively. But finding the next *I Love Lucy* has proved tougher than many had thought. Two much-hyped new FOX comedies, *Luis* and *The Ortegas*, featured Hispanic actors in the lead roles but failed to connect with a prime-time audience. Meanwhile, *The O.C.*, a glossy new series that centered on the travails of wealthy white teens in California's affluent Orange County but also featured full-blooded Latino characters as part of the plot, was the season's smash hit. The lesson of *The O.C.* is that, for the moment at least, Latinos do best on network TV when they are presented as one element of a multicultural mix rather than the main focus.

At the same time, according to another Initiative Media Services study, the TV viewing tastes of blacks and whites are moving closer together, paving the way for a new wave of shows that are designed to attract a multiethnic audience. The study, which was based on an analysis of ratings data from Nielsen Media Research, counted fifty-one shows introduced in the 2002–2003 season that featured multiethnic casts, the most in twelve years. Of the twenty prime-time series watched most by blacks in the fourth quarter of 2002, nine were also among the shows most watched by whites. The overlap was the highest since 1992, when the study started tracking viewer habits by race. The nine programs were *Monday Night Football, CSI, Law & Order, Without a Trace, Law & Order: SVU, ER, CSI: Miami, 60 Minutes,* and *Judging Amy.* Of the ten prime-time series watched most by blacks, eight had black leads or cast members, while shows that scored in the top ten for whites but did not feature black cast members tended to do much worse. For example, *Friends,* which ranked second for whites, ranked in a tie for thirty-ninth among blacks; and *Everybody Loves Raymond,* which ranked third for whites, ranked sixty-fourth among blacks. Advertising spent on programs watched by black viewers in the fourth quarter of 2002 rose by 33 percent compared with the same period in the previous year. Yet there is evidence that suggests programs in which people of color are the mains stars still need to attract a broad base of multiethnic viewers to succeed. The Initiative Media Services study found that in the 2002–2003 season, only 16 percent of the audience watching *George Lopez* was Latino, and 25 percent of the audience watching Damon Wayans's ABC comedy *My Wife & Kids* was black.[21]

In a medium where each rating point can represent millions of viewers—and millions of potential advertiser dollars—the TV ratings system itself is coming under fire from ethnic leaders who allege that their methodology is faulty and undercounts black and Hispanic audiences. In early 2004, Nielsen Media Research abruptly postponed its plan to begin testing a local version of its electronic "people meters" in New York City after a broad coalition of black and Hispanic media and business organizations claimed that it would hurt Spanish-language networks and undercut the economic viability of TV shows that feature or are popular with people of color. According to critics, the new system would not only lower the prices for ads on shows watched by ethnic viewers, but would discourage networks from developing or continuing to air such shows. The protesters were joined by the National Association of Broadcasters and the News Corporation in charging that the new generation of set-top ratings boxes—which would replace pen-and-paper diaries in the top ten urban U.S. markets—undercounted young and minority viewers by as much as 25 percent. In a hastily called news conference in Harlem, Nielsen announced the formation of a special task force with the aim of "assuring the accurate counting of African American and Latino viewers." [22]

Regardless of how the Nielson ratings flap is eventually resolved, the increasing demographic and economic leverage of ethnic viewers means that the networks and the myriad businesses that support them can no longer take ethnic viewers—or their silence—for granted and the prime-time trend toward New Mainstream programming that appeals to a diverse audience is irreversible. Tapping into a TV tradition that dates back to *I Love Lucy*, *The Redd Foxx Show*, and *All in the Family*, the programs are set in a social milieu where ethnic and class stereotypes are often flipped on their heads and culture wars are fought with verbal jabs and wisecracks. On *Whoopi*, the actress Whoopi Goldberg plays Mavis Rae, the owner of a run-down hotel in New York City who isn't afraid to speak her mind, even if that means being less than politically correct. When an Iranian handyman complains to Mavis that jittery post-9/11 New Yorkers seem to suspect him of being a terrorist, she replies: "If I see three or four of you guys on an airplane—I'm off it." One of the most interesting characters in *Whoopi* is not even a minority—at least not in the traditional sense. Actress Elizabeth Regen, who is white, plays Rita Nash, a hip-hop princess in denim miniskirt and dangling gold earrings who is also white. Nash, who has been described by the show's own producers as "extroverted and culturally confused," is that increasingly common phenomenon known as a "wigger," a once derogatory term for white people who willingly take on the cultural attributes and style of a black person.[23]

Hip-hop lite can be played for laughs, as it was in the film *Bringing Down the House*. Everybody gets the joke when Eugene Levy, playing a middle-age, middle-class white man, incongruously exclaims, "You got me straight trippin', boo." Ditto the version of "Rappers Delight" performed by Ellen Dow, who is an elderly white lady, in the film *The Wedding Planner*. But to a younger generation who grew up watching MTV and listening to P. Diddy and Eminem, there's nothing particularly funny or even strange about a young white person wearing baggy jeans and speaking ghetto slang. For Regen, who grew up in New York City in a multicultural environment that included Japanese, Puerto Ricans, and African Americans, playing Rita Nash is anything but a cultural stretch. Unlike the blackface performers from the nineteenth-century who used race as a costume to enhance the pathos of their performance, white wiggers regard hip-hop as an integral part of their identity. It's not an act; it's simply who they are.

Hispanic professionals in the cable and news business also confirm a positive shift in the way the media portrays ethnicity. Nowadays, producers are more likely to assign stories with an ethnic slant, if only to document the way society is evolving. For Maria Hinojosa, a correspondent for CNN since 1997, the new emphasis on multicultural programming at CNN and other news outlets is a delayed reaction to changes that have already taken place. She rejects the notion that reporting on Latino topics is something that exists outside the cultural mainstream. "I have always said from the beginning in my travels as a journalist that I am not telling 'Latino stories,' " she says. "I am not telling 'minority stories.' I'm telling *American* stories." For Hinojosa, who was born in Mexico and became a U.S. citizen in the late eighties, the multicultural perspective she brings to her reporting is automatic and reflective of the world around her. "For me, it's just about telling stories of lives that are, for my experience, organically multicultural, organically diverse," she explains. "It's the way I live my life and the way I think a lot of people will live their lives ten years from now, twenty years from now. It's all part of the transformation."

Mario Bosquez, a coanchor of *CBS News This Morning* at WCBS in New York City, has also noticed a new assertiveness on the part of viewers to offer feedback on how people of color are portrayed in the news. "The multicultural consumer, in my opinion, is better versed now than ever before in 'analyzing' the media for messages that are both positive and negative regarding minorities," he says. "The next two decades, I expect, will bring more changes as the industry brings in more technology and programming that will require personnel with knowledge of the multicultural consumer."

But while brown and black faces are appearing more frequently on TV screens, changes behind the camera have been much slower to arrive. Jesus Trevino, who has produced and directed prime-time TV shows as well as prize-winning programs and documentaries with Latino themes, points out that the percentage of Latino directors working in Hollywood today remains lamentable. Today, Latinos represent only 2 percent of the directors working on TV and film, 1 percent of the writers, and 4 percent to 6 percent of the acting roles. "In 1970, I produced a three-part study of the Latino presence in the motion picture and television industry," Trevino recalls. "Although we were virtually nonexistent on American television, at the time I thought that a breakthrough that would see many television shows featuring Latinos on American television and many Latino feature films was right around the corner. Unfortunately, it has taken more than thirty years for these changes to come about, and they have come about only after many Latino producers developed our own films and television programs. Is this the beginning of a new era for Latinos? I believe it is. Clearly the fact that we have had television programs like *Resurrection Blvd.*, *American Family*, and *The Brothers Garcia* and successful films such as those directed by Robert Rodriguez, Gregory Nava, Miguel Arteta, Luis Mandoki, and others points to a growing acceptance in the industry of the viability of programs about and for Latino audiences. Too, we now have Latino entrepreneurs who can muster the resources to produce our own films and television shows. But even with the advent of more shows, our presence in the motion picture and television industry is likely to remain low, simply because we have so much 'catch-up' to do."

Meanwhile, a new generation of Latino actors and filmmakers—most of them still in their twenties and thirties—have already taken up *la causa*. Hollywood's new Latino wave includes directors such as Alejandro Gonzàlez Iñárritu *(21 Grams)*, Jessy Terrero *(Soul Plane)*, and Alejandro Amenabar *(The Others)* and producer-actors like Gael García Bernal *(Y Tu Mamá También)*, Diego Luna *(Havana Nights)*, Freddie Rodriguez (HBO's *Six Feet Under*), and Jay Hernandez *(crazy/beautiful)*. These young guns and others like them are bound by a pan-American perspective that makes no distinction between their creative contributions and the global, multicultural audiences that increasingly drive the film industry. They also share a conviction that gratuitous sex and violence can be transcended by focusing on human matters of the spirit and heart—values that recall a more innocent era when filmmakers viewed their craft as a higher calling. "There is a sense of integrity, a soulfulness that comes from who they are and where they come from," observes Sergio Aguero, a co-producer of *Y Tu Mamá También* who is exploring projects with several Latinos. "And that quality naturally manifests itself in their work."

Eduardo Verástegui, who emigrated from his native Mexico in 2001 and was hailed three years later on the cover of *People en Español* as one of Latino Hollywood's up-and-coming stars, hasn't lost his idealism since becoming a poster boy for Hollywood's New Mainstream. "*Chasing Papi* was a great opportunity, but it's exactly the kind of film I don't want to do anymore," he says. "Because of *Chasing Papi* and the *People en Español* cover, I'm getting lots of offers to play the Latin lover, the Casanova. But who is that? It's just somebody who doesn't respect women, and who tries to get all the girls that he can. It doesn't mean anything. Doing Don Juan is not an option for me anymore; I want to make films that touch people's hearts and consciences. No matter how long it takes, that's what I'm going to do. That's my new personal version of the American dream."

There are other signs, both obvious and subtle, that Hollywood is waking up to the connection between diversity and dollars. Warner Bros. and 20th Century–Fox are just two of the major studios that have recently

launched new divisions aimed at cultivating movies for multicultural audiences. But the complexion of big-budget movies is also changing. After
years of speculation on whether or not a Hispanic actress would get the
chance to portray Mexican artist Frida Kahlo on film, Salma Hayek, a
Mexican, performed the title role in Julie Taymor's Academy Award–
winning movie. In the Jim Carrey film *Bruce Almighty*, the African American actor Morgan Freeman plays God, literally.[24] First appearing in
worker's overalls and later dressed in an immaculate white suit, Freeman's
God is personable, wise, and kind. By transferring his divine powers to
Carrey's character, he helps him transcend his selfish proclivities and grasp
the greater rewards of self-sacrifice and altruism. The 2003 film, which
grossed more than $200 million in the United States alone, implicitly
tapped a theological concept put forth in 1929 by Robert Alexander, who
in his "Ethiopian Manifesto" envisioned a "black Messiah" who would arrive from heaven to free the slaves. Since then other black leaders, theologians, and anthropologists have challenged the idea that Jesus was a white
man with European features. Albert Cleage, a black theologian and close
associate of Malcolm X, stated categorically that Christ was black and that
his mother, Mary, was a black woman. His argument centers on the fact
that Mary was an Israelite of the tribe of Judah and that Judeans were a
"mixture of Chaldeans, Egyptians, Midanites, Ethiopians, Kushites, Baby-
lonians and other dark peoples, all of whom were already mixed with Black
people of Central Africa."[25] Cleage argued that since God created man in
his own image, then "we must look at man to see what God looks like . . .
if God created man in his own image, then God must be some combination of Black, red, yellow and white . . . we must think of God as Black."
The film's writers and director have said that their decision to cast Freeman was based on his acting skill, not his race. But while Freeman's performance was generally praised, some African Americans criticized *Bruce
Almighty* for depicting a black God whose raison d'être is to help a white
man become a better person, thus perpetuating the stereotypical image of
black people—even if they're God—being subservient to, and ultimately
in the business of serving, whites. A year later, Mel Gibson caught flak for
casting a white actor in the lead role of his blockbuster epic, *The Passion of
Christ*. Gibson's film, which took such pains to be authentic that it fea-

tured dialogue in the ancient language of Aramaic, was criticized by scholars for portraying Christ as an Anglo despite the fact that the inhabitants of biblical lands during the time of Jesus were ethnic Africans.[26]

Still, things have come a long way in Hollywood since 1949, when a masked white do-gooder known as the Lone Ranger galloped across the American West with a Native American sidekick named Tonto, whose name, in Spanish, means "stupid." These days, when a white and a minority join forces to battle evil—most commonly in a crime-fighting action genre known as the "buddy film"—the nonwhite character is likely to be faster, smarter, or more stable than the white partner. Modern buddy films are socially progressive in that they either ignore the racial divide altogether or use it as a source of humor. And because they are designed to appeal to black and white audiences alike, they are more profitable than buddy films with a monoracial cast. According to *Premiere* magazine, during the fifteen years between 1987 and 2002, the average gross of a black-white buddy movie was $101,939,175, versus $67,091,163 for buddy films with a monoracial cast.[27]

In interracial buddy movies, the mismatched partners—after an obligatory initial distrust and/or dislike—inevitably move on to grudging respect and mutual admiration, usually after saving each other's lives and vanquishing the bad guys. In *Lethal Weapon 2*, for example, Danny Glover is the stable, law-abiding family man and Mel Gibson is an emotionally volatile loner. The villains just happen to be a band of ruthless South African white supremacists, underscoring the natural connection between racism and evil. In the *Men in Black* series, Will Smith is young and hip; Tommy Lee Jones is seasoned and square. The fantastical outer space creatures they battle are a kind of macrocosm of the multicultural population—the first *Men in Black* movie opens with a scene in which extraterrestrials try to sneak into the United States by stowing away on a truck full of illegal immigrants. In *Beverly Hills Cop*, one of a string of Eddie Murphy interracial buddy films that includes *Trading Places* (costarring Dan Aykroyd) and *48 Hours* (with Nick Nolte), Murphy plays Axel Foley, an uppity urban black cop from Detroit who is the demographic and cultural antithesis of the white Beverly Hills cops with whom he predictably clashes—and eventually bonds. Seann William Scott plays the flaky sidekick to the Rock's solid bounty hunter in the action-adventure film *The Rundown*. And in *Once upon a Time in Mexico*, Antonio Banderas and Johnny Depp team up against a drug cartel kingpin played by Willem Dafoe in the third installment of Rodríguez's *El Mariachi/ Desperado* film trilogy. Part of the social-ethnic appeal of such movies is that as the two partners come to terms with—or simply ignore—their racial and cultural differences, the audience participates in their emotional assimilation. If Chris Rock and Anthony Hopkins (*Bad Company*) can bridge the gap, and if Jackie Chan and Chris Tucker (*Rush Hour*) can bond, then anyone can. What's more, by putting these ethnic odd couples in mortal danger and then having them rescue each other, those movies tell us that, as Americans, it's not only possible to get along and help one another out, it's something we should do for our own mutual survival.

Cinderella Stories

When James L. Brooks, the Oscar-winning writer-director of films like *Broadcast News* and *As Good as It Gets*, decided that his new film would center on the relationship between a Latina maid and the affluent white couple who employ her, he knew that the authenticity of the Hispanic character was critical to the story's success. To help him research the Latina role in *Spanglish*, he turned to Christy Haubegger, a Texas-born Mexican-American who built a career out of understanding Hispanic women as the founder and publisher of *Latina* magazine.

"*Spanglish* is about a Latina who goes to work with this crazy American couple, played by Adam Sandler and Téa Leoni," says Haubegger, who is one of the film's executive producers. "Jim is such a wonderful writer, but it takes him years to write a script. He's very committed to the research process. He interviewed all these women, who were Mexican immigrants generally, and asked them about their expectations and aspirations, what they expected from America, and their hopes when they got here. All of a sudden he realized that she doesn't have to be every Mexican woman. She's just one person—she's a real flesh-and-blood character. But what she goes through is very emblematic of what's happening. And she has these kids who are assimilating against her will and trying to navigate two worlds and two languages. The experience is sort of universal among a whole bunch of us, or our parents. There's this great moment when you see her humanity and her dignity and all these other things that you'd want to see in any character. And it's not remarkable anymore; you realize that it's what we all aspire to—it's the normalness of humanity."

For Haubegger, normal was growing up as an orphan in Houston with American foster parents of German extraction. As an ambitious Latina with no role models, she had to navigate a path to her own sense of identity. Magazines that years later would open the door to professional and personal fulfillment made her feel excluded. "I didn't realize then that teen magazines make everyone feel unattractive and left out," she says. "I literally never saw anyone who looked like me. At the time it was about being really thin and really blond. It was something I couldn't even imagine being." After graduating from the University of Texas and Stanford Law School, Haubegger managed to get an appointment with Ed Lewis, Chairman and CEO of Essence Communications (the publisher of *Essence* magazine), and pitched him the idea for a magazine for Hispanic women. "I said something along the lines of, 'There's going to be more Hispanic women than African American women in about twenty minutes, and we don't have a magazine for us yet,' " she recalls. "And that's it, that's the whole story. He believed in the opportunity enough to do some testing. We did focus groups, we did direct-mail tests, and they all came back positive. We put together a joint venture to launch the magazine in 1995, and we launched it a year later in 1996."

The debut issue of *Latina* featured an up-and-coming actress named Jennifer Lopez on the cover. At the time, Lopez had just won a nationwide talent search for the title role in *Selena*, a film about the photogenic Tejana singer that would establish her as a Hollywood star. The rest of the issue, which was bilingual, featured a mix of celebrity interviews, self-help articles, and a Miami-inspired fashion spread. *Latina*'s target market— young professionals, newlyweds, and working women with children who bought more than their share of clothes, cosmetics, and baby products— was receptive to the magazine, but getting advertisers to grasp the implications of their interest was another story. "The business plan had called for fifty pages of advertising, and we had only about sixteen in the first issue," Haubegger recalls. "It was like, 'Oh my God, how are we going to keep this going?' "

Over time, advertisers began to understand the value of marketing to bilingual Latinas, but the track record for English-language publications aimed at ethnic audiences is spotty at best. Among magazines for African Americans, *Essence* magazine has a circulation of about 1 million, while *Black Enterprise* is just below half a million. General-interest publications for Asian Americans have generally fared less well. *aMagazine*, an Asian lifestyle and entertainment magazine that launched in 1989, reached a peak circulation of two hundred thousand in 1994 before debts incurred by the launch of its Web site forced it to close in 2001. Lately, long-running Asian magazines like *AsianWeek*, *KoreAM Journal*, and *Filipinas* have been joined by trendy start-ups like *Noodle* and *Yolk* that appeal to a younger, hipper Asian readership.[28]

Latinos stand out, not just in their ability to span races and languages, but also in their pattern of assimilation, which, owing to a near constant influx of immigrants, is less like the proverbial lump in the snake than a river or a spring that is being constantly replenished and refreshed by its source. What that means is that even as second-, third- and fourth-generation Latinos become increasingly acculturated and move up the socioeconomic ladder, the bottom rungs are refilled by Latin Americans seeking work and a chance to do the same. Owing to a variety of factors, including proximity to Latin America, the relatively porous U.S.-Mexico border, and the large numbers of Spanish-speaking people already living in major urban areas, not all Latinos who come to the United States feel the need to assimilate at the same rate or in the same way. And their adoption of American values, habits, and customs may be a matter less of language than of cultural affinity and choice.

"We are a community that comes here and is very optimistic about the future," observes Lisa Quiroz, *People en Español*'s founding publisher and current vice president of corporate responsibility for Time Warner. "We come here with a very self-sacrificing attitude: we say, 'I'll work in a factory so my kid can go to Harvard.' We tend to be socially conservative. We're pretty darn religious and almost more patriotic than most Americans. There's a real desire to fit in, which I don't think someone who's black necessarily feels." At the same time, however, Hispanics are very comfortable with a dual cultural identity that might seem contradictory to others but is perfectly natural to them. "There is something very different about the Latino experience," says Quiroz, a Latina of Puerto Rican and Mexican descent who grew up in Staten Island and graduated from Harvard University before joining Time Inc.'s consumer marketing department in 1990. "It makes us very comfortable with saying, 'I'm Latino, and I'm a citizen of this country' all in the same breath. And that is the concept that is the hardest thing for me to explain to a group of non-Hispanic people who work in corporate America."

Launched in 1996, *People en Español*, with a readership of 4.2 million, is the largest Spanish-language general-interest publication in the country and the best-selling magazine targeted to Hispanics in any language. *Reader's Digest*, *National Geographic*, *Glamour*, and *Men's Health* also publish Spanish-language editions. Yet while other Spanish editions of U.S. magazines are mainly translated versions of the same editorial content, *People en Español* creates about 80 percent of its content specifically for its audience, reflecting the uniquely transnational character of the U.S. Hispanic reader, particularly in the celebrity-fueled realm of movies, TV, and music that is *People*'s primary focus. Nineteen percent of the magazine's subscribers are U.S.-born, and 81 percent are foreign-born. "It's not about English versus Spanish, it's about a cultural translation," says *People en Español* marketing executive Joaquim Rebeiro. "In the beginning it was 80 percent direct translation from the English edition of *People* and 20 percent original content. Now it's the other way around."

In its 2002 Hispanic Opinion Tracker (H.O.T.), *People en Español* and Cheskin Research conducted six thousand telephone interviews to probe linguistic and cultural characteristics of the U.S. Hispanic population. When asked how they saw themselves in terms of being Hispanics or Americans, 29 percent said they were Hispanics and not Americans; 21 percent said they were Hispanics first and Americans second; 36 percent said they were equally Hispanics and Americans; 9 percent said they were Americans first and Hispanics second; 3 percent said they were Americans, not Hispanics; and 3 percent didn't know or declined to answer. The

H.O.T. study defined 56 percent of the market as "Hispanic dominant," or those who displayed a preference for Spanish and a strong Hispanic identity; 20 percent were "bicultural," or fully bilingual and comfortable in both worlds, with a Hispanic cultural orientation and an economic and academic alignment with the United States; and 23 percent were "U.S. dominant," with attitudes and behaviors that mirror the general market, but maintaining a respect for and identification with their Hispanic heritage. This group was also identified as the most likely to "demonstrate retro-acculturation," or to rediscover or reaffirm the importance of their ethnic roots. Hispanic dominants were also the most likely to feel the "need to demonstrate and sustain my heritage, traditions, and symbols," to listen to Latin music, to have a spouse or partner who was also Hispanic, to have five of their closest friends be Hispanic, and to plan to raise their children bilingually. U.S.-dominant Hispanics were most likely to own their own home and celebrate the Fourth of July and the least likely to be married to a Hispanic or have five Hispanic best friends.[29]

Bicultural Hispanics were the most likely of the three groups to observe Cinco de Mayo and listen to hip-hop. Lou Lopez, the marketing executive who coordinated the H.O.T. study for *People en Español*, believes that for Spanish-speaking Hispanics in the United States, the Latin American film and music stars who often appear on the magazine's cover have a sociological impact that goes far beyond entertainment. "The role of Spanish celebrity, and by extension Spanish celebrity media, is one of affirmation, appreciation, and connection," he observes. "It affirms the importance of Hispanic culture without and within the United States. It allows for appreciation of Hispanic talent across national boundaries, and it provides a connection to the past and a bridge to the future."

That future includes deeply felt values that have much wider social implications. Overall, the H.O.T. study found that 95 percent of the Hispanic respondents backed bilingual education and 87 percent identified education as "the key" to their children's success. Seventy-three percent of Hispanics rated "allocating funds for building affordable housing" extremely or very important, compared with only 39 percent for non-Hispanics. Seventy percent of Hispanic respondents felt that "appointing a Hispanic/minority to the U.S. Supreme Court" was very or extremely important, versus 22 percent for non-Hispanics. Sixty-seven percent said they preferred the term *Hispanic* to *Latino*, and a majority expressed strong support for a slew of public policy initiatives, including child care assistance, helping impoverished countries, gun control, after-school programs, and drug control.[30]

Politically, Hispanics in the United States continue to be something of a conundrum. While the H.O.T. study found that 53 percent of the Hispanics polled identified themselves as Democrats and only 17 percent as Republicans, a significant percentage of Latino votes went to George Bush in the 2000 presidential election and to Arnold Schwarzenegger in the 2003 California recall.[31] In New York City alone, there is a considerable cultural gap between Puerto Ricans, who have lived in the city for generations, and Dominicans, who have arrived in the last few decades. And both groups differ greatly from Mexicans, who have also migrated to New York in recent years. While agreeing that Hispanics in the United States are linguistically and culturally diverse, Quiroz nonetheless believes that the common culture that unites Hispanics is stronger than national or ethnic disparities. "The sense of Hispanic identity runs pretty deep," Quiroz says. "In terms of our social values and attitudes, we haven't found a lot of differences in terms of ethnicities—where we see the bigger differences between people who are born here versus those that were not."

As advertisers pursue an increasingly multitiered approach to reach New Mainstream consumers, local ethnic media is gaining traction as one of the most effective ways to get the attention of the non-English market. A study by Bendixon and Associates, a Florida-based survey, management, and communications consulting group, entitled "New California Media" found that ethnic television stations, radio stations, and newspapers reach 84 percent of all Californians who self-identify as Hispanic, African American, or Asian American. The study's definition of Asian included Koreans, Chinese, Vietnamese, Asian Indian, Japanese, Filipino, Thai, Cambodian, and Laotian. Bendixon found that ethnic media outlets reached their audience with substantial frequency, as 67 percent of Hispanics, 51 percent of African Americans, and 55 percent of Asians reported using an ethnic media source at least once a day. News was the favorite type of programming watched on ethnic television, music was most popular on ethnic radio, and international news was the most popular section of ethnic newspapers. More than half (53 percent) of the respondents said they preferred ethnic TV, radio, or newspapers to their "general market" counterparts. Fifty-nine percent of the respondents also said that they paid "more attention" to ethnic TV, radio, and newspapers, compared with 33 percent who said they paid more attention to general media, and 63 percent of Hispanic respondents said they were "more likely to buy a product or service advertised in a Latino-oriented publication or program." Among African Americans, 58 percent agreed that "businesses that advertise in media that focuses on African American themes and content seem to understand my needs and desires better than other companies." And 68 percent of the Asians polled felt that companies that advertised in media that focused on Koreans, Vietnamese, and other Asian groups "really care about me and my community."[32]

For Monica Lozano, president of *La Opinión*, the nation's largest Spanish-language newspaper, those statistics translate into a golden opportunity for advertisers seeking a foothold in the Hispanic community through her 680,000 readers. Founded in California in 1926 and owned jointly by the Lozano family and the Tribune company, *La Opinión* is a trusted and familiar media brand to the state's Hispanics, who make up roughly a third of California's population of 34.5 million. In 2003, the U.S. Census Bureau reported that between 2000 and 2002, Los Angeles County had the nation's largest Hispanic population (4.5 million) and numerical increase (300,000). In 2002, Latinos made up 45 percent of L.A. Country's nearly 10 million residents, versus 31.1 percent for non-Hispanic whites. Lozano likes to point out that if ranked by economic clout, U.S. Hispanics would represent the world's tenth largest economic power. Lozano is leveraging *La Opinión*'s credibility with Hispanics to offer an array of possibilities for clients who want to make an impression with Latino consumers and business owners. In its campaign for Beech-Nut, the paper used the Latino community's affinity for family and health issues to devise a multimedia vehicle that included a "Beech-Nut baby" picture contest and expert advice on infant care, pregnancy, nutrition, and baby shower ideas that was promoted in the newspaper and on a co-branded micro–Web site. "This is the future," says Lozano, who points to rising rates of Latino home ownership, political participation, and bilingualism, especially among Latino youth, as signs that California's Hispanics are poised to flex their growing demographic muscle.[33]

The potential for immense profits is drawing other media players into the field. In 2003, plans were announced to launch Spanish-language newspapers in Dallas, Orlando, and Chicago. The *Dallas Morning News* spawned *El Día (Today)*, a six-day-a-week publication aimed at the city's 1 million Latinos that will compete for readers with the Knight Ridder chain's *La Estrella (The Star)*. And *El Nuevo Día (The New Day)*, Puerto Rico's largest newspaper, is starting a daily tabloid version in Orlando, where some 140,000 Puerto Ricans live and work. In March of 2004, the Tribune Company launched a Los Angeles edition of *Hoy*, a Spanish-language newspaper also published in Chicago and New York. *Hoy*'s debut came two months after *La Opinión* joined forces with *El Diario/La Prensa (The Diary/The Press)*, New York's oldest and largest Spanish-language daily, to create Impremedia, a publishing partnership with a combined total of 10 million readers.[34] And Edward Schumacher, a former managing editor of *The Wall Street Journal* Americas edition and a former correspondent in Madrid and Buenos Aires for *The New York Times*, left the *Journal* to help raise $20 million in seed money from investors for Meximerica, a new U.S.-based publishing company hoping to capitalize on the rising number of Latino newspaper readers by blending news from Mexico and Latin America with localized reporting. Schumacher, who has recruited a number of other top U.S. journalists to help run Meximerica, is planning to publish newspapers in several Texas cities in 2004 before branching out to other heavily Hispanic communities.[35]

The challenge—and financial lure—of cobbling together regional and national networks from ethnically and economically disparate U.S. Hispanic populations is hardly limited to print. The linguistic duality of U.S. Hispanics—and the economic and cultural importance of Latinas in the typical Hispanic family—has had a formative influence on the evolution of Spanish-language TV, as well as new bilingual and English networks targeting more assimilated Latinos. In the fall of 2003, Telemundo unveiled a Spanish-language version of ABC's *Bachelorette* called *La Cenicienta*

(*Cinderella*). The program followed the basic girl-picks-boy dating format, but with a uniquely Hispanic twist. In this case, the protagonist, a twenty-four-year-old Mexican American from Texas named Minerva Ruvalcaba, was a twice divorced mother of a two-and-a-half-year-old girl, a fact that stayed a secret from Ms. Ruvalcaba's suitors until the very end of the show. In a culture where unwed mothers are still looked upon to a certain extent as social lepers, the suspense of whether or not love would triumph over propriety was part of the program's appeal. The show also raised issues of race, class, and nationality by having its Cinderella choose from a pool of prospective husbands that included a black Cuban American, a Jewish Mexican, and men from various other nationalities and ethnic and socio-economic backgrounds. Finally, the contestants were subjected to grilling by not just Ms. Ruvalcaba, but also her parents, a priest, an astrologer, and a fairy godmother played by daytime soap star Eva Tamargo Lemus. Early episodes of the show exceeded Telemundo's average viewership for eighteen- to forty-nine-year-olds by 54 percent and proved that English entertainment formats could be carried over into the Spanish market, if offered within the proper context.

For Nely Galán, one of the show's producers and a longtime advocate of programming created by and for Hispanics in the United States, the buzz created by *La Cenicienta* was also a personal vindication. "Sometimes you have to wait a while for redemption to come—everything I did before helped me learn and enabled me to get to that point," said Ms. Galán, who at the time of *La Cenicienta*'s debut had a three-year-old son, born out of wedlock to the Latino comedian Paul Rodriguez. "NBC finally realizes that they have to create original programming to compete."

Born in Cuba, Galán immigrated to the United States in 1965 at the age of two and grew up on a tree-lined street in Teaneck, New Jersey. After a series of television jobs both in front of and behind the camera, she co-founded Tropix, a joint venture with HBO aimed at developing Latino-themed shows for the growing U.S. Hispanic audience. In late 1994, she formed Galan Entertainment, a multilingual advertising and marketing firm that quickly morphed into a media production company. Galán, who based her new company in a renovated warehouse in Venice Beach, California, explored different graphical and thematic approaches for Hispanic audiences in the United States and Latin America. One of the people who shared Galán's vision was Gabriel Reyes, a Mexico-born TV actor who joined Galán's company in 1991 to work on public relations and content development. "At the time, the two Spanish-language networks, Univision and Telemundo, were doing a very poor job of delivering programming that reflected the Latino experience in the United States," Reyes recalls. "Their programming, which to this day remains largely unchanged, consisted largely of imported *telenovellas*—daily soap opera told within a four- to six-month story arc. The programming resonates with older, more traditional Latinos—parents and grandparents. We wanted to make shows for young, upwardly mobile Latinos who had been brought up as American. We knew there was a market for this type of entertainment, because we ourselves *were* the kind of Latinos we were trying to reach."

Galán got her chance in 1998 when she became president of the entertainment division of the Telemundo network, the number two U.S. Spanish television network, making her the nation's most powerful Latina TV executive. Even though the network's market share rose from 16 percent to 18 percent during Galán's tenure, her reign was short-lived. Industry insiders say that Galán fell out of favor with her bosses after trying to cut back on the foreign-produced Spanish-language soaps, or *telenovellas*, that continue to be a staple at both Telemundo and Univision. Galán left Telemundo in the fall of 1999 with a deal to produce three shows, including *Padre Alberto*, a weekday talk show hosted by a hunky Catholic priest from Miami.

The success of *La Cenicienta* has given Telemundo, which was purchased by NBC in 2001, some much-needed traction in its lopsided battle with Univision, which currently reaches over 95 percent of all Hispanic households in the United States and controls the lion's share of Spanish-language television viewers and ad revenue. Founded in 1961 by Mexican media mogul Emilio Azcarraga and several investors, Univision, in addition to its station group and network, owns Galavision, a Spanish-language cable network with six million subscribers, and operates TeleFutura, a sixteen-station Spanish-language TV network, and several Latino music labels and Internet sites. In 2003, Univision acquired Hispanic Broadcasting Corp., the largest Spanish-language radio chain in the United States, thereby creating a virtual monopoly on Spanish-language news and entertainment content in the United States America.

Both networks are pursuing the reality TV craze, hoping to repeat the ratings bonanza of their English-language antecedents. Other Telemundo reality-style shows include *Protagonistas de Novela (Protagonists of a Soap Opera)*, a variation of *American Idol* in which twelve contestants vie for spots on a Telemundo soap opera. A spinoff scheduled for the 2004 season will apply a similar formula to contestants who can sing, dance, act, and do comedy. Univision, for its part, has *La Pesera de Amor (The Love Bus)*, a variation of ABC's *The Bachelor* aimed at an older audience. Telemundo executives initially worried that *La Cenicienta* was too worldly for a show named after a character in a fantasy fable of romantic love. But, demographically, at least, the show was bound to resonate: census figures show that 28 percent of all Hispanic families with children in the United States are headed by a single mother.

Galán took *La Cenicienta*'s Cinderella premise a step further—and into the English TV market—with her next project, a makeover-cum-beauty pageant reality show called *The Swan*. The program, which debuted in the spring of 2004 immediately following *American Idol* and melded the unabashed emotionality of Spanish soaps with the cutthroat competition of the *Survivor* series, won a 12 share on its first night, or an audience of roughly 19 million viewers. Galán, who appeared on the show as a "beauty coach," described it as the "most loving 'lottery for women' show in the world." What she has proved without a doubt is that psychologically charged themes of fantasy and transformation, when shaped to fit the fast-food formats of network TV, can serve an aspirational need that transcends culture and language.[36]

As the U.S. Latino population approaches a cultural and economic tipping point, there is no dearth of media strategies that attempt to straddle the myriad ways in which Hispanics are influencing and redefining life in the United States. Fernando Espuelas, who built the Spanish-language Web portal StarMedia into a hemispheric brand before the dot.com collapse took the wind out of its stock—is spreading his chips with VOY, a "multitiered lifestyle and entertainment company aimed at the English-language Latino market." VOY—Spanish for "I go"—intends to act, according to the company's press release, "as a cultural bridge between Latinos and the mainstream" by producing branded content packaged for television, publishing, music, film, and other media products. Uruguayan-born Espuelas, who will be the CEO of the privately funded miniconglom-erate, envisions VOY as "the preeminent 'home' for the New Generation Latino consumer." VOY, which has partnered with Hollywood's Endeavor talent agency, has completed a pilot for a talk show featuring "entertaining stories of success and triumph over adversity." Its first book, VOY: I Go, to be published by Tarcher/Penguin books, is described as "an inspiring story of optimism and self-empowerment," VOY plans to offer a continuing se-ries of fiction and nonfiction titles that will "inspire and provide 'tool kits' for consumers looking to improve their lives" and to, as Espuelas puts it, "build a brand synonymous with self-empowerment, optimism and suc-cess."[37] Whether or not Espuelas can survive in an industry that already has a number of established Latino players, he deserves credit for daring to bet his future on the notion that a media company can create products that reflect and appeal to the optimism of an entire demographic phenom-enon. The historical ascendance of Hispanics and their transformative ef-fect on the American mainstream is palpable but still largely unarticulated. If Latinos go with VOY, it will be because Espuelas was able to sell them the self-fulfilling story of their own success.

4. diversity.com

On the morning of January 10, 2000, I was awakened in my São Paulo hotel room by a phone call that carried mind-boggling news: America Online, the world's largest Internet service and the company that I worked for, had just announced it was buying Time Warner for $165 billion. The AOL–Time Warner deal was a transaction of historic proportions. Not only was it the biggest merger ever, but it signaled the triumph of new media and certified the Internet as the medium of the twenty-first century. The cybergeeks and computer nerds had won; revered brands like Warner Music, HBO, Cartoon Network, CNN, Time Inc., and New Line Cinema were now divisions of AOL. The new company, which would be dubbed AOL Time Warner, was estimated to have a combined worth of almost $319 billion. At the time, long before the dot.com collapse and mismanaged expectations turned the deal into one of history's greatest business fiascoes, it was seen as a transformational moment with implications that went far beyond the exploding popularity of e-mail. We all sensed that nothing would ever be the same again, and, of course, we were right.

For me, the merger had a personal relevance that dated back to my days in old media as a *Time* magazine staff writer. While at *Time*, I had written a 1988 special issue cover story on Edward James Olmos subtitled "Hispanic Culture Breaks Out of the Barrio." The idea that Hispanic culture was somehow imprisoned in the barrio and thus needed to "break out" seems ludicrous today, but back then, coming from a mainstream publication like *Time*, the pronouncement seemed enlightened and empowering. A few years later, research I conducted in Mexico and Guatemala for my second novel, *Obsidian Sky*, which featured a Chicano protagonist who was studying anthropology in Mesoamerica, would lead to a *Time* cover story on the Maya. In between, I kept a lookout for stories that reflected what I already felt in my gut: that Latinos were part of a multifaceted and fascinating story, a story about a nation that was changing and evolving in innumerable ways, a story about America and its demographic and cultural destiny. After leaving Time Warner in the early 1990s to finish *Obsidian Sky*, and later as a cofounder and content director of a Web 'zine called *Total New York*, I became a part of that story. But the lessons I learned during my tenure at *Time*, about how magazines and media don't just reflect the world but also help to shape it, had molded and transformed me as well.

Meanwhile, in the uncharted wilderness of the Internet, a new American territory had opened up. This new terrain, in the words of Internet guru and Wyoming rancher John Perry Barlow, was an "electronic frontier" where computer code and a kind of abbreviated techno-English was the lingua franca. The unrestricted, democratizing force of Internet tools, terms, and protocols was creating a new definition of community that transcended borders and cultural boundaries. As the Web's early adopters quickly learned, people in India, Argentina, and Singapore had computers, too, and they were eager to use them to join the digital revolution. The user community, predicted MIT's Nicholas Negroponte in his 1995 book, *Being Digital*, "will be in the mainstream of everyday life. Its demographics will look more and more like the demographics of the world itself. . . . The true value of a network is less about information and more about community. The information superhighway is more than a shortcut to every book in the Library of Congress. It is creating a totally new, global social fabric." [1]

The door to this wired new world swung open for me in the fall of 1994 at a friend's birthday party, where I met John Borthwick, a Wharton grad and business consultant who was planning to launch a local Web site about New York City. At the time, I hardly knew a Web site from a construction site (eventually I learned how similar they actually are), but from what I already knew, I had an inkling that the Internet could have a significant and lasting impact on publishing and other media. So when Borthwick invited me to become an equity partner and the site's editorial director, I joined the founding team. Launched in the spring of 1995, Total New York was part of a pioneering breed of local Internet sites that sought, as we became fond of saying, to "connect cyberspace with real space."

One of our projects was an avatar-based virtual world created in partnership with the downtown pop artist Kenny Scharf. Total Cosmic Cavern, as we called it, was a surreal universe unto itself where Web surfers could assume the zany personas of Scharf-designed characters, converse with other residents via speech balloons, order virtual drinks from an automated "bot" bartender, and ride Dr. Seuss–like spaceships to wormholes, neon planets, and glowing galaxies. One day, a Total New York staffer came into my office with a perplexed look on his face. "There are a bunch of people on the second level of the spaceship hanging out and speaking Portuguese," he reported. "I think they're Brazilian." Sure enough, for reasons that escaped us at the time, the basement of the Cosmic Cavern starship had become a meeting place for Brazilian cybernauts. We shrugged off the incident as just another inexplicable Internet phenomenon, but years later I would remember the adventurous colony of Brazilians in Cosmic Cavern with a new level of respect.

Even after AOL bought Total New York in 1997, and I became the content director and editorial architect of AOL's Digital City New York service, I continued chronicling various aspects of the Latino phenomenon in *Rolling Stone, The New York Times,* and other publications. During the Internet frenzy that had engulfed America in the late 1990s and was now sweeping the rest of the world, that story had taken on an interesting new twist. A new Spanish-language portal based out of New York was getting attention from the press and a positive reaction from Wall Street. Back then, for most people, even smart Web techies, the idea that Latin America might join the digital revolution was a revelation. Was it really possible that the continent of cocaine farmers, Maoist guerrillas, and seething Amazonian jungles could get wired? Did enough people even have telephone lines down there? And how do you say "Yahoo!" in Spanish, anyway? (The answers: Yes, Yes, and StarMedia).

In the summer of 1999, as AOL's levitating stock defied gravity and all known business models, a colleague informed me that the company was looking for someone to head content and programming for its new Latin American division. AOL Latin America (AOLA), as the new entity would be called, was a $100 million joint venture between AOL and the Cisneros Group, a family-run media empire based in Caracas that controlled, among many other things, one of Latin America's largest television production companies. The idea of helping to launch AOL services across Latin America was simply too tempting to pass up. The Internet would come to Latin America only once, I knew, and I was determined not to miss the opportunity to help make it happen. Not to mention the rumored plans for an AOL Latin America initial public offering, a financial rite of passage that in those days was practically akin to obtaining a license to print money.

The operational assumption, which seemed pretty reasonable at the time, was that AOL's proven model of making the Internet accessible to the masses would follow the same trajectory in Latin America that it had in the United States. After all, as just about anyone with a modem and a high school education knew, the Internet had grown mushroomlike on the digital remains of a defunct U.S. Defense Department plan to create an emergency communications network that could survive a nuclear attack. More important, the whole concept of the World Wide Web as a mass commercial enterprise, made popular by a browser built and marketed by Netscape Communications, as well as the Wall Street frenzy that followed, had been cultivated in America. In the late 1990s, the majority of all users and Web sites were based in the United States, and AOL was the world's biggest and most successful Internet service. In fact, AOL's success in the United States was a key factor behind its international push; with some 24 million registered users, the domestic U.S. market was quickly approaching the saturation point. To fuel the subscriber growth that Wall Street expected and demanded, AOL had initiated a series of joint ventures in Europe and Japan. Now it had turned its attention to Latin America and Mexico, which together represented a tantalizing market of nearly 500 million people. So what if nearly half of them lived in poverty and only a fraction of them spoke English? The world-famous AOL brand, allied with the powerful Cisneros Group and guided by the demonstrated marketing savvy of then AOL president Bob Pittman, was a couldn't-miss proposition. Shortly after joining AOLA, I found myself at an offshore board of directors meeting at Jamaica's Round Hill resort, where Pittman had a vacation home. I had met Pittman briefly when our careers overlapped at Time Warner and had watched in awe like everyone else as he led AOL from near disaster to unimaginable success. To me, the fact that he was personally involved in AOLA was just another sign of kismet. We spent most of the day discussing strategy and presenting our plans to the board, which included Pittman, various AOL senior executives, and Gustavo and Ricardo Cisneros. The talk was sober, but spirits were high. Later that evening, before a lavish torchlit dinner on the beach, we were shuttled up the hill to Pittman's multitiered house, where we sipped tequila shots and savored the inevitable success that lay before us. With Pittman himself helping to shape the AOLA brand, there was no way we could possibly lose. It was no accident that AOLA's affable president, Charles Herington, had cut his teeth as an executive for the Latin American divisions of Revlon and Pepsico. Like Coke, General Motors, and dozens of American corporations before it, AOL would repackage and market its product for the Latin American market *en Español.* And Portuguese, too, for that matter. The only problem, we at AOLA eventually, painfully learned, was that Latin America wasn't waiting for AOL to lead it into the Internet age. It was already there.

The day after the AOL–Time Warner merger announcement, during a flight to our offices in Buenos Aires, I stared at the pictures of Steve Case and Gerald Levin that were splashed across the front page of every newspaper in Latin America. Clearly, the deal of the century was being saluted as an event of global significance, and there was no question in my mind that it would have a considerable impact on AOL Latin America. Two months earlier, with a splashy party that featured hundreds of VIP guests, bands, and celebrities, AOLA had launched AOL Brazil. Along with Mexico and Argentina, Brazil represented almost three-quarters of Latin America's user base, making it a key piece of AOLA's regional strategy. Even Pittman had flown down for the event, signaling AOL's commitment to Latin America and AOLA. For the AOLA executive staff, it was an exhilarating moment and the culmination of months of hard work.

But along the way to the well-deserved handshakes and champagne toasts, we had come to the dawning realization that conquering Latin America would be no cakewalk. The local competition, which had used AOL as an inspiration and model for its own Internet services, had been aggressively building their user bases and amassing exclusive content deals and advertising war chests with the help of local banks, telephone companies, and media partners. The largest of them, Universe Online or UOL, even sounded like an AOL clone. But just like Superman's evil twin, UOL was our worst nightmare. *America is big, but the Universe is even bigger.* UOL was owned by a consortium of investors that included the Folha Group, which own *Folha de São Paulo,* Brazil's version of the *New York Times,* Editora Abril, Brazil's largest magazine publisher, and Portugal Telecom. Even before AOL Brazil launched, our competitors had used their ties to the government and local media to drum up bad press and specious lawsuits. Since most of the major Brazilian media were already aligned with the major Brazilian Internet service providers (ISPs), signing up credible content partners was an uphill battle. Further complicating matters was IG, or Internet Gratis, a new ISP that was giving its service away for free, a move that threatened to undercut AOL Brazil's business model before it even got started. Ominously, as we geared up for AOL launches in Mexico and Argentina, our next two core markets, we were already encountering signs of similar drawbacks and obstacles.

In this context, the AOL–Time Warner deal had arrived out of the blue as something of a godsend. In several of our target markets, Time Warner brands like Warner Bros., Warner Music, CNN, HBO, and Cartoon Network were well known and respected. By cutting synergistic deals with our new corporate siblings, we suddenly had a competitive advantage and a shot at leveling the content playing field. For me, the deal also carried a personal significance that dated back to my days as a *Time* staffer. In my eyes, the merger not only made business sense, but was like two parts of my family finally coming together. Everything I had ever done or dreamed of was suddenly under one gigantic corporate umbrella. What were the odds that the two companies I had spent most of my professional life working for would suddenly merge into one multimedia behemoth? I couldn't shake the feeling that there was something inevitable and cosmic in what was happening and that it would be a long time before I understood the true significance of it all. Like everyone else at the time, I had no inkling how true that would prove to be.

In the aftermath of the AOL–Time Warner meltdown, the dearth of actual synergy among the company's various divisions has become the stuff of corporate legend, but AOLA and Time Warner's international divisions shared many of the same goals and corporate concerns. There was also an in-the-trenches camaraderie and a common perspective and knowledge of the Spanish- and Portuguese-speaking world that drew us together and made us natural collaborators. Even before the merger, I had helped to initiate content and cross-promotional deals with the Latin American divisions of Warner Music, HBO, and Cartoon Network, but now the possibilities seemed almost endless. Voces/Voices of Latin America, a collaboration of *Time*'s Latin American editions to simultaneously publish original essays by leading Latin American intellectuals and writers on the AOLA service in Spanish and in print in English, had received attention in the upper ranks. Now that we were all in the same corporate family, it seemed there should be a way to do something innovative with my old alma mater, the flagship domestic edition of *Time* itself. But what could possibly link *Time*, with its mainstream U.S. editorial focus, to the interactive barrio of AOLA's Spanish- and Portuguese-speaking subscriber base?

Back in the fall of 1999, as I traveled across Latin America for meetings with prospective content partners for the AOLA service, a question invariably came up. The question, which was sometimes delivered in Spanish and sometimes in English, was nevertheless always the same: "What are you doing for U.S. Hispanics?" We invariably answered that extending the AOLA network to include the U.S. Hispanic population was part of our plan, even though at the time it was unclear how or when. But there was no question that the perceived connection between AOL Latin America and the U.S. Latino market was a distinct plus in the eyes of our partners and a key advantage over our competitors. There was a time when Latin Americans regarded U.S. Latinos as half-breed oddities, brown-skinned gringos who had left their homelands behind and were no longer relevant. But that had obviously changed. The growing size and wealth of the U.S. Hispanic population had begun to grab the attention of Latin American entrepreneurs and businessmen who sensed its importance, and AOL Latin America was perceived as a bridge to that group. AOL, it turned out, had already signed up almost half of the estimated 3 million Hispanics who were online at the time. Leveraging the natural linguistic and cultural affinity between U.S. Latinos and their Latin American homelands and relatives not only made business sense, it was the pan-regional embodiment of what the Internet was supposedly all about.

I began to envision a digital version of Simón Bolívar's dream of a united Latin America, a network of English- and Spanish-speaking Internet users that would transcend borders and unite the Spanish-speaking world in a hemispheric AOL community extending from Canada to Tierra del Fuego. Soon afterward, in a keynote speech to the U.S. Hispanic Chamber of Commerce at the Waldorf hotel in New York, I described a pan-Latino future where "a boy from East L.A. can chat with the girl from Ipanema and book a vacation in Cancún without ever leaving his chair." Not surprisingly, I was not the only executive at AOLA thinking along those lines. In fact, the Cisneros Group already owned a stake in Univision, which had its own plans to launch a Spanish-language Web site. All of us at AOLA agreed that creating a seamless worldwide community of Spanish-speaking AOL members was a good idea. The only problem was that the original AOLA business charter granted it the license to market the AOL brand and sign up subscribers in Latin America only. In a weird replication of the actual tortilla curtain, AOL's networks allowed members to cross through the international channel into Latin America, but not the other way around. Opening America Online's digital border would require a modification of the original AOL-Cisneros deal, something that would be difficult, if not impossible, to do.

The catalyst for change came in the form of a phone call from a business affairs executive at AOL headquarters in Dulles, Virginia. He was calling to get my opinion about a Web site for U.S. Hispanics called Qué Pasa. Based in Phoenix, Arizona, and funded by the Telemundo TV network and others, the site had recently made waves by signing Miami Sound Machine singer Gloria Estefan as an investor and spokesperson. Qué Pasa, my colleague explained, was offering a large sum in exchange for the right to develop and program content for AOL's U.S. Hispanic area. As calmly as I could, I explained that AOLA was planning its own area for U.S. Hispanics and that selling the area to a competitor would be shortsighted and self-defeating. "I'd hate to be the one to explain to Bob Pittman that AOL's $100 million venture in Latin America has been undermined by the chance to score a few hundred thousand dollars," I told him. The call ended on a friendly note, but my pulse was racing.

At the next AOLA staff meeting, I reported that AOL's U.S. Latino site was up for grabs and that we had to make a move or risk the chance of losing a critical financial and psychological link to the U.S. Latino population. Luckily, I was not the only AOLA executive who felt that we were uniquely qualified—and almost morally entitled—to program AOL's U.S. Latino area. A lobbying campaign was initiated at the highest levels, and a few weeks later, with the blessing of the AOLA board, John Gardiner, AOLA's then vice president of business affairs and general counsel, began negotiations to make AOL Latin America the primary content provider for a new U.S. Latino site. By early 2000, we had devised a plan for a bilingual site for U.S. Hispanics that would serve as a bridge between AOL's Latino membership and the Spanish-speaking networks of AOL Latin America. Phase one would consist of a bilingual content and community area with channels for Latino-oriented entertainment, news, sports, and lifestyles as well as links to the AOLA services in Mexico, Argentina, Puerto Rico, and Brazil. U.S. Hispanic AOL members would also have access to Spanish-language editions of Web search, online directories, AOL Instant Messenger, and other tools developed for AOLA. Phase two would feature a completely Spanish version of the AOL service and Web-based expansion into AOL's Netscape and CompuServe brands. Meanwhile, I learned that *Time* was planning a special issue on the U.S.-Mexico border with the cover line "Welcome to Amexica." *Time*'s special issue was planned to coincide with a week-long series of pieces on the U.S.-Mexico border by CNN. The *Time*-CNN reports and the upcoming launch of AOL Latino were a perfect fit. The project also capitalized on the cross-promotional multimedia possibilities, which would harness print, cable, and the Internet to reach millions of people in two languages across at least half a dozen countries.

On June 5, 2001, just a few months after a deal anointing AOLA as AOL's primary U.S. Hispanic content provider was finally signed, AOL Latino was born. The launch was kicked off by a day-long "town meeting" at the University of Texas at El Paso (UTEP) called "La Frontera: A Day on the Border." The event included a panel discussion titled "Culture and Society of the New Frontier: How Will It Change the U.S. and Mexico?" Moderated by myself and CNN correspondent Maria Hinojosa and carried live by the AOL Time Warner local cable affiliate, the panel included Latino filmmaker Cesar Alejandro, writers Denise Chavez and Ruben Martinez, and Mexican techno-*norteño* musician Pepe Mogt. By signing on to a special AOL Instant Messenger screen name appearing on the crawl text accompanying the live feed, viewers could join the panel and audience discussion in real time as their questions were projected onto a screen inside the UTEP auditorium. At the same time, AOL subscribers in the United States and Mexico could click on an interactive border zone map, which featured geographically accurate links to *Time* articles, CNN video clips, AOL Mexico editorials, chats, and other online content. After the town meeting, in a fitting grace note that took place at a gala reception, the AOL Time Warner Foundation presented a sizable check to a local border zone charity. As a mariachi band played and I toasted my colleagues from Time, CNN, and Time Warner Cable, I couldn't help feeling that this was the definition of the merger's much-ballyhooed synergy.

Despite its auspicious start, however, AOL Latino was hamstrung by resource limitations and logistical problems, not the least of which was the unwieldy structure of the AOL Latino deal itself. Because AOLA was precluded from signing on new subscribers inside the AOL Latino area, it never had a strategic incentive to enlarge its Latino offerings. And because AOL's Virginia-based programming staff never understood the value of programming for U.S. Hispanics in the first place, AOL Latino never got the promotion it deserved. Liked but never nurtured by its estranged corporate parents, AOL Latino languished in an organizational limbo. The collapse of dot.com stocks, which hit Latin America first, only made matters worse. After leaving AOLA to become a vice president at AOL's international division, I was instructed not to waste my time on AOL Latino. Eventually, that myopic attitude changed. Faced with a suddenly shrinking subscriber base and an increasingly wired ethnic consumer class, AOL was forced to acknowledge the importance of Latinos and other once marginal communities to its bottom line. In 2003, it reorganized its U.S. Hispanic efforts and later that year relaunched AOL Latino along with a version of the AOL service in Spanish. By then, of course, the Internet— and AOL itself—was no longer the same place.

But along the way, something else had changed, too. Despite dire predictions that Spanish-speaking Web surfers would never catch up to their more affluent, technically savvy predecessors, a surprising number of Latin Americans were able to get online anyway. In the less developed nations of Latin America and other parts of the world, those who couldn't afford computers improvised with Internet-enabled cell phones and increasingly ubiquitous cybercafés. By erasing national boundaries and accelerating the speed of communication and information dispersal, cultural interaction intensified and took new forms. With just a few clicks of a mouse, a soccer fan in Japan could watch a match in Buenos Aires and chat with a fellow fan in England. In the disembodied realms of cyberspace, skin color, gender, and geographic location became irrelevant, and foreign languages began to creep into U.S. chat rooms. The nature of community became fluid and voluntary. Negroponte's notion of a new global social fabric was becoming a reality, but in a way that no one outside the New Mainstream could have anticipated or expected.

Bytes, Pods, and Blogs

Even in midst of the dot.com collapse, it was clear that the Internet was— in terms of sheer number of users, at least—more popular and integral to people's lives than ever. Between 2001 and 2003, thousands of Web sites failed and stock market investors abandoned the Internet in droves, but the online population kept on growing in size and diversity. For most people, having an e-mail address and access to the Internet became a necessary part of cosmopolitan life, and instant messaging replaced the telephone as the fastest, most convenient way to trade short bits of gossip and information. Minorities and women, once relegated to the sidelines, became part of the cyberspace mainstream. Not that online definitions of gender and race were necessarily even relevant anymore. One of the fascinating—and to some disconcerting—dimensions of the Internet was the way it allowed people to create alternate or multiple personas, which might or might not resemble their "meat space" counterparts. Depending on whether you were looking for a lover, a mortgage, or a chance to masquerade as the opposite sex, this aspect of the Net could be, depending on your goals and point of view, disappointing, alarming, or disgusting. But for most Web surfers, the relative anonymity of cyberspace merely confirmed and reflected a newfound flexibility and fluidity in how they actually perceived themselves in real life.

A survey of data on Internet computer domains by the Center for the Next Generation Internet, an Internet software consortium, found that between August 1999 and March 2001, the number of Internet hosts, or computers connected to the Internet, grew worldwide from 56.2 million in 222 countries to 109 million in 230 countries. The report cited "especially notable increases" in the number of hosts in Hong Kong, Argentina, and Portugal and projected that if the same rate of growth was sustained, "the Internet would cross the 1 billion host mark in mid-2005."[2]

In 2003, Nielsen/Net Ratings, Inc., counted the "current digital media universe," or people two years or older with a computer and the means to connect to the Internet, in the United States at 185,813,238. The U.S. "active digital media universe," or people two years or older who had visited a Web site or launched an Internet program tracked by Nielsen, was 131,052,267. Nielsen found that Americans were going online at an average of thirty-one times per month at home and sixty-one times from work. The average time spent on a PC was twenty-seven minutes at home, seventy minutes at work, and just under a minute on any single Web page.

The change in behavior, and the potentially isolating effects of continuous computer use, was regarded by some as a threat to human interaction, while others hailed it as a new dawn of social evolution. But some of the most interesting changes were happening behind the glowing screens, in the ways that cyberculture was transforming notions of work, community, and class. Ethnicity and culture, rather than being left behind as relics of another age, began to seep into the social fabric of cyberspace.[3]

In terms of language, a 2004 study compiled by Global Reach estimates that 280 million people, or 35.6 percent of the global online population, are native English speakers. Non-English native speakers total 474.3, or 64.4 percent. The leading non-English languages are Chinese (12.2 percent), Japanese (9.5 percent), and Spanish (8 percent), followed by German (7 percent), Korean (4 percent), and French (3.7 percent). Other significant language groups include Italian (3.3 percent), Portuguese (2.6 percent), Russian (2.5 percent), Vietnamese (2.2 percent), Scandinavian languages (1.9 percent), Dutch (1.8 percent), Malay (1.2 percent), and Arabic (1.2 percent). Outside the United States, the largest ISPs include Germany's T-Online and AOL Deutschland, with about 8 million and 3 million subscribers, respectively, Italy's Tiscali (7 million), Japan's Nifty (5.1 million) and So-net (2.2 million), France's Wanadoo (4.9 million), Korea's Telecom (3.8 million) and Hanaro (2.2 million), and Spain's Terra (2.7 million).[4]

Demographic and technological trends are accelerating growth of the non-English Internet. Some studies project that 50 percent of the world's Web users will be Chinese by 2007. The implications are so profound that some foreign governments have begun to question American dominance over the technological protocols and regulations that govern cyberspace. At a United Nations conference in December 2003, five thousand representatives from more than sixty nations gathered in Geneva, Switzerland, to discuss greater United Nations involvement in the Internet Corporation for Assigned Names and Numbers, or ICANN, a nonprofit group established by the U.S. government in 1998 to oversee technical coordination issues for site domains and other protocol standards. Talal Abu-Ghazaleh, a Jordanian businessman and vice chairman of the United Nations' Information and Communication Technologies Task Force, is

proposing that ICANN be placed under the umbrella of the UN communications task force with the aim of giving a greater voice to the international Internet community and balancing priorities and interests of the
private, public, and nonprofit sectors.[5]

Some U.S. companies, meanwhile, are discovering that online overseas audiences can be lucrative both at home and abroad. Blackboard,
Inc., a Washington, D.C.–based company that sells online software plat-
forms to universities and colleges, recently closed a deal with the Chinese
education company Cernet to provide its software to one thousand Chinese universities. Blackboard, which has already served more than six hundred foreign clients in five other languages, expects from $3 million to $5
million in revenue from the first year alone.[6] YesAsia.com, an online retailer based in San Francisco and Hong Kong, has built a business on selling Asian pop CDs, Korean DVDs, and Japanese comic books to the 10
million Asian Americans in the United States. It also markets English-
language books to English-speaking Asian expats in Japan and Korea.[7]

The brand-building and economic opportunities presented by international and domestic ethnic audiences are altering the way American
companies present themselves online. In an effort to connect with the
growing number of overseas football fans, the National Football League
has rolled out a Mandarin Chinese version of its official site with com-
mentary by Chad Lewis, a Philadelphia Eagles tight end who learned to
speak Mandarin in his twenties during a two-year stint as a Morman mis-
sionary in Taiwan. The National Basketball Association is also going
global. Partially in response to the rise of foreign-born players such as
China's Yao Ming, a center for the Houston Rockets, the NBA has nine
foreign-targeted Web sites, including Chinese and Portuguese versions.
Foreign users represent 42 percent of traffic going to Walt Disney Internet
Group's sites, which include ABC.com, ESPN.com, and Movies.com. Disney is also offering Toontown, a multiplayer online game, to international
audiences with broadband or high-speed Internet connections.[8]

Content providers are discovering that foreign online audiences are
sources of multiple revenue streams, including fees for specially licensed
videos and sports scores, cross-promotions with affiliated companies, and
brands and advertisers eager to reach international Internet users. Surveys

had found that 40 percent of *The Washington Post*'s foreign online readers have incomes that are higher than 90 percent of their countrymen, making them particularly desirable to advertisers and sponsors like British Airways, Nokia, and Royal Dutch Shell. In the third quarter of 2003, Yahoo! reported that 60 percent of its 230 million monthly visitors came from outside the United States, traffic that generated 17 percent of the company's total revenues.[9]

Inside the United States, the vision of the Internet as a realm that represents, in the words of social commentator George Gilder, "a rainbow parade of all colors and wavelengths,"[10] has been a subject of debate ever since cyberspace was acknowledged as the global medium of the future. The disproportionate number of white affluent males that made up the early Web population raised concerns that women, Hispanics, African Americans, and other minorities would be left behind as the rest of the wired world advanced. The so-called digital divide became a social and political hot button and the subject of a statistical tug-of-war that pitted free market advocates against those who saw the Net as the latest tool of capitalist exploitation and oppression. During the late nineties, a number of studies fueled worries that the Internet would exacerbate existing social and economic disparities. During the Clinton administration, a government-sponsored report titled "Falling Through the Net: Defining the Digital Divide" found that despite the fact that access to computers and the Internet "has soared for people in all demographic groups and geographic locations," its analysis of 1998 Department of Commerce data uncovered "significant disparities" between whites and nonwhites, urban high-income households, and lower-income rural households.[11] The study found that gaps between whites and Hispanics and blacks had widened by 5 percent between 1997 and 1998 and that, over the same period, the digital divide between those at the highest and lowest education levels had increased by 25 percent and the divide between the highest and lowest income levels had increased by 29 percent. "Establishing and supporting community access centers, among other steps, will help ensure that all Americans can access new technologies," the report stated. "As we enter the Information Age, access to computers and the Internet is becoming increasingly vital. It is in everyone's interest to ensure that no American is left behind." [12]

But recent data suggests that the digital divide, as such, is narrowing. A study from the Center for Communications Policy at the University of California at Los Angeles found that U.S. Hispanics were going online at a faster rate than any other group. The percentage of Latinos using the Web at least once a month rose 25 percent between 2000 and 2003, the study found. African Americans were the second-fastest-growing group, with a 22 percent increase over the same period. A report by comScore Media Metrix placed the number of U.S. Hispanic Internet users in 2003 at 12.4 million, or approximately one-third of the total U.S. Hispanic population. The U.S. Hispanic population is currently 11 percent larger than the total online population of Spain and 4 percent larger than the total online population of Mexico, Argentina, and Colombia combined. The average amount of time spent online by U.S. Latinos (85.9 minutes per day) is roughly equal to the general U.S. online population (86.4 minutes per day). In other ways, though, U.S. Hispanic Internet users are markedly different from the general online population. They are generally younger, with 60 percent being thirty-four years old or younger, versus 50 percent for the general online population. Latinos online also tend to live in larger households, with 39 percent living in households of five or more, compared with 18 percent for all other online households. U.S. Latinos online tend to have lower household incomes than general U.S. users, but higher incomes than most U.S. Hispanics, with 26 percent of online Hispanics reporting household incomes of $40,000–$59,999 compared with 20 percent for U.S. Hispanics overall. Of U.S. Hispanics with incomes of $60,000–$74,999, 13 percent were online versus 10 percent overall; of those reporting incomes of $75,000 or more, 21 percent were online versus 17 percent overall. The comScore data also revealed that 51 percent of the U.S. online Hispanic population preferred English as their language of choice at home, with 21 percent preferring Spanish and 27 percent reporting equal use of English and Spanish. The study also found that the top ten Spanish-language Internet sites reached more than 91 percent of the Spanish-preferred users in a single month. The leading sites for Hispanics online are AOL, Yahoo!, MSN, Terra Lycos, eBay, Google, Gator Network, About/Primedia, CNET networks, and Amazon. In its report, comScore suggested that "since Hispanic Web users tend to be younger and live in larger households, they are likely to be more comfortable with technology and exercise influence over other family members for purchases and other key decisions." [13]

The online U.S. Hispanic market was estimated at $4.3 billion in 2002, about 6 percent of total online spending. In February 2003, 1.2 million Hispanics, or 10 percent of the Latino online population, visited an automotive site. Nearly 6 million Latinos visited travel sites, with Mapquest .com receiving 2.2 million unique visitors in July 2003 and Expedia.com and Orbitz.com receiving more than 1 million each during the same month. Hispanics online also show a strong affinity for purchases in categories like computer hardware, consumer electronics, online ticket sales, and apparel and accessories. A "Hispanic cyberstudy" conducted by America Online and RoperASW in 2002 found that 60 percent of U.S. Latinos online had begun using the Internet in the previous three years. The AOL cyberstudy also found Hispanics to be avid users of instant messaging, videos, music, and educational materials and sources. Latino online shopping rates were only slightly lower than Internet users overall, and 37 percent reported that they were planning to increase the number of online purchases. [14]

Gay Internet users, who have been credited with contributing to the early success of AOL by congregating in its community chat rooms, are also more likely to make online purchases than the general online community. A survey by Harris Interactive found that "32 percent of Lesbian/Gay/Bisexual/Transgender (LGBT) Internet users now go online for over 21 hours a week, up from 25 percent in 2000. Only 17 percent of nongay Internet users spend over 21 hours a week online. Sixty-three percent of LGBT respondents said they were likely to buy goods or services over the Net, in comparison with 59 percent of nongay respondents." [15]

Hispanics and gays are not the only minority groups making strides online. The percentage of African American households online is roughly equal to that of Hispanics, at around 51 percent, according to comScore. In a response to the 82 percent growth rate of the U.S. Vietnamese population over the past ten years, New York Life has launched a native-language site offering financial information. Asian Americans lead other ethnic groups in online shopping, according to data by Forrester Research. On average, Forrester found, Asians make an online purchase 6 times a year, versus 3.2 times a year for whites, 3 times a year for Hispanics, and 1.8 times a year for blacks. Asians are also more likely than either Hispanics or African Americans to use the Internet to track shipping and delivery of mail and consumer purchases. According to *Wired News*, 30 percent of new companies in Silicon Valley between 1995 and 1998 were founded by Chinese or Asian Indian immigrants. And the Corporation for Public Broadcasting found that between 2000 and 2003, the percentage of African American children using the Internet had risen from 19 percent to 58 percent.

The New Mainstream is also having a transformative effect on Internet service providers and the nature and number of sites that reach them. A 2002 report by the Insight Research Corporation found that "the rapidly growing ethnic population represents a substantial opportunity for ISPs and Web portals that can attract these consumers with in-language, in-culture messages and specialized content. By 2005, Insight predicts U.S. ethnic groups will spend $3.1 billion on Internet access, an amount nearly equal to the $3.3 billion total U.S. Internet access market in the year 2000." Insight projects that Internet access revenues will "more than triple" in the first few years of the 21st century, reaching $11.1 billion by 2005.[16]

Those numbers have caught the attention of the leading Internet service providers, who see segmented audiences and ethnic-targeted content as a key to their ability to retain and recruit new subscribers. Just weeks after relaunching AOL Latino as a Spanish-language service, AOL announced an expansion of Black Focus, its content area for African Americans. The site, which exists inside the proprietary AOL English-language service, will feature added content and community features, as well as areas devoted to news, spirituality, and relationships. According to AOL executives, features will cover topics ranging from the dearth of black fashion models to a profile of gospel singer CeCe Winans. There will also be content leveraged from affiliated Time Warner properties, including

Entertainment Weekly and Africana.com, and partnerships with Black-Voices.com, NiaOnline, and Black Enterprise.

With about five hundred thousand visitors, Black Focus is the number three site for African Americans, behind BET.com and BlackPlanet, which boasts 1.6 million members. BlackPlanet is a division of Community Connect Inc. (CCI), an independent company specializing in ethnic community sites that includes AsianAvenue and MiGente ("My People"), a site for U.S. Hispanics. Founded on July 21, 1997, in the one-bedroom apartment of President and CEO Benjamin Sun, CCI has grown to a company with eighty-five employees who tend and cultivate CCI's community sites in a loftlike office in New York's Flatiron district, aka Silicon Alley. All of the Community Connect sites share spare, welcoming interfaces and a suite of tools designed to re-create a social environment where people can meet, relax, date, or even get a job. "The essence of it is the social aspect," said Omar Wasow, BlackPlanet's executive director. "What it means is that the site is alive. There's hustle and bustle. There are living and breathing people at the site. Most of the other sites feel like being alone in the library. We've built ourselves from the ground up to be much more like a café than a library. We focus on the conversation."[17] On all three CCI sites, that conversation takes place in English. The choice reflects the multicultural perspective of its U.S.-born founders: young, assimilated, technologically savvy, and comfortable in a diverse society that sees no contradiction between ethnic identification and American identity. In 2003, Community Connect partnered with New York Times to develop the Diversity Job Market, which offers prospective employers a chance to browse four hundred thousand profiles of minority applicants from AsianAvenue, BlackPlanet, and MiGente. CCI's founders liken the their sites to "town squares," says Wasow, "where people are working, meeting old friends, spouses, and making new friends in a trusted environment."

The idea of community is itself evolving as technology and the urge to congregate spawn new forms of human interaction. Inthefray.com, a site that describes itself as "an online magazine devoted to issues of identity and community," divides its forums and discussions into six basic areas: belief, class, gender, physique, race, and sexuality. Members are invited to "identify," "imagine," "interact," and "image." Inthefray is dedicated to "understanding, reporting on, and acting upon issues" that define the new demographic and social realities of the twenty-first century and the "need for a broad-minded sense of identity, one that is comfortable with diversity and yet also envisions a richer, more complex humanity than can be found in nationalism or consumer culture." By nurturing a conversation that is "frequently controversial but ruthlessly honest, often inspired but ever independent," Inthefray's mission is "nothing less than the transformation of the political scene, rethinking multiculturalism and making it a mainstream concern, not just a problem for the minority to talk about and the majority to retreat from."

To be sure, the intersection of new media and shifting codes of cultural and national identity are not just symptoms of intellectuals and activist elites. If anything, it is one of the defining—and definitive—experiences of an entire generation that came of age when the information economy was not just a trendy catchphrase, but a mode of expression and a vehicle for self-discovery. Adriana Kampfner, born in Mexico to a Mexican father and a Syrian Lebanese mother, left her banking job in Chicago to take a senior marketing and sales position in StarMedia just as the company was taking off. "A big driver in the creation and momentum of StarMedia was in fact the idea of selling the future of Latin America," she recalls. "But it was not just to the U.S. investor market, it was to Latin America itself. The messages of empowerment and owning your own future were driving forces." For Kampfner, who left Mexico at the age of two months and spent most of her life growing up in England and the United States, the chance to open StarMedia's Mexico City office was both a homecoming and a catalyst for a new sense of identity. By living and working in Mexico, she was able to validate a cultural connection to the country of her birth while appreciating the ways in which she was inalterably American. "By exploring how Mexican or not Mexican I really was, I found that I have much in common with the growing community of Hispanics here and am personally committed to contributing to its success. I fully expect my sense of identity to change over the course of my life, as I have a family and raise them as Mexican Americans."

Her personal journey has also given her a unique perspective on the evolution of the Internet in Latin American, a trajectory that, if anything, has reaffirmed her conviction that new media remains key to the social and economic future of Latin Americans inside and outside the United States.

"The Internet business in Latin America has lost its wind," Kampfner says. "Although the number of users and the sophistication of users continues to explode, there are fewer companies and initiatives meeting them on the other side. Bottom line, the market is there but has many untapped opportunities. Serving as a global platform that can enhance awareness and communication among the proliferation of Hispanics nationwide and worldwide, the Internet remains a key tool in what lies ahead."

The advent of high-speed Internet connections, or broadband, is bringing changes not just to the type and amount of content that users can access, but also to how and why they interact with media and one another. As photography and music became digital mediums, new networks and communal hubs have sprung up to allow users to trade, share, and manipulate pictures and songs. Shutterbugs know how to edit, upload, and print; music fans are adept at "ripping and burning" songs to transfer them to mp3 players and Apple iPods. All of a sudden, ten-year-olds are talking about "gigs" and "bytes," terms used to describe units of digital storage. More than ever before, people have become the producers and editors of their own digital media experience.[18]

But something else is happening, too. Taking a cue from the reality TV shows that have taught us nothing is too mundane to be entertainment, tech-savvy youths are turning their personal experiences into content. Web logs, or "blogs," frequently updated online journals that often refer to current events and social issues, with excerpts from news reports and links to other blogs, are just one way that people of all stripes are learning to broadcast their feelings to the world at large. As part of an online series called P.O.V., the Public Broadcasting Service has launched a project called "Borders," which features a group of video diaries made by three students from Elsa, Texas, a working-class Mexican American border town where getting an education is one of the few routes of escape to a better life. One of the Borders diaries is a collection of video clips by a nineteen-year-old Columbia University sophomore named Cecilia Garza, who documents a *carne guisada* plate" sale put on by her hard-pressed family in a public park to raise $550 for her education fund. At Columbia, Garza, who doesn't have the money to pay for textbooks, is seen getting a credit card rejection letter and otherwise struggling to get by in an environment that she can barely afford.[19]

Despite statistics showing that minorities from lower-income families are less likely to have access to the Internet, online forums like a Scholastic .com site called "Writing with Writers" are being used to motivate grade school students with substandard writing skills by letting would-be authors post their work to be read and critiqued by their peers. By posting and automatically distributing students' work, the program has proved successful at giving budding writers a sense that the quality of the work they do matters and can even have an impact on other kids like them. Giving disadvantaged youths an equal shot at a good education is also the goal of a bilingual CD-ROM by Ember Media that has been distributed to hundreds of U.S. high schools with large Latino student enrollments. Sponsored by MTV Networks, Mastercard International, HBO Latino, *Urban Latino* magazine, the Hispanic College Fund, and other organizations and corporations, *An Interactive Guide to the Top Colleges and Universities for Hispanics* features a free SAT and ACT online test prep course, hundreds of college profiles, college essay and application tutorials, and financial aid resources and information, as well as testimonials and tips from former president Bill Clinton and Latino celebrities like Miss USA 2003 Susie Castillo and TV personality Bob Villa. Anna Liza Bella, one of the CD-ROM's producers, came to the United States from the Philippines when she was six years old. "It's amazing working with these young people and seeing how they think and trying to address some of the shortcomings of the educational system in this country," she says. "One can truly see how race and ethnicity still play a role in how people perceive themselves, but it's more subtle, not just a matter of black and white."

The wired generation is also learning new lessons from how they play on computers and other devices—and the makers of those games are beginning to realize the importance of diversity in their products and workforce. On popular games like 007 Nightfire and Enter the Matrix, players can choose their identity from a variety of gender and ethnic combinations. Some games allow the players to adjust the clothing, hairstyle, and skin tone of their game personality or even to temporarily adopt the persona of their favorite hip-hop artist. In Def Jam Vendetta, a street-style wrestling game from Electronic Arts (EA), players can bash and stomp one another in the pumped-up guise of Ludacris, DMX, Method Man, N.O.R.E., and other Def Jam rap stars.

In 2002, the video game industry earned $28 billion and is growing in the United States at the rate of 20 percent a year. Americans now spend more time playing video games than watching rented videos and DVDs, and a single hit title like FIFA Soccer can earn more than $1 billion.[20] The fact that minorities represent a growing percentage of the youth market for games is not lost on video companies like Electronic Arts, which is applying a multicultural awareness to the way it markets and develops new offerings for its increasingly pan-ethnic and international audience. At the company's offices in Orlando, Florida, a demographically varied mix of young people in shorts and flip-flops ambles around Xbox game stations and life-size cardboard cutouts of Steve Madden and clusters around glowing computer screens where EA games are dreamed up and developed. "Cultural diversity is important for developing a creative community inside the company," explains José Martin, EA's vice president of human resources for the Americas. "Our goal is to give the end user control over who they want to be and who they think they are."

The menu of virtual identities to choose from is becoming increasingly open-ended. In Star Wars Galaxies, an online "persistent world" developed jointly by Sony and Lucas Arts, players are given the option to be a human, a Wookiee, a Mon Calamari (Admiral Ackbar), or a Zabrak (Darth Maul). Once a life-form has been chosen, players can alter their gender, skin color, musculature, height, weight, and body fat. Adjustable facial features include eye, hair and skin color, and the shape of cheekbones, nose, and jaw.

The latest games and software go one step farther, allowing players to project their own image into the action. EA's Tiger Woods game lets people insert their own face onto the bodies of tournament pro golfers. Eye Toy camera, a software add-on for Sony's PS2 game player, lets the viewer enter the game environment and interact with the digital environment to bounce balls or swat at swarms of flying ninjas. Other programs let the player enter detailed dream worlds where they can fly, lift large objects, and take on other superhuman powers. Some PC-based games combine time travel with scholarly research by rendering amazingly detailed environments based on ancient civilizations. In Microsoft's popular PC game series Age of Empires, players are immersed in historically accurate recreations of the past, where each civilization displays attributes unique to its culture, from authentic weaponry and dress to architecture and real-time battles of charging warriors and burning villages. Players are required to wisely balance their resource allocation between domestic and imperialist agendas: for instance, a ruler who invests in farming and education will be rewarded with more food for soldiers and hence a bigger army, as well as more technologically advanced weapons. As the game's designer, Bruce Shelley, explains on the Age of Empires Web site:

> The twelve cultures in the game use four different building sets. The buildings of an Asian culture will look quite different from those using the Egyptian or Greek set. Each culture has a unique tech tree. No culture has all the possible technologies. Some have better soldiers, some better cavalry, some better ships, some better priests, and some have economic advantages. For example, Shang (Chinese) villagers move faster than the villagers of other cultures, making them more efficient in resource gathering. The Egyptian priests can develop the greatest range, making them more useful for converting enemy units. Each culture has to be played differently to take advantage of its strengths and overcome its weaknesses.

The sequel, Age of Empires II: The Conquerors' Expansion, introduces five new civilizations, the Huns, Aztecs, Mayans, Koreans, and Spanish. It's hard not to imagine a young Hispanic boy sitting at his computer and ordering his Aztec and Mayan armies to annihilate the Spanish conquistadors in an emotionally satisfying revision of historical fact. No matter that the Maya and Aztec civilizations existed in different eras, a detail that is duly noted in the studiously researched profile of each culture that is included with the game.

Intercultural conflict takes a disturbingly modern turn in Command and Conquer: Generals, a similarly realistic war game where players can lead or fight against three different forces: the U.S. Army, the Chinese, or the GLA, an al-Qaeda-like organization whose members vow to destroy the "infidels" with an arsenal that includes angry mobs, tanks, armor-piercing rockets, bomb-wielding "terrorists," and "anthrax toxin shells." During the fighting, as an ominous sound track of Middle Eastern drums plays in the background, a GLA commander exclaims, "The time has come, our cause is just! We will fall upon our foes like lightning from a cloudless sky!" Rated "Teen," Command and Conquer: Generals is not for the faint of heart or for anyone who thinks negative depictions of Arab terrorists serves only to stoke militarism, hatred, and ethnic stereotyping. On the other hand, the Sims, a virtual reality game built around the activities of seemingly ordinary people, probably does just as much damage with its subversively dysfunctional portrait of suburbia. On New Year's Eve 2002, EA reported that half a million virtual kisses were exchanged by Sims online avatars during five thousand online parties. (When Peter Ludlow, a professor at the University of Michigan, published reports of Sims avatar sex orgies in his virtual newspaper, the *Alphaville Herald,* which itself was part of the online Sims metaworld, his persona was abruptly unplugged by EA.) Or perhaps, as the defenders of online virtual worlds claim, having a place to act out our dreams and nightmares defuses feelings that might otherwise find more dangerous forms of expression. What is certain is that these interactive environments are becoming more immersive and lifelike by the day. Inevitably, these digital entertainments will merge with online player networks, videocam feeds, and real-world databases, measuring everything from traffic patterns and stock market fluctuations to birth rates and the weather.

A new breed of games even allows the player to explore the territory within. The Journey to the Wild Divine: The Passage includes a biofeedback device that measures the player's heart rate and perspiration. Instead of hand-eye coordination, Wild Divine explores mind-body coordination by requiring different levels of bioactivity and relaxation to make things happen. As the journey unfolds, the player is confronted with a series of obstacles and tasks that can be overcome only by focusing the power of one's mind. Breathing evenly will cause a magical stairway to appear; relaxing will open the door to a roomful of belly dancers. By synchronizing their breathing and heart rate, players can awaken a woman and make her slowly levitate. Virtual gurus appear from time to time to guide players on their journey.

In the "mirror worlds" foreseen by Yale computer expert David Gelernter and others, the line between fiction and fact, fantasy and reality, will blur.[21] Like a time machine that moves simultaneously in both directions, interactive entertainment will fuse the history and myths of ancient peoples with space age effects and gadgetry. As the exploration of virtual realms and selves becomes ordinary, transcultural identities and environments will morph into a seamless projection—and reflection—of the real thing and a lens into what lies beyond it. The New Mainstream will shape the companies that build and sell the virtual worlds of tomorrow, because the ultimate success of those companies depends on how well they understand the multicultural world of today.

Relativity

People are social animals. An individual's sense of security or fear, happiness or grief, wealth or impoverishment, his or her very conception of the world and just about everything in it, is defined through relationships to other human beings. For our primordial ancestors, status in the tribe, the ability to count on others as allies, lovers, or friends, was not just a key to social identity, but the difference between life and death. A grasp of social dynamics—and our ability to communicate and process the complex variables of multiple relationships with other individuals and their consequences—is the key differentiator between higher primates and the rest of the animal kingdom. Our ability to build and navigate complex social networks is, to a very real extent, the essence of what makes us human. It is also the key to understanding the emotional ecology of existing consumer markets and those that are still in the process of being formed.

The biological imperative to reproduce and the consequences of natural selection, or the natural cost-benefit analysis of any biological mutation or change, are key components in the theory of evolution put forth by Charles Darwin in *On the Origin of the Species* in 1859. Darwin's theory of evolution holds that the benefits of any mutation, a bigger brain or longer neck, for example, must exceed the costs required to support it, to become evolutionary. If the benefits of change do not exceed the costs, natural selection, or the genetic advantage of those individuals who successfully reproduce as opposed to those who do not, will favor the status quo, and the mutation—and those who embody it—will die out.

In the early 1900s, Darwin's theories were distorted into "social Darwinism," a movement espoused by the social philosopher Herbert Spencer that attempted to rationalize racism and justify the wretched fates of the genetically mixed masses at the bottom rungs of the socioeconomic ladder. If anything, the social Darwinists' argument that the ethnic impurity of the lower classes was diluting the viability of the human species was the opposite of what Darwin believed. Genetic and social diversity are critical components in the process of natural selection; a species devoid of genetic variation will eventually become trapped in an evolutionary cul-de-sac, unable to innovate or adapt to a changing environment. Without genetic mutation and diversity, in other words, our simian forefathers would never have left the trees.

In his book *Grooming, Gossip, and the Evolution of Language*, Robin Dunbar, a professor of psychology at the University of Liverpool, makes the case that, contrary to popular wisdom, language was not created to help *Homo sapiens* hunt, make tools, or otherwise assert their superior intelligence over nature.[22] Instead, Dunbar contends, language emerged as a way to maintain connection, status, and social cohesion among primate groups who, owing to the increasing size of their clans, no longer had the luxury of communicating with other members of the group through direct physical contact. Among male primates, the role of grooming, and its ability to help an individual build and maintain alliances and gain status, is a critical factor in their ability to mate and pass their DNA to future generations. For female primates, grooming creates bonds with other females, who in turn help to defend them from aggressive males and share the responsibilities and burdens of caring for their young. As baboons, macaques, and chimpanzees moved from the trees into more terrestrial, open habitats on the edge of savannah, the increased risk from predators and the need to forage over ever larger territories led to an increase in the average size of their groups, making social alliances even more important. But for baboons and chimpanzees, the largest group they could possibly have grooming relationships with was about fifty to fifty-five, or slightly more than the thirty-six-person limit in an AOL chat room. "We do seem to use language in establishing and servicing our relationships," writes Dunbar. "Could it be that language evolved as a kind of vocal grooming to allow us to bond to larger groups than was possible using the conventional primate mechanism of physical grooming?"[23]

Dunbar suggests an affirmative answer to that question for a number of compelling reasons, not the least of which is his finding that in mammals, the size of the neocortex—the part of the brain devoted to thinking and reasoning—can be correlated to the size of the group they live in. Not only does language allow humans to exchange information over a much wider network of individuals than monkeys and apes, but the attitudes, preferences, and assumptions embedded in that information also convey the "tribal" association of the speaker. Finally, what psychologists call "theory of mind," or the human ability to understand that other individuals can have a similar yet different mental state or belief system, allows humans to develop the complex interpersonal strategies required for advanced forms of cooperation and social progress. Studies have shown that human beings are capable of verbally processing up to a maximum of six orders of "intentionality," or the ability to track and internalize different mental states. The first order of intentionality, for example, is expressed by the statement "I believe this to be true," followed by "I believe you believe this to be true" (the second order), "I believe you believe I believe this to be true" (the third order), and so on.

Theory of mind, which usually becomes apparent in children at age four or five, allows us to engage others with a unique dimension of understanding and sensitivity. People don't just communicate with other people; they strive to relate and identify, opening the door to empathic behaviors that include generosity, friendship, and love. Dunbar found that up to two-thirds of all casual human communication is devoted to social subjects, which is to say, the business, activities, and feelings of other humans. Books, magazines, television, and other media are similarly dominated by information about people or news that could have an effect on people we know, or people we know they know. "Our much-vaunted capacity for language seems to be mainly used for exchanging information on social matters," he writes. "We seem to be obsessed with gossiping about one another. Even the design of our minds seems to reinforce this."[24]

Human beings, it seems, are actually hardwired to interact with one another in overlapping circles of social interconnection. When Dunbar plotted the mean group size for different genera of monkeys and apes against the relative size of their cerebral cortex, he found a consistent correlation between cognitive ability and the optimal size for any given animal group. When he calculated the neocortex ratio for humans (4:1) and added it to the chart, he found that the corresponding group size for humans was 150. That number, he notes, corresponds to the size of tribal clans, which are the largest social groupings in which "everyone knows everyone else, in which they know not simply who is who but also how each one is related to the others." Which means it is the maximum number in which humans can share a visceral, physical connection with others that does not require governing systems of hierarchy, protocol, or other psychosocial constraints. Not surprisingly, it is also an optimal number for tasks that require an intense, coordinated effort and strong bonds of trust and mutual respect.

It's probably not coincidental that 150 matches archaeological estimates of the size of the earliest agrarian communities founded in the Near East around 5000 B.C. as well as most rural villages. It is the most effective fighting size for military companies, the ideal church congregation size as defined by the Church of England, and the number of individuals most people said they would be willing to ask for a favor. One hundred and fifty, it turns out, is roughly the number of living descendants who would be able to trace their heritage back to a single couple after four generations, which is the farthest back that any living member of the clan could have had personal contact with prior generations. In other words, 150 marks the mean number for the living genetic web that surrounds any single human being—or, to put it another way, their extended family.

Dubar's insights put a revealing spin on the origins of the Internet as a mass medium, an unplanned and unforeseen phenomenon apparently born out of a primordial urge for human beings to communicate in ever larger networks. His theories also help to explain the mushrooming popularity of online communities like Friendster, Craig's List, Tribes, and Social Circles—all of which use relational databases and community-building tools to digitally replicate different aspects of inherent human social behavior. Social networks help strangers find one another by identifying and organizing subscribers around common interests and activities. The growth of these sites has been exponential. Between January and October of 2003, the number of listings on Craig's List, a free bulletin board service with branches in several U.S. cities, jumped from 1,600 to 3,500, and the number of people viewing those posts ballooned from 651,000 to 950,000 over the same period. Friendster and Tribes are more clannish, requiring participants to be invited by a friend, just as it might happen at a party or at the house of an acquaintance. Such sites also attempt to evoke the "six degrees" model—or the number of human relationships said to be separating any single person from anybody else on earth—by helping to identify and reinforce the overlapping connections among different social circles. Friendster, for instance, allows subscribers to meet people up to four degrees away—friends of your friends of your friends of your friend. Many of the new sites also allow members to post public comments—or gossip—about other members, adding to the small-world ambience of familiarity, safety, and communal relations while allowing people to explore a social universe that can number in the hundreds of thousands or even millions.

As digital networks have expanded in reach and depth, so has the vocabulary used to describe them. Social scientists and network theorists now talk of how electronic "nodes," "hubs," and "links" mimic the patterns found in natural ecosystems, macroeconomies, and social movements. Then there are "memes," which are contagious ideas that resemble DNA in their ability to replicate and spread to the minds of other people, just as a virus jumps from host to host. As first defined in Oxford zoologist Richard Dawkins's 1976 book, *The Selfish Gene*, a meme is an idea that takes hold in the mind, not because it is necessarily more true than other ideas, although that may be the case, but because it triggers a recognition in our psyche that it could have a Darwinian impact on our ability to compete, mate, or otherwise survive and multiply. Memes, like DNA, are subject to a kind of natural selection; a good idea produces more benefit than cost for the belief system of the mind that holds it by contributing a net gain to the believer's sexual, material, social, or physical well-being. A meme like "Immigrants take jobs away from American workers" gets its power from the insecurities of the white and black working classes; right or wrong, these people fear they will be eliminated by the competitive threat of cheap foreign labor. The best meme is a thought that people are ready to hear, because the path of previous thinking—that is, other memes—have already paved the way for it. In order to succeed, a meme must compete and prove itself superior to competing notions and counterthoughts. It is an idea, in the popular vernacular, whose time has come.

In the early months of the 2004 U.S. presidential elections, Democratic candidate Howard Dean proved impressively effective at using in-person networking sites like Meetup.com to recruit volunteers, raise money, plan political rallies, and mobilize a wired constituency that was widely regarded as a glimpse of the political future. Dean's goal of using the Internet and other unconventional political tactics to draw 8 million "new voters" to the polls in the November election depended on his ability to rally a New Mainstream coalition of tech-savvy youths, affluent anti-war liberals, and minorities. Regardless of the fact that his presidential bid ultimately sputtered, Dean deserves credit for ushering in a new era of Internet-powered "movement politics." Another idea that crystallized in the 2004 election race was the recognition that Hispanics can no longer be taken for granted by anyone seeking national office. Even incumbent president George W. Bush's campaign managers have openly admitted that their candidate can't win without increasing his share of the minority vote, particularly Latinos. The president's announcement of an immigrant guest worker program in early 2004 was considered a calculated nod to Latino voters, as was the Democratic Party's decision to deliver its rebuttal to the president's State of the Union address in Spanish, allowing it to be carried live by the Univision TV network.

"The multicultural wave is upon us, whether conservatives want to admit it or not," asserts Ember Media's Anna Liza Bella. "We hit a bump on 9/11 in terms of acceptance of Arab and Middle Eastern minorities, but I do believe that the generations of other immigrants who had to live through the same issues (the Japanese internment during World War Two) has helped to bridge the gap somewhat. Right after 9/11, I attended a number of community meetings held by AALDEF (Asian American Legal Defense and Education Fund), and I was overwhelmed by the support that the other Asian subgroups (Chinese, Korean, Japanese, Filipino) were giving to South Asians and Central Asians. I thought it was a true testament on how things had changed and for the better. I believe that as we have more interaction with a wide range of ethnicities and cultures, both here in the United States and globally, we are truly going to have a much improved society, one that adapts the best things from all its parts and slowly creates a New Mainstream culture where the differences are not as important as the commonalities."

Yet despite our ability to recognize and process information that encompasses ever larger networks of people and relationships, our emotional universe remains quite small. Studies have found that when people are asked to list the names of others whose death tomorrow they would find devastating, the respondents invariably listed between eleven and twelve. Similarly, Dunbar found that when asked to name the number of people a person counted as intimates—friends and relations they contacted at least once a month—the list averaged ten to fifteen names. Groups of around twelve also characterize juries, inner cabinets, Christ's apostles, governmental inner cabinets, and most sports teams. "We may live in the centre of enormous modern conurbations like New York or Karachi, but we still only know about the same number of people as our long-distant ancestors did when they roamed the plains of the American Midwest or the savannahs of eastern Africa," Dunbar writes. "Psychologically speaking, we are Pleistocene hunter-gatherers locked into a twentieth-century economy."

For that reason, Dunbar, who wrote his book in the mid-1990s, was skeptical about the vaunted potential of the Internet to radically transform human society, as many cybervisionaries were then claiming. To him, innovations like e-mail would accelerate but not fundamentally change

the underlying imperatives of direct association to which we are genetically predisposed: "Suspicion of the unknown and the fear of being duped
by untrustworthy strangers will continue to dictate our decisions. As a result, negotiations in large amorphous populations are more likely to be
conducted under the straitjacket of the rule book rather than by intuition.
And where it is really important, we will resort to the trusted age-old machinery of direct personal contact."[25]

What Dunbar failed to fully anticipate at the time was the extent to
which cybernetworks would tether themselves to physical space and find
ways to mimic the "trusted age-old machinery" of human interaction. He
couldn't have foreseen that a then fledgling auction site called eBay would
grow into a giant that incorporated subscriber-generated reviews to keep
fraud in check and give traders a motive to live up to their online bargains.
Or the extent to which chat communities would voluntarily police themselves to uphold consensual standards and codes of conduct. Or the way
that online social networks and dating sites would position themselves as
go-betweens and matchmakers who help people find each other and make
plans to meet face-to-face in public and in private.

In the multicultural mindscape of the New Mainstream, human beings will work best in social environments that build cohesion and trust.
Any tribe—or company—that rejects diversity is undermining its own
ability to grow and create alliances with other groups. The instinct to
reach out ultimately overrides the impulse to pull back because construc-
tive contact is the best defense. Social networks, and the consumer markets they breed and foster, are inherently collaborative. Any company that
resists diversity is not just out of step with the New Mainstream; it is pit-
ting itself against the same social dynamics that will allow it to compete
and win. Diversity is not a corporate goal; it is a process that acknowledges
and incorporates the genetic imperative of innovation and evolution. Diversity is individual and social, personal and public. It is manifested not
just in *what* is being said, but in *how* it is being said—whether it's a conversation between colleagues or a companywide announcement. Diversity
is not a committee that reports back to the company; it is an economic
and social fact that must be recognized and internalized in order to ensure
maximum rates of productivity and return on investment. When an orga-

nization of any size decides that it wants to understand diversity, the first step is realizing that it has embarked on a journey to understand itself.

In the end, what matters most is how Dunbar's insights suggest that the atavistic urges that divide us are the same ones that bind us together. Culture can push people apart or bring them together. If language developed to help human beings bond and relate to one another as they organized into ever larger tribes, then the Internet is merely a new form of communal tongue, one that serves a similarly unifying purpose in an increasingly interrelated world. Seen from that perspective, cyberspace is merely a high-tech manifestation of a tribal imperative to communicate and a primordial reminder that all human beings are distant relatives who remain dependent on one another for their mutual survival.

The convergence of tribalism and technology is strongest and most evident in younger Americans who, not coincidentally, are also the population segment most likely to see ethnic and racial diversity as something to be taken for granted. Their postethnic perspective—the assumption that identity and ethnicity are optional and flexible, as opposed to preordained and fixed—is already challenging the social assumptions of their elders and forcing marketers to rethink how they present their products and brands. According to a study by Harris Interactive entitled "Youth Pulse," members of "Generation Y" (also called "echo boomers"), or young people born between 1982 and 1995, have annual incomes that total $211 billion.[23] Spending levels rise with age, along with the ability of teens and young adults to earn extra income through part- and full-time jobs. Per capita spending is lowest for preteens (ages eight to twelve), followed by teens (ages thirteen to nineteen) and young adults (ages twenty to twenty-one). Echo boomers are significantly more numerous than the Gen X–ers who preceded them and are generally considered less cynical and more optimistic than their older brothers and sisters. For advertisers and the entertainment industry, teens and young adults have a value that goes far beyond their actual spending power as tastemakers and style setters. This is also the age when young consumers are forming brand loyalties than can last the rest of their lives.

Urban ethnic youths are considered by many to be the key to Generation Y, not just because of their disproportionate numbers, but because they tend to skew younger and be concentrated in the major cities, where fashion, music, and other cultural expressions are forged and transmitted to the rest of the population and around the world. In 2000, Hispanics made up 12.5 percent of the U.S. population, but Hispanics under eighteen years old made up 17.1 percent. And since the number of Hispanic teens is growing faster than the number of non-Hispanic whites by a margin of 34 percent to 6 percent, respectively, the Latino proportion of the population will only increase as they get older.

Roger Selbert, vice president of strategic planning for Latin Works, a multicultural advertising and marketing agency based in Austin, Texas, found that 74 percent of the Hispanic teens it surveyed in Los Angeles said that they spoke Spanglish. "It's the voice of a new generation," Selbert predicts. "Spanglish will enter the mainstream." Common examples of English and Spanish grafted together include "parkiar *el carro*" ("park the car") and editorial copy from *Latina* magazine, which enjoins women to have "gorgeous *ojos*" ("gorgeous eyes"). A growing number of books are being written in Spanglish, and, for better or worse, there's a Spanglish translation of Cervantes's classic novel, *Don Quixote*. David Perez, the chairman of Cultural Access Group, a Hispanic consumer insight and marketing firm based in New York City, has identified a "multicultural commonality" among U.S. Latino youth, a third of whom live in either Los Angeles, New York City, or Miami. In a study that included 250 telephone surveys and 50 qualitative interviews with fourteen- to twenty-four-year-old Hispanics living in Los Angeles and New York City, Perez found that a solid majority expressed a preference for English, but more than 70 percent said they also spoke Spanglish, mainly at home or when with friends. Perez also found that rather than fitting into any existing demographic or language-based segmentation scheme, Latino urban youths identified with lifestyle "tribes" that revolved around a particular music style and the fashion, attitudes, and other social cues that went with it.

The urban youth market that emerges is less a demographic segment than a constellation of interconnected networks and subcultures that construct their identity from a variety of sources and media. In Los Angeles, New York City, and Miami, they are already the New Mainstream, and most of the rest of the country is not far behind. The cultural fusion they represent is both local and international, and the reverberations of that mix amplify and echo signals that are being picked up in Des Moines and New Delhi, as well Caracas, São Paulo, and Mexico City. As they fearlessly combine cultural ingredients, stitching together new ways of sounding, looking, and being from everything and anything in their reach, they are turning the urban youth market into a plugged-in global bazaar where a hot new idea or trend can zip across town—or the world—in the time it takes to type an instant message. Instinctively testing and reformulating the social glue that holds their tribe together, they are the de facto vanguard of the American present and the owners of its destiny.

PART II

The History of the Future

5. Melting Pots and Salad Bowls

The New Mainstream was not born in a vacuum. It did not form overnight. Its tributaries reach back to the earliest moments of the republic, and its principles are tied to the economic and philosophical foundations of the American experiment. It is a commonplace to say that the United States is a nation of immigrants, but without the successive waves of newcomers who arrived on American shores, or were absorbed as a consequence of territorial expansion, our culture and economy would not be what it is today—or what it will become tomorrow. The New Mainstream is not alien or foreign; it is intrinsically American. The New Mainstream is both imported and homegrown, assembled from foreign parts and made in the United States. To anticipate the multicultural economy of the future, it's necessary to remember the past. To understand who we are becoming, it's essential that we understand who we have always been.

The multicultural fabric of the New Mainstream is woven from the monochromatic threads of history. All Americans are united by a common experience of immigration that began when the first Native Americans crossed the Bering Strait, and continued with the Spanish explorers, with the English, French, and Dutch settlers, and with successive infusions of people seeking religious, economic, and cultural freedom in the New World. Rather than a steady trickle of immigration and assimilation, the newcomers have arrived in torrents triggered by domestic and international events, often followed by paroxysms of xenophobia and a spate of anti-immigration laws that attempt to turn off the immigrant spigot. The naturalization law passed by the first United States Congress in 1790 was quite clear about limiting citizenship to free white persons.

In nineteenth-century America, however, some whites were more equal than others, and sociocultural distinctions were far from absolute. Discrimination against non-Anglo European immigrants, particularly Irish Catholics, was severe enough that it contributed to one of the most fascinating footnotes in American history during the U.S.-Mexican War of 1846–1848. The war—which has been variously portrayed as either a righteous defense of the sovereignty of the United States or a shameless land grab fueled by racist delusions of manifest destiny—was triggered by a dispute over the status of Texas, which declared its independence from Mexico in 1836 and was annexed to the United States nine years later despite Mexico's denunciation of both events. Declaring that Texas was still part of Mexico and that therefore U.S. troops based near Matamoros under the command of General Zachary Taylor had invaded Mexican territory, the Mexican government demanded their withdrawal. When Taylor refused, Mexican forces led by General Pedro de Ampudia attacked. Not long after the fighting began, a group of more than 150 U.S. Army deserters and their allies joined the Mexican army under the command of John Riley, a blue-eyed Irishman from County Galway who had enlisted in the U.S. Army in Michigan in 1845. Known by the Mexicans as *El Batallón de San Patricio*, or Saint Patrick's Battalion, Riley and his men, many of whom were Irish and fought under a shamrock-emblazoned flag, were reviled as traitors by the Americans and hailed as heroes by the Mexicans.[1]

Like the seeds of a social transformation that would not take root until more than a century later, the San Patricios proved that shared experience could create alliances that transcended national and political divisions—

although not always in ways that governments could anticipate or tolerate. While the motives behind the San Patricios' defections varied from man to man and included material incentives promised by the Mexican government and romances with Mexican women, there is little doubt that discrimination and harsh reprisals against Irish foot soldiers by their mostly Protestant and often abusive American-born officers were a factor. In his book *Shamrock and Sword: The Saint Patrick's Battalion and the U.S.-Mexican War*, Robert Ryal Miller notes that the decade before the U.S.-Mexican War was a period of intense nativism and anti-Catholicism in the United States. "Nativist prejudice, which frequently was combined with contempt for Roman Catholicism, was widespread in the American army," Miller writes. "Foreign born soldiers were taunted—Irishmen were disparagingly called 'micks' or 'potatoheads'—and discriminated against, often being passed over for promotion. Although immigrants constituted the bulk of the recruits for the infantry, they generally were excluded from elite units such as dragoons and engineer companies. While based in Mexico, a number of Protestant officers and soldiers disparaged the Catholic Church there, calling its rituals 'absurd' and 'flummery.' Some Americans robbed chapels or churches, others stabled their horses in religious buildings, and a few disrupted religious processions. These outrages, along with crimes perpetrated against Mexican civilians by unruly Yankee soldiers, were cited by Mexican propagandists who tried to persuade foreign-born Catholic soldiers to desert from the invading army."[2] Riley and the Saint Patrick's Batallion fought the American army until the end of the war. They were eventually defeated and captured by U.S. forces in Mexico City, where a monument erected in their memory by the Mexican government still stands. The surviving San Patricios were court-martialed. Fifty were executed; the others were whipped and branded. Mexico's defeat resulted in its loss of not just the disputed Lone Star Republic, but also most of what is now California and New Mexico. A hundred and sixty years after the battle of the Alamo, a big-budget Hollywood dramatization of the fight became an embarrassing box office flop. Despite—or possibly because of—their attempt to create a historically balanced account of the conflict, the filmmakers missed their target by underestimating the ambivalence all Americans have come to feel about an episode that has no obvious heroes or victims, winners or losers.

The U.S.-Mexican War was hardly the last time that economics and race would shape American attitudes towards non-Anglo immigrants. Fifteen years later, Abraham Lincoln, who was a freshman congressman at the time of the U.S. war with Mexico, would send Union troops to fight the armed forces of the southern Confederacy, a group of states opposed to the abolition of slavery on the grounds that it would devastate the agrarian economy of the South. And despite the considerable legal and political gains that came with northern victory and emancipation, the subsequent enactment of segregationist codes, or Jim Crow laws, in many southern states allowed social discrimination and institutionalized racism to fester for decades, sowing the seeds of a black separatist subculture that survives in various forms to this day.

Asians have also taken their turn on the dark side of the American dream. While some Chinese and Filipinos came to the Americas as crew members on Spanish galleons during the early seventeenth century, Asians did not begin arriving in the Americas in large numbers until the mid–nineteenth century. Chinese immigrants were seen as a convenient and cheap way to replace freed black slaves and were recruited as contract laborers to work in agriculture and on the railroads. The California Gold Rush and the prospect of instant wealth was another lure for young Chinese hoping to make a better life for themselves. The U.S. Congress responded by passing the Chinese Exclusion Act of 1882,[3] which barred Asians from becoming U.S. citizens. Around the same time, antimiscegenation laws, which made it illegal for Asians and other nonwhites to marry whites and propagate "hybrid races," were enacted in Virginia and California. Meanwhile, California laws based on the "separate but equal" segregationist codes of the South forbade Asian and Native Americans from attending the same schools as white children.

American bigotry toward Asians took a military turn in 1899, when the United States purchased the Philippine archipelago from Spain for $20 million as part of a treaty that ended the Spanish-American War. When

Philippine nationalists refused to submit to American rule without a fight, the United States embarked on a bloody campaign of pacification that some have called America's first Vietnam. The war was vehemently opposed by a number of prominent Americans, including writer and humorist Mark Twain, who decried the immorality of armed aggression against a fledgling republic. "I thought we should act as their protector—not try to get them under our heel," Twain told the newspaper *New York World* in October 1900. "But now—why, we have got into a mess, a quagmire from which each fresh step renders the difficulty of extraction immensely greater."[4]

Meanwhile, out on the battlefield, African American soldiers listened with mixed emotions as their white comrades used the word *nigger* to describe the insurgent natives. In a South Pacific echo of the *San Patricios*, a number of African American soldiers defected to the Filipino side and fought against the U.S. Army. Hundreds more married Filipino women and adopted the islands as their permanent home.[5] In 1912, a decade after the end of the conflict, fears that the election of Woodrow Wilson as president could accelerate Philippine independence prompted a fresh wave of bigotry from developers who worried that the policy change could undermine their plans to profit from commercial development of the islands. In an effort to galvanize public opinion against Philippine independence, agents for the American-Philippine Company disseminated propaganda materials that suggested Filipinos would revert to banana leaf–wearing savages without the civilizing presence of the United States.[6]

In the early twentieth century, as immigration reached what was up until then an all-time high and the influx of immigrants shifted from English and Northern Europeans to a more Southern and Eastern European mix that included Russians, Italians, and Austro-Hungarians, Congress again tried to stanch the flow. By 1929, U.S. immigration policy was defined by country- and race-based quotas designed to preserve a Northern European ethnocentric population. During the 1930s and early 1940s, immigration tapered off considerably, reaching a nadir of thirty-four thousand immigrants per year between 1941 and 1945, then began climbing again, mainly because of changes in public attitudes and immigration policies during and after World War II. Despite domestic hate-mongering against Germans and Japanese—and the forced internment of 120,000 Japanese Americans after the attack on Pearl Harbor—America's opposition to the racist regimes of Nazi Germany and imperial Japan and its alliances with Germany and Russia led to the repeal of the Chinese Exclusion Act in 1943. Meanwhile, in an effort to address the wartime labor shortage, the U.S. and Mexican governments entered into an agreement allowing Mexican laborers to migrate across the border temporarily to fill low-level jobs in agriculture and other industries. Over the next two decades, the policy, which came to be known as "the *bracero* program," gave millions of Mexicans a taste of U.S.-style capitalism and introduced them to the benefits—and drawbacks—of large-scale cross-border migration.[7]

World War II also heightened America's awareness of itself as a bastion of freedom and opportunity and as a haven for the defenseless victims of the world's totalitarian and Fascist regimes. Nazi persecution of the Jews, the Communist revolution in Russia, and the ensuing cold war all gave an ideological imperative to America's self-image as an open, racially and culturally tolerant society and put additional pressure on immigration law reform. The McCarran-Walter Immigration Act of 1952 lifted what was left of immigration race restrictions and allowed U.S. citizens to bring their spouses into the country regardless of country of origin quotas. During the 1950s, immigration rose again, to more than two hundred thousand per year and climbed to nearly three hundred thousand per year during the early 1960s. The racial and cultural makeup of the immigrants themselves was also changing. Asylum seekers from Eastern Europe and other parts of the Communist bloc prompted Congress in 1953 to allow two hundred thousand refugees to enter the United States. Six years later, two hundred thousand Cubans who were seeking to escape Fidel Castro's Communist revolution were allowed into the United States on temporary visitor's visas. By 1965, the same year that national origin quotas were finally abolished and replaced with an annual quota of twenty thousand for every nation in the Eastern Hemisphere, Canada and Mexico, at almost forty thousand immigrants apiece that year, were contributing more than any European country.[8]

The influx of new immigrants coincided with a time when U.S. social

values and institutions were being openly questioned. The political activism of the 1960s, fueled by the Vietnam War and the "Black Power"
movement, further accelerated the evolution of multicultural consciousness. As African Americans challenged the superiority of Eurocentric
white culture, "Black is beautiful" became a rallying cry for nonwhite ethnic pride. In California, inspired by the media shock tactics of the militant
Black Panthers, a group of Mexican American activists formed the Brown
Berets. Both groups, convinced that the white-dominated establishment
would never change voluntarily, advocated social reform and racial parity
by whatever means necessary. Martin Luther King Jr. and César Chávez,
who provided a unified voice and a moral legitimacy to the civil rights aspirations of African Americans and Mexican Americans, respectively, became national folk heroes and provided an ideological and tactical bridge
between minorities and reform-minded whites. By the end of the decade,
the realization that marginalized factions could gain leverage by banding
together to celebrate their uniqueness had sparked similar ethnic identity
movements among Asians, Native Americans, and other minorities and
paved the way for women's liberation, Gay Pride, and other shadings of
the Rainbow Coalition.

And while the issue of race has always been—and will probably continue for some time to be—the final acid test for tolerance, there are signs
that the once indelible division between black and white is giving way to
something less absolute. In his book *From Margin to Mainstream: The Social Progress of Black Americans*, sociologist Sethard Fisher argues that
African Americans have moved out of the stage where their race and social
status automatically relegate them to a lower social stratum and have thus
acquired many of the traits and options of other ethnic groups. "In the
transition from caste to class, blacks have now reached an intermediate
stage, to which I refer to as ethnic status," he writes. "Black have now
achieved a resource—ethnicity—that for most other ethnic groups in
America has been available for a much longer time."[9]

Even some whites are reevaluating the value of their own cultural past.
Laura Muller White, an instructor with the Diversity Management Institute at Montgomery College in Rockland, Maryland, has detected a new
willingness among Americans of European ancestry to recognize their Eu-

ropean roots. "It's not enough to be inclusive, you have to step out of the middle," says White, who traces her own heritage to the Netherlands. "I realized one day that my own cultural awareness was defined by some windmills I kept in my house that were made in Malaysia. When you drop your heritage, all that's left are these centuries-old icons." White, who travels around the country lecturing to students and professionals on how to nurture and enhance cultural diversity in their workplaces and schools, had a sobering experience at a high school in Washington State, where the majority of the students were of European or Scandinavian extraction. "I asked one kid to describe his culture, and he answered: 'Nike, McDonald's, Nordstrom's, Starbucks.' It was amazing." At another high school north of Seattle, White found that when the students were asked to identify their race, they made a point of describing themselves as "Norwegian" or "German." "They all avoided the word *white*, or they did it apologetically," she says, "because for them white pride is associated with white supremacy."

The rise of identity politics—the blatant rejection of the "melting pot" and all that it represented, as well as efforts to compensate for past injustices—is still regarded by some as a step down the road to social chaos and an affront to the idea of America itself. Multiculturalism, in this context, became a tug-of-war between those who held that the established cultural canons of the Anglo-American experience were the essential pillars of American identity and others who saw them as devices of historical distortion and social repression. The primary battleground was in the classroom—particularly over the content of high school and college curriculums—but by the 1980s, the dispute had widened into an ideological standoff between conservative and liberal visions of the United States. In his book *The Disuniting of America: Reflections on a Multicultural Society*, Arthur M. Schlesinger Jr. acknowledges that "the United States has been from birth a multicultural nation," then goes on to bemoan the emergence of a new "militant form" of multiculturalism that "opposes the idea of a common culture, rejects goals of assimilation and integration, and celebrates the immutability of diverse and separate ethnic and racial communities. Extreme separationists, while often flourishing the multicultural flag, in fact rush beyond true multiculturalism into ethnocentrism, the belief in the superior virtue of their own ethnic group." [10]

Ironically, it was Anglo-Americans in the United States who first practiced the kind of exclusionary ethnocentrism that Schlesinger so deplores, but it would also be unfair to dismiss his concern as mere hypocrisy. Clearly, it was no longer the case that Americans, as John Jay wrote in *The Federalist Papers*, were "one united people—a people descended from the same ancestors, speaking the same language, professing the same religion, attached to the same principles of government, very similar in their manners and customs." But many still clung to notion that America was a place where, in the words of the French immigrant J. Hector St. John de Crèvecoeur, "individuals of all nations are melted into a new race of men" and that this melting of peoples, a shedding of personal identity that was a prerequisite for the creation of this quintessentially American alloy, was not only the secret source of America's strength but an unspoken requirement of true citizenship.[11] It followed that anyone who refused to shed their personal (read: foreign) identity—or questioned the legitimacy of the identity being offered to replace it—was by definition un-American.

By the end of the twentieth century, Americans who still subscribed to such restrictive notions of nationalism were themselves a numerical minority. Their reaction has been to declare a cultural holy war against those who favor creating a social agenda more reflective of the nation's ethnic and racial mix. Neoconservatives, sensing that the demographic tide has turned against them, have adopted the tactic of portraying themselves as ideological Custers, desperately retreating to higher ground as the yelping savages close in for the kill. In a 2001 article for the online 'zine *Salon*, David Horowitz decried "the triumph of 'multicultural' thugs" who harassed right-wing cover girl Ann Coulter during a talk at Cornell University, proving that "fascism is alive and well on U.S. campuses."[12] Never mind that, significantly, Coulter's harasser was a white man of Scottish ancestry. "The police will remove obstructors and thugs, but the administration will not discipline them," Horowitz fumed. "It knows the organizations and individuals who are the source of the problem but will take no action against them because they are either minorities or 'progressives'— and usually both. This tolerance has the effect of encouraging the delinquent behavior that requires the police, while relegating conservatives to the role of a harassed minority element in the campus community."

If you strip away the polemics from Horowitz's rant, it's clear that conservatives are quite aware of their shrinking demographic base and are trying to use claims of their status as a "harassed minority" to stoke the fears of the white majority. It's equally obvious that the real threat to the neoconservatives, and the trend that poses the greatest danger to their sociopolitical agenda, is the natural alliance between "minorities"—that is, immigrants, people of color, outsiders, women, and gays—and the creative class, encrypted by Horowitz in the term *progressives*. It's no accident either that Horowitz uses "tolerance"—the binding glue of the New Mainstream and the antonym of bigotry—as a slur.

Luckily, most Americans intuitively understand that tolerance is not capitulation to politically correct fascists, but a necessary component of liberty and social stability, and that it is ultimately in the national interest to foster and promote it. In his book *We Are All Multiculturalists Now*, Harvard sociologist and *Beyond the Melting Pot* coauthor Nathan Glazer, asked, "Will multiculturalism undermine what is still, on balance, a success in world history, a diverse society that continues to welcome further diversity, with a distinctive and common culture of some merit? I believe things will not come to that pass because the basic demand of the multiculturalists is for inclusion, not separation, and inclusion under the same rules—stretching back to the Constitution—that have permitted the steady broadening of what we understand as equality."[13]

The boundaries of American social equality were broadened again in 2003 when the U.S. Supreme Court struck down antisodomy laws directed against homosexuals. The court's ruling in *Lawrence vs. Texas* was compared by attorneys on both sides of the issue as comparable in scope and impact to *Brown vs. the Board of Education*, which banned school segregation, and *Roe vs. Wade*, which legalized abortion. Observers also predicted an inevitable legal battle over the right of homosexuals to legally marry. Less than a month later, the Anglican Church approved the election of its first gay Episcopal bishop. In both cases, gay advocates were not challenging the mainstream practices of consensual adult sex, marriage, or religious worship but were merely fighting for the legal right to engage in the same behaviors and rituals as the heterosexual majority if they chose to do so.

The Supreme Court's highly anticipated ruling on affirmative action the same year was more equivocal but no less definitive. In a split decision on two separate but interconnected cases involving the University of Michigan, the Court ruled that race could be used as a contributing factor in university admissions decisions but struck down a point system used by the school's undergraduate program on the grounds that it failed to provide equal protection to white students by making race a "decisive" factor. The legal strategy of the team defending the university, to the dismay of some minority activists, was based not on any moral obligation to correct past injustices, but on the fact that affirmative action was in the nation's self-interest because a diverse student body in the nation's colleges was a crucial ingredient in higher learning and would help keep the United States economically strong and globally competitive. In her majority opinion in the University of Michigan Law School case, Justice Sandra Day O'Connor cited numerous studies that "show that student body diversity promotes learning outcomes, and 'better prepares students for an increasingly diverse workforce and society, and better prepares them as professionals.' These benefits are not theoretical but real, as major American businesses have made clear that the skills needed in today's increasingly global marketplace can only be developed through exposure to widely diverse people, cultures, ideas and viewpoints."[14]

The business case for diversity was underscored in an amicus curiae brief filed on behalf of General Motors, Inc. The company, which has annual revenues exceeding $175 billion and employs 388,000 people in more than two hundred countries on six continents, argued that "the Nation's interest in safeguarding the freedom of academic institutions to select racially and ethnically diverse student bodies is indeed compelling: the future of American business and, in some measure, of the American economy depends on it."[15] Citing the importance of diversity in academia to promote "speculation, experiment and creation" and to prepare a new generation of managers for an increasingly heterogeneous work environment, the GM brief warned that a ruling proscribing the consideration of race and ethnicity in admissions decisions would hobble the company's ability to compete in increasingly critical global markets. GM's brief—and dozens of others like it submitted to the Court by other Fortune 500 companies—illustrates how the economic imperatives of profit and market share are merging with demographic trends to mold a new social order. In a society where the consumer is king, corporations will do everything they can to protect their interests in domestic and overseas markets, if that means changing the rules or, in this case, defending existing rules that, however imperfectly, foster social diversity.

E Pluribus Plural?

But the economic dividends of the New Mainstream are not limited to the domestic consumer market or even giant multinationals. Diversity also gives the United States a competitive edge against all other nations in ways that go beyond corporate communication and staffing. The multicultural, transnational nature of the New Mainstream, so quintessentially American in spirit and manifestation, is what sets the United States apart from the rest of the world and provides the real source of its global stature and authority. In the coming decades, thanks to the unflagging influx of foreigners, the U.S. population—and the economic and intellectual vitality it represents—will continue to thrive and expand, even as the relatively hermetic, ethnically homogeneous societies of Japan and Europe age and shrink.

In other words, the New Mainstream will keep America young and strong even as the world's other major industrial powers become older and weaker. Demographers estimate that by the middle of the twenty-first century, Japan will have 30 percent fewer people and, as deaths exceed newborns at an annual rate of eight hundred thousand, more than 1 million one-hundred-year-olds. By the end of the century, the United Nations predicts that Japan could lose as much as half of its population of 120 million. The UN report estimates that Japan will need up to 17 million new immigrants to hold back the trend, but Japan's entrenched tradition of cultural and racial insularity will make that goal socially and politically impossible. The side effects of such a sharp drop in population include economic deflation, a shrinking tax base, and the collapse of its national pension system.[16]

Europe is facing an equally dire scenario. According to a study by William Frey, a demographer at the Brookings Institution and the University of Michigan's Population Studies Center, the median age in Europe is expected to rise from 37.7 years of age to 52.3 by 2050. By contrast, the median age in the United States will rise only slightly to 35.4 during the same period. With European fertility rates currently at 1.34 children per woman, well below the 2.1 children-per-woman rate needed to sustain a stable population, Europe will continue to lose demographic ground to the United States, China, and Latin America.[17]

A similar demographic shift is happening within the United States as native-born migrants of varying nationalities and economic strata redraw the lines between young and old, rich and poor, those who represent the future and those who cling to a diminishing past. Data from the 2000 U.S. census reveal a nation moving in several directions at once.[18] Frey has identified at least three different subnations within the United States, each of which has its own geographic, ethnic, and demographic personality:

"MELTING POT" AMERICA
- California, Texas, Florida, New York, New Jersey, Illinois, Hawaii, Alaska, and New Mexico.
- 40 percent of the U.S. population; 70 percent of all immigrants.
- Hispanics and Asians are concentrated here and already make up a majority of the population in cities like Los Angeles, Miami, and San Antonio.
- Growing faster than the rest of the country.
- Younger median age.
- Home to a higher percentage of recent immigrants, although large numbers of U.S.-born Hispanics and Asians also live here.
- Democratic strongholds.

THE NEW SUNBELT
- Oregon, Washington, Nevada, Utah, North and South Carolina, Georgia, and Pennsylvania.
- 20 percent of the U.S. population.

- Magnets for white U.S.-born migrants who are moving away from large metropolitan areas to the suburbs and exburbs.
- Growth due mainly to domestic migration from other states.
- Southern states in this group have the highest concentrations of African Americans, who are migrating there from other states as well.
- Politically leans to the center and center right.

THE HEARTLAND

- Idaho, Michigan, Nebraska, North and South Dakota, Wisconsin, Oklahoma, Arkansas.
- 40 percent of the U.S. population.
- More likely than other Americans to be white and of European extraction.
- Older than other states.
- Poorer than other states.
- Politically conservative.
- Traditionalists who share a nostalgic vision of America epitomized by icons like Ronald Reagan and John Wayne.

This snapshot of new demographic patterns goes far beyond the so-called white flight from large metropolitan centers. African Americans are also on the move—mainly back to the South. At the same time, the immigrant population can be divided into two main groups, which show divergent migration patterns. One group, made up of immigrants who arrived in the United States after 1990, is gravitating to the large cities of the melting pot states, where large established ethnic populations make the transition to U.S. society less jarring. A large percentage of immigrants who arrived before 1990, meanwhile, are moving along with other native migrants to the New Sunbelt states. The continued inflow of recently arrived foreign immigrants—most of whom are from Mexico, the Caribbean, or Latin America—to Texas and Florida is likely to accelerate the multicultural evolution of those states, even as that trend continues at a less rapid pace in California, New York, and the other "melting pot" states.[19]

According to Frey, as affluent creative class whites move to states like Nevada, Arizona, Colorado, Idaho, Georgia, North Carolina, and Utah in search of better housing and schools and lower congestion, they in turn "increase the demand for construction, service and retail jobs that are increasingly filled by immigrants."[20] In other words, the economic conditions for social diversity are created by the very same people who are leaving the cities to escape the downside of urban life—traffic, congestion, pollution, and thinly stretched city services. The immigrants are not only attracted to the jobs created by economic growth—they make that growth possible. And once new communities are established, immigrants take many of the service and maintenance jobs that allow it to operate smoothly. The degree to which affluent and middle-class Americans rely on immigrants to maintain their way of life was satirized in the "mockumentary" 2004 film A *Day Without a Mexican*, which depicted a California paralyzed and thrown into chaos by the sudden disappearance of the state's 14 million Latinos. "How do you make something invisible visible?" asks a character on the film's promotional Web site. "You take it away." A plot synopsis explains: "The realization that what has disappeared is the very thing that keeps the 'California Dream' running—cooks, gardeners, policemen, nannies, doctors, farm and construction workers, entertainers, athletes, as well as the largest growing market of consumers—has turned Latinos and their return into the number one priority in the State."

This economic symbiosis, which is one of the prime drivers of the New Mainstream, not to mention the U.S. economy overall, has a paradoxical effect on the statistical makeup of the New Sunbelt states. The resulting "barbell" economies—a simultaneous ballooning of the upper and lower socioeconomic strata—are an increasingly common feature of the New Sunbelt states. Between 1990 and 2000, for example, Las Vegas showed a poverty population increase of 86 percent. Other high-growth metropolitan areas such as Raleigh-Durham, Atlanta, Charlotte, Greensboro, and Phoenix all saw their poverty populations go up by more than 25 percent. The same areas have also seen a jump in the number of people who speak Spanish at home but do not speak English very well. Frey reports a rise in segregation between non-Hispanic whites and Hispanics in the New Sunbelt states, although the disparity is sharper in the South than in the western states.

The implication of Frey's analysis is that the fast-growing New Sunbelt states are in danger of becoming two-tiered societies, where a lower, mostly immigrant class serves the needs of an affluent, mostly white middle and upper class, with little or no contact between the two—raising the specter of a kind of "Juan Crow" nightmare that combines the worst of the urban inner city with oppressive social discrimination. "The new waves of foreign-born immigrants dispersing into domestic migrant states such as Nevada, Georgia, and North Carolina appear to reflect a mirror image of domestic migrants with respect to education and income," Frey observes. "This influx of foreign-born migrants with less selective socio-demographic attributes, coupled with rising levels of residential segregation, may be setting the stage for emerging 'barbell economies' in these fast-growing states."[21]

It is of course possible, if not inevitable, that the disparities between poor, non-English-speaking foreigners and affluent native whites will cause tension and challenge local institutions and infrastructures. But it's just as likely and inevitable that the same process of assimilation and integration that has already occurred in "melting pot" America will seep steadily into New Sunbelt communities. If anything, tolerance and acculturation will come faster in the New Sunbelt than in the Old Sunbelt—if only because of the widespread existence in those states of national corporations, institutions, and retail chains that have already joined the New Mainstream and accepted diversity as a social fact and a sound business strategy.

The prognosis for what Frey calls the Heartland is, at least from a statistical viewpoint, considerably less upbeat. As younger people gravitate to large cities and other creative centers that satisfy their hunger for diversity and fulfilling careers, and affluent retirees and middle-class families migrate to the New Sunbelt, the midwestern section of the nation faces declining social vitality along with an aging population. Out of touch with—or even hostile to—the cultural and economic trends of the New Mainstream, Heartland holdouts may suffer a self-perpetuating cycle of political retrenchment, economic stagnation, and cultural marginalization.

Amber Waves

Today, the United States of America is a nation of unprecedented economic and military power, able to protect and project its interests, desires, and dreams across the world. Yet it remains oddly invisible to itself. Instead of recognizing and celebrating this amazingly diverse nation in our midst, we often try to ignore or deny it. For every glimpse of this marvelously multicultural America, there is a countereffort to suppress or obscure it with a business-as-usual nostalgia for an idealized, ethnically homogenized society that exists only in old movies and the minds of politicians keen on impersonating the Lone Ranger.

In its most extreme and virulent manifestation, this reactionary impulse takes on a shrill, almost apocalyptic tone that doesn't even try to hide its underlying xenophobia. In his book, *The Death of the West: How Dying Populations and Immigrant Invasions Imperil Our Country and Civilization*, right-wing columnist and onetime presidential candidate Pat Buchanan warns of an "immigration tsunami" that will drown all that is good and right (and white) in America. "In little more than fifty years there will be no majority race in the United States," he fumes. Warning that the subversive notion of diversity will turn the United States into "a Third World America," he proclaims: "Uncontrolled immigration threatens to deconstruct the nation we grew up in and convert America into a conglomeration of peoples with almost nothing in common—not history, heroes, language, culture, faith or ancestors."[22]

If all immigrants were as ethnocentric as Mr. Buchanan, we would indeed have something to worry about. But despite record rates of immigration over the past two decades and the presence of an estimated 8 million undocumented immigrants, the United States has remained pretty much intact. The flag still waves, the republic stands. What is truly remarkable is how *little* ethnic and racial strife has occurred in the United States in spite of so much immigration. The reasons for this are myriad, but it could be that the glue that holds America together is neither skin color nor a love of English literature, but a shared commitment to hard work, cultural tolerance, and the promise of an equal chance to improve one's life and the lives of one's children. The great majority of immigrants come to America to escape repression, find work, or build a new life, and America itself invariably gets rebuilt—and culturally enriched—in the process. A 2003 survey of U.S. Latinos by the Pew Hispanic Center of the Kaiser Family Foundation found that immigrants from Latin America were over-whelmingly committed to strong family ties, religious beliefs, education, and hard work and were actually worried that coming to the United States would have a negative impact on the moral values of their children.[23]

Some African immigrants have gone a step farther, deciding that the only way to protect their children from the distractions and dangers of being black in America is to send them back to their ancestral homes for schooling. About 20 percent of the students enrolled in Akosombo International School, a boarding school in northeastern Ghana, are from families who live outside of the country, many of them African Americans sent there by their African-born parents, who have remained in the United States. Parents and students agree that dress codes, acceptable social conduct, and academic standards are all superior to what they would have experienced in the United States. Some of the students, many of whom returned to the United States for college, are grateful for what they perceive as an edge over their U.S.-educated peers when it comes to academic preparation, social manners, and self-discipline. While no figures exist on what percentage of the estimated 1 million African immigrants living in the United States send their children to attend preparatory schools in countries like Ghana, South Africa, Senegal, and Kenya—which have relatively stable economic and political systems—the practice is catching on. Academic experts say the trend began to take hold in the 1970s and 1980s as African-born parents with the means to send their children to Africa saw it as a way of shielding them from bad habits, drugs, and crime, particularly in the impressionable precollege years.[24]

In fact, one of the most profound—and no doubt to some surprising—aspects of the New Mainstream may be in how the national psyche is continually resuscitated by immigrants whose commitment to religious values, family ties, and upward mobility through hard work exceeds that of most native-born Americans. According to a New York Times/CBS News poll of more than three thousand Americans conducted during the summer of 2003, Hispanics living in the United States were more optimistic about their chances for a better life for themselves and their children than the general population. More than 70 percent of the foreign-born Hispanic respondents said that they identified more with the United States than with their country of origin, even though many continue to send money to their families in their home countries. Sixty-six percent of the foreign-born Hispanics said that they came to the United States in search of work, and the same percentage said that they still believed it was possible to come to the United States poor, work hard, and manage to become rich. Eighty-three percent of the recently arrived foreign-born Hispanics said that they believed life would be better for the next generation, while only 64 percent of the Hispanics born in the United States felt the same way. The poll shows that the American dream is alive and well, particularly among those immigrants who are willing to endure discrimination, loneliness, and, in the case of illegal immigrants, incarceration for the chance to improve their lot.

The signs of the entrepreneurial energy of America's ethnic immigrants are everywhere. In New Brunswick, New Jersey, where the Mexican percentage of the foreign-born population grew from 5 percent to 37.8 percent between 1900 and 2000, immigrant-owned shops and businesses have revitalized the city's declining downtown district. A few miles away, in Iselin, the Asian Indian population has gentrified the Oak Tree Road area near Mahatma Gandhi Plaza, where the streets are lined with Indian-owned and -run jewelry stores, clothing shops, and restaurants. African Americans have made a similar mark in Maryland's Prince George County, not far from Washington, D.C., where an ethnic mix that is 63 percent black, 27 percent white, 7 percent Latino, and 4 percent Asian American is driving up property values (from an average house price of $200,000 in the early 1990s to around $700,000 today) and attracting major retailers such as Ikea and Barnes & Noble.[25]

In an article published by the Knight Ridder/Tribune newspapers, Hector Barreto of the U.S. Small Business Administration noted that 1.2 million of America's small businesses are owned by Hispanics and that the number of Hispanic-owned firms is growing at a rate of 30 percent. Barreto, who has stated publicly that "small businesses are going to have to lead us out" of the current economic slump, has restated his commitment to help Hispanics assimilate and achieve the American dream. He also cited recent studies that show most Hispanics see no contradiction in maintaining a strong Latino cultural identity while working, living, and even raising families in the United States. "This dual desire to assimilate while also maintaining cultural identity, priorities and pride is not dissimilar from other groups who came here as immigrants," wrote Barreto, who is himself the son of Mexican immigrants. "From the Scottish family whose fifth-generation American men wear a kilt on their wedding day, to the Chinese American family who celebrates Chinese New Year, maintaining cultural traditions while assimilating is what has made this country such an incredible, diverse place."[26]

Naturally, not all the economic and social effects of immigration are positive. Large numbers of immigrants strain the social and physical infrastructure of local communities and breed resentment by those who feel threatened by abrupt change or see themselves losing ground to the new arrivals. Most blacks and Latinos trail non-Hispanic whites in income, education, and health care. Dropout and teen pregnancy rates for African American and Hispanic high school students are alarmingly high. And outdated and inefficient policies toward illegal immigrants fuel a self-fulfilling cycle of discrimination and resentment. A 2003 study by Lisa Catanzarite, a sociologist at the University of California at Los Angeles, found evidence that the 10 million Hispanic immigrants who work in the United States were dragging down wages for a large number of blue-collar jobs in big cities and towns where they compete with other "brown collar" workers for jobs as gardeners, dishwashers, construction day laborers, janitors, and roofers. In U.S. cities where Hispanic immigrants made up more than 25 percent of the workforce in any given field, Catanzarite found that white workers earned about $200 less based on an average annual income of $21,600. Yet the downward pressure on wages was much greater for the immigrants themselves, who earned as much as $2,900 less per year in the same jobs as their nonimmigrant co-workers.

Concerns that immigrants compete with native-born workers and create an undue burden on taxpaying citizens were two of the arguments used to justify California's Proposition 187—a 1994 ballot measure, later struck down by the courts, that would have restricted public services for illegal immigrants. In a rather sad but understandable example of the human propensity to shut the door behind them, even some Latinos favored the passage of Proposition 187—fearing that new waves of poor, unskilled Mexicans could hurt their chances for economic and social advancement.

Another common but flawed assumption about minorities in general—and Latinos in particular—is that they are politically liberal. But, as anyone who has ever spent any time in Miami knows, Hispanic political affiliations are diverse and complex, with ideological footholds in both major parties. The New York Times/CBS News poll of U.S. Latinos found that while Hispanics viewed the Democratic Party as better equipped to manage the economy, create jobs, and improve the nation's school system, they also had a favorable view of George W. Bush. A majority of Hispanics polled also sided with Republicans' more conservative views on social issues like gay rights, taxes, and abortion. Hispanics were less likely than the general population to support the legalization of homosexual relations between consenting adults and were twice as likely—44 percent versus 22 percent—to oppose the legalization of abortion.

Such data flies in the face of charges that Hispanic immigration is contributing to the disintegration of American society. To be sure, an influx of newcomers—particularly illegal workers who must live and work in the shadowy margins of the underground economy—is bound to put pressure on local institutions and infrastructures. And large population shifts, whether prompted by immigration, economics changes, environmental factors, or war—have always exacerbated regional, racial, and class tensions. In his book *Bowling Alone: The Collapse and Revival of American Community*, Robert Putnam, a professor of public policy at Harvard University, traces a steep decline in recent decades of participation in civic and professional associations like the Rotary Club, the National Association for the Advancement of Colored People (NAACP), the Masons, 4-H, the Elks, and the American Bowling Congress. He also shows how "social capital," or the organizations and customs that reflect and foster social connection and cohesion, has been undermined and eroded by the anti-communal effects of television, the Internet, two-career families, suburban sprawl, and generational shifts in morality and social responsibility. Drawing parallels between the present and the so-called Gilded Age, or the first two decades of the twentieth century, when large-scale economic and technological change was accompanied by a major spike in immigrants, Putnam notes that newcomers contribute to the overall building of social capital by transplanting their own networks and interpersonal relationships. "Generally speaking, emigration devalues one's social capital, for most of one's social connections must be left behind," Putnam writes. "The immigrants rationally strive to conserve social capital. So-called chain migration, whereby immigrants from a given locale in the 'old country' settle near one another in their new homeland, was and remains one common coping strategy. In addition, the benevolent society for mutual aid was the bedrock of many immigrant communities, providing financial security, camaraderie, and even political representation."[27] This dynamic has been illustrated in recent decades by the congregation in New York City of Mexicans from the state of Puebla and by the Hmong community in California. A Southeast Asian agrarian mountain people, the Hmong were persecuted in their homeland by the Communists after the U.S. withdrawal from Vietnam. More than three hundred thousand were admitted to the United States during the 1970s, a third of whom settled in California. The Hmong American Community, Inc., a nonprofit organization based in Fresno, California, was formed by the Hmong community to assist its people in finding affordable housing and health care, provide assistance in education and economic development, and serve as a sounding board and advocate for community needs and social issues. Inevitably, such organizations evolve into business associations that in turn create jobs and contribute to the tax base.

In Los Angeles, home to an estimated 1.1 million undocumented immigrants, issues around the short- and long-term economic and social costs of the city's foreign-born population have become a political hot button. Native residents—including many U.S.-born Latinos, Asians, and African Americans—worry that the influx of foreigners is straining the city's physical infrastructure and overwhelming health, education, law enforcement, and other public services. Los Angeles County officials estimate that as many as 800,000 of the 2.5 million people who receive public health care each year are undocumented aliens. The Los Angeles Sheriffs' Department estimates that as much as a quarter of the county jail's inmate population is made up of illegal immigrants. And since California state law requires every child between the ages of six and eighteen to attend school regardless of immigrant status, undocumented aliens also make up a sizable percentage of the public school student body. At the end of 2003, newly elected governor Arnold Schwarzenegger fulfilled a campaign pledge to repeal a law allowing undocumented workers in the state to obtain diver's licenses. In a state where cars are part of the ecosystem, the move only insured that a significant percentage of California's population would continue to drive outside the law without rights and privileges.

The perception that state coffers were underwriting health and education for undocumented aliens, the majority of whom are Mexican, is widely acknowledged as a key factor behind the state's recent history of tax revolt. In 1994, voters passed a referendum known as Proposition 187, which barred illegal aliens and their children from receiving public money. Though the proposition was eventually ruled unconstitutional on the basis that it conflicted with federal authority to set immigration laws, the perception by Californians—and most Americans, for that matter—that they are footing the bill for foreigners persists.

Yet there is ample evidence that the portrayal of immigrants as a negative drag on the economy is at best a gross oversimplification of a far more complex truth. A 1997 study by a panel of economists and demographers assembled under the auspices of the National Academy of Sciences designed to measure the net impact of immigration concluded that immigrants "actually make a net fiscal contribution" to the U.S. economy. Its study, titled "The New Americans: Economic, Demographic, and Fiscal Effects of Immigration," found that the negative effect of Latino immigrant households, which tend to have lower incomes and include more children than other immigrants, is balanced out over time by the incomes of other immigrants and native-born households for three reasons. First, the new immigrants who are a net cost to the public sector due to the cost of educating their offspring may ultimately offer a positive contribution as the children finish school and become coemployees and taxpayers. Second, the fiscal gain or loss caused by the immigrant population is determined by government fiscal policies, which may shift short-term deficits to future generations. Finally, as corroborated by the Urban Institute and other surveys, the ages, socioeconomic skills, and cultural backgrounds of new immigrants is far from homogeneous. The positive effects of older, professionally trained immigrants such as, say, Filipino nurses, may cancel out the negative drag of Mexican laborers in the short term, while the opposite could occur in the longer term.

What's more, immigration policies favoring higher-skilled immigrants could skew their economic contributions upward, even though lower-skilled laborers contribute to business growth by filling menial jobs and holding down wages. In addition, the rate of assimilation also varies among ethnic and socioeconomic groups, although several studies suggest that the evolution of the current immigrant wave will eventually follow historical patterns. "Despite fears in the past about the effects of immigration on the social fabric of the nation, few socioeconomic differences now separate the descendants of immigrants from Europe," noted the National Academy of Sciences. "Whether the same generational progress will characterize present-day immigrants and their children remains to be seen. Early readings suggest that some recent immigrants and their children, especially Asian Americans, match native-born whites in education and occupation, although not incomes, fairly quickly." Another factor contributing to the net positive effect of immigration is that younger working-age immigrants tend to make a positive contribution, while those in their late sixties and older tend to do the opposite. The fact that the overwhelming majority of current immigrants are in the former category adds to the overall positive net balance.

The National Academy of Sciences also debunked the notion that immigration contributes to overall crime rates. Noting that national crime rates rose from the 1960s until about 1990, even while immigration rates continued to rise, it found "no obvious link" between immigration and crime during this period, adding, "Studies at the local level have found no association of immigrant concentrations with crime rates, with the exception of high rates of non-violent crime near the borders."

While the overall net effect of immigration on a national level was deemed to be positive, the National Academy of Sciences did offer some caveats, namely that the negative effects were concentrated at state and local levels, particularly in areas with disproportionate immigration levels. The downside explains why "melting pot" states like California also tend to be centers of anti-immigration sentiment and legislation. Not surprisingly, the academy found that despite competition for jobs and political influence, Americans from ethnic and racial minorities were more likely to see immigration in a positive light. "In the past 50 years, polling data have charted a deepening opposition to immigration, linked in part, it appears, to economic concerns," the study said. "Interethnic tensions have surfaced, especially in areas of high unemployment and poverty. Attitudes are by no means monolithic, however: Americans of African, Hispanic and Asian descent are more accepting of immigration than non-Hispanic whites are." People with higher education levels also tend to be more accepting of immigrants than their less-educated counterparts, which dovetails with research indicating that highly educated professionals seek ethnic and racial diversity in their communities and work environments.

There is also a new understanding of the historical role that once marginalized non-European minorities have played in the definition and validation of core American values such as liberty, equality, and freedom of speech. By resisting marginalization and exclusion, and using the institutions and tools of American democracy to press their case, African Americans, Hispanics, Asians, women, gays, and other minorities have over the years reinforced and deepened the power and meaning of those institutions. By opposing injustice and oppression, they in effect were testing and safeguarding those protections for all Americans and for future generations to come. "Although situating itself at the core, the mainstream is not the center that embraces and draws the diverse nation together," Gary Y. Okihiro, a historian and director of the Asian American studies program at Cornell University, asserts in his book *Margins and Mainstreams*. "The mainstream derives its integrity from its representation of its Other. And despite its authorship of the central tenets of democracy, the mainstream has been silent on the publication of its creed. In fact, the margin has held the nation together with its expansive reach; the margin has tested and ensured the guarantees of citizenship; and the margin has been the true defender of American democracy, equality, and liberty. From this vantage, we can see the margin as mainstream."[28]

Time and again, racism, bigotry, and intolerance have been overcome by America's remarkable ability to absorb and incorporate new cultural tributaries, even as the mainstream is itself transformed by them. Now, due to the latest surge of immigration that began after World War II and accelerated during the 1970s and 1980s, the United States is home to an increasing number of people from Asia, East Asia, the Caribbean, and Mexico. Like the waves of immigrants who preceded them, these new arrivals are entering and transforming the existing social order. And just like the immigrants who came before them, these newcomers, with their unfamiliar manners and customs, are triggering an immune reaction from those who feel threatened or confused by change, no matter how inevitable or irreversible. Adding to the unease are socioeconomic disparities, language barriers, and the geographic proximity—and psychological distance—of the Caribbean and Mexico, our "distant neighbors." It's almost understandable that those who represent and have a vested interest in the old mainstream might want to cling to the status quo—or their idealized conception of it—rather than deal with complex and confusing new cultural realities.

The American "melting pot"—the storied forge of assimilation where, in the words of the Russian-Jewish playwright Israel Zangwill, "all the races of Europe are melting and reforming"—was actually more of a simmering stew, with spicy chunks of nationalism and a racist broth that sometimes boiled over into the streets of early-twentieth-century America. Though it's rather hard to believe now, back then it was Italians and Irish and Jews who were considered the nonwhite invaders. In their book, *Remaking the American Mainstream: Assimilation and Contemporary Immigration*, sociologists Richard Alba and Victor Nee remind us that the idea that the pathway to assimilation for Irish and Italian immigrants during the early 1900s "was smoothed by a white racial identification is an anachronism, inappropriately imposing contemporary racial perceptions on the past. There is ample evidence that native-born whites perceived some of the major European immigrant groups, such as the Irish, Jews and

Italians, as racially distinct from themselves and that such perceptions flowered into full-blown racist theorizing during the high-water period of mass immigration in the early decades of the twentieth century."[29]

Over time, despite facing many of the same social and structural obstacles that confront immigrants today, Irish, Italians, and Jews eventually came to be seen as a part of the "white" majority. The other remarkable thing about the American "salad bowl," which has become a preferred metaphor for the nation's zesty multiethnic mix, is how the bowl itself always grows to accommodate another ingredient. The problem with people like Pat Buchanan is that they are so busy drawing a line in the sand, they've forgotten that the American ability to redraw that line is one of the things that makes it so resilient and great.

In a 2004 article in *Foreign Policy*, Samuel Huntington resurrected the bugaboo of invading alien hordes, arguing that the geographic proximity of Mexico and the rest of Latin America and the concentration of those immigrants in the U.S. made them different—and therefore more dangerous—than previous immigrant groups. To hear him describe it, the growing percentage of Spanish-speaking Latins is nothing less than a national emergency that threatens to sweep away everything Americans hold near and dear. For a glimpse of the Latino-ized America that Huntington so fears, one need only visit Santa Fe, New Mexico, or Miami, Florida—two of the most economically dynamic and culturally vibrant cities in the nation. "There is no Americano Dream," he proclaims. "There is only the American dream created by Anglo-Protestant society. Mexican Americans will share in that dream and in that society only if they dream in English."[30]

But if there is no "Americano Dream," then there is no English Dream, either. Huntington, just like Buchanan, makes the myopic mistake of assuming that assimilation is a one-way street that leads only to England, completely ignoring the mutual transformation of immigrant and mainstream that has always characterized the American experiment. Huntington's assumption that Hispanics will become a malignant lump in the American body politic is equally dubious and superficial. As Harvard's Alba and Nee point out, the newest American immigrants, for all their cultural and geographic uniqueness, are still following a path to acculturation roughly similar to the one followed by ethnic groups before them.

They also argue that the American mainstream has a long history of transforming itself even as it transforms those who enter it and that that quintessentially American pattern is now repeating itself. "Perhaps the single
most important conclusion to take from the social assimilation of Europeans and Asians descended from the nineteenth- and early-twentieth-
century immigration is that racial/ethnic boundaries can blur, stretch, and
move, as the current emphasis on the social construction of race implies,"
they write. "Indeed, were it not for the fluidity of boundaries, there might
be no racial/ethnic numerical majority in the United States today. Only
between a quarter and a third of the population can trace some ancestry to
Protestants from the British Isles, the former 'majority' group. Thus, were
the ethnic definition of the majority group limited to the original Anglo-
American core, it would already have become a minority of the population; only because of past assimilation can one say that an ethnic majority,
in all senses of that term, exists in the United States."[31]

In other words, the ability of the American mainstream to accommodate new groups into its political and social fabric has led to a refor-
mulation—and redefinition—of the mainstream itself. This mutual
transformation of perimeter and core, of insider and outsider, is what
allows America to absorb immigrants without sacrificing its stability or
social cohesion. The majority remains the majority by widening the definition of itself to include the margins that would otherwise overwhelm it.
This mutual transformation of native and newcomer, participant and observer, is the active agent in the American social experiment and the cultural catalyst at the core of the New Mainstream.

6. Cowboys and Indians

The image is timeless and prototypically American, immortalized in countless dimestore novels and Hollywood movies: a man on a horse, dressed in buckskins and armed with a gun, galloping across the open range. He rides into the sunset, west, toward the unknown, in pursuit of his destiny. Behind him is home: wife and family, the civilized colonies, Europe, the past. Before him lies the future: an unexplored frontier, full of danger and possibility—a lawless terrain of untamed animals, unscrupulous bandits, and savage Indians. The American cowboy is stoic, fearless, and self-sufficient. He is an expert horseman and knows how to live off the land. He sleeps under the stars and sings ballads by the flickering campfire. He is equally adept with a branding iron and a gun. He works on ranches and moves with the herds, or wanders from town to town, seeking adventure and dispensing justice. Sometimes he wears a sheriff's star, but the law he most represents is moral, personal, absolute. He speaks bluntly and keeps his word. He will fight for what he believes is right. And he is almost always right—and white.

Such is the cowboy myth, but history tells a different story. In fact, the first cowboys, or vaqueros, were Mexican, and the buckeroo culture of the American West is rooted in traditions that reach back to the Spanish conquest. The skills, manners, equipment, and dress we associate with cowboys were born on the great *ranchos*, or ranches, of northern Mexico, where horses and equipment imported from Europe were adopted by the mestizo workers for the rugged open ranges of New Spain. The haciendas, a term that refers to both the great estates and the grand houses built on them, were created during the sixteenth century, when the Spanish crown awarded huge tracts of land to conquistadors and noblemen in recognition of service or social status. The *vaqueros*, or cowboys, many of whom acquired their equestrian and musical skills during stints in the army, patrolled and managed the vast holdings and livestock herds of their wealthy *jefes*, or bosses, who spent much of the year in Mexico City or Europe. To keep track of the herds, the vaqueros branded cattle with red hot *fierros*, or irons, that bore the owner's initials or a unique design associated with their *rancho*. The vaqueros wore large sombreros, or hats, broad leather belts with silver buckles, buckskin jackets, tight canvas trousers, half boots, and *chaparreras*, or chaps. They used reatas, or lariats, to rope cattle and wild *mestenos* (mustangs) and showed off their riding and cattle-roping skills during public gatherings called rodeos. They prized valor, loyalty, and strength but also revealed a poetic streak in their plaintive ballads, or *corridos*, heartfelt tales of battles fought and loves lost sung over the twang of a strumming guitar.[1]

Cattle and horses were introduced to south Texas in the sixteenth century by Spanish explorers and military expeditions searching for French intruders. The roaming herds were augmented by runaway cattle and horses from settlements and haciendas located along the lower Rio Grande, and soon the grazing lands of south Texas were teeming with millions of cattle, which were butchered for their hides and for tallow, used for making candles. In wasn't until after the U.S. Civil War, and the construction of a railway line connecting Texas to the meat-packing markets of Chicago, that the commercial value of the herds became apparent and the era of the great cattle drives began. Between 1866 and 1900, the cowboy buckeroos drove more than 10 million cattle from south Texas to northern rail heads and pastures. Many of the cowboys were Hispanic Tejanos, who used Mexican herding techniques and riding equipment and a vocabulary inherited from the vaqueros of colonial Mexico. After a hard day on the range, the cowboys would gather for a barbecue, a derivation of *babracot*, a word and cooking technique borrowed from the Carib Indians of the West Indies, who seared meat over a grill made of green sticks placed over a fire. The barbecue sauce they used on their meat had its origins in the Creole and Cajun cuisines of Louisiana, where food was often accompanied by a spicy tomato-based puree that combined French, Spanish, and Afro-Caribbean flavors.[2]

The cowboy, both mythical and real, has always loomed large in the American psyche. From the Lone Ranger to the Marlboro man, from John Wayne to George W. Bush, the cowboy has been a core component of America's self-image. Cowboys are rugged and strong. They are quick on the draw and slow to back down from an argument. The upright figure on horseback embodied the westward migration of the white man and the notion of manifest destiny, a term coined in 1845 by the journalist and diplomat Louis O'Sullivan to describe and promote the American propensity for territorial expansionism. Manifest destiny became a catchphrase used to propagate the notion that it was America's God-given right to take possession of the North American continent. Advocates of the policy argued openly that the racial and cultural superiority of white Americans over Indians, Mexicans, and blacks gave them a moral obligation to seize and settle their lands by any means necessary.[3]

In fact, by 1845 American expansionism had proven itself to be a successful political and economic strategy. James Polk, who was elected president in 1844 on a platform that supported manifest destiny, believed that the United States needed to reach the Pacific to become a great power. His resolve to make that happen resulted in the doubling in size of the United States during his presidency. Shortly after the annexation of Texas, which Congress admitted as a slave state in 1845, Polk negotiated successfully with Britain to secure ownership of the Oregon Territory. In early 1846, after Polk's attempt to buy California from Mexico for $25 million was rebuffed by the Mexican government, Polk sent four thousand troops under the command of General Zachary Taylor, best known for his role in the war with the Seminoles, to the Texas-Mexico border, near the town of

Matamoros. Polk, fully aware that the Mexicans had never recognized the Lone Star State's succession from Mexico, ordered Taylor to establish a fort on the northern bank of the Rio Grande. On April 12, 1846, Major General Pedro de Ampudia, who commanded a force of several thousand men, demanded the immediate withdrawal of the American forces. Taylor responded that his orders did not allow him to withdraw. On April 25, 1,600 mounted Mexican soldiers crossed the river to cut the supply line at Fort Texas and ambushed an American scouting party, killing eleven, wounding six, and taking sixty-three prisoners. In his report on the skirmish, Polk told legislators that Mexico had "passed the boundary of the United States . . . invaded our territory and shed American blood upon American soil. . . . War exists notwithstanding all our efforts to avoid it."[4] Not everyone agreed. Among the vocal minority of Americans who opposed "Polk's war" were president of the former Republic of Texas Anson James, Henry David Thoreau, Daniel Webster, John Quincy Adams, Abraham Lincoln, and Ulysses S. Grant, who in his memoirs referred to the conflict as "one of the most unjust ever waged by a stronger nation against a weaker nation."[5] Abraham Lincoln, who at the time was a freshman congressman, joined those who decried the conflict as unnecessary and begun by the president under pretexts that were "the sheerest deception." Following the congressional declaration of war on Mexico on May 13, thousands gathered in New York, Philadelphia, Louisville, Cincinnati, Richmond, New Orleans, and other cities to hear military bands and listen to speakers who argued that prosecution of the war would benefit the Mexican people by liberating them from the oppressive domination of the aristocracy, the military, and the Catholic Church.

As the U.S. Army advanced into Mexico, there was a movement in the United States advocating the U.S. annexation not just of the disputed parts of Texas, but of the entire country; others, however, worried that the absorption of so many mixed-race mestizos would undermine the Anglo majority. In 1848, after almost two years of battle and the invasion and occupation of Mexico City by forces under the command of General Winfield Scott, Mexico signed the Treaty of Guadalupe Hidalgo, which called for Mexico to relinquish all claims to Texas and agree to a new frontier with the United States. The new border ran from the mouth of the Rio Grande to the southern boundary of New Mexico and then west to a point just south of San Diego, an area encompassing the present-day states of California, New Mexico, Nevada, and parts of Texas, Arizona, and Utah. The United States, for its part, agreed to pay $15 million for the land ceded by Mexico, which amounted to 529,000 square miles, or roughly two-fifths of its total territory. Adding insult to injury, only weeks before the treaty was signed, gold was discovered at Sutter's Mill on the American River. The prospecting frenzy that ensued helped to populate California and laid the foundations for the development of the even more valuable mineral and agricultural industries that help drive the American economy to this day. "The combination of mineral and animal wealth the Anglos found on the annexed Mexican lands, plus the Mexican laborers Anglo businessmen recruited to extract it, provided the underpinnings of twentieth century western prosperity," writes Juan Gonzalez in *Harvest of Empire.* "That combination made possible the vast expansion of our country's electrical, cattle, sheep, mining and railroad industries. Yet this historic Mexican contribution has been virtually obliterated from popular frontier history, replaced by the enduring myth of the lazy, shiftless Mexican."

Anglo resentment against Mexican Americans and other immigrants, which had been exacerbated by the Alamo and the U.S.-Mexican War, took a virulent turn in the mid-nineteenth century with the rise of the Know-Nothings. Also known as the American Party, the Know-Nothings spearheaded a nativist political movement in the Northeast to oppose the wave of mostly Irish and Catholic immigrants, who they believed were a threat to the Anglocentric American way of life. A million Irish had already immigrated to the United States in the decades before 1845, the year of the great potato famine; between 1855 and 1920, 3 million more left Erin to seek a new home in America. The Irish, who competed for jobs with Chinese immigrants lured from Asia to help build the railroads and work in the nation's agricultural sector, were viewed by nativists as "a race of savages" who were the social and ethnic equivalent of blacks and threatened to swamp the country in a tide of papist immorality. Begun as a clandestine movement that would secretly mobilize to support candidates who shared their views, the Know-Nothings, when asked about their political activities, would often answer, "I know nothing." The group, which had a strongly Anglo-Saxon definition of an ideal society, advocated curbs on immigration, the limiting of office holding to native-born Americans, and a twenty-one-year wait before an immigrant could be naturalized or allowed to vote. They also sought to limit the sale of liquor, restrict public school teaching to Protestants, and teach Protestant versions of the Bible in public schools.[6]

The Know-Nothing movement quickly spread to the South and West, where Mexican and Chinese immigrants were easy targets. The Know-Nothing ideology of intolerance found adherents among those who felt abandoned by the two major parties, which were distracted by political arguments over the future of slavery. In San Antonio, Texas, where the American Party became a serious political force in the early 1850s after Know-Nothings won the mayor's office and a majority on the city council, Hispanics and Anglo Democrats joined together against a common threat. In 1855, José Antonio Navarro, a native Tejano and Hispanic signer of the Texas Declaration of Independence, gave an impassioned speech denouncing what he saw as "an attack on everything [George] Washington stood for":

> A new and direful party has arisen to the shame of liberty. They call themselves Know Nothings, and true to their name, know nothing about just and generous feelings, know nothing about thrusting a fratricidal steel in the breasts of all who helped make them free Americans. . . . They proclaim an equality of rights, a refuge, and liberty to all of humanity, but at the same time proscribe Catholics because of their religious beliefs, and at the same time that they wish unbounded latitude for themselves. . . . The die is cast, the Mexico-Texans are Catholics and should be proud of the faith of their fathers and defend it inch by inch against such infamous aggressors.[7]

In 1856, Millard Fillmore, a former U.S. vice president who had served as president from 1850 to 1853 after the death of Zachary Taylor, ran for president as the American Party candidate in 1856. As president, Fillmore had negotiated a compromise over the statutes of slavery in the new states of California (declared a nonslavery state), Utah, and New Mexico, whose slavery status was left undetermined. As the American Party candidate, Fillmore received 21 percent of the popular vote, losing to James Buchanan, who deplored slavery but did little to stop the secession of the Confederate states. After the American Party lost the presidential race, external opposition and organizational discord took its toll. Within a few years, the Know-Nothing movement had fragmented over its own internal disagreements over slavery, and its members dispersed to other parties as the nation girded itself for civil war.[8]

Ironically, Polk's success in expanding America to the Pacific had led to his own political undoing and sowed the seeds of southern secession. But it had also laid the groundwork for the American Industrial Revolution and had inadvertently planted the seeds of a multicultural society. Two hundred years before the buying power of Latinos, blacks, and Asians would transform the American economy, the interdependence of immigration and prosperity was already apparent. Much as it is today, the drive for profits and new markets trumped racism and xenophobia, triggering a historical transformation of American society. It would be decades before the depth and breadth of that transformation could be fully understood or measured. Meanwhile, manifest destiny had unleashed other historical and economic forces that were shaping a society that was uniquely and distinctly American.

The Final Frontier

America's westward expansion also brought new urgency to the status of the surviving Native American tribes, which were scattered across the country in a patchwork of reservations and ancestral enclaves, some of which abutted white settlements, others of which were still isolated and relatively unscathed by progress. As a result of their encounter with the Lewis and Clark expedition and other explorers at the beginning of the nineteenth century, fur trading had become an important part of the economic and social life of the Sioux Nation and Oglala Lakota tribes, whose influence reached from what is now North and South Dakota to the Big Horn Mountains in Wyoming and the Platte River in Nebraska. In 1868, the U.S. government signed the Treaty of Fort Laramie, which gave the Sioux unrestricted control over 60 million acres of land in the Black Hills, as well as federal supplies and provisions. The treaty, much of which was negotiated by the Sioux chief Red Cloud, stipulated that "the United States now solemnly agrees that no person except those herein designated and authorized so to do . . . shall ever be allowed to pass over, settle upon, or reside in the territory described in this article, or in such territory as may be added to this reservation for the use of said Indians."[9]

But when claims of gold in the Black Hills surfaced in 1874, the U.S. government sent one-thousand horse soldiers of the Seventh Cavalry under the command of General George Armstrong Custer to investigate. The government outlawed the Sioux religion shortly thereafter in an effort to peaceably drive the Indians off the land. But the Indians held their ground and rebuffed invitations to renegotiate the treaty. In March 1876, as federal troops led by Colonel George Cook took positions in the area, Sitting Bull called a meeting of the Lakota, Cheyenne, and Arapaho at his camp on Rosebud Creek in the Montana Territory. There he led the group, which included Crazy Horse, in a sun dance, offering prayers to Wakan Tanka, the Great Spirit. During the ritual, Sitting Bull had a vision in which he saw U.S. soldiers falling into the Lakota camp like grasshoppers falling from the sky. Inspired by Sitting Bull's vision, on June 17 Crazy Horse and five hundred warriors staged a surprise attack on Cook's troops, forcing them to retreat. To celebrate the victory, the Indians moved to the valley of the Little Big Horn River, where they were joined by three thousand more Native Americans who had left the reservations to follow Sitting Bull. On June 25, believing that he was moving against a small Indian force, Custer charged into Sitting Bull's camp. In his famous "last stand," Custer retreated to a ridge near the Little Big Horn, where he was annihilated. But the victory was short-lived; in 1889, Congress annexed the Black Hills, setting the stage for an incident that would become known as the massacre at Wounded Knee.[10]

Even before the battle of the Little Big Horn, finding a balance between military force and diplomatic appeasement with native tribes was a tricky and dangerous business owing to the overwhelming number of tribes and the varying degrees of opportunity and risk that they represented to American nationalism. Francis Amasa Walker, who served as commissioner of Indian affairs during the early 1870s under president Ulysses S. Grant, approached the task of dealing with the three hundred thousand Indians who were still living in the United States with an attitude that combined scientific detachment with compassionate condescension. While he was mindful of the fact that America had developed and grown at the expense of the land's indigenous peoples, he also openly admired the bravery of Indian warriors "that have utterly disappeared from the continent, happy that their long, savage independence and their brief, fierce resistance to the encroachments of the pale-face were not to be succeeded by a dreary period of submission, humiliation and dependence."[11] Walker found the existing reservation system both unwieldy and ill-suited to the task of pacifying and civilizing the Indian population. Instead, he proposed a consolidation of existing reservations and the establishment of new ones, whereby natives and whites could be better kept apart. Walker, who had served as a brigadier general during the Civil War and went on to become a distinguished economist and director of the 1880 U.S. census, divided the natives into three distinct groups: those who were "civilized," those who were "semi-civilized," and those who were "wholly barbarous."

In his essay "The Indian Question," Walker argued that segregation would ensure the safety of both Indians and whites by minimizing the danger of misunderstandings and conflict. He was also concerned that without proper education and federal supervision, even fierce warriors "who shook the infant colonies with terror" would become dissolute and degenerate into "diseased wretches, who hang about the settlements, begging and stealing." Walker's ultimate goal was assimilation of Indians into white society, with the reservations acting as a kind of holding tank, where Indians could gradually be acculturated. When deemed to be sufficiently Americanized, they would then be introduced to civilized society. His confidence that such a plan could work sprang from the example of "tribes, once warlike and powerful, [that] have, by a fortunate turn of character and circumstance, become so rich and respectable as to not only deprive them of all romantic interest, but practically to take them out of the scope of the Indian question."[12]

When peering ahead toward the future, Walker was impressively pre-scient about America's looming multicultural society—and the bleak prospects for Native Americans who had not already been exterminated. "Are the Indians destined to die out?" he asked. ". . . Or are the original in-habitants of the continent to be represented in the variously and curiously composed population which, a century hence, will constitute the political body of the United States? If this is to be in any appreciable degree one of the elements of our future population, will it be by mixture and incorpora-tion; adapting himself, as he may be able to do, to the laws and customs of his conquerors, but preserving his own identity and making his separate contribution to the life and manner of the nation?"[13]

Whatever the answer, Walker made no apologies for presenting his case "bluntly" and subjecting the nation to the "whole naked truth." The Indian question, after all, was a matter of "life and death to thousands of our own flesh and blood" and citizens deserved to know "what becomes of the seven million dollars" collected annually in taxes and disbursed to the Bureau of Indian Affairs:

> In good faith and good feeling we must take up this work of Indian civilization, and, at whatever cost, do our whole duty by this most un-happy people. Better that we should entail a debt upon our posterity on Indian account, were that necessary, than that we should leave them an inheritance of shame. We may have no fear that the dying curse of the red man, outcast and homeless by our fault, will bring bar-renness upon the soil that once was his, or dry the streams of the beau-tiful land that, through so much of evil and good, has become our patrimony; but surely we shall be clearer in our lives and freer to meet the glances of our sons and grandsons, if in our generation we do jus-tice and show mercy to a race which has been impoverished that we might be made rich.[14]

Not everyone shared Walker's definition of "justice and mercy," how-ever. Other white reformers, in a foreshadowing of the segregation battles of the twentieth century, argued that the isolation of Indians on reserva-tions was unduly harsh and would only delay their assimilation into the

American mainstream. In 1887, eleven years after the battle of Little Big Horn and three years before the massacre at Wounded Knee, the reformers' views became law with the passage of the Dawes Act, which reversed Walker's policy by breaking up the reservations and mandating the allotment of 160 acres of reservation land for each Indian family. The lands would be non-negotiable, or "inalienable," for twenty-five years, protecting the Indians from real estate swindlers and giving the Indians ample time to develop the land for farming or other productive uses.[15]

Even as Walker was making his case for an Indian management policy that would avoid leaving future generations an "inheritance of shame," the Indian nations of North America, while not yet defeated, were disorganized, defensive, and desperate. The Great Spirit that had granted them so much for so long seemed to have abandoned them to the onslaught of the paleface invaders. It was around that time that a Paiute mystic named Tavibo prophesied that the whites would eventually be swallowed by the earth, but Native Americans would emerge to enjoy a world free of their oppressors. Tavibo, whose movement spread to parts of Nevada, California, and Oregon, urged his followers to dance in circles, as was already customary in the Great Basin region, as they sang religious songs. In the late 1880s, an Indian from western Nevada called Wovoka began to make similar prophecies. Orphaned at the age of fourteen, Wovoka was raised by a white rancher named David Wilson. Wovoka's teachings, which merged Christian notions of resurrection with Paiute mysticism, foresaw the dawning of a new age in which whites would disappear, leaving Indians to flourish in a paradise of material abundance, spiritual renewal, and everlasting life, which would be led by a Christ-like Supreme Being, or "Big Man." The coming Indian messiah was to be greeted by prayer, upright living, and ritual celebration.[16]

The ghost dance, which spoke directly to the bitterness and frustrations of Indians everywhere, was quickly embraced by the Lakota and other Great Plains tribes. When ghost dancing began at the Pine Ridge reservation in South Dakota, federal agents became alarmed and called for help. Indian police were sent in to arrest tribal leaders whom it accused of fomenting civil unrest, among them Sitting Bull, a Sioux chief and holy man under whom the Lakota had united in their struggle to survive on the northern plains. After defeating Custer at Little Big Horn, an event he had foreseen in a vision, Sitting Bull had found sanctuary from pursuing federal troops in Canada. Four years later, with his people facing starvation in the harsh Canadian wilderness, he surrendered to U.S. authorities. In 1885, he was allowed to leave the reservation to join Buffalo Bill's Wild West Show, earning $50 a week for riding once around the area in traditional garb.[17]

Sitting Bull had returned to the Standing Rock reservation and was living peacefully in a cabin near the Grand River, not far from where he had been born, when a Lakota Indian named Kicking Bear came to tell him of the ghost dancing at Pine Ridge. In another vision a few years earlier, Sitting Bull had foreseen himself being killed by his own people. Worried that Sitting Bull, who was revered by the Lakota as a great warrior and holy man, would join the ghost dance movement, the authorities sent forty-three Lakota tribal policemen to arrest him. Shortly before dawn on December 15, 1890, the police burst into his cabin and dragged him outside, where a group of followers rushed to his defense. In the scuffle that followed, Sitting Bull was fatally wounded by a bullet fired by the tribal police. Hearing of Sitting Bull's murder, another Lakota chief, Sitting Elk, aka "Big Foot," tried to flee from Pine Ridge with a band of 350 followers. They were intercepted by the U.S. Seventh Cavalry and detained in a camp at Wounded Knee. Captain James W. Forsyth ordered Spotted Elk and his people to surrender their arms, which they refused to do. A shot was fired, and federal troops unleashed a fusillade of bullets from rifles and rapid-fire Hotchkiss guns. Many of those not killed in the first attack were hunted down and shot. The Sioux casualties were 153 dead and 44 wounded, half of them women and children. Charges were later brought against Colonel Forsyth for his role in the massacre, but he was eventually exonerated. In 1973, members of the American Indian Movement, an Indian rights activist group, occupied the village of Wounded Knee for seventy-one days to call national attention to civil rights abuses and claims that elements of the Lakota Tribal Council had conspired with FBI and other U.S. agents in the deaths of more than forty followers of traditional Lakota culture.[18]

The killing of Sitting Bull and Spotted Elk and their people at

Wounded Knee is generally regarded as the last major military confrontation of the Indian Wars. While it was by no means the last armed clash between Indians and white men, the ability of Native Americans to pose a serious threat to the white population had been neutralized, their spirit broken. The same year, the superintendent of the 1890 census declared the closing of the American frontier, pointing out that the continent's "unsettled area has been so broken into by isolated bodies of settlement that there can hardly be said to be a frontier line." Though more territory would be added to the Union, the boundaries of the continental United States were set. The white settlers' dream of imposing their ways on the untamed lands and people of North America had been realized from sea to shining sea. But once again, the transformation had been mutual. The Americans who set out from the colonies to seek their destiny were not the same people who fulfilled it. On the journey from Massachusetts and Virginia to Texas and California, they had changed; the journey itself had changed them. And the consequences of that transformation would remold the nation, and the very meaning of the word *American*, for generations to come.

The importance of this transformation was first articulated in 1893 by a young historian named Frederick Jackson Turner. In his essay titled "The Significance of the Frontier in American History," he argued that the nation's western expansion, and the difficult and bloody task of taming the wilderness and the people who lived in it, was not only a distinctive feature of American history, but the defining factor in the molding of the American identity:

> The frontier is the line of most rapid and effective Americanization. The wilderness masters the colonist. It finds him a European in dress, industries, tools, modes of travel, and thought. It takes him from the railroad car and puts him in the birch canoe. It strips off the garments of civilization and arrays him in the hunting shirt and the moccasin. It puts him in the log cabin of the Cherokee and Iroquois and runs an Indian palisade around him. Before long he has gone to planting Indian corn and plowing with a sharp stick, he shouts the war cry and takes the scalp in orthodox Indian fashion. In short, at the

frontier the environment is at first too strong for the man. He must accept the conditions which it furnishes, or perish, and so he fits himself into the Indian clearings and follows the Indian trails. Little by little he transforms the wilderness, but the outcome is not the old Europe, not simply the development of Germanic germs, any more than the first phenomenon was a case of reversion to the Germanic mark. The fact is, that here is a new product that is American.[19]

It was as if the "melting pot" had itself melted and joined the other ingredients to create an entirely new flavor. In Turner's eyes, the frontier was not a static boundary demarking the line between insider and outsider, cowboy and Indian, white man and red man, but a dynamic wave of cultural mutation that absorbed previous waves before rolling forward again. For Turner, the frontier, in effect, *was* America. The zone of cultural incorporation and conquest, the place where opposites met and exchanged places, for better or worse, had become more American than any pilgrim could ever be, because the process of becoming American was also its definition:

At first, the frontier was the Atlantic coast. It was the frontier of Europe in a very real sense. Moving westward, the frontier became more and more American. As successive terminal moraines result from successive glaciations, so each frontier leaves its traces behind it, and when it becomes a settled area the region still partakes of the frontier characteristics. Thus the advance of the frontier has meant a steady movement away from the influence of Europe, a steady growth of independence on American lines. And to study this advance, the men who grew up under these conditions, and the political, economic, and social results of it, is to study the really American part of our history.[20]

The West had shaped the American experience in several critical ways, Turner argued. Unlike the national borders of Europe, which divided densely settled and culturally distinct societies from one another, the American frontier was the doorstep to a seemingly unlimited expanse of open, relatively uninhabited terrain. In order to survive, the pioneers initially adopted a lifestyle not much different from that of the Indians, but they quickly evolved into communities derived from European-style values, customs, and technology. The result was a pattern of settlement that re-created the "universal history" of mankind, or nothing less than an accelerated leap from primitivism to modern industry in a few years. The process began with "pathfinders," a few individuals or families who braved the unknown to establish outposts on the fringes of Anglo-American civilization. Salt, which was essential for the preservation and seasoning of meat, had initially limited the range of the early pioneers to within a few days of the coast. But the discovery of salt springs and licks in Kentucky and western New York freed the pioneers to move farther inland and cross the mountains. The first waves of settlers used materials at hand for shelter and relied on the fur trade and cooperation with Indians to survive. In time, the western outposts were solidified and trading was joined by ranching and farming, which provided jobs for new arrivals. The ranchers and farmers were followed by speculators, entrepreneurs, bankers, and other professionals who helped build the social and industrial infrastructure that connected the new community with the rest of the nation.

As the white settlements inched westward, first to the Ohio and Mississippi valleys, then on to the Great Plains, the Rockies, and California, the traders' path in the woods inevitably widened into a road, which then became a railroad line, which was joined by a highway. Army posts and forts, built to protect settlers from hostile Indians and foreign troops, acted as a wedge into the wilderness, encouraging more development and often serving as the core of the new community. The rail and road system connected the frontier towns to the industrial urban centers of the East and brought the means to extract natural resources and transport them to market, making real estate more valuable and solidifying economic and social ties to the cities. Once a new community was firmly established, the pathfinders would pick up stakes and move west again to civilization's new fringe, repeating the process. "American social development has been continually beginning over again on the Frontier," Turner wrote. "This perennial rebirth, this fluidity of American life, this expansion westward with its new opportunities, its continuous touch with the simplicity of primitive society, furnish the forces dominating American character."[21]

German, Dutch, Scottish, and other immigrants, initially brought to the colonies as servants, became the shock troops of manifest destiny. Their search for gainful employment and the possibility of owning land drove them to the Frontier, where opportunity was limited only by a person's daring and willingness to carve out a new home in the wilds. Their relationships with Anglos, Indians, and other immigrants "promoted a composite nationality" for the American people. "In the crucible of the frontier the immigrants were Americanized, liberated, and fused into a mixed race, English in neither nationality nor characteristics," Turner wrote, noting that by the mid-eighteenth century, Edmund Burke worried that Pennsylvania was "threatened with the danger of being wholly foreign in language, manners, and perhaps even inclinations." Concluded Turner: "Such examples teach us to beware of misrepresenting the fact that there is a common English speech in America into a belief that the stock is also English."

Though many Anglo-Americans would continue to confuse English stock with being American, Turner grasped that American identity was defined no longer by any particular racial or cultural group, but by a set of shared values, institutions, and aspirations. The ever evolving intersection between the known and unknown, and the consequent encounter, domination, and assimilation of territories and peoples, had forged a uniquely American brand of social diversity.

As the frontier continued to push West, and the previous boundary line was reabsorbed, the new "composite" became part of the American mainstream. The mind-set of the pioneer—the attitude of self-reliance, cultural incorporation, and unfettered movement and thought—became an integral part of the national character. Over time, the pioneer experience, and its "restless, nervous energy," had an equally formative effect on the nation's political and social institutions. The "national republicanism of Monroe" and "democracy of Andrew Jackson" reinforced the spirit and legitimacy of individualism, opportunity, entrepreneurialism, and social and economic mobility—core components of the American dream. "Since the days when the fleet of Columbus sailed into the waters of the New World," Turner wrote, "America has been another name for opportunity,

and the people of the United States have taken their tone from the inces-
sant expansion which has not only been open but has even been forced
upon them." Yet despite the closing of the frontier, "he would be a rash
prophet who should assert that the expansive character of American life
has now entirely ceased." By then, in fact, the pioneer experience had
been solidly ingrained in American culture; the cowboys and Indians of
the West had become part of the mainstream mythology, as integral to the
national psyche as the notion of freedom itself.

Yet the libertarian populism of the West did not always translate into
justice or equality for all—nor did it bring an end to exploitation or prejudice. The cult of the gun, the rule of the mob, the gold digger, and the
renegade are all-too-enduring aspects of Wild West excess. The Indian
Wars, albeit in a different form, continue to this day, with skirmishes
occurring on various economic, legal, social, and cultural fronts. Poverty,
alcoholism, and unemployment plague the reservations. Of 470 Indian
treaties signed by Congress, almost all have been broken. As younger Native Americans abandon tribal life to take their chances in the urban marketplace, the old ways are in danger of being lost. In Oklahoma, where
most Cherokee children attend schools located off the reservation, fewer
than eight thousand of one hundred thousand Cherokees speak the native
language. A similar concern has prompted the Passamaquoddy Indians of
northern Maine to record their language on CDs to be distributed to local
schools and preserved for posterity. Casinos built on Indian lands in New
York, California, and other states have brought wealth to some tribes,
although disagreements over development and investment policies have
divided some Native American communities. In Montana, a tussle over
management of the nineteen-thousand-acre National Bison Range has
broken out between members of the surrounding Flathead Indian Reservation and the U.S. Fish and Wildlife Service, which wants to maintain
control over the preserve and the hundreds of federally protected bison
that live on it. There are some bright spots. Thanks to a farsighted decision to develop its own natural gas reserves, the Ute Indians of southwestern Colorado are reaping windfall profits from assets estimated to be
worth as much as $1.45 billion. Still, while some tribes are flourishing,

many remain destitute, and ethical issues raised by mining, gambling, and other business ventures that seem at odds with core tribal values are still being resolved.

At the same time, Native Americans have begun to question their cultural role in a nation that in many ways still treats them as outsiders in their own land. For some the answer still lies in the stories and creation myths that guided the lives and ways of their ancestors. By reaching back to the past, Indians can once again hope to understand what lies ahead. Gerald Vizenor, a University of California professor and mixed-blood member of the Chippewa tribe of Minnesota's White Earth reservation, has turned history and his own anger into fodder for fiction and scholarly research into the spiritual implications of the Native American predicament. In books like *Wordarrows: Indians and Whites in the New Fur Trade* and the American Book Award–winning *Griever: An American Monkey King in China*, Vizenor resurrects sacred metaphors to probe modern conundrums. By refusing to relinquish the "American" in Native American, Vizenor stands his ground: a clearing in the psychocultural undergrowth that functions as a modern-day refuge for values and dreams that have become another kind of endangered species.

In his book *Earthdivers*, Vizenor uses *Me'tis*, the French term for a person of mixed blood, and the Native American myth of the earthdiver to illuminate stories about contemporary Indian characters. In Native American creation myths, the earthdiver creates the world by bringing up the land from the primal water. For Vizenor, the earthdiver is "an imaginative metaphor" for healing meditations on the contemporary Indian condition. "The earthdivers are . . . mixedbloods or Me'tis, tribal tricksters and recast cultural heroes, the mournful and whimsical heirs and survivors from that premier union between the daughters of the woodland shamans and white fur traders," he explains. "The Me'tis, or mixed blood, earthdivers . . . dive into unknown urban places now, into the racial darkness in the cities, to create a new consciousness of coexistence."[22]

Vizenor's "word warriors," Native Americans who have been psychologically skinned and branded by the white man's language and literalism, are trapped in a postmodern world drained of sacred meaning. Robbed of their license to roam the open range, they run free with their imaginations "in a tireless tribal drama." Like the tribal shaman-trickster, they use humor and wry subterfuge to undermine surface realities and uncover deeper truths: "So here we are now, translated and invented skins, separated and severed like dandelions from the sacred and caught alive in words in the cities. We are aliens in our own traditions; the white man has settled with his estranged words right in the middle of our sacred past."

For Indian intellectuals like Vizenor, the final frontier is internal; the genocide that continues is the extermination of the imagination and the slow suffocation of the human spirit. Native Americans are forced to use the weapons of their former enemy—words—to defend themselves, even though that process itself acknowledges defeat. The cowboy war is no longer on the land, but with the land, which white men regard as something to own, conquer, a resource from which to extract value. The "word warrior" has no choice but to hurl verbs, nouns, and adjectives; he cannot retreat from the metaphysical battlefield that has moved from the villages and open plains to universities, libraries, and art galleries:

> We all turn to books and machines, new politics and noise, when we move from reservations to the cities. Words relocated from sacred places became the shape of our visions, not the source of our dreams. We became word and mouth warriors, shadowless memories in the cities. No mountains or rivers or birds without words, no water sounds or wind without weather reports. The common tribal metaphors we once shared stand now in abstract places, statues, eventless in descriptive words. My name is not an event, her name is not an event from dreams. We are translated, invented, and transformed now in plain grammars, not in visions as animals and birds.

Vizenor's earthdivers and tricksters are "the metaphors between new sources of opposition and colonial ideas about savagism and civilization." In the Indian creation myth, the earthdiver asks animals and birds to help him dive for the earth, "but here, in the metaphor of the Me'tis earthdiver, white settlers are summoned to dive with mixedblood survivors into the unknown, into the legal morass of treaties and bureaucratic evils, and to swim deep down and around through federal enclaves and colonial economic enterprises in search of a few honest words upon which to build a new urban turtle island."[23]

By diving deep into his personal past, Vizenor emerges with a communal, multiracial vision of the future. Vizenor's vision, like the "composite nationality" that Turner saw being formed in 1893, is based on historical realities and recognition of an interdependent, if not necessarily manifest, destiny. By the end of the nineteenth century, the boundless horizon of the West would be replaced by the material panoramas of the Industrial Revolution; the same pioneer can-do spirit that tamed the continent would fuel unprecedented technological innovation. Americans would harvest factories instead of farms, and expansion would be measured in net profits, not acres. More than two hundred years after the closing of the frontier, the mavericks and the pathfinders continue to lead the way, probing the outer boundaries of the known in search of new opportunities. Now as before, the shared experience of the postmodern economy is profoundly shaping the national character into something quintessentially American. Now as before, American identity is being defined not by any particular racial or cultural group, but by a set of shared values, institutions, and aspirations that transcend ethnicity and race.

The conquered Indian lands and annexed Mexican territories not only provided the natural foundation of America's economic future, they were absorbed into the national bloodstream, a cultural transfusion that has generated enormous wealth along with the priceless gift of ecological conscience. The manifestations of this exchange, this fusion of materialism and myth, past and future, define the headwaters of the New Mainstream and provide insights into the instincts and attitudes of the multicultural consumer. In the New Mainstream, products that are natural, organic, and ecologically responsible will increasingly outsell those that aren't. Companies are also learning that it pays to "give back"—through philanthropy or programs that contribute to the general well-being of communities and individuals who buy their products. Purity commands a premium in everything from cosmetics to water. In 2004, annual sales of filtered H_2O soared to $8.3 billion and Americans were imbibing twenty-two gallons per person. At a time when the fragility of nature is forcing us to rethink unchecked development and seek a sustainable relationship with the environment, Vizenor invites the white man to reconnect with the earth and join Native Americans in a mutual rediscovery of America. "Me'tis earth-divers and the new urban shamans now summon the white world to dive, to dive deep and return with the sacred earth," Vizenor writes. "The Me'tis wait above the chaos at common intersections in the cities for the white animals to return to the earth, enough to build a new urban turtle island. Earthdivers, tricksters, shamans, poets, dream back the earth." [24]

7. Amexica

The two-thousand-mile border between United States and Mexico, the Mexican novelist Carlos Fuentes has written, "is not really a border, but a scar." [1] The wound is as old as the Alamo, and it still bleeds people, money, and hope. The "tortilla curtain" begins in Texas at the Gulf of Mexico and follows the crooked line of the Rio Grande west to New Mexico, Arizona, and California, where it heads in a straight line to the Pacific Ocean. It is both a barrier and a looking glass that reflects the fantasies, fears, and aspirations of the observer.

The duality that the U.S.-Mexican border represents is confirmed by the paired cities that straddle it, different yet permanently joined together, like siblings from different parents strung along a two-thousand-mile umbilical cord: Brownsville and Matamoros, McAllen and Reynosa, Laredo and Nuevo Laredo, El Paso and Ciudad Juarez, Douglas and Agua Prieta, Nogales and Nogales, Calexico and Mexicali, San Diego and Tijuana. The border is at once physical and symbolic, a country of 24 million that is equal parts Mexico and the United States, an industrial powerhouse with its own history, culture, and language. More than eight hundred thousand people cross the border daily, coming and going for work, study, and play. The Wal-Mart in Laredo, one of the many border towns where booming Mexican maquiladoras, or assembly plants, are churning out everything from Siemens electric motors to baby toys, is the nation's highest grossing. With Mexico poised to replace Canada as America's largest trading partner, the intertwining of north and south is provoking ambivalent emotions. A Time/CNN poll of more than one thousand U.S. citizens conducted in May 2001 by Harris Interactive found that while 45 percent of the respondents agreed that Canada "is more important to the U.S." than Mexico, versus 35 percent who disagreed, a majority thought that Mexico had "more of an impact on the U.S." in the realms of the economy, culture, and politics. And while 53 percent thought it should be "harder for people to cross the border from Mexico," versus 21 percent for Canada, 78 percent said they would encourage their children to learn Spanish.[2]

Yet Anglo-American assumptions of social solidarity with its northern neighbor may no longer be mutual. If England and America, as the old saying goes, are two peoples divided by a common language, then the United States and Canada may be two countries divided by a common culture. As Canada's social and political center moves closer to Europe and away from the United States, it is increasingly at odds with U.S. policies on everything from the Middle East to gay marriage. Once the slightly stodgy, boringly homogeneous stepsister of the richer, sassier United States, Canada, a nation of slightly more than 30 million, has emerged in the twenty-first century as the hemisphere's most unabashedly multicultural state. An ethnic diversity survey conducted by the Canadian government in 2002 found that 23 percent of Canada's population aged fifteen and over, or 5.3 million people, were born outside Canada, the highest percentage of "first generation" Canadians since 1931. Of that group, 46 percent, or 2.4 million people, had only non-European ancestry. The leading places of origin included Southern Europe, the United Kingdom, eastern and southern Asia, Arabia, the Caribbean, and Latin America. After Canada's two official languages, English (59.21 percent) and French (23.26 percent), 16.12 percent, or 4.5 million people, reported speaking other languages, including Chinese, Italian, German, Spanish, Punjabi,

Arabic, Tagalog, Vietnamese, and Cree. Yet the study reported that "the vast majority of all Canadians," or 93 percent, said they had "never, or rarely, experienced discrimination or unfair treatment because of their ethno-cultural characteristics."[3]

In his book *Fire and Ice: The United States, Canada and the Myth of Converging Values*, Michael Adams argues that social tolerance reflects a divergence between America and its largest trading partner in everything from ethnic and linguistic diversity to the role of religion and women. Yet for Canadians that split, if anything, seems to have strengthened many of the democratic ideals that the United States has always championed for itself and other nations.[4] During a visit to Toronto, Pico Iyer, who describes his own heritage as a mix of South Asian Indian, British, and American, was struck by the city's openness to people of other cultures and backgrounds. It was as if Toronto, he writes in *The Global Soul: Jet Lag, Shopping Malls, and the Search for Home*, "had embarked upon a multicultural experiment with itself as guinea pig. . . . It was daring to dream of a new kind of cosmopolis—not a melting pot, as people in Toronto politely reminded me, but a mosaic" that "offered the prospect of uniting all the fragments in a stained-glass whole."[5]

The cultural commonalities between the United States and Canada are assumed to be so strong that 58 percent of Americans think that the lightly regulated border between the two countries is "about right." Yet when it comes to attitudes about marriage, homosexuality, and religion, Americans are generally more aligned with their Mexican neighbors to the south. In a 2003 poll by the Pew Research Center for the People and the Press, 66 percent of Canadians said that "marriage is more satisfying" if both the husband and wife share household and child care duties, while only 55 percent of Americans felt the same way. Sixty-nine percent of the Canadians polled believed that "homosexuality should be accepted by society," versus 51 percent of the Americans. When asked if "it is necessary to believe in God to be moral," 58 percent of the American respondents said yes, while only 30 percent of Canadians agreed. The implications are eye-opening but clear: non-Hispanic Americans identify with Canada despite the fact that their values are actually closer to those of the Latin American immigrants they consider a cultural threat.[6]

The same sense of cultural paradox—the disorientation of stereotypes being flipped onto their heads—is apparent along the Mexican frontier with California, where undocumented and legal immigrants are crossing the border in such numbers that they are altering the local culture beyond recognition. In this case, though, the migrants are affluent white Americans seeking to escape the crowds, regulations, and high prices of their native land for a better life in Mexico. At least six hundred thousand Americans live in Mexico, more than any other foreign country, though the real number is unknown because some have crossed the border illegally. In the Mexican state of Baja California, an eight hundred-mile-long peninsula that juts south of California into the Pacific, dollars are the coin of the realm, English is the local tongue, and new housing developments cater to American professionals in their thirties and forties. No longer just a haven for American retirees looking for warm weather and a favorable exchange rate, Baja is becoming a California suburb. State officials have recorded more than 30 million trips by Americans who are willing to commute from their jobs in San Diego and other U.S. border communities to live in Mexican towns like San Felipe, where one-quarter of the city's thirty thousand residents are Americans. The holds true for Rosarito, where a nice house near the sea can cost as little as $150,000 and property taxes are less than $100 a year. In Nopalo, a planned community under construction near Laredo on Baja's east coast, a consortium of American and Canadian developers are investing $2 billion to build five thousand new homes that will cost up to $2 million each. The Nopalo housing development is part of a master plan by Fonatur, the Mexican government tourism agency, to create a complex of grand homes, megaresorts, and luxury yacht marinas its calls La Escalera Náutica ("The Nautical Ladder"). When completed, Escalera Náutica will generate millions of dollars for the local economy, create jobs for Mexicans who otherwise might have migrated to El Norte, and lure thousands of tourists, some of whom will no doubt decide to stay. In time, more money and Americans will follow, leading inevitably to a new cycle of development, congestion, and higher prices, until the Americanization of Baja reaches the point where it becomes indistinguishable from the places the gringos left behind.[7]

The border's bicultural economy is spawning opportunities and conflict as entrepreneurs and corporations compete for the hearts, minds, and wallets of the evolving social ecosystem. In El Paso, a city of 670,000 that is 78 percent Hispanic, plans for a U.S.-targeted bilingual expansion of *El Diario*, which is currently published across the border in Juarez, have touched off a newspaper war that pits one of Mexico's successful publishers against Arlington, Virginia–based Gannett Company, which owns the *El Paso Times* as well as *USA Today*. Charging that the *El Paso Times* has failed to adequately service the needs and sensibilities of its Latino community, Mexican publisher Osvaldo Rodríguez Borunda sparked a local fracas when he challenged the El Paso media establishment by asking the city for $750,000 in municipal tax breaks in exchange for opening a newsroom and printing plant for a bilingual edition of *El Diario*.[8] Whatever the outcome, the complacency of the local Anglocentric elite has been permanently shaken. Rodríguez, who has also announced plans to launch a bilingual newspaper in the demographically similar San Diego–Tijuana market, is merely one of dozens of large and small media players who have gotten a whiff of the border's new business realities. In Dallas–Fort Worth, where Latinos already account for 22 percent of the area's 5.9 million residents and the Hispanic community is projected to grow 21 percent by 2007, Knight Ridder beefed up the size and frequency of *La Estrella*, its Spanish-language offshoot of the *Fort Worth Star Telegram*. Knight Ridder's move was at least partly motivated by the announcement of plans by its rival, the *Dallas Morning News*, to launch its own Spanish-language edition, *El Día*. Knight Ridder's publication, renamed *Diario La Estrella*, has partnered with other Spanish-language newspapers, hired new staff, and gone from publishing twice weekly to five days a week.[9]

In an era when Mexican politicians campaign in U.S. cities to raise their political profile and the president of the United States feels it's necessary to assure Latinos that *"mi casa blanca es su casa blanca,"* the Spanish accent of American publishing has implications that go far beyond the bottom line. Print media serves as a news source and social sounding board, but also shapes the perceptions and cultural assumptions of its audience, which in turn illuminates and empowers those who had formerly lived on the margins. "There's a myth that Latinos don't read," proclaimed Javier Aldape, *Diario La Estrella*'s publisher. "We're out there to shatter that myth."[10]

The border is changing the way Americans and Mexicans read, shop, work, eat, and think. But the border doesn't stop there; the division it represents extends thousands of miles in every direction and deep into the minds and hearts of the millions who carry its duality inside of them. The border is not just a line in a map, but a way of life and a state of mind. In his book of poems *Scene from the Movie* Giant, Tino Villanueva describes the indelible anguish he experienced when, as a boy of fourteen sitting in a darkened movie theater in 1956, he watched a fight scene between a character, played by Rock Hudson, named Bick Benedict and a racist Texas café owner who refuses to serve the Mexicans that Benedict brought in with him. For Villanueva, the struggle between the two men, which takes place as "The Yellow Rose of Texas" blares on the jukebox, forces him to face the conflict inside of himself. For a flickering instant, the images on the screen illuminate and become the border—between the United States and Mexico, between American and Mexican, between right and wrong, between hope and despair.[11]

When it was released in 1956, *Giant* was hailed as a bold social statement that dared to expose the racism and small-mindedness of the Lone Star State. The saga of a sprawling Texas ranch called Benedict Reata, the film is both a sweeping, melodramatic epic and an allegory for America. The story, which begins in the 1920s and chronicles the surge of wealth brought to the region by the discovery of oil, traces a decades-long trajectory of idealism, the corrupting influence of money and unrequited love, and finally a bruised, world-weary kind of wisdom. Along the way, Benedict, who is the Reata's owner, finds personal redemption in his realization that discrimination against Mexicans and women is morally wrong. Nominated for eleven Academy Awards, and best remembered as the last movie made by James Dean, *Giant* today seems obvious, even quaint.

In a twenty-first-century remake of *Giant*, the jukebox would be playing Mexican *banda* or Santana's latest hit, and the diner where Benedict makes a stand for ethnic tolerance would be Latino owned and staffed, serving huevos rancheros with a chipotle-mango salsa on the side. Yet

Giant, in spite of its flaws and after all this time, still resonates. Overt expressions of bigotry have been replaced by more subtle forms of discrimination, but the feeling that Mexicans, native-born or not, are still not quite Americans, persists. Even worse, large numbers of Latinos and other minorities have voluntarily ceded their claim to American identity and, by extension, their claim on America itself. The internal struggle that Villanueva so poignantly describes has morphed from feckless yearning to willful denial. No one can say you're not an American if you reject the label first. But the price of that gesture is a retreat into a kind of self-imposed marginalization that confuses ethnic pride with nationalism and ultimately does a disservice to both.

In his essay for *The New York Times* op-ed page on September 16, 2003, Mexican Independence Day, Oscar Casares, a Mexican American from Brownsville, Texas, eloquently describes the border within. Despite the fact that his parents and grandparents were born in the United States, he rejects the terms *Hispanic* and *Mexican American,* preferring simply to call himself Mexican. "I didn't want to be Hispanic," he writes. "The word reminded me of those Mexican-Americans who prefer to say their families came from Spain, which they felt somehow increased their social status."[12]

Casares describes the annual tradition in his predominantly Hispanic community known as *"charro* days," a festival in which men grow beards and compete in jalapeño-eating contests, and mothers paint mustaches on little boys to make them look like Mexican peasants. The event opens with traditional *gritos,* boisterous cowboy calls exchanged by men on opposite sides of the International Bridge that marks the Brownsville-Matamoros border. The yelps commemorate and reaffirm the connection between the two cities and the people who live in them, but no amount of shouting can reconcile the internal split between national and cultural identity that Casares shares with millions of other U.S.-born Latinos who deny the hyphen and the bridge:

> Away from the border, the word Mexican had come to mean dirty, shiftless, drunken, lustful, criminal. I still cringe whenever I think someone might say the word. But usually it happens unexpectedly, as though the person has pulled a knife on me. I feel the sharp words up

against my gut. Because of my appearance, people often say things in front of me they wouldn't say if they knew my real ethnicity—not Hispanic, Latino or even Mexican-American. I am, like my father, Mexican, and on this day of Independence, I say this with particular pride.[13]

The mistake Casares makes is that cultural identity is indelible and inalienable, while social participation and political empowerment are not. By refusing to label himself "American," Casares is unwittingly agreeing with ethnocentric exclusionists who argue that "white" and "American" are interchangeable (they are not) and that therefore Anglo-Europeans are the only real, legitimate Americans (also untrue). Nothing is more un-American than cultural exclusion, and nothing could be more self-defeating than voluntary disassociation. It goes without saying that the mind-set of the cultural outsider contributes to the lamentable voter registration levels among Latinos, which are the lowest of any ethnic group, including African Americans. If the laws and policies enacted by elected officials had no effect on the lives and well-being of native-born Americans who consider themselves Mexicans, none of this would matter. But of course they do, and it does.

When Hispanics—or any other native-born ethnic or cultural group—identify themselves as something other than American (as opposed to something *in addition* to American), they disengage psychologically and symbolically from their civil responsibilities and rights as full-fledged citizens. They are also making the exact same mistake as the descendants of white settlers who confuse their Anglo heritage with the prerogatives and privileges of being American. Anglo and American are not synonymous. Americans are brown, black, white, and yellow. Americans eat chili peppers and sushi and hummus.

Americans have roots in every nation. But Latinos or other people of color who are citizens and refuse to call themselves Americans are reinforcing the myth of a Euro-white America that tolerates the "Mexicans" and "Chinese" and "Indians" in their midst. By relinquishing their Americanness, they undermine their ability to influence local, state, and national policies with the same authority and weight as any other U.S. citizen, so they have no one to blame but themselves when those policies fail to address their own needs and concerns. "Mexicans" don't have to share responsibility for America's strengths and weaknesses or find solutions for its problems. "Mexicans" can blame their own problems and predicaments on "Americans," the white oppressors, the ones who own the place. But real Americans understand that democracy is a shared responsibility that transcends ethnicity and requires participation by all to be meaningful. Americans, for better or for worse, are the native-born and naturalized citizens of the United States, regardless of their cultural background or proximity to the border. To pretend anything else is to intentionally turn oneself into a tourist, a squatter, a foreigner. At a time in history when Anglo-Americans are the numerical minority, it is more important than ever for Americans of every ethnic extraction to acknowledge and exercise their legitimate claim to the term *American* and accept their rightful role in helping to define it.

Wal-Mex

The border zone blurring of communities and markets, along with the growing spending power of middle-class minorities, is having an impact on industries as diverse as retailing, sports, agriculture, and travel. Owing to a combination of perceived post-9/11 danger in Asia and Europe and relatively favorable currency exchange rates, U.S. travel to Latin America in 2003 was up 14 percent even as tourist traffic to Europe and Asia had declined by 15 and 38 percent, respectively. As the growing influence and visibility of ethnic communities in the United States helps to cultivate a heightened awareness of the cultural riches of the Western Hemisphere, Americans who would have formerly gone to, say, the Egyptian pyramids at Giza are showing a new interest in alternative—but equally awesome—destinations like Machu Picchu.

At the same time, affluent minorities seeking to get in touch with their cultural roots are becoming a lucrative market for savvy tourist boards and Latin American governments. In Brazil, the government of the state of Bahia, which has one of the most vibrant Afro-derived cultures in the world, has begun a multimillion-dollar marketing campaign aimed at

African Americans who want to get closer to their African roots but may find Africa itself too distant, expensive, or dangerous. Bahia's state tour operator estimates that 60 percent of the forty-five thousand Americans who visited the region in 2002 were African American.

Tour operators in Latin countries and the United States are waking up to the potential profits in pitching cultural destinations to U.S. minorities, who represent an expanding market of tens of millions. Mexico alone is investing $1.3 billion in its tourism sector, which accounts for 8.9 percent of its GDP. In order to take advantage of the increasing ethnic diversity of U.S. tourists, who accounted for nearly 92 percent of all visitors to Mexico, America's southern neighbor has begun to market itself as a destination that offers much more than margaritas and great beaches. The importance of music, dance, and the arts as a conduit for greater mutual understanding among the diverse communities of the United States and Mexico was the formative idea behind the "Gateway to the Americas" initiative, a collaborative effort between the Association of Performing Arts Presenters (APAP) and Cultural Contact, an independent nonprofit organization established in 1991 by the Rockefeller Foundation, Mexico's National Fund for Culture and the Arts, and the Bancomer Cultural Foundation. The Gateway initiative, which was kicked off in New York in January 2003 with a reception at the Harvard University Club hosted by the Mexican embassy, involved hundreds of Mexican dancers, musicians, and performers and binational conferences in both countries with the goal of creating "a bridge for learning and exchange opportunities that will improve and contribute towards resolving our neighboring countries' complex relationship, irrespective of political, economic, and social encounters and conflicts."

Changing demographics and a Latin affinity for U.S. sports are also transforming the complexion of the quintessential American pastime. In 2003, Arturo Moreno, a fourth-generation Arizona native of Mexican heritage, became the first Hispanic owner of a major league sports franchise when he purchased the Anaheim Angels from the Walt Disney Company for $184 million. Moreno, who made his fortune in billboard advertising, promptly signed Dominican pitcher Bartolo Colón to a four-year $51 million contract; Colón teams with Ramon Ortiz and other players to make what *Orange County Weekly* columnist Matt Coker has called "the Latinest starting rotation in baseball."

The Latinization of major league baseball is simply another sign of how demographics and transnational marketing trends are transforming the economics of professional sports. The National Association for Stock Car Auto Racing (NASCAR) has launched a "Drive for Diversity" program to develop and showcase minority drivers and mechanics in an effort to tap the expanding ethnic sports fan base. According to an ESPN sports poll, NASCAR's white fan base had declined by 14.6 percent between 1995 and 2001, compared with increases of 631.3 percent for Hispanics, 111.7 percent for Asians, and 17.8 percent for blacks. NASCAR, which claims a fan base of 75 million and runs about ninety races a year in twenty-five states, hopes to build on the 6.4 million Latinos and 2 million African Americans who follow the sport. NASCAR races are currently broadcast in about one hundred countries. The association, which acknowledges that its diversity effort is aimed at boosting audiences in the United States and abroad by making itself more reflective of multicultural audiences, is planning to run its first race in Mexico in 2005. Meanwhile, the Championship Auto Racing Teams (CART) has pulled ahead of NASCAR in both diversity and in establishing a presence among U.S. Hispanics and in Mexico by showcasing Mexican drivers like Michael Jourdain Jr., Mario Dominguez, and Adrian Fernandez. CART, which lost market share and visibility after a 1996 split with the Indy Racing League (IRL) has aggressively positioned itself as the unofficial sports association of the North American Free Trade Agreement (NAFTA). During the 2003 season, a Mexican finished among the top three in all six CART races. CART, which holds races in Vancouver, Toronto, Montreal, Mexico City, and Monterrey, estimates that almost a quarter of the estimated ninety-five thousand spectators at the 2003 Toyota Grand Prix in Long Beach, California, were Latinos. "The Hispanic element of our market is huge," said CART CEO Christopher Pook. As a result, CART has been able to leverage its transnational fan base to sign up Mexican sponsors eager to reach the U.S. Hispanic market, including Corona, Tecate, the supermarket chain Gigante, and the salsa manufacturer Herdez. In a reverse NAFTA spin that few saw coming, Mexican advertisers like corn flour maker Maseca, fruit juice distributor Jumex, and construction materials giant Cemex, are pouring millions into Spanish-language marketing campaigns aimed at the 22 million U.S. residents with Mexican roots and the growing numbers of Hispanics and non-Latinos who buy and enjoy Mexican products.

At a time when American companies are bracing for a backlash in European, Asian, and Middle Eastern countries from their association with U.S. government policies, Latin Americans are embracing U.S. brands as their own, and vice versa. The Modelo Group, thanks to aggressive marketing and a strategic partnership with Anheuser-Busch, has turned Corona into the best-selling imported beer in the United States and one of the most popular beers in the world by positioning it as a lifestyle beverage that evokes the carefree, escapist allure of basking on a deserted, sun-struck beach. Modelo was cofounded in the wake of the Mexican revolution by a penniless Basque immigrant named Pablo Aramburuzabala. In 2000, María Asunción, who became Modelo's chairman after her father's death, bought 20 percent of Univision, which coincided with a decision to expand its brand awareness among U.S. Hispanics. Meanwhile, U.S. companies, like McDonald's, Domino's Pizza, Procter & Gamble, Sara Lee, and Frito-Lay have invested more than $2 billion in Mexico's food industry.

Wal-Mart, which is already the biggest corporation in the United States with 1.2 million domestic employees, launched international divisions during the 1990s in Mexico, Canada, China, Brazil, Argentina, Puerto Rico, and South Korea. Wal-Mart has 633 stores and employs more than one hundred thousand workers in Mexico, where it is responsible for 30 percent of all food sales and 6 percent of all retail sales. In 2002, when it became Mexico's number one employer, it added eight thousand new jobs, or about half the new permanent positions generated by the entire Mexican economy. In 2003, Levi's jeans announced that it would move all of its manufacturing operations to factories in the Caribbean, Latin America, and Asia, where lower labor costs will allow it to remain competitive with other jeans makers. In the post-NAFTA economy, in other words, it's entirely possible for a person who lost her job at the Levi's factory in San Antonio to have a relative in Monterrey who gets hired to do the same work for a fraction of the cost, with the resulting savings passed back to U.S. consumers, whose pursuit of rock-bottom prices only increases pressure on American companies to continue cutting costs.

The economic underpinnings of the immigration debate were spotlighted on October 23, 2003, when federal agents from the Division of Immigration and Customs Enforcement raided sixty Wal-Mart stores in twenty-one states and arrested 250 illegal immigrants who were employed as janitorial workers by the world's largest retailer. The workers, who were mostly from Latin America and Eastern Europe, were technically employed by a subcontractor, who in turn provided cheap janitorial labor for the Wal-Mart chain. In addition to hiring the illegal aliens, the Wal-Mart contractors stand accused of violating overtime, Social Security, and workers' compensation laws. Wal-Mart officials have denied responsibility, but federal agents, who also carted away boxes of files and documents from the company's headquarters in Bentonville, Arkansas, said they believed company executives are culpable because they intentionally used subcontractors as a cover for illegal hiring practices that allow them to maximize shareholder profits and benefit customers by offering lower prices. Wal-Mart has been subsequently sued by a group of immigrants who accuse it of discrimination, failure to pay overtime, and other violations. It is also facing a class action suit charging it with conspiring to cheat the janitors out of wages owned to them, failing to pay Social Security fees, and other transgressions. The undocumented workers, who face deportation, could theoretically find themselves rehired by one of Wal-Mart's foreign divisions for a fraction of what they earned in the United States, while still contributing to the company's bottom line.

Soul-Searching

"Tell me how you die," the Mexican poet Octavio Paz once wrote, "and I will tell you who you are." [14]

Once each year, during the holiday known as Día de Los Muertos, or the Day of the Dead, Mexicans remember who they are—and who they were—in a series of vivid rituals that evoke the beauty, horror, and humor of the afterlife. From dusk to dawn on the evenings of October 31 and November 1, Mexicans put aside their modern selves and, in Paz's words, "poke fun at life, affirming the nothingness and insignificance of human existence."

A fertile fusion of pre-Columbian and Christian traditions that dates back to the arrival of the Spaniards in Aztec Mexico, the Day of the Dead is a time when Mexicans—and Mexican communities across the United States and as far north as Canada—honor their ancestors by placing fruit, candles, flowers, and skull-shaped candies on the graves of their departed loved ones. The offerings, which are often also displayed in elaborate altars, or *ofrendas*, for public viewing, can include music, photographs, and plaster Virgins, a bottle of tequila, or a favorite article of clothing that once belonged to the deceased and are meant to console and provide sustenance to their souls during the long journey to heaven. The pageants, artifacts, and religious displays that surround the Day of the Dead—at once a recognition of death and a savoring of the pleasures of life—are a visual feast that has inspired generations of Mexican artists, from the painter Frida Kahlo to the novelist Juan Rulfo.

The Day of the Dead traces its earliest roots to the ancient pre-Columbian civilizations of Mexico and Central America and during the sixteenth century became mixed with the Christian tradition of All Souls' Day. Over the last few decades, as Latino populations have migrated north, the holiday has steadily spread to the United States and even parts of Canada. In the U.S. Southwest and cities with large Latino populations, Day of the Dead traditions are reenacted in private homes, community centers, and cemeteries. Chicago's Mexican Fine Arts Center Museum boasts what it calls the largest Day of the Dead exhibition in the nation. Entitled *"Puerta de la Eternidad"* ("The Door to Eternity"), the exhibit features paintings, mixed media displays, sculpture, photography, and folk art. In Phoenix, Arizona, Day of the Dead activities include lectures, concerts, gallery shows, food fairs, altar exhibitions, poetry reading, and "demon masquerades." In Los Angeles, at the Spanish historical center of Olvera Street, visitors can watch Xipetotec Indian–style dancers take part in events that include sugar skull decorating, piñata breaking, or *pan de los muertos* baking. A few miles away, the Hollywood Forever Cemetery features authentically decorated graves, live performances, food, and art installations. Educational institutions sponsoring Day of the Dead programs include the University of Texas, which offers an overview of Day of the Dead rituals through its Latin American Studies Department, and Utah State University, which offers special curriculums for grade schools and colleges.

The artistic contemplation of life and death, and of man's relationship to both, is a recurring theme in Asian and Latin folk cultures and one that is increasingly evident in the creative life of multicultural America. Popular Hollywood movies like *The Sixth Sense* and *The Others*, featuring characters who seem even more poignantly alive because they don't know they're already dead, are direct descendants of the unknowingly deceased narrator in Rulfo's novel *Pedro Páramo*, one of the seminal works in Mexican literature. The protagonist of Rulfo's postmodernist ghost story wanders through a dust-caked dreamscape of God-forsaken villages, recoiling in terror from the other lost souls he encounters, searching for a destination he will never be able to reach. That haunted sense of limbo, in this case felt by those who survive the death of others, surfaces again in *21 Grams*, a film by Mexican director Alejandro González Iñárritu that takes its name from the weight of the human soul, or whatever it is that leaves the body at the precise moment of death. Mortality, and its ability to affirm and enhance the understanding of life, is a recurring motif in the art of Julie Taymor, who studied mythology and folklore at Oberlin College and used her knowledge of shamanistic rites and ethnic cosmologies in theater works like *The Lion King* and movies like *Frida*. While living in Bali, Indonesia, she witnessed a ritual being performed by Balinese musicians and dancers who didn't know she was watching. Realizing that the dancers were engaged in pure expression for its own sake, without any need for an audience, she thought to herself, This is what it means to perform for God! In Taymor's work, kites, cloth, and color take on symbolic, ritual significance. Taymor believes that art should hold "a skewed mirror" up to the public. "Don't hold the mirror up to their face," she says, "show them the back of their heads." By undermining assumptions, and re-creating, rather than appropriating, indigenous art forms and techniques, Taymor seeks to conjure the "spiritual, healing power of art."

The paintings made by Australia's aboriginal artists evolved from designs and symbols used in clan ceremonies to represent "creation ancestors," supernatural beings, and "rainbow serpents" that ruled the earth and controlled the forces of nature. For fifty thousand years, the aborigines created intricate pictures, or "dreamings," from ocher and plant fibers to be experienced as part of a communal storytelling ritual before they were rubbed away. It was not until the 1970s, after forced resettlement had decimated tribal life, that white social workers introduced the indigenous artists to paint, and the dreamings took on a permanent form, partly as a way to preserve traditions that the natives feared were in danger of disappearing. The aborigines believed that the paved roads and mines built by white men had stripped the earth of its *mangi,* or the spiritual traces of human beings who had died or gone away. For artists like Pijaju Peter Skipper, painting restored the land's *mangi* through *wangarr,* or shadow images of what had been before. For the aborigines, the *wangarr* paintings were a link to the spirit world and a way to stay connected to the untrammeled lands they had lost.[15]

For many immigrants in the United States, reconnection to one's ancestral homeland takes a literal form, even after death. R. G. Ortiz Funeral Homes, a mortuary chain with fifteen locations throughout New York City, offers a special package for families who wish the remains of their loved ones to be returned to Mexico. The service, which costs between $2,200 and $2,500, includes embalming, a cloth-covered pine coffin, and transportation to a new resting place south of the border.[16] The reasons vary from a desire to be interred in one's native land or with other family members, to a feeling that a proper Mexican wake is not practical or feasible in the United States. It's not uncommon for a Mexican wake to last as long as nine days. On the final day, the entire town accompanies the body to the cemetery. Afterward, the mourners gather at the family home for a meal and shared remembrances. In the summer of 2003, the remains of 419 colonial-era slaves took a much shorter journey to a new burial ground in lower Manhattan, not far from the site of a market where they had once been sold as slaves. The remains, which were discovered in 1991 by construction workers during the building of a federal office tower near the

South Street Seaport, were determined to have been in a burial ground for people of African American descent that was closed in 1794. The reburial ceremony, which was attended by New York City mayor Michael Bloomberg, was used by African American community leaders as a time to reflect on the hardships and inequities that were suffered by their enslaved ancestors.

Death in the United States is becoming an increasingly multicultural affair. As the U.S. ethnic population ages and the demand for ethnically specific services increases, funeral directors are finding that traditional arrangements might not be enough. According to the Bureau of Labor Statistics, out of the fifty-eight thousand funeral directors in the United States, about 10 percent are African American, 2 percent are Latino, and 24 percent are women.[17] Burial traditions can vary widely among different ethnic groups. For instance, West Indian tradition calls for the singing of hymns during visiting hours, while Portuguese treat funerals as a time for quiet prayer and reflection. Buddhists, on the other hand, believe in having a procession from the visitation room to the cremation room, and South Asian Indian traditions require that the males of the family begin the process of lighting the cremation fire. Some Asian families, wishing to preserve the memories and remain near deceased family members they left behind when they migrated to the United States, arrange for the remains of their relatives to be brought to America. Frank Woo, a Chinese immigrant who settled in San Francisco, paid to have his father's and mother's remains, which had been buried separately in Asia, brought to the United States and reburied near his home at Skylawn Memorial Park in San Mateo. For many Chinese, where ancestral plots are often displaced or overrun by industrial development, being reburied in the United States is seen as something admirable. "Going overseas is everyone's dream," Qian Yaping, a funeral director at the cemetery where Woo's father rested between 1988 and 2000, told *The New York Times*. "And it isn't easy getting to America, whether you are alive or dead."[18] Frank Woo, who has ten children, most of whom live in the United States, had a more pragmatic attitude. "I know that America is where the Woo family home is going to be from now on," he said. "I don't want my children and grandchildren to forget about our ancestors, or forget about me."[19]

The acute consciousness of mortality and eternity that permeates Latin and Asian ethnic cultures resonates anew in the art, theater, and literature of the New Mainstream, not just because all human beings are, ultimately, on a journey from birth to death, but also because the quintessential immigrant experience is defined by arrivals and departures, away from the places and people they left behind and toward the people they became even before they reached their destination.

8. Destinations

The United States is a nation forged in flux. The explorers' fearless search for gold and virgin lands, the Pilgrims' transatlantic lunge for spiritual freedom, the pioneers' intrepid push into the wilderness, are all hallmarks of a people defined by the crucible of change. Just as the geographic frontier of the West shaped the American character and economy during the nineteenth century, the Industrial Revolution of the twentieth century generated new opportunities for personal realization and upward mobility in factories and teeming cities. Today, the transnational markets of the information age are accelerating and accomodating demographic and economic trends that are simultaneously local and global. Domestic migration, free trade, and a continuing influx of immigrants from Latin America, Asia, and the Caribbean are reshaping the American dream even as the dreamers themselves become more culturally diverse. The new frontier is in the telemarketing call centers of India and in the borderless economics of NAFTA; the "old country" is across the ocean and in the ethnic enclaves that serve as buffers and assimilation centers for recent arrivals. The wilderness of marginalization is giving way to the postethnic outposts of transnational markets, cultural cross-fertilization, and mass migration in both real space and on the Internet, where digital settlers are founding virtual communities that transcend color, culture, and gender. As the population shifts and morphs and identity becomes a fungible commodity, borders are blurring and community is psychographic, pan-racial, and tribal.

The number of immigrants in the United States has more than tripled since 1970, when the census put the number at 9.6 million, or 4.7 percent of the population. If current immigration policies and trends continue—an annual influx of 700,000 to 900,000 legal immigrants and 300,000 to 500,000 undocumented immigrants—the foreign population in the United States will become 15 percent of the U.S. population by 2050,[1] or approximately the same as the historical high point reached around 1900. Then as now, the rising percentage of foreigners was seen as a threat to American life. Then as now, xenophobes and racists clamored for new immigration controls and a closing of U.S. borders. Then as now, immigrants have invigorated and transformed the economic and cultural landscape of the nation they have chosen as their new home. Then as now, the salutary effects of the immigrant wave are downplayed, ignored, or misunderstood as the media and social reactionaries focus on the immigration "problem."

In her book *From Ellis Island to JFK: New York's Two Great Waves of Immigration*, Nancy Foner points out that "an elaborate mythology" about the immigrant population that came to New York City at the turn of the twentieth century has distorted the past and colored our perceptions of the current wave of newcomers. "A century ago, many native-born Americans viewed newly arrived eastern and southern European immigrants with fear and loathing, as 'repulsive creatures' who menaced the very foundations of American civilization," she writes. "These negative attitudes have long been forgotten in a haze of history, replaced by images that glorify the past. For many present-day New Yorkers, their Jewish and Italian immigrant forebears have become folk heroes of a sort—and represent a baseline against which current arrivals are compared and, unfortunately, often fail to measure up." During the last great immigration wave, between 1880 and 1920, close to 1.5 million people arrived in New York, so that by 1910, "fully 41 percent of all New Yorkers were foreign born."[2]

Today's immigrants make up more than a third of the city's population and are continuing to arrive at a rate of more than one hundred thousand a year. Unlike their predecessors, who were mostly of Southern European and Russian-Jewish extraction, they are predominantly Asians, Latin Americans, and West Indians, from the Dominican Republic, China, Mexico, and Jamaica. The majority arrive in the United States not by taking a boat to Ellis Island, but by taking a plane to JFK International Airport. *The New York Times* responded in 2004 by publishing its own *Guide for Immigrants in New York City*.[3] Produced in partnership with the city's Lower East Side Tenement Museum, the guide, which is available in English, Spanish, and Chinese editions, provides information on a range of logistical issues and public services, including applying for a green card, finding an apartment and a job, enrolling in school, getting medical insurance, and setting up a bank account.

The new immigrants are coming for many of the same reasons that drew them here a century ago. "Population growth and economic disruptions, attendant upon industrialization, urbanization and agricultural development, set the stage for large-scale migration from Europe in the past and still operate as underlying causes of migration in many developing countries today," Foner writes. Like those who came before, the immigrants who come in search of work or to seek asylum or to escape crowding or calamity arrive with personal histories and a web of relationships that connect them to their home. In a pattern established by the first European colonists, once the new settlers get their footing, they send word of opportunities and encourage others to follow in a "chain migration." Writes Foner: "If Russian Jews a century ago were escaping political oppression, so, too, many of today's immigrants are in a flight to freedom. Whatever the initial causes, once set in motion, immigration movements become self-perpetuating, so that today, as in the past, migration can be thought of as a process of progressive network building."[4]

Yet despite the déjà vu of current immigration patterns, there are important differences between now and the turn of the twentieth century. Despite perceptions of the new immigrants as being mostly unskilled laborers, the fact is they represent more educational and occupational variety than their predecessors. Disparities in income and educational levels range across ethnic groups and within them. In 1990, one out of five of working-age, post-1965 Chinese immigrants had a college degree or more, while one out of four had failed to complete the ninth grade. While undocumented immigrants are more a factor than a hundred years ago, they still make up a relatively small percentage of the city's immigrant community (540,000 in 1996, or roughly one-fifth of the total immigrant population). Most of them arrive, not by crossing porous borders, but by flying to New York as tourists and simply staying after their visas expire. Studies also show that illegal immigrants usually share the same attributes of self-selection as their legal counterparts, arriving with a willingness to work and an ambition to improve their economic lot. A study of Dominican immigrants conducted in the 1980s found that the undocumented Dominicans were more likely to have been professionals or managers in their home country. The flow of European immigrants, while not nearly as great as in the late nineteenth and early twentieth centuries, remains ongoing. In 1990, Italy, the USSR, and Poland were among the top ten home countries for foreign-born New York residents, ahead of Trinidad, Korea, and India. For many immigrants, New York City has become synonymous with America; an almost mythical place where a person can realize his dreams and achieve personal fulfillment. As a result, the current wave of immigrants is more diverse than ever before. "Diversity, the buzz word of the 1990s, is an apt description for the newest New Yorkers," Foner writes. "In almost every way—economically, educationally and culturally—they are more diverse than their predecessors a hundred years ago."[5]

They are also more likely than ever to migrate away from the major immigration hubs of the past. In postethnic America, immigration has moved from the cities to the suburbs to the exburbs as ethnic populations take root in cities and towns in Minnesota, Georgia, Nevada, and Ohio. Communities that saw little or no immigration as recently as 1990 are learning to accommodate doctors from India, unskilled laborers from Mexico, and engineers from China. Although immigrants continue to be drawn to "melting pot" states, the foreign-born population is also migrating to states in the Midwest, South, and Pacific Northwest. In 1990, nearly three-quarters of all immigrants lived in six states: California, New York, Texas, Florida, Illinois, and New Jersey. During the 1990s, the same states saw their share of the immigrant population drop to about two-thirds, while twenty-two other states saw their immigrant populations surge by as much as 90 percent, owing to both direct immigration and secondary migration from "melting pot" states. The "new growth" states with the greatest immigrant population increases were North Carolina (274 percent), Georgia (233 percent), Nevada (202 percent), Arkansas (196 percent), Utah (171 percent), Tennessee (169 percent), Nebraska (165 percent), Colorado (160 percent), Arizona (136 percent), and Kentucky (135 percent). Drawn to employment opportunities created by new construction and jobs in the service sector, the new immigrants are shadowing the domestic migration of native-born and naturalized Americans in search of a better life, a quest that is defined by some as a better job, by others as an escape from the crowded urban jungle. As a consequence, the settlement patterns of immigrants in the "new growth" states vary from region to region. In Rhode Island, for example, immigrants tend to cluster in the capital city of Providence and surrounding suburbs, while the immigrant population of Atlanta is dispersed in outer suburbs, or exburbs, and semirural communities in Clayton, Cobb, DeKalb, and Fulton counties.[6]

The Atlanta Metropolitan Statistical Area provides an illuminating snapshot of how immigration is affecting "new growth" areas. The Federation for American Immigration Reform projected that if population growth continued at the 1990–2000 rate from 2000 until 2025, the population of Greater Atlanta would increase by 127.5 percent to 9,356,000.[7] It also quoted a *Washington Post* story claiming that the Atlanta area was suffering from record levels of smog and traffic congestion, due largely to population increases attributable to "transplanted northerners, residents from all over the Southeast and large communities of Asians and Hispanics . . ."[8] In a column posted on the Online Athens Web site, a Georgian wrote that "most of us have noticed the sudden rise in Hispanic workers in this area." Warning that unchecked illegal immigration would strain social services, turn English into a "second language," and lead to "job losses" and "criminal activity," the author called on his fellow Georgians to "demand immediate corrective action from Washington to save us from this dilution from our American way of life."[9]

Even more telling, however, was an incident that occurred in Vidalia,

Georgia, in 1998, when forty-five officers from the Immigration and Naturalization Service (INS) raided farms and packing houses in the heart of Vidalia onion country. During the operation, dubbed "Southern Denial," twenty-one suspected undocumented immigrants were detained during the height of the onion harvest. When growers, who represent a $90 million agribusiness that spans nineteen south Georgia counties, complained that the INS raids were threatening to put them out of business, the government agreed to grant the workers amnesty in exchange for cooperation from growers in enforcing immigration laws.[10]

The incident highlights the complex web of conflicting interests between business owners who rely on cheap immigrant labor and those who see the foreigners as a social threat. In fact, immigration and economic interests have been intertwined throughout American history. As Ronald Takaki notes: "Many diverse ethnic groups have contributed to the building of the American economy, forming what Walt Whitman saluted as 'a vast, surging, hopeful army of workers.' They worked in the South's cotton fields, New England's textile mills, Hawaii's cane fields, New York's garment factories, California's orchards, Washington's salmon canneries, and Arizona's copper mines. They built the railroad, the great symbol of America's industrial triumph."[11] And in the postethnic economy of the twenty-first century, they not only wash and bus the dishes, weed the gardens, build the houses, and watch the children, they also contribute to the social and ethnic diversity that stimulates and nourishes the multicultural appetites of the creative class.

When a particular ethnic group shows an affinity for a certain kind of occupation or line of work, the acculturation process can be mutual. Japanese gardeners, Korean grocers, and Irish policemen are examples of professions that have been indelibly marked by the minorities who dominated them. As the ethnic makeup of the immigrants has changed, so have professional associations as the newcomers find their own niche in the workplace. In New York City, Filipinos have become the largest ethnic group among nurses at many hospitals throughout the region. According to the 2000 census, 30 percent of the city's 173,000 Filipinos work as nurses or health practitioners. American hospitals, which prize Filipinos for their English-language skills and U.S.-style training, have aggressively recruited Filipino nurses for decades, often using bonuses and other perks to lure them to the United States. Filipinos are also valued for their honesty, work ethic, and tenderness toward patients, which stems from a culture with a tradition of caring for their own sick and elderly. The Filipinos, in turn, receive a solid financial and social footing that helps to speed assimilation and economic advancement for the entire community.[12]

One of the most common arguments against immigration from non-English-speaking countries in Latin America and elsewhere is that foreigners with strong ties to their native cultures are unable or unwilling to assimilate. Yet studies on immigrant assimilation tell a different story. The Urban Institute notes that because immigrants settling in the "new growth" states tend to be more recent arrivals, they are also "more likely than less recent arrivals to be undocumented, to have relatively low incomes, and to speak a language other than English at home. They are also *less* likely to be citizens, homeowners and proficient in English." Nevertheless, "As immigrants live longer in the United States, they tend to become more fully integrated, in other words they grow increasingly similar to the native-born population in social and economic status." The Urban Institute found that while only 25 percent of the most recent arrivals own their own homes, immigrant home ownership matches that of natives (67 percent) after twenty years of residence in the United States. Median family income also rises over time. Immigrants who entered the United States after 1990 have a median family income of $39,600, compared with $52,000 for natives. But immigrants who entered the United States after 1980 have a median family income of $43,500, and those who arrived before 1980 have a median family income of $53,000. "Even when effect of aging is taken into account," the study concludes, "these trends do not disappear, showing that immigration integration is a process that occurs gradually over time, and that the amount of time spent in the United States is key to analyzing immigrant populations' characteristics, contributions and needs."[13]

The new immigrants are amazingly diverse, reflecting America's enduring ability to attract a global mix of races and cultures. An analysis of 2000 census data shows that the population of 31.1 million foreign-born in the United States comprises individuals from almost one hundred different countries. The largest single source is Mexico, representing 30 percent, or 9.2 million people, followed by Asia, with 26 percent (8.2 million), and "other Latin Americans" (22 percent, or 6.9 million). Immigrants from Europe and Canada make up 18 percent (5.7 million) and "Africa and other" 3 percent (1.0 million). The proportionate size of the Mexican population in the United States is not unprecedented. The Urban Institute noted that in the middle and late nineteenth century, Irish or German immigrants accounted for more than 30 percent of the U.S. population and that "in some decades, both exceeded 30 percent."

The institute's survey of immigrant families found that the population of Los Angeles County represented 75 different countries of origin and that New York City's immigrants came from 109 countries. The extent to which the current immigrant flows are undocumented differs by region of origin. A large number of Central American immigrants are also undocumented, although many have been granted temporary protected status as they fled war, hurricanes, and earthquakes in the region. Other Central Americans and a large number of Cubans have been admitted permanently as refugees. Still other Latin Americans have been admitted for permanent residency under employment and family reunification provisions. Most Asians, by contrast, have been admitted as permanent residents or as refugees. Southeast Asians constituted over half of all refugees during most of the 1980s and at least a third until the mid- to late 1990s. Most European and Canadian immigrants were admitted as permanent residents, although a large number of immigrants from Russia and other former Soviet republics entered as refugees during the 1990s.[14]

By contrast, undocumented immigrants are estimated to number between 7 million and 11 million, or about 25 percent of the total immigrant population, with most of them coming from Mexico. Although about 2 million Mexicans became legal permanent residents under legalization provisions declared in 1986, several million more remain undocumented owing to ongoing large-scale migration from Mexico. According to most estimates, the undocumented population doubled during the 1990s, from somewhat less than 4 million to more than 8 million. Children in immigrant families are generally poorer, in worse health, and more likely to live in substandard, crowded housing conditions than children of natives.[15]

In an effort to quantify racial and ethnic diversity in a single number, Phil Meyer of the University of North Carolina and Shawn McIntosh of *USA Today* created a "diversity index" that used probability theory to calculate the likelihood that any two people chosen at random from a given census area would be of different races or ethnicities. Applying their formula to the 1980 and 1990 census, they found that the diversity index of the United States had increased 20 percent over the decade.[16] Community leaders and social activists across the country have begun to realize that the fate of immigrants impacts the quality of life for all residents and that getting those newcomers on a path to naturalization is the first step in the process of making them productive citizens. In Atlanta, Families and Advocates for Immigrant Rights (FAIR), a coalition of religious, ethnic, and social service groups, sent a letter to the state Office of Planning and Budget asking Georgia to "embrace our new immigrants" by allotting funds for English-language instruction, citizenship classes, and help in preparing for the immigration and naturalization interviews and civics tests related to naturalization. "The face of Georgia is changing," said a FAIR spokesperson. "Since citizenship is now a defining criteria for social service benefits, we see it in the best interests of the state to help get people naturalized."

In December 2003, the United States held a lottery for fifty-five thousand legal resident documents, or "green cards," representing a fraction of the immigrants seeking legal resident status. To help cover the gap, municipalities and states are devising new ways to track and deliver civil services to illegal aliens who may have fallen between the cracks. During the summer of 2003, several midwestern U.S. cities with growing Hispanic communities began recognizing the *matricula consular*, which in Spanish means "consular registration," an identity card issued by the Mexican government to undocumented Mexican nationals living in the United States, as a valid form of identification for a range of civic and commercial services. Since the 1870s, Mexico has offered the card to its citizens in the United States so it could give them consular assistance with U.S. employers, police authorities, and transporting deceased relatives back to Mexico. The card has only recently been perceived as a way to reach Mexican immigrants who otherwise would have been impossible to locate or identify. It is also increasingly seen as a way to boost the economies of towns and cities with growing immigrant populations.[17]

In Indianapolis, the card can be used to apply for building licenses and permits to drive taxis and operate vending carts. Local businesses like the National City Bank in Minneapolis see the cards as a way to expand their customer base and will accept them as identification to open an account. In East Chicago, Indiana, immigrants can use the card to check out library books or open an account with the local water utility. The number of U.S. cities and banks that recognize the card has grown from a handful to more than one hundred cities, nine hundred police departments, one hundred financial institutions, and thirteen states, including Indiana, New Mexico, and Utah.

The *matricula consular* is not without its detractors. Police departments in New York, Connecticut, and New Jersey have yet to accept the card as a valid form of identification, and Colorado has barred its use, citing concerns about reliability. Officials at the FBI and the Department of Homeland Security, citing the possibility of fraud or counterfeiting, have voiced concern that the cards pose a potential security risk. Never mind that it was post-9/11 restrictions that spurred the use of the card as undocumented workers found themselves unable to enter buildings where they worked when photo identification became mandatory for entering many buildings and hospitals, buying train tickets, and wiring money. The Mexican government, for its part, has begun issuing a new version of the card with enhanced security features. In July 2003, the House of Representatives approved a measure that would allow the U.S. Department of State to regulate all consular identification cards issued by Mexico and other countries. And a recent move by the Treasury Department to give banks discretionary power to accept the cards was rescinded after protests by several Republican lawmakers. Yet other politicians are convinced that the benefits of the card outweigh any risks. Senator Richard G. Lugar, a Republican and chairman of the Senate Foreign Relations Committee, has expressed his support for the cards, stating that they "pose no risk to our anti-terrorism efforts. In fact, cards that simplify identification of immigrants and facilitate their contact with Americans and our institutions are a benefit to public safety, not a liability." [18]

A growing recognition that immigration is not only not a threat to national security, but actually in the nation's self-interest, is sparking political action designed to address that fact. Legislation introduced in 2003 by Republican congressmen Jim Kolbe and Jeff Flake in the U.S. House of Representatives and a similar bill sponsored by Arizona senator John McCain in the Senate seek to bring some sense of order and realism to a process that has been a political albatross and an embarrassing human rights disaster for decades. In a letter to John Hostettler, chairman of the House Judiciary Subcommittee on Immigration, Kolbe and Flake voiced an urgent need to act and begin congressional hearings. "Deaths of illegal immigrants as they attempt to enter the country (mostly for the purpose of finding work), a general environment of lawlessness enveloping the southwest border, and an illegal U.S. population of at least 7 million people are problems that must be addressed by federal legislators," they wrote. [19]

Despite the common refrain that illegal immigrants take jobs away from taxpaying Americans, the evidence shows that not only are immigrants a boon to the economy by taking lower-paying, unskilled jobs that would otherwise go unfilled, but their contribution helps support the economic and physical infrastructure that creates higher-paying, white-collar jobs. And those who claim that undocumented immigrants are an undue burden on American society need only ponder the fact that these people are actually willing to risk their lives for the chance to work and build a better life for themselves and their children. There is also reason to believe that granting work visas or some other legal status to immigrant workers would not dramatically increase the flow of newcomers, since studies have shown that historically the immigrant workforce has ebbed and flowed depending on the availability of jobs north of the border. In a 2002 paper entitled "Willing Workers," Dan T. Griswold, associate director of the Cato Institute's Center for Trade Policy Studies, describes the problem as a clear-cut case of mismatched supply and demand. "Demand for low-skilled labor continues to grow in the U.S. while the domestic supply of suitable workers inexorably declines—yet U.S. immigration law contains virtually no legal channel through which low-skilled immigrant workers can enter the country to fill the gap."[20]

Up until recently, that channel was a two-thousand-mile-long porous membrane that allowed Mexican workers to cross back and forth almost at will. If anything, increasing border security only adds to the number of permanent resident workers by making the trip back to Mexico too dangerous. And even if it made economic and moral sense, effectively sealing the border is too expensive and impractical. Kolbe and Flake are proposing changes that take into account the fluctuating needs and motives of the illegal immigrant worker population, including new temporary visa categories that distinguish between those who are looking only for daytime jobs and those who seek to live permanently in the United States. Instead of granting blanket amnesty to those who have already entered the United States, the government would give them a chance to apply for legal resident status, but only after paying a fine for breaking the law. Unless changes in the current immigration system are made, Griswold warns of a continuing pattern of "smuggling, document fraud, deaths at the border, artificially depressed wages and threats to civil liberties."[21]

In the autumn of 2003, a growing sense of frustration among immigrants found its voice in a form of social protest that resurrected tactics from the civil rights movement of the 1960s. In an effort to call attention to immigration issues and rally support for policy reform, hundreds of undocumented workers riding eighteen buses made promotional stops in more than one hundred U.S. cities as part of the "Immigrant Workers Freedom Ride." The protesters were backed by a coalition of politicians, labor unions, religious leaders, and African American organizations like the Congressional Black Caucus, the Coalition of Black Trade Unionists, the NAACP, and other groups that saw the event as a tribute to the freedom rides of the civil rights era and a way to help immigrants from Africa and the Caribbean. Carrying white crosses representing those who had died crossing the border and singing "We Shall Overcome," the riders met with local leaders and staged rallies calling for a granting of amnesty to undocumented workers similar to the one enacted in 1986, stronger civil rights protections for illegal immigrant workers, and the issuing of additional visas for reuniting family members.

By the end of 2003, Homeland Security Secretary Tom Ridge, who became the U.S. government's chief spokesman on immigration policy after his department was given the job of protecting the nation's security in the wake of the 9/11 terrorist attacks, signaled that he was ready to consider granting legal status to undocumented aliens already living in the United States. Speaking at a town hall meeting in Miami, Secretary Ridge said, "The bottom line is, as a country, we have to come to grips with the presence of 8 to 12 million illegals, afford them some kind of legal status some way." The prospect of granting legal status to undocumented aliens living in the United States, the majority of whom are Mexicans, had been the cornerstone of initially warm relations with Mexican president Vicente Fox, who saw a kindred soul in George Bush. It was understood, for both economic and humanitarian reasons, that easing border tensions with America's number one trading partner by loosening immigration restrictions was in the mutual interest of both countries. But 9/11, and Mexico's refusal to endorse the U.S.-led attack on Iraq, changed all that. Now the Bush administration was suddenly showing a renewed interest in immigration reform, but the rationale was noticeably different. "The secretary acknowledges that we have several million people here illegally, and he understands that for homeland security reasons, at some point in time, there needs to be a better way to identify those who may be a threat to our country." [22]

While offering no details on what kind of status might be offered to the illegal immigrants, it had been previously suggested that the government might consider giving immigrants the right to apply for a driver's license and a work permit. Secretary Ridge did, however, rule out the possibility of granting the undocumented residents U.S. citizenship. "I'm not saying make them citizens, because they violated the law to get here," he said. "So you don't reward that kind of conduct by turning over a citizenship certificate." [23]

Meanwhile, old-fashioned bigotry and lingering paranoia over the terrorist attacks on the World Trade Center continue to breed atrocities both large and small. In 2003, *New York Times* columnist Bob Herbert wrote about the plight of Elizabeta Markvukaj, an Albanian immigrant and businesswoman who came to the United States in the mid-1990s and now owns the Al Laghetto restaurant in Congers, New York. Her fiancée, Vaso Nikpreljevic, a fellow Albanian refugee who fled the Communist regime of his native country and worked with Markvukaj at the restaurant, was pulled over for a speeding violation on the Connecticut Turnpike. When a computer check revealed that his immigration papers were not in order, Nikpreljevic was handcuffed, arrested, and sentenced to deportation. Nikpreljevic's history of interaction with the United States immigration authorities is a Kafkaesque tale of approved petitions for an alien resident green card, denied requests for political asylum, deportation and illegal return via Canada, fines, and finally a limbo of uncertainty. He had never been in trouble with the law, and since his brother and fiancée had both secured legal residence without any problems, he had understandably assumed that it would eventually all work out for the better. Instead, a tight-knit family of entrepreneurs has been torn apart, a man who believed he was living within the law of the land has been jailed, and their business is in danger of failing. "Mr. Nikpreljevic and his relatives are exactly the kinds of productive individuals who help a society to thrive," Herbert wrote. "They have been a boon to their local community and are assets to the U.S. as a whole. But the law, especially in times of great fear, does not always leave room for wise decisions. And where immigrants are concerned, the system becomes more of a crapshoot than ever."[24]

The tribulations that immigrants face can be fatal. A Portuguese dairy farmer in California's San Joaquin Valley was charged in 2003 with violating worker safety regulations when two Mexican immigrants drowned in a sump hole filled with cow manure and water. The case was intended to call attention to lax workplace safety standards, with the goal of preventing future job-related deaths for all of the state's dairy workers. The human toll of existing border policies is also well documented. According to the University of Houston's Center for Immigration Research, between 1985 and 2000, more than four thousand people died along the U.S.-Mexico border. The U.S. Border Patrol reported 336 fatalities in 2001 and 320 in 2002. By the middle of 2003, an estimated 318 Mexicans had died on the border. Some drown, others succumb to exposure in the desert, and still others are the victims of "coyotes," who prey on their victims' hunger for the north. The "coyotes" charge hundreds or even thousands of dollars to smuggle their human cargo across the border in trucks, sometimes leaving them locked inside in the hot desert sun to suffocate and die.

Others willingly risk their lives as soldiers in the U.S. armed forces, ready to die for a country that is not yet their own. Diego Rincon, an eighteen-year-old immigrant from Colombia, was killed in Iraq in March 2003 in a suicide car bombing. Rincon, a green card legal resident who decided to join the army in his hometown of Conyers, Georgia, after the September 11 terrorist attacks, was granted citizenship posthumously at the age of nineteen. According to the Pentagon, some thirty-seven thousand immigrants currently serve in the U.S. armed forces, making up about 3 percent of the active duty population. U.S. military personnel who are legal U.S. residents are eligible to apply for citizenship after three years, compared with a waiting period of five years for civilians. President Bush has waived the waiting period for immigrants who joined the military after September 11, allowing them to apply for U.S. citizen immediately as long as the war on terrorism continues. Meanwhile, Congress is considering no fewer than six different bills designed to ease restrictions for immigrants who fight for the United States. Among the changes being proposed are shortening the waiting period by one or two years, the waiving of naturalization fees, and allowing soldiers to conduct citizenship interviews at U.S. embassies during tours of duty, versus having to fly back to the United States at their own expense, which is now the case.

Some legislators also want the spouses and children of soldiers killed in the line of duty to be allowed to apply for citizenship immediately. "This is a chance to do the right thing for those who are doing the right thing for America," said Representative Doc Hastings, a Republican from Washington. Hastings has proposed that immigrants who join the military should be allowed to apply for citizenship immediately. But other lawmakers are wary of changing the rules. Representative John Hostettler, chairman of the House Judiciary Subcommittee on Immigration, reasserted that immigrants currently serving in the U.S. armed forces, despite their willingness to give their life for America, "must demonstrate their character and their loyalty for three years" before they can become U.S. citizens.[25]

If fighting for one's country is a measure of national valor, then military statistics show that minorities are at least as patriotic as other Americans. In recent decades, the percentage of minorities and women in the military has increased even as the total number of soldiers has decreased from 776,000 in 1981 to 406,000 in 2002. Between 1981 and 2001, the percentage of women increased from 11 percent to 16 percent, while minorities rose from 38 percent to 42 percent during the same period. A number of studies show that a greater proportion of Hispanics were killed in the U.S. war with Iraq than non-Hispanic whites. According to the Pew Hispanic Center fact sheet, "Hispanics in the Military," while Latinos make up 9.5 percent of the actively enlisted forces, they are overrepresented in the categories that get the most dangerous assignments—infantry, gun crews, and seamanship—and make up over 17.5 percent of the front lines. As of August 28, Department of Defense statistics show a casualty rate of more than 13 percent for people of Hispanic background serving in Iraq.[26]

While the Pew study found that Latinos in the U.S. military are underrepresented overall, they are overrepresented in the lower ranks and pay grades and are more likely to have duties that put them in harm's way. Aggressive army recruitment efforts in inner-city schools and in states with large Hispanic populations have led some community activists to accuse the government of waging a "recruiting war" on lower-income minority youths with a "poverty draft" that preys on disadvantaged minority youths. Despite the grain of truth in such polemics, the history of minorities in the military is much more complex. What is certain is that generations of Latinos, African Americans, and other ethnic Americans have served in the military with honor and distinction and have willingly taken on a disproportionate share of the burden of bearing arms to defend the American way of life and all that it represents. Since the abolition of the draft and the institution of the volunteer army in the early seventies, the education level of conscripts has risen from 54 percent of recruits having a high school diploma in 1980 to 98 percent by 1991. The increasing diversity of the military is also accelerating the acculturation of immigrants and forcing Americans to acknowledge that patriotism is not determined or defined by ethnicity or race. In a polyglot world of ethnic strife and quickly shifting battlefields, a multicultural army is literally America's best defense.[27]

When the Pilgrims set out for America in the *Mayflower*, the charter they carried entitled them to settle in Virginia. They never made it. Instead they veered north to the coast of modern-day Massachusetts, eventually landing at Plymouth. They came ashore in the New World with little more than what they could carry, willing to risk everything for the dream of a better, nobler life. They arrived uninvited by the natives, with no visas or passports. Like so many other undocumented immigrants, they did not speak the local language, and their habits and customs were strange and ill-suited for their new surroundings. At first they kept to themselves, forming an insulated community bound by a common language, religion, and culture. But in order to survive and thrive they were forced to adapt and learn, and in time they assimilated, changing their new home even as it changed them, until the two became indistinguishable and their journey became the journey of all travelers, all immigrants, all survivors, all Americans.

PART III

The Unfinished Pyramid

9. Liquid Assets

The U.S. dollar is the official currency of the most powerful nation in the history of the world, a global symbol of American wealth, security, and stability. It also has a mythic power, not just for Americans who spend so much of their time and energy pursuing and spending it, but also for the foreigners and immigrants, past, present, and future, who were lured across oceans and borders by the chance to earn it. For millions around the world, the dollar represents a free pass to financial independence and a ticket to personal fulfillment. For others, it evokes all that is superficial, artificial, and corrupting. But in a market-driven, consumerist society, the dollar—and the material aspirations it represents—is the definitive expression of economic achievement. On the world stage, the flow of greenbacks, in or out, can make or break a country's economy. Its fluctuations are felt in London, Tokyo, Cairo, Buenos Aires, and Beijing.

The dollar greases the wheels of the world economy, and vice versa. More than ever before, its fate and value are tied to the external machinations of international trade, which more than ever before is linked to

America's internal ethnic economy. In 2003, 20 percent of America's national debt—which totaled $6,460,686,804499.03 on April 14—was held by non-Americans. Foreign trade as a percentage of the U.S. gross domestic product accounts for about one-quarter of the nation's total GDP and continues to rise. At the same time, the U.S. ethnic market is the fastest-growing segment of the U.S. economy and an increasingly critical component in the projected growth of the United States and many other foreign economies. As these two megatrends intersect and feed each other, the changes that have already begun will accelerate and expand in myriad ways. More than ever before, the dollar is not just a barometer of American prestige and a projection of its long-term prospects, but an index of the global economy overall and America's stature in the international community. If the dollar is white, it is because white is not a color per se, but the visible result of the simultaneous presence of all colors. In a very real sense, the dollar is the color of all countries, all races, all peoples.

Remarkably, the ambitious vision of America as a proud and prosperous bastion of freedom-loving democracies is encoded directly on its money. Designed in 1957 and measuring roughly six by two and one-half inches, the one-dollar bill is printed on a cotton and linen blend with minute red and blue fibers running through it and stamped with an ink whose formula is a closely guarded secret. The U.S. Bureau of Engraving and Printing produces about 16,650,000 one-dollar bills each day, and there are billions more in circulation.[1] The dollar bill is ubiquitous, familiar beyond notice, yet few Americans understand the meaning of the words and images that appear on it. In fact, many of the core values and ideals of the founding fathers are documented on the dollar, in plain view for all to see. Anyone with a buck holds the symbolic key to America in his pocket.

The front of the dollar bill is printed in black ink. It pictures George Washington, the first U.S. president, and carries the seal of the U.S. Department of the Treasury. Inside the green seal are scales representing a balanced budget. In the middle of the seal is a carpenter's square, a precision tool used for an even cut, and below it is the key to the U.S. Treasury. The back of the dollar bill is dominated by the two faces of the Great Seal of the United States. The Great Seal was commissioned by the delegates of the First Continental Congress on July 4, 1776, just a few hours after adopting the Declaration of Independence. The delegates, who believed that an emblem and national coat of arms for the new nation would underscore its authority, sovereignty, and idealism, entrusted Benjamin Franklin, Thomas Jefferson, and John Adams to devise a suitable design. It took four years and several iterations of the original committee to get the design done and another two years to have it approved. The final version, which combined elements of all previous designs, was approved by Congress on June 20, 1782. The same day, Charles Thomson, secretary of the Congress, submitted a blazon, or list of key elements, and a written companion report, "Remarks and Explanation."[2]

The obverse, or front side, of the Great Seal is used on official documents to authenticate the signature of the president and appears on national proclamations, warrants, and treaties. The right side of the one-dollar bill shows a bald eagle grasping a bundle of arrows in its left talon and an olive branch in the other. The bald eagle is crownless, signifying the colonies' hard-won independence from the British throne and an ingrained distaste for monarchs. It grasps the arrows of war, but its beak faces the olive branch. A scroll in its beak reads "E Pluribus Unum," or "Out of Many, One." Thirteen, a number of transformation and rebirth, recurs throughout the Great Seal: there are thirteen stars above the eagle's head, thirteen arrows in its left talon. In the official description of the seal, the thirteen vertical stripes on the eagle's shield "represent the several states all joined in one solid compact entire, supporting a chief, which unites the whole & represents Congress. The motto alludes to this union."[3]

The reverse, or back, of the Great Seal displays a pyramid with thirteen steps. "If you look behind that pyramid, you see a desert," noted the mythologist Joseph Campbell. "The desert, the tumult in Europe, wars and wars and wars—we have pulled ourselves out of it and created a state in the name of reason, not in the name of power, and out of that will come the flowerings of the new life. That's the sense of that part of the pyramid." The pyramid's face is lighted, but the western side is dark—the rest of the continent at the time was still unexplored, an unknown yet to be discovered. The pyramid, a symbol of duration and everlasting life dating back to the ancient Egyptians, and echoed by the ceremonial temples of the Aztecs and Mayas, is uncapped. On the final design of the Great Seal, it is described as "a pyramid unfinished." Above the pyramid's zenith floats the eye of providence and the Latin words *Annuit Coeptis*: "It [providence] looks favorably on our undertakings"; below it, a scroll displays the words *Novus Ordo Seclorum*, announcing a "New Order of the Ages." At the base of the pyramid are the Roman numerals for 1776, the year of American independence.[4]

Franklin and Jefferson had both been influenced by the philosophers of the Enlightenment, including John Locke, who argued that human beings had "natural rights" to life, liberty, and property. Franklin and Jefferson were also influenced by Thomas Paine's pamphlet *Common Sense*, in which he laid a rationale for the colonies' break with England and asserted, "The cause of America is in a great measure the cause of all mankind."[5] In his response to a pamphlet written by John Pemberton on behalf of the Quaker community and in opposition to armed rebellion, Paine defends religious tolerance and the separation of church and state: "Sincerely wishing, that as men and christians, ye may always fully and uninterruptedly enjoy every civil and religious right; and be, in your turn, the means of securing it to others; but that the example which ye have unwisely set, of mingling religion with politics, may be disavowed and reprobated by every inhabitant of America."

Campbell explains why the founding fathers' definition of providence in the Great Seal was not referring to God in the strictly Christian sense. "This is the first nation in the world that was ever established on the basis of reason instead of simply warfare," Campbell writes. "These were eighteenth-century deists, these gentlemen. Over here we read, 'In God We Trust.' But that is not the god of the Bible. They did not think the mind of man was cut off from God. The mind of man, cleansed of secondary and merely temporal concerns, beholds with the radiance of a cleansed mirror a reflection of the rational mind of God. Reason puts you in touch with God. Consequently, for these men, there is no special revelation anywhere, and none is needed, because the mind of man cleared of its fallibilities is sufficiently capable of the knowledge of God. All people in the world are thus capable because all people in the world are capable of reason. All men are capable of reason. That is the fundamental principle of democracy."[6]

The First Amendment holds that "Congress shall make no law respecting an establishment of religion, or prohibiting the free exercise thereof" not because it's the morally correct thing to do, but because freedom of worship is necessary for democracy to function. In other words, it is not Christianity per se that provides the philosophical foundation of American democracy, but a recognition that all men—regardless of the flavor of their faith—are capable of reason and, by extension, are prepared and willing to respect the rights and opinions of others as equal to their own. The motto "One nation under God," in this context, signals that all men are blessed equally by the power of reason and are thus able to share the responsibilities and rewards of democracy, regardless of their specific religious affiliations. It is therefore rather fitting that the symbols of the American social contract would appear on the currency that defines and drives the engines of the American economy, engines that perform best when the largest possible number of consumers are working, buying, and spending, regardless of their ethnic or religious background.

The decision to put the Great Seal on the dollar bill was made by President Franklin Delano Roosevelt in 1935. The seal was brought to Roosevelt's attention by then secretary of agriculture and future vice president Henry A. Wallace, who surmised correctly that Roosevelt would be intrigued by the seal's implication that the United States was a nation still in the process of being completed, a nation that was continually being redefined by new immigrants, cultures, and races—all of them created equally in God's own image. Roosevelt, Wallace later recalled, "looked at the colored reproduction of the Seal and was first struck by the representation of the 'All Seeing Eye,' a Masonic representation of the Great Architect of the Universe. Next he was impressed with the idea that the foundation for the new order of the ages had been laid in 1776 but that it would be completed only under the eye of the Great Architect. Roosevelt like myself was a 32nd degree Mason. He suggested that the Seal be put on the dollar bill rather than a coin and took the matter up with the Secretary of the Treasury."[7]

In an Armistice Day address at the Tomb of the Unknown Soldier on November 11, 1940, Roosevelt referred to the Great Seal and the significance of "A New Order of the Ages," which he interpreted as an evolution of civilization culminating in an enlightened era of freedom and equality for all mankind. At a time when Fascism and Communism were both vying for control of the world, he saw the role of the United States as one of "spreading the gospel" of democracy and protecting weaker nations from tyranny and expansionist empires. Said Roosevelt: "We, alive today—not in the existent democracies alone, but also among the populations of the smaller nations already overrun—are thinking in the larger terms of the maintenance of the 'New Order' to which we have been accustomed."[8]

The idea of the United States as an unfinished nation was grounded in the founding fathers' conviction that democracy was a by-product of the evolution of human civilization and therefore part of a process that would necessarily continue ad infinitum. The signing of the Declaration of Independence signaled not the end—but the beginning of the American experiment; democracy and America would evolve together, laying the foundation for a new society in which all men are "endowed by their Creator with certain unalienable Rights, that among these are Life, Liberty and the pursuit of Happiness." A society seeded with these principles, the signers reasoned, would ensure the success of democracy. "A generation that commences a revolution rarely completes it," Thomas Jefferson wrote in a letter to John Adams in 1823.

The cause of American progress and transformation would be taken up again more than thirty years later by Walt Whitman, considered by many to be the first truly American poet. "America, having duly conceived, bears out of herself offspring of her own to do the workmanship wanted," he wrote in a letter to Ralph Waldo Emerson, which was included in the 1856 edition of *Leaves of Grass*. Whitman understood that America's genius and true promise lay in its future generations, its ability to constantly reinvent itself. Without growth, without change, the United States would lose its soul and, in a sense, cease to exist. "The architects of These States laid down their foundations, and passed to further spheres," he wrote. "What they laid is a work done, as much more remains. Now are needed other architects, whose duty is not less difficult. Each age forever needs architects. America is not finished, perhaps never will be; now America is a divine true sketch."

The "other architects" whom Whitman refers to were by definition a far cry from the Anglocentric revolutionaries who laid the first foundation of U.S. democracy. In fact, Whitman, who was probably gay or bisexual and spent his whole life exploring and celebrating artistic diversity, was one of the first American multiculturalists. Born near Huntington, Long Island, to Quaker parents, he spent his early years as a journalist and worked for several newspapers in Long Island and New York City, including the *Brooklyn Eagle*. As a newspaperman in New York, during the mid-nineteenth century, Whitman would have been exposed to the eclectic waves of immigrants arriving on American shores. In 1855, Whitman self-published his first edition of *Leaves of Grass* and mailed a copy to the noted philosopher and transcendentalist Ralph Waldo Emerson, whose praise of Whitman launched his career. Ten years earlier, Emerson had heralded America's ethnically diverse social tapestry, which had expanded to include "Irish, Germans, Swedes, Poles and Cossacks, and all the European tribes" and also "of the Africans, and of the Polynesians," all of whom were coming together in the creation of "a new race, a new religion, a new state, a new literature, which will be as vigorous as the new Europe which came out of the smelting pot of the Dark Ages."

Whitman would take up that theme in his own exuberant prose, adding a dimension of patriotic fervor. The new Americans, he ardently believed, were not just enriching the United States with their energy and spirit, but helping to forge an entirely new culture, a supremely American expression that was unlike anything that had existed before. "These States, receivers of the stamina of past ages and lands, initiate the outlines of repayment a thousand fold," he wrote. "They fetch the American great masters, waited for by old worlds and new, who accept evil as well as good, ignorance as well as erudition, black as soon as white, foreign-born materials as well as home-born, reject none, for discrepancies into range, surround the whole, concentrate them on present periods and places, show the application to each and any one's body and soul, and show the true use of precedents. Always America will be agitated and turbulent. This day it is taking shape, not to be less so, but to be more so, stormily, capriciously, on native principles, with such vast proportion of parts!"

Whitman, who was a great admirer of Abraham Lincoln, became known not just as a groundbreaking writer of free verse, but also as an egalitarian free thinker and advocate of social tolerance. His poetry took its cadence from nature, the "thought-rhythms" of Old Testament poetry, and sacred Indian texts like the Bhagavad Gita. After the Civil War, he became somewhat disillusioned by what he saw as the increasing materialism of an America on the cusp of the Industrial Revolution, yet he never gave up hope that humanist ideals would triumph over insouciance and greed.[9]

Just as the vision of the United States as an egalitarian democratic community—not a "melting pot" in which immigrants lost their ethnicity and became second-class imitations of Anglocentric whites, but the multi-hued "new race" of Emerson and Whitman—has existed almost since its inception, so has the fear that America might lose its moral compass, that its very success and wealth could corrupt it. Throughout its history, the United States has seesawed between idealism and pragmatism, myopia and farsightedness, ruthless self-interest and courageous altruism. As a result, the world has always regarded us with ambivalence, an uneasy mix of admiration and fear that can be as unsettling to our allies as it is to our enemies.

In the dark, early dawn of the twenty-first century, America's fortitude and forbearance—and its ability to project and embody democratic institutions and ideals—are once again being tested. Throughout much of the world, the image of the United States as defender of freedom and liberty has been replaced by a perception of America as an arrogant and ruthless bully. Even America's allies have begun to see it as an imperialist empire willing to wield its unmatched power to pursue its interests without respect or regard for the concerns or cooperation of the international community.

A 2003 poll of fifteen thousand respondents in twenty countries conducted by the nonpartisan Pew Research Center found a widening rift between the United States and members of the transatlantic alliance and a growing mistrust of the United States by many formerly friendly nations.

Some of the most dramatic changes were in non-Arab Muslim countries such as Turkey, where unfavorable views of the United States had risen to 83 percent from 55 percent the previous year, and Indonesia, where a 75 percent favorable opinion in 2000 had deteriorated to an 83 percent unfavorable view. Other countries in which favorable views of the United States between 2000 and 2003 slipped included Brazil (from 56 percent to 34 percent), Morocco (77 percent to 27 percent), and South Korea (58 percent to 46 percent). The Pew poll also saw a significant loss of faith in two international institutions—NATO and the United Nations—that had symbolized stability and cooperation in the post–World War II era. A survey conducted by *The New York Times* three months later found that many of the anti-American feelings held in other nations were centered on George W. Bush, whom they regarded "at best, as an ineffective spokesman for American interests and, at worst, as a gun-slinging cowboy knocking over international treaties and bent on controlling the world's oil, if not the entire world." In October 2003, a panel appointed by the Bush administration found that "hostility toward America has reached shocking levels" among Arabs and Muslims around the world, concluding: "What is required is not merely tactical adaptation but strategic, and radical, transformation" in how U.S. policies are communicated to other countries.

On the home front, meanwhile, a lack of ethnic diversity within the FBI was cited as a contributing factor in the failure of U.S. intelligence agencies to anticipate the 9/11 attacks. During his testimony to Congress in 2000, former FBI director Louis Freeh said that the FBI lacked the foreign language expertise to translate "conversations and documents" it obtained during investigations. During prosecution of individuals charged in the 1993 World Trade Center bombing, the FBI discovered that elements of the plot had been outlined in Arab-language documents gathered during its investigation into the murder of Rabbi Meir Kahane in 1990. "Ethnocentrism is one of the agency's biggest faults," said Emanuel Johnson, a former FBI agent. "Everything is judged by a white-male mentality." [10]

At the same time, the Patriot Act, a piece of legislation granting law enforcement agencies expanded powers, and the Department of Homeland Security, a new cabinet-level agency charged with countering terrorism on U.S. soil, were alarming civil rights organizations and alienating immigrants, Arab Americans, and other ethnic groups that found themselves under new scrutiny as potential terrorist agents. The charges of insensitive and possibly illegal actions by the Immigration and Naturalization Service ranged from accusations of gross violations of human rights to petty bureaucratic harassments. Not only had U.S. visas become much harder to get, but compulsory registration requirements and other new regulations made it difficult for immigrants to work in the United States without living in constant fear of arrest or deportation. Even those who supported the U.S. invasion of Iraq as necessary and justified are openly worried about the human and financial price tag of keeping the peace and the international erosion of America's moral authority.

Americans and their allies *should* be concerned—and the reasons are pragmatic and economic. All the political huffing and puffing about not bowing to world opinion can't change the fact that America's security and prosperity are tied to our ability to work and trade in friendly, stable international markets. There are other ways in which the international perception of aggressive U.S. unilateralism runs against America's own self-interests: the prosperity and strength of the United States has always depended on its ability to attract the best and the brightest from all over the world. American preeminence in such disparate fields as filmmaking, digital technology, bioengineering, molecular science, physics, robotics, pharmacology, pop music, and architecture owes an enormous debt to foreign-born immigrants. The list ranges from Albert Einstein (Germany) and An Wang of Wang Laboratories (Korea) to Google cofounder Sergey Brin (Russia), and Yahoo!'s Jerry Yang (Taiwan). Thousands of other scientists, inventors, artists, and entrepreneurs came to the United States because they believed in what it stood for and where it was going. One can hardly imagine an America without the likes of former secretaries of state Madeleine Albright (Czechoslovakia) and Henry Kissinger (Germany), author Isabel Allende (Chile), dancer Mikhail Baryshnikov (Russia), composer Irving Berlin (Russia), TV news anchor Peter Jennings (Canada), director Mike Nichols (Germany), architect I. M. Pei (China), musician Carlos Santana (Mexico), baseball player Sammy Sosa (Dominican Republic), and *The Sound of Music*'s Von Trapp family (Austria). One imagines a twist on the Christmas classic *It's a Wonderful Life,* in which America looks back on its past without the presence of immigrants, a sad scenario that wouldn't even exist in such a fantasy, since the film's director, Frank Capra, himself immigrated to the United States from Italy.

These people were drawn to the image of an America that championed the rights of the oppressed and the powerless, a nation that embraced newcomers and encouraged innovation and creativity. America is still the world's most powerful and influential nation—the place where the best of the world's best come to prove themselves But the swaggering, gun-toting America of George W. Bush has become a scary place to the young artists, scientists, scholars, engineers, and entrepreneurs who will discover, design, and build the transformative technologies and industries of the future. If anything, there is evidence that the "brain drain" that other countries used to complain about as their best minds gravitated to the United States is in danger of reversing its direction.

In an age when the world's tallest buildings are in Kuala Lumpur and the *Lord of the Rings* film series was photographed and produced by a company in New Zealand, the United States is no longer the only game in town. The fast-growing economies of India and China, which have a combined total of about 2.2 billion people, or about a third of the world's total population, are providing homegrown options for many who traditionally assumed life was better in America. Chinese and Indian workers are showing a newfound reluctance to brave what they see as an increasingly hostile environment in the United States for jobs that they can now find closer to home. At the same time, high-speed communication and data-transferring techniques are making it easier for foreigners to work for U.S. companies without ever leaving home.

The new dynamics of the international labor market are giving even proponents of globalization pause. At the 2004 annual meeting of the World Economic Forum in Davos, Switzerland, business, government, and academic leaders from around the world expressed concern that the new global economy may not produce as many high-paying jobs in rich countries as once believed. For decades, the argument for globalization was based on the assumption that lower-paying manufacturing jobs lost to countries where wages were lower would be replaced by higher-paying jobs that required education and skills that less-developed nations couldn't provide. The net gain for developed countries was even higher, since boosting the economies of less-developed nations would grow new markets for the services and markets of richer nations. That model is starting to show cracks. IBM, for example, recently announced plans to shift three thousand high-paying programming jobs from the United States to China, India, and Brazil.

Outsourcing, which transfers skilled service and technology jobs to developing countries, and a rising class of educated workers in nondeveloped nations are making it harder than expected to replace high-paying jobs in the developed economies of the United States and Europe. As manufacturing and service jobs shift to overseas markets, defensive tariffs may appease affected constituencies but only postpone the pain. The longer-term solution, most economists agree, is for developed countries like the United States to "move up the development chain" by developing the innovative new technologies and services of the future that will in turn spark and drive new markets. In a competitive global marketplace, that means continuing to attract and keep the best talent from around the world—reaching out, in effect, to an international "creative class."

In an article in the *Washington Monthly*, Richard Florida warns that the United States is slipping into a "creative class war" in which government policy is undermining America's ability to compete by alienating the people it now needs more than ever. "In the 1990s, the federal government focused on expanding America's human capital and interconnectedness to the world—crafting international trade agreements, investing in cutting-edge R&D, subsidizing higher education and public access to the Internet, and encouraging immigration," Florida writes. "But in the last three years, the government's attention and resources have shifted to older sectors of the economy, with tariff protection and subsidies to extractive industries. Meanwhile, Washington has stunned scientists across the world with its disregard for consensus scientific views when those views conflict with the interests of favored sectors (as has been the case with the issue of global climate change). Most of all, in the wake of 9/11, Washington has inspired the fury of the world, especially of its educated classes, with its my-way-or-the-highway foreign policy. In effect, for the first time in our history, we're saying to highly mobile and very finicky global talent, 'You don't belong here.' "[11]

Restrictive immigration policies are only adding to the problem. Florida points out that between 2001 and 2002, the number of visas issued to immigrants for work in science and technology dropped 55 percent, from 166,000 to 74,000. Even more disturbing is the fact that a significant portion of the decrease was due to a drop in applications. Florida has found that the recent tendency of the United States to ignore or dismiss widely held views and accords on global warming and other issues has undermined America's credibility with the international scientific community, which has in turn damaged its reputation as a leader in research and development. "In the post-1990s global economy, America must aggressively compete with other developed countries for the international talent that can spur new industries and new jobs," Florida contends. "By thumbing our nose at the world and dismissing the consensus views of the scientific community, we are scaring off that talent and sending it to our competitors."[12]

The international creative class is attracted to many of the same things as their American-born counterparts: cultural diversity, social tolerance, an unfettered opportunity for personal, and professional growth. They are also looking for familiar comforts of their home country. If they can't find them, they create them, American-style. James Chih-Cheng Chen, a Taiwanese immigrant who moved to Los Angeles in 1971, was visiting Las Vegas with a friend's mother when he realized the gambling mecca had no Chinatown. In 1990, Chen invested $10 million of his own money on the bet that Asians were ready for a shopping center that spoke to their cultural needs. He was right. Today, Chinatown Plaza is the epicenter of a booming Asian American community that includes residential homes and a burst of commercial development, including a hair salon, jeweler, florist, pharmacy, and bookstore and the editorial offices of the *Las Vegas Chinese Daily News.* The new neighborhood is attracting other investors and more immigrants, who become assimilated themselves as they join the rising economic cycle.[13]

The increasing interdependence between local demographics and global economics is changing the way money moves and putting a multicultural premium on international immigration and trade. Since the middle of the last century, the number of immigrants has nearly doubled to 175 million, or almost 3 percent of the global population.[14] About 12 percent of the U.S. population is foreign-born, a segment that is growing 6.5 times faster than their native-born counterparts. Yet the long-term upside is enormous, especially for a multicultural state like California. For every 1 percent increase in the number of first-generation immigrants from a given country, California exports to their ancestral home rise nearly .5 percent. As America's ethnic communities continue to multiply and grow, the economic dividends of diversity will become exponential.[15]

Due to the recession in the United States during the early 2000s, as well as tighter visa requirements, the immigrant stream from Latin America has started spilling over into Europe. The legal and illegal Latino immigrant population on the continent is projected to reach 3 million in 2003. Lured by jobs, less stringent visa requirements, and linguistic ties, Latinos are the fastest-growing immigrant group in Italy, Switzerland, Spain, and Britain. In Switzerland, nearly 1 million residents now speak Spanish, which is close to passing Italian as the country's third-most-spoken language, after German and French. According to Washington's Inter-American Development Bank, cash remittances from Europe to Latin America doubled between 2000 and 2002, to $2 billion annually. By 2003, Spain was receiving more than two hundred thousand Latin immigrants per year, up from less than fifty thousand in 1985. Spain, which has elaborate economic and cultural ties with its former colonies, has long granted special status to immigrants from Latin America, who are eligible to become Spanish citizens after twenty-four months of residency.

The United States, of course, remains the prime destination of Latin American immigrants, who are a kind of human glue in the increasingly bonded economies of the Western Hemisphere. Since the signing of NAFTA, trade between the United States and Mexico alone has risen to more than $1.7 billion a day. Mexico's share of total U.S. imports has doubled to 12 percent, making it America's second largest trading partner. The recognition that Latin America is a key to future U.S. economic growth was behind the push for a Free Trade Area of the Americas (FTAA) extending from Canada to Tierra del Fuego. Yet the days when Washington could dictate trade terms to its Latin neighbors have given way to a climate of guarded reciprocity. Organized resistance by trade unions in the United States and Latin countries, immigration issues, regional security pacts, and international relations have joined goods and services as bargaining chips in a high-stakes poker game where ad hoc alliances and unlikely coalitions are rewriting the rules of engagement.

The breakdown of World Trade Organization talks in Cancún, Mexico, in 2003 was further evidence that the old paradigm of "rich" (developed) countries and "poor" (underdeveloped) countries no longer describes the global neighborhood. Nor does geography determine destiny. The Central American Free Trade Agreement, or CAFTA, a deal with four Central American countries concluded by the Bush administration in late 2003, failed to include Costa Rica, which boasts Central America's largest economy and highest education levels. Ad hoc trading blocs, like the Group of 20+, a consortium of not-so-poor, large, resource-rich countries that includes Brazil and India, are reaching across oceans and languages to bypass the leading industrial powers in favor of mutually beneficial biateral arrangements. Trade has itself become culturally and ethnically diverse—a process requiring a higher level of cross-cultural cooperation and understanding in the interests of mutual gain.

But the ultimate upside of international trade, which makes up about one-quarter of the U.S. economy and continues to grow, goes far beyond obvious economic interest. At the 2003 conference on NAFTA and the future of regional trade agreements, Myles Frechette, a former U.S. ambassador to Colombia and president and CEO of the Council of the Americas, underscored the collateral benefits of trade with Latin American nations, pointing out that governments "attempt to monitor and control the flow of people and goods and information, while business try to move more people, more goods and more information in less and less time." He also noted that "increased trade is critical in promoting democracy and the rule of law abroad, while generating the wealth that promotes and underwrites reforms. As such, trade expansion is a national security imperative for each of our countries."

The traditional one-way perspective on how trade can further the political and cultural goals of the United States in other countries, however, is giving way to a far more complex relationship of give-and-take. The delicate and politically charged trade-off of tariffs and subsidies, immigration and transnational marketing, is affecting the United States even as it uses its economic clout to pursue other agendas. The plight of Mexican yam farmers can affect America's ability to protect itself from terrorist attacks, just as Wal-Mart's treatment of undocumented workers in the United States can affect its expansion into lucrative Latin American markets. In the postethnic economic order, the transfer of goods and services and the flow of human and intellectual capital are inextricably bound, and the transnational, multicultural markets of the twenty-first century are indistinguishable from America's own economic destiny.

Patriot Dreams

The United States is at a critical crossroads. It can continue to pursue an agenda that turns the world against it and alienates those who will define and drive the economy of the twenty-first century, or it can learn from the symbols on the dollar bill and usher in a new age of American strength and leadership. The American multicultural consumer is a microcosm of—and a bridge to—the emerging global economy. The true value of the dollar is not in what it can buy, but in its message that America's wealth lies in the energy and diversity of its people.

Writing in 1961, a time when the United States was engaged in a global struggle with the Soviet Union and Communism, the Mexican poet and essayist Octavio Paz observed:

> I think that every time a society finds itself in crisis it instinctively turns its eyes toward its origins and looks there for a sign. Colonial American society was a free, egalitarian, but exclusive society. Faithful to its origins, in its domestic and foreign policies alike, the United States has always ignored the "others." Today, the United States faces very powerful enemies, but the mortal danger comes from within: not from Moscow but from the mixture of arrogance and opportunism, blindness and short-term Machiavellianism, volubility

and stubbornness that has characterized its foreign policies during recent years and which reminds us in an odd way of the Athenian state
in its quarrel with Sparta. To conquer its enemies, the United States
must first conquer itself—return to its origins. Not to repeat them but
to rectify them: the "others"—the minorities inside as well as the marginal countries and nations outside—do exist. Not only do we "others" make up the majority of the human race, but also each marginal
society, poor though it may be, represents a unique and precious vision of mankind. If the United States is to recover fortitude and lucid-
ity, it must recover itself, and to recover itself it must recover the
"others"—the outcasts of the Western World.[16]

More than forty years later, Paz's words are uncannily relevant. The
United States is again engaged in a global struggle that is as much ideological and philosophical as it is military and economic. Despite its unprecedented power, it feels naked and vulnerable to an enemy that lives in the
shadows and feeds off of the resentment and ignorance bred by inequity
and marginalization. Just as it was in the sixties, battles will be fought with
bombs and guns, but the war will be won only by waging an effective
peace, which also means unleashing America's most powerful weapon: the
egalitarian vision of a just and decent society where all men and women,
regardless of race, religion, or color, can thrive and prosper.

America will never be safe or secure until it is again admired and respected for its restraint and prudence, instead of feared for its military and
economic might. Now as then, the key to America's legitimacy and security lies in its sincerity as a bastion—not a truncheon—of liberty and as
"a golden door" for "the huddled masses yearning to breathe free." Now
as then, America is a nation made rich by the cultural and economic
contributions of immigrants and ethnic minorities, and one whose financial future is dependent on the hard work and entrepreneurial zeal of its
breathtakingly diverse population.

The architects of the new America are both native and immigrant,
local and global. The international creative class and its domestic counterparts are becoming mirror images of each other; they are complementary
expressions of the same demographic and cultural forces, and they are

both critical components of America's social and economic future. As their interests and priorities intersect and overlap, they will steer ever larger portions of the global economy. The ballooning buying power of America's ethnic marketplace is merely the tip of the iceberg; below the surface, tectonic shifts are laying the groundwork of the next economic revolution, the seeds of which have already been planted. As the new hybrid cultures of the United States achieve critical mass, the margins will move to the center of American life, which, just as in decades and centuries past, will itself become transformed. The multicultural consumer is not limited to a single race or minority group, nor is any race or minority group excluded; the choosing and merging of identities and affiliations is an ongoing process that will continually redefine the mainstream and, by extension, what it means to be an American.

10. Creative Consumption

The New Mainstream is both local and global, geared to the future yet rooted in the past. Multicultural consumers are influenced by how they see others, but even more by how they see themselves. Self-image—and the way they define that image—determines what people choose as careers, where they live, whom they vote for, what kind of car they drive, where they shop, eat, and vacation. Consumers gravitate to brands, products, and activities that reinforce their established sense of self or allow them to test-drive a new persona. At a time when identity is becoming recognized as a key driver of consumer behavior, understanding how people see themselves—and the myriad new ways in which they can do it—is imperative for corporations, organizations, and institutions. Multicultural consumers are the key to the new American economy because their perception of the world is what the world has already become. And any company or entrepreneur who can see the world through their eyes is getting a glimpse of the future.

Consumer profiling is a booming business, serving industries as diverse as airlines, health clinics, Web sites, publishers, retailers, car manufacturers, food and beverage companies, and political parties. People's core beliefs are the psychic pillars of their personalities, the filter through which they perceive reality and respond to the world around them. It's no longer enough to know who people think they are; we need to understand who they want to be. In the consumer democracy of the New Mainstream, products and services that fail to connect emotionally with their customers will fall by the wayside. New Mainstreamers seek brands, products, and services that affirm their sense of self-worth and well-being and validate their personal definition of the American dream. It is a dream that celebrates cultural diversity, corporate accountability, and social responsibility.

But what about attitudes and stereotypes of which they are not even aware? What if it were possible to measure the unconscious biases regarding race, culture, and society that guide our behavior? What if Americans harbored prejudicial attitudes that clashed with their conscious beliefs? What if politicians who pledged to uphold the egalitarian ideals of America could be scientifically shown to have an implicit bias against them? And what would be the implications for businesses, social institutions, civic organizations, and the future of American democracy?

During the late 1990s, psychologists Mahzarin Banaji, from Harvard University, and Anthony Greenwald, from the University of Washington at Seattle, began working on a groundbreaking technique to provide answers to those questions. In their Implicit Attitude Test, or IAT, subjects are asked to click on two sets of images (for instance, the picture of a white person's face and the word *good* or a black person's face and the word *bad*). Then the paired sets are switched (for example, white and *bad*, black and *good*). By measuring the difference in time it takes a test subject to click on the different pairings, a pattern of unconscious, or "implicit," bias, can be discerned. Since then, the IAT has been used to show how implicit bias affects our judgment of others based on factors like race, sex, and age, irrespective of our conscious or "explicit" attitudes and beliefs.

In a series of studies titled "American = White?" conducted with Thierry Devos from San Diego State University, Banaji investigated the degree of association between white, Asian, and African Americans and the concept "American." "We asked, What is it that makes somebody an

American?" Banaji recalls. "And there are three different factors that come out, but mostly it's the civil component that people believe is important to be an American. Not so much whether you hold a passport, but if you abide by a certain set of principles that make up what people call the American creed."

In one experiment, students at Yale University were shown a set of images that symbolized "America" (the U.S. flag, the one-dollar bill, a bald eagle, Mt. Rushmore, and so forth) and another set of images that represented foreign nationalities (a Ukrainian bill, the Flemish lion, a twenty-cent Swiss coin, and so on). Students were then asked to pair both sets with pictures of white, Asian, and African American faces. The results showed that despite the respondents' explicit "allegiance to universalistic values, especially equality," both Asians and African Americans were "less associated with the national category 'American' " than were white Americans. Even though images of African American Olympic athletes were explicitly regarded as "more American" than whites, the implicit bias revealed the contrary. And while Asians shared the American = white bias, African Americans did not. "Importantly, the American = White association predicted the strength of national identity for White Americans: the more they personally identified with being American, the more they excluded Asians from the category," the authors concluded. "Together, these studies provide the first evidence that to be American is implicitly synonymous with being White."

Banaji and her colleagues have found similar implicit attitudes regarding gender and age, suggesting that most people go through life with a kind of parallax view of the world—unaware of the subconscious reactions they are having to literally everything around them. But while implicit biases are held deep in the primordial part of the brain, they are not etched in stone. Banaji has gathered evidence that a person's IAT can be altered by adjusting environmental factors, such as the race, age, or gender of the person administering the test, or simply by making people aware of their unconscious attitudes and how it might be affecting their behavior.

"What I see to be the central message of our work is that there are constraints in the way we see things that lead us to do harm without us knowing it," Banaji says. "If we know this, then people of goodwill should behave differently. And both groups need to know this: those who seemingly are harmed and those who are harmed, because everyone is doing it and being harmed by it. It's just disproportionate to some groups of people as opposed to others. If you take that message, then there are certain things it applies to very readily."

The possibility of measuring other types of implicit biases—including those that might be found in industries like health care, law enforcement, and education—are intriguing to Banaji, not least because of the IAT's ability to raise awareness among those entrusted with delivering crucial services and care to the public. Meanwhile, the applications of the IAT as a marketing tool are equally profound—and could result in a new understanding of how people subconsciously react to not just products and messages, but also particular symbols, words, colors, and sounds. One merchandiser has already used the IAT to help it decide which of its products should be offered to customers online and which should be available only in stores. The payoffs included greater processing efficiency, fewer returns, and better shopper satisfaction. It's a no-brainer, as it were, to imagine how the IAT could be used to discern cultural biases that are subconsciously guiding the purchasing decisions of, say, Hispanic women with a Cuban heritage versus a Korean man in New York or a black teenager in Chicago.

But the IAT's ultimate application may be its ability to reveal an individual's subconscious feelings about social codes of conduct and other psychological filters that define their sense of self. "It would be interesting to develop implicit measures on a concept like Freedom," Banaji notes. She is also curious about the possible ways in which implicit biases might change over time as the nation's population becomes increasingly multiethnic. "One of the questions that is interesting to me in these tests is the power of numerical majorities," she says. "That is to say, fifty years from now, will whites still control more of the wealth proportionately than other groups?"

And, perhaps more important, what in fifty years will be the definition of "white"? Banaji speculates that a coalition of Caucasian ethnic groups, including lighter-skinned Latinos, will most likely continue to dominate the nation's social and economic agenda for decades to come. "I think even if the U.S. is half white and non-white, the non-white groups are still seen as very distinct from each other, Asians from Mexicans and blacks, whereas among whites, the differences between Irish, German and Italian are gone, and so they are still perceived as a majority because they are one, and we are many different ones," says Banaji. "That's an interesting thing in itself, that the ring doesn't get drawn in a certain way around these different brown groups."

That scenario assumes, of course, that ethnicity will continue to be the defining factor that delineates the New Mainstream from the old margins. And for at least some African Americans, race may continue to shape social attitudes and identity for generations to come. Yet the current blurring of brown and white, along with the acculturating effects of media and consumer marketing, suggest a much more complex picture. In its 2003 MONITOR Multicultural Marketing Study, Yankelovich found that when asked if it was "cool" to be part of their own ethnicity or race, 91 percent of Hispanics, 87 percent of African Americans, and 40 percent of non-Hispanic whites agreed. The study also found that more than half of African Americans and Hispanics and about 40 percent of non-Hispanic whites are spending most of their leisure time with people from varied ethnic and racial backgrounds. What this means is that the old mainstream perception that anyone who celebrates their own culture is by definition biased against other cultures is giving way to a more fluid social ethos characterized by mutual cultural appreciation and respect.[1]

In fact, there are signs that ethnicity as a sociopolitical movement may be fading. A 2002 analysis of U.S. census data showed that when respondents were asked to identify their "ancestry or ethnic origin" on question ten of the 2000 long form, 20 million people identifies themselves as "American," a 54 percent increase from 1990. The "American" response, which was spread evenly across income, education, or other demographic factors, is seen by some demographers as a sign that the assertion of ethnic identity that dominated the latter half of the century has finally run its course. The reasons behind the so-called unhyphenating of America include accelerating intermarriage between various ethnic groups, an aging of the immigrant population, and a general feeling that "now that people's ethnicity is established and acknowledged, we can go on to identify with a larger cultural fabric."[2]

But if neither race nor ethnicity is the glue that ultimately holds America together, what is the source of its social cohesion? And how does that trend jibe with the growing awareness and power of ethnic consumers? Time and again, in numerous national polls, nine out of ten Americans describe themselves as "patriotic," "proud," or "very proud" to be an American. But when they are asked to express their nationalism in specific social or political terms, it turns out that there are many kinds of patriots with contradictory images of the country they all love.

In *The American Dream*, Jim Cullen provides a clue by defining the title of his book as "Life, liberty, and as much entertainment as digitally possible." It would probably be accurate to add: "and as many consumer markets as socially feasible." The dream of America as a place of new beginnings, religious freedom, and a land where it was possible for one's children to have a better life than one's own dates back to the Pilgrims. But there are other, equally compelling and indelible dreams: the dream of racial equality and free speech, the dream of upward mobility, the dream of the good life. All of these dreams, at various times for various people, have been equally true and valid. "The American Dream would have no drama or mystique if it were a self-evident falsehood or a scientifically demonstrable principle," Cullen writes. "Ambiguity is the very source of its mythic power, nowhere more so than among those striving for, but unsure whether they will reach, their goals."[3]

The genius of the American dream, much like that of the Declaration of Independence that spawned it, lies in its very elasticity and nebulousness, its ability to be simultaneously specific and vague, universal and individual, to stretch in ways that address the needs and social mores of any given era. "If there is one constant in the Declaration of Independence, it lies in the way no version of the status quo is ever completely acceptable," Cullen writes. "It provides us with often imperceptibly shifting standards by which we measure success but simultaneously calls attention to the gap between what is and what we believe should be, a gap that defines our national experience. A piece of wishful thinking composed in haste, the Declaration was born and lives under the charter of the American Dream. It constitutes us."[4]

One of the great secrets of American democracy is that the very same market forces that allow immigrants to participate in the U.S. economy also help to make them American. More than language or nationality or race, capitalism assimilates immigrants and outsiders by turning them into consumers, which in turn gives them a stake in the evolving social order. What, after all, could be more thoroughly acculturating, more quintessentially American, than a day of shopping at Wal-Mart or Sears? In that sense, the bottom-line ballot of modern American democracy is the dollar, and in a multicultural economy voter turnout is always 100 percent. At the same time, the political ecology of democratic capitalism requires a baseline of social responsibility, if only to prevent unrest on a scale that could undermine the authority of the status quo. Chaos is unpredictable and expensive, which is why equal access to the pursuit of happiness is ultimately in everybody's interest.[5]

From the very beginning, Americans granted the same freedom to others that they would wish for themselves—albeit not always willingly and sometimes not without a fight—because the logic of their own desires demanded it. Americans, as a whole, will always allow others to share in their dreams because it is in their self-interest. The instinct to exclude will always succumb to the inclusive forces of commerce. The promise of profit will always trump social oppression because free enterprise thrives in an open, egalitarian economy. There is no single American dream; there are as many American dreams as there are dreamers to dream them. The freedom to make that dream our own, to fill it with our deepest desires and highest aspirations, is ultimately what binds all Americans and keeps us dreaming together.

Sound Effects

As New Mainstreamers continue their climb up the socioeconomic ladder, their ethnicity, nationality, or sexuality may matter less than how they feel about children, electronic media, and what kind of car they drive. By using powerful new computer programs to cross-index zip codes and other public records with demographic and other personal data, marketers are targeting customers by their habits and lifestyle choices, the neighborhoods they live in, and even their weakness for fast food. In the neomarketing slang of "geo-demographic segmentation," consumers are categorized under labels like "Young Digerati," "Cosmopolitans," "White Picket Fences," "Bohemian Mixers," "Upper Crusters," and "Urban Achievers." These categories cut across race and ethnicity, yet many of these psychographic groups are actually defined by their affinity for—or embodiment of—multicultural lifestyle choices.

New Mainstreamers are naturally drawn to ethnic accents in the music they listen to, the movies they see, and the books they read. As American audiences have become open to culturally diverse forms of entertainment, the medium itself is increasingly mixed. The 2004 Lincoln Center Festival in New York City featured a multimedia interpretation of three stories by Japanese writer Haruki Murakami, a 7-hour "spiritual journey" by Britain's Sir John Tavener that featured sounds made by Tibetan horns, Indian harmoniums, and Buddhist temple bowls, and "Transmetropolitan," a globally-hip video and sound set curated by Paul D. Miller, aka. "DJ Spooky," that incorporated performances by video artists Eclectic Method, South Asian pianist-composer Vijay Iyer, and African American author Colin Wilson. At Joe's Pub in New York City, the club's urban clientele reflects—and expects—an eclectic format that can range from Brazilian electro–bossa nova and South Asian–inflected jazz to Mexican techno and southern blues guitar—sometimes all in the same night. Bill Bragin, the club's musical director, books a diverse mix of artists that mirrors New York's multicultural population.

"Audiences are much more adventurous than a lot of people give them credit for," says Bragin, who also moonlights as a DJ under the name Acidophilus, as part of GlobeSonic, a DJ collective devoted to playing and promoting electronic world music. "I think what has happened is that audiences have come of age," Bragin says. "You've got artists coming from their own specific local traditions, and at the same time globalization, and the Internet, radio, all of that. People are listening to music from all over the world—from American pop, funk, and techno to Asian and European versions of the same. It's all part of the vocabulary, so they create these hybrids that are natural, because it's all part of the information. This has been happening for fifty years, but lately it has accelerated."

A few nights later at an East Village club called NuBlu, Bragin is bent over a CD turntable, cueing up a techno-samba-break-beat mix for a multiethnic crowd. Along with his DJ partners, Fabian Alsultany, who founded GlobeSonic in 2000, and Derek Beres, Bragin is part of an international network of DJs, musicians, cultural anthropologists, music critics, and industry executives who are passionately dedicated to the creation, promotion, and enjoyment of world music in all its myriad forms. In a couple of months, Bragin will present GlobalFEST, an ambitious showcase of world music organized in conjunction with the Association of Performing Arts Presenters (APAP), which represents 1,500 music, theater, and dance promoters who book acts at festivals, theaters, and colleges across the United States.

GlobalFEST is part of a growing movement toward world music, an umbrella term for international, folk, and new fusion forms that range from Eastern European Gypsy music to the Blind Boys from Alabama, a Christian country-blues roots outfit, to Malian singer Salif Keita, to Nortec and Kinky, Mexican techno-rock bands that fuse Mexican *norteño* and mariachi traditions with rock guitar, electronica, and house rhythms. At the same time, clubs and concert halls across the country are throbbing with a slew of new musical hybrids and transnational sounds, from Desis—or second-generation South Asian Indians—writhing to the bhangra-rap fusions to reggaeton, a fast-spreading mix of rap and Caribbean dance music that is popular among New York's Puerto Rican community. Nonminority hipsters looking for the next cool trend are seeking out the cutting-edge hybrids that are transforming the sound of mainstream American music, adding to an atmosphere of cross-cultural appreciation that transcends races, nationalities, and politics. As Latin American, South Asian, and other ethnic communities in the United States have grown, their numbers are attracting the attention of record labels, concert promoters, and even foreign governments seeking a bridge to America's lucrative and increasingly influential ethnic markets.

Hybrid music is the sound track of the New Mainstream, and it is changing not just what people buy and listen to, but also why. In Brooklyn, Polish Americans bob to polka-tinged rock at a dance hall called Warsaw, while in Manhattan, pan-ethnic nightcrawlers revel to Latin-tinged techno- and bhangra-house mixes at clubs like Taj, Lotus, and S.O.B.'s. In Los Angeles, Miami, Houston, Chicago, and dozens of other major U.S. cities, people can take tango, cha-cha, hip-hop, or belly-dancing lessons. They can munch on Spanish *tapas* while they listen to Afro-Cuban salsa, dance to a Ukrainian brass band, or watch *César and Rubén: A Musical Celebration of the Life and Work of César Chávez*, which features songs by Rubén Blades, Peter Gabriel, Carlos Santana, Enrique Iglesias, David Crosby, and Joni Mitchell. Rock and jazz bands routinely beef up their rhythm sections with Indian tabla drums, Latin congas, or both. Latin and Jewish elements merge alternative rock and rap in the music of the Hip Hop Hoodios, whose name is a twist on *judío*, the Spanish word for Jew. The West Coast band Bayu fuses world, Latin, Brazilian, and funk, while Caramelize reflects the ethnic mix of two Chicanos and two African American Jews who, in the words of their publicist, "write songs of social justice, scorched love affairs, and *abuelita*'s recipe for the perfect flan."

For the South Indian fusion percussionist Ravish Momin, redefining the relationship between American jazz and the South Asian rhythmic traditions of his native India not only has opened the door to other cultures, but has provided a key to his own cultural roots. He is proud of Indians who have had an impact in the cinema, such as Ismail Merchant, M. Night Shyamalan, and Gurinder Chada, and writers, such as Salman Rushdie and V. S. Naipaul, but he feels that most media images of Indians are still stereotypical. Nevertheless, he is optimistic about the popularity of rap-bhangra fusion among younger people and the rising acceptance and appreciation for Indian food, fashion, fragrances, henna tattoos, and yoga.

"I, for one, also feel that booking agents are now more interested in presenting a 'world music' band, featuring exotic instruments and grooves, and have had a better run at booking myself at venues across the United States," says Momin. "No doubt Indians are getting more and more involved in music, without giving up their racial identities. This is an important move, a different route from simply becoming 'Americanized.' My generation has begun to find their own voice, their own identity. So it's great that the cultural diaspora has begun to embrace our contributions, and we hope to keep our traditions evolving and adapting to new paradigms, and reclaiming what once we forsook."

Rock and pop have incorporated foreign musical influences since the sixties, when the Beatles experimented with South Asian Indian sitars and tabla drums in "Revolver" and "Sgt. Pepper's Lonely Hearts Club Band." More recently, Brazilian and Middle Eastern elements have cropped up in the music of Sting, David Byrne, and Peter Gabriel. The difference now is that foreign musicians who grew up listening to mainstream pop, techno, and rock are creating their own hybrids, which then join the global mix in a more open spirit of cross-pollination and mutual transformation. Bragin points out that Panjabi MC's original mix of "Mundian To Bach Ke" ("Beware"—"Beware of the Boys")—was already popular with South Asian nightclubbers when Jay-Z's remix turned it into an international mainstream hit. Café Tacuba, a quartet from Mexico, graft *norteño* and Mexican folk to post-punk rock on their album *Cuatro Caminos*, while guitarist Gary Lucas combines Chinese folk, Western-style swing, and the blues on his record *The Edge of Heaven*.

In a similar vein, hip-hop's global popularity is inevitably spawning polyethnic permutations that cement its status as a pan-global sound. South Asian bhangra, Indian ragas, and hip-hop break beats are fused in the category-defying mixes of Timbaland, Talvin Singh, Asian Dub Foundation, and DJ Suhel. Spiraling Middle Eastern riffs surface in Beyonce Knowles's video for *Baby Boy*, which shows her belly dancing to an Arabic hip-hop mix. And Vannes Wu, a member of a Taiwanese boy band who performs a duet with Knowles on her CD *Dangerously in Love*, is boosting sales in his home turf of Asia and Hong Kong. Jin, a Chinese American rapper, rhymes about interracial dating and the Asian experience in the United States on his debut CD, *The Rest Is History*. On the song "Learn Chinese," he raps: "Every time they harass me, I wanna explode / We should ride the train for free / We built the railroads."

"In the purest sense, hip-hop is a form of folk music," Bragin notes. "If you look at the creation and transmission of hip-hop music, it started as a populist form created by musicians using the tools at hand that was transmitted orally—all of those things are the hallmarks of folk music. And as hip-hop evolves, in that process of dissemination other things filter in, and again it all ultimately becomes part of the vocabulary, the same way Cuban music became part of the West African vocabulary. And there's an element of exoticism—that's always part of it. But what's happening is that the artists themselves are doing it."

For Bragin, world music has benefits that go beyond the novelty of a new sound. He points to Pakistani singer Nusrat Fateh Ali Kahn, whose music transcends national and linguistic boundaries. Khan, who died at the age of forty-nine in 1997, was a master of Sufi devotional music, or *qawwali*, an Islamic mystical tradition that uses strings, harmonium, and nonverbal vocalizations to attain a sacred realm of expression that goes beyond language. *Qawwali*'s devotional themes date back over seven hundred years to the spiritual Samah songs of Persia. During his career, Kahn, who was Pakistan's most revered singer, collaborated with Eddie Vedder, Peter Gabriel, and the British trip-hop band Massive Attack. On songs like "Must Must," he added techno dance beats, which helped him expand his fan base to a younger international audience. The Orchestra of Fez, an ensemble from Morocco that plays Arab Andalusian music dating back to the ninth century, reflects Spanish, Muslim, and Jewish musical influences in its choice of instruments, which include an Egyptian six-stringed oud, a *darbuka* drum, and a tambourine played with violins and violas. "There's a sensitizing that happens even if you don't know the words," Bragin says. "One of the things I learn from that is that the transporting aspect of *qawwali* music is that it's not necessarily predicated on knowing the words as much as it is on catching the feeling. As it is with American gospel music, a lot of religious music transcends the linguistic."

As the audience for indigenous and world music grows, so does its ability to foster cross-cultural understanding and grease the wheels of international diplomacy and economics. Mexico: Gateway to the Americas is a joint initiative launched in 2003 by the U.S. and Mexican governments to promote Mexican culture in the United States and to develop the arts as a tool to enhance cultural, economic, and diplomatic ties. The initiative is an ambitious attempt by leading cultural and political institutions in the United States and Mexico to "develop comprehensive responses to a cultural situation created by globalization" and to address "issues concerning cultural diversity, the reconstruction of identities, the growing number of cultural initiatives and agents, and the influence of new dialogues and aspirations."

But at a time when the domestic and international importance of cross-cultural initiatives like GlobalFEST and Gateway to the Americas are more obvious than ever, post 9/11 U.S. policies are threatening to hold them back. Recent U.S. immigration restrictions have forced a number of promoters to cancel or reduce visits from foreign artists. "The true potential of world music is being stunted right now by government policies and the closing of our borders," says APAP president Sandra Gibson, who has joined a national coalition of cultural organizations committed to speeding the processing of granting visas for visiting performers and easing restrictions for performers from countries on a State Department hot list that includes many Muslim and Middle Eastern nations. "Just when being exposed to other cultures is more vital than ever," says Bragin, "we're closing the door."

Beat Streets

If the immigrant experience is reflected in the music immigrants listen to and make, then what would be the sound of a culture that forged its fractured identity in the agitated rhythms and defiant voices of the urban ghetto? The fact that rap rules is old news, but it's telling that, even before it broke into the pop consciousness, its leaders knew that they were the inheritors of a new order built on the primordial beat and that the creative torch once carried by jazz and the blues and rock and roll had now been passed to them. Just as the first DJs—who couldn't afford instruments but had easy access to turntables and vinyl records—turned a limitation into a creative breakthrough, rappers used street slang and rhyme to transform their stories of desperation and neglect into anthems of cultural empowerment. While hip-hop historian Raquel Rivera, a sociologist and a member of the Latin rap group Yerba Buena, has chronicled the role of Puerto Ricans in the early development of rap, the movement quickly coalesced into an expression of African American politics and identity.

The call to pump up the volume was heard, and not just by beat-box-toting youths with a social ax to grind. In her book *Black Noise*, Tricia Rose, a former professor of history and African studies at New York University who now teaches at the University of California at Santa Cruz, made the definitive academic case for rap and hip-hop, arguing that its reflection of the urban experience transcends linguistic and socioeconomic barriers because it invokes a far more universal picture of reality than, say, a John Denver song. Because of its ability to crystallize and address the issues and emotions of urban life from the perspective of the marginalized masses, hip hop, according to Rose, has become "black America's most dynamic contemporary popular cultural, intellectual and spiritual vessel."[6]

Hip-hop's authority and potency as a bass-boosted megaphone for black anger and frustration was established long before Run-DMC scored rap's first gold record in 1984. References to police brutality, drugs, drive-by shootings, gang warfare, crushing poverty, and graffiti-streaked streets were staples of the simmering inner city depicted in "gangsta" rap and in the music of Run-DMC, Ice-T, NWA ("Niggers with Attitude"), and, perhaps most memorably, Grandmaster Flash's "The Message."

In the late eighties, critical acclaim for Spike Lee's *Do the Right Thing*, MTV's decision to air rap videos, and the commercial success of the Beastie Boys, Vanilla Ice, Tone-Loc, and MC Hammer settled the question of whether hip-hop could speak to a nonblack audience. Hip-hop's antiauthoritarian tone made it the new music of rebellion for a generation of white suburban kids who were looking for a cool new sound to call their own. By 2002, rap had become a multibillion-dollar industry, selling more than 80 million records in the United States alone. It also became a force to be reckoned with in Hollywood and on Broadway. *Russell Simmons' Def Poetry Jam on Broadway* won raves for presenting rap and a spoken-word performance through a nine-person cast that included an African American from Philadelphia, a Palestinian American from Brooklyn, and a Chinese American from Oklahoma City.

In *8 Mile*, a film that took its name from the street that divides Detroit's black neighborhoods from the northern mostly white suburbs, a rapper named Rabbit overcomes racism, poverty, and prejudice for the right to rap and dream of a life beyond the ghetto. The fact that Rabbit was a white man played by a rapper named Eminem underscored the universal acceptance of hip-hop's sound and motivational message. A year later, even Rodgers and Hart were hip-hopized in *Da Boyz*, a rap-infused East London revival of *The Boys from Syracuse*, the 1938 toe-tapper that was itself a reworking of Shakespeare's *Comedy of Errors*. And Tom Sanford, a thirty-one-year-old white artist from Westchester, New York, has documented his willful transformation into slain rapper Tupac Shakur—including Tupac-inspired body tattoos, shaved head, and other artifacts of rap-star worship and devotion—in a multimedia show titled *Thug4Life*.

Yet despite—or perhaps because of—hip-hop's enormous commercial and cultural clout, voices from inside and outside the black community wonder aloud if rap's antisocial subtext is empowering or merely self-defeating. No less disturbing to some is the idea of rappers as role models for a generation of American youths. Def Jam Vandetta, a video game released in 2003 by Electronic Arts, sets the music—and faces—of some of hip-hop's biggest names in the "underground circuit of hardcore brawling." Players can choose from over forty pumped-up personas and face off in the ring to a sound track of Def Jam artists that includes DMX, Ludacris, Method Man, Redman, Scarface, and WC. The game's instruction manual invites players to "get your props as you hook up with the local legends and battle for ultimate supremacy."

Cultural prudes and grandstanding politicians learned long ago that picking a fight with violent entertainment is a no-win proposition. The bigger question for some African Americans is whether hip-hop's pugilistic posturing may be teaching a generation of youths how to win the virtual battle while losing the real war against discrimination, disempowerment, and poverty. In an article in the summer 2003 edition of *City Journal*, an urban policy magazine based in New York, John H. McWhorter, an associate professor of linguistics at the University of California at Berkeley and author of *Losing the Race: Self-Sabotage in Black America*, questions the redeeming social value of hip-hop and what it represents for the African American community. McWhorter points out that many of the earliest iterations of rap, like Sugar Hill Gang's "Rappers Delight," had a noticeably upbeat vibe that had typified black rhythm and blues and pop for decades. He traces the turning point to the "angry, oppositional stance that 'The Message' reintroduced into black culture," which took its defiant tone from the black nationalist movement of the 1960s. He bemoans the gangsta poses and real-life rap sheets of millionaire role models like 50 Cent, Mobb Deep, Busta Rhymes, East Side Boyz, and Sean "P. Diddy" Combs, and questions the value of glorifying and reinforcing ghetto stereotypes and lifestyles in hip-hop records and videos. As a middle-class black man who is proud of the social and economic progress African Americans have achieved in recent decades, he worries that for all its chest-beating bluster, hip-hop actually represents a cultural step backward.

"The attitude and style expressed in the hip-hop 'identity' keeps blacks down," he writes. "Almost all hip-hop, gangsta or not, is delivered with a cocky, confrontational cadence that is fast becoming—as attested by the rowdies at KFC—a common speech style among young black males. Similarly, the arm-slinging, hand-hurling gestures of rap performers have made their way into many young blacks' casual gesticulations, becoming integral to their self-expression. The problem with such speech and mannerisms is that they make potential employers wary of young black men and can impede a young black's ability to interact comfortably with co-workers and customers. The black community has gone through too much to sacrifice upward mobility to the passing kick of an adversarial hip-hop 'identity.' . . . Hip-hop creates nothing."

Speaking in Tongues

But not even McWhorter would argue that hip-hop *says* nothing, or even that the way rappers say it lacks linguistic logic or validity. In *Losing the Race*, McWhorter, who is a linguist, flatly states, "Black English is not Bad English," pointing out that the grammatical structure of black English, aka "African American vernacular English" or "Ebonics," shows it to be a variation of standard English that evolved over time within the African American community. For that reason, McWhorter sees black English as a "dialect," essentially no different (better or worse) from the variants of English spoken in Appalachia or certain outlying areas of England. McWhorter opposes the recognition of black English in schools as a "second" or alternate language for African Americans, not because standard English "is somehow 'better' or 'more correct' in the eyes of God, but because it happens to be the one spoken where the center of power coalesces."[7] In other words, standard English is better simply because African Americans who speak it are more likely to advance economically. Black Americans, McWhorter argues, should be prepared to give up their dialect in order reap the material rewards of greater assimilation.

The same logic has been used against advocates of bilingual education for Spanish-speaking Latinos and immigrants from Latin America. Spanish, of course, is not a dialect of English, but the rationale for the adoption of English is identical and equally compelling, since countless studies have shown that immigrants and minorities who speak English do better than their non-English-speaking counterparts on a variety of socioeconomic fronts, including income, high school graduation, and home ownership. Even so, the sheer size of the Spanish-speaking population in the United States, which is estimated to be as high as 20 million, has nurtured an entire Spanish media universe that includes broadcast and cable TV, radio, magazines, newspapers, and a new breed of bilingual pop stars who jump back and forth across the language barrier in their search for creative fulfillment and adoring audiences. Jon Secada, Ricky Martin, Marc Anthony, and Enrique Iglesias all established singing careers in Spanish before venturing into the English market. Some, like Jennifer Lopez and Martin, have recently reached back to their roots in canny moves for inspiration and authenticity. On her 2002 hit single "Jenny from the Block," Lopez sings: "Don't be fooled by the rocks that I got / I'm still I'm still Jenny from the block / Used to have a little, now I have a lot / No matter where I go, I know where I came from." For Martin, knowing where he came from meant singing in the language of his native Puerto Rico. In 2003, after a two-year hiatus from performing and recording, he released *Almas del Silencio (Souls of Silence)*, his first record in Spanish since his 1998 Grammy-winning album, *Vuelve*. The *Almas* CD completed a linguistic round trip for Martin, who detonated the "Latin boom" of the late 1990s with his chart-topping, genre-bending ode to the fast lane, "Living La Vida Loca." The song was an instant international hit, propelling the album *Ricky Martin* to sales of 14 million. With his chiseled features and

party-boy moves, Martin was the perfect vessel for a culture ready to acknowledge Latinos as long as it didn't take too much effort. But the global
response to his unabashed blend of Buddhist spirituality, sexual ambiguity, and multicultural identity was also a testament to the commercial and
cultural potency of the New Mainstream.

For Steve Drimmer, a music producer and talent manager based in Los
Angeles, Martin's ascent remains the model for media stars who can straddle the burgeoning bilingual market. "Ricky Martin is a white guy with a
white name and no accent coupled with a huge built-in audience from
selling millions of Spanish-language albums around the world," Drimmer
says. "He was acceptable to all market segments. But, he was nonethnic,
an assimilated Latino." Drimmer, who has managed Latino talent and
worked with Motown's Berry Gordy, Interscope's Jimmy Iovine, and other
recording industry chieftains, sees Spanish-language media as a minor
play compared with the long-term potential of English and bilingual
Latino entertainment. Drimmer believes that the Latinization of the U.S.
music industry is only beginning, but that several major obstacles must be
overcome for it to reach its true potential. Because English-language radio
is largely hostile to anything besides mainstream pop and hip-hop, and because most Latino youths shun the old-world programming of Latin radio
networks, Drimmer believes that Latin artists must build a solid base in
Mexico and Latin America before they can launch a successful foray into
English. And even then, Latin artists lacking a universal look and sound
that appeals to both Latinos and non-Latinos—and a depth of talent to
sustain the initial buzz—will inevitably fail. As proof, Drimmer points to
the careers of Paulina Rubio and Shakira, two Latin singers who made bids
for U.S. megastardom with English-language releases. Rubio, a former
member of the Mexican teen pop group Timbiriche, released *Border Girl*
in 2002; Colombia's Shakira, whose funkified poprock has a Middle Eastern tinge thanks to her Lebanese father, launched *Laundry Service* a year
earlier.

"Paulina is the perfect example of a premature assault on the English
market," says Drimmer. "She came here armed with only one successful
Spanish album, so her Latin audience was not nearly solid enough to rely
on for support for the English record. Having no voice is somewhat of a

problem—but, once again, she abandoned her Latin base to go English. The correct move for her would have been to make another great Spanish album, build on her previous success, and then go English. Shakira is the best example of all of the changing public taste. An album with lyrics barely understandable, *Shakira* had a solid worldwide base and the entire resources of Sony Music behind her. The songs were mediocre, with no real standout singles. But she went sexy, and I think that sexy Latin women can be sold all day long if they have the whole package. Shakira wrote all the songs and produced the album. Paulina wrote none of her songs, and her label hired all the usual top-name producers who know nothing of Latinos or Latino music. Shakira is the real deal, Paulina is a pretender, and the results prove it: 15 million in sales of *Laundry Service* versus less than 1 million of *Border Girl*."

Drimmer envisions a future where a diminishing immigration flow from Mexico and Latin America brings consolidation in the Spanish media sector, while a growing English-dominant Latino community becomes an important component of the media mainstream. In fact, changing demographics are already sparking competition among Latino groups for representation in Spanish media outlets. In New York, La Mega WSKQ, the city's most popular Latin music station, was picketed by Dominican listeners who objected to a shift in the station's programming, which reduced the amount of merengue to make room for new styles like reggaeton and *bachata*, a softer Dominican rhythm. Meanwhile, La Mega's sister station, WPAT-FM, which traditionally plays Mexican pop and ballads, is contemplating a move to increase the amount of *ranchera, norteño, banda*, and other Mexican regional styles favored by the city's growing population of Mexican immigrants.

Nationalistic competition for media exposure within the U.S. Latino community has also plagued the Latin Grammys. Launched in 2000 by a consortium of backers led by Cuban immigrant and Latin music producer Emilio Estefan, the event, which was held in Los Angeles, was criticized as a vehicle for the personal wealth of its organizers rather than a positive step forward for U.S. Latinos as a whole. There were also charges that music from Cuba and the Caribbean had been featured and promoted at the expense of Mexican American bands, despite the fact that more than half of the Latin records sold in the United States are made by Mexican artists. In 2001, plans to move the show from Los Angeles to Miami were abandoned after organizers and anti-Castro protesters failed to agree on security issues. Two weeks later, the terrorist attacks in New York forced the cancellation of the show, which was scheduled to take place on September 11.

In 2003, the Grammys finally moved to Miami, where organizers braced themselves for demonstrations by Cuban Americans who objected to the nomination of Cuban musical groups because of their vehement opposition to Fidel Castro. After extensive negotiations, the protesters were granted a permit to stand 168 feet from the entrance to Miami's American Airlines Arena. The awards, which were broadcast to 110 countries, included a tribute to salsa diva Celia Cruz, who died earlier that year, and performances by Bacilos, a Miami-based group with members from Colombia, Brazil, and Puerto Rico, and the regional Mexican brass band Banda El Recodo. The evening's major awards were swept by Juanes, a Colombian singer-songwriter known for his artful mix of salsa, rock, and socially conscious lyrics. Part showcase for Latin pride, part targeted marketing vehicle, the Latin Grammys were welcomed by some as a sign that Hispanics had finally arrived. But for others, including a fair number of Latinos inside and outside the music industry, it was a misguided detour that, just like bilingual education, only delays the acceptance of Hispanics into the American mainstream.

"The Latin Grammys is an inherently flawed idea, trumped up by Emilio Estefan and [Latin Recording Academy president and CEO] Michael Greene," says Drimmer. "Instead of lobbying for increases in the number of categories in the real Grammys, a separate Grammys was created for Latin music. Why? For a market segment of 5 percent of total U.S. sales. It diminishes the Grammys for Latin categories in the real Grammys, it hurts the Grammy brand, and its TV show is designed to fail. It was a bad idea—totally contrary to the power of joining the mainstream. It is ghettoization in its most elementary form."

While the assimilation of Latinos may take several generations, Drimmer is convinced that they will inevitably follow the same cultural trajectory as Jews, Irish, Italians, and other ethnic immigrant groups. "The

American fabric has benefited from all the minorities that have been woven in over the generations," he says. "The same will apply for the Latino experience, but with huge implications and effects—due to the size of the Latin component of our population and the explosive birthrate. Latin food, music, vocabulary, and dancing will all make their mark. The most important thing for American industry is to learn how to produce and sell to the new Latino. Latinos will retain vestiges of Latin culture. But the pressures of assimilation will cause them to diminish over time. We'll see what percentage of 'Latin derived' families end up speaking Spanish after thirty to fifty years in the United States. I predict that the percentage will be small. Nobody in my generation speaks Yiddish."

Pan-American

As the recording industry struggles to adjust to bilingual market trends, some Latin musicians are exploring pan-cultural avenues of expression that don't even require a record label. Panamanian singer-actor-politician Rubén Blades has melded cutting-edge technology with ancient cultural traditions in an effort to break new ground and connect with younger audiences and musicians. To gain creative freedom, he turned to the Internet for his latest musical venture: a bilingual collection of original and rerecorded songs that included collaborations between Blades and various musicians from around the world, including the Panamanian rock band Son Miserables, Brazil's Boca Livre, Costa Rica's Editus Ensemble, the Celtic fusion composer and bagpipe player Eric Rigler, the American singer Luba Mason, and the Utah-based Debi Gibson band. Blades, who saw the project as a platform for showcasing material by world music artists and lesser-known bands that might otherwise never get the attention they deserve, has made the tracks available for downloading on his Internet site.[8] Fans who download the material are asked to voluntarily pay for the music they take or donate what they think it is worth. "There's pirating on the Internet because records are expensive and people think artists are greedy," Blades remarked several month later, standing in the kitchen of his brownstone home in New York City. "So now let's turn the tables. I'm asking my fans, How much is this record worth to you, and will you pay for it? Here's your chance to exploit me—or make a trade."

Most of the musicians showcased on Blades's Web site appeared on *Mundo*, a disc that mixed Celtic folk, swinging salsa beats, fusion jazz, and Middle Eastern riffs and won him his fifth Grammy, for Best World Music album, in 2002. In the CD notes, on a page that faces a red handprint bisected by a double helix of the human genome, Blades writes: "The earth was not born with political divisions. Nature pays no attention to where a country begins or ends. The spirit is universal. Life flows from a common fountain. In support of these premises, artists from Argentina, Brazil, Costa Rica, the United States, Mexico, Panama and Puerto Rico have joined in the creation of this work. We believe that music is the ideal expression of the human character. In celebration, and united in the hope that we all share, to the ancient memory that resides within us, we offer *Mundo* (*World*)."

Blades is fully aware that making music available online is a controversial move in the music industry and that by doing so he has joined the likes of Janis Ian, Courtney Love, and other musicians who have championed the Internet as a viable alternative to traditional music distribution and promotion channels. "We are convinced people are going to respond," says Orosman de la Guardia, the Panamanian graphic designer who, along with Son Miserables bass player David Bianco, administers rubenblades.com. "What we are proposing to our friends out there is that we are going to bypass the process of manufacturing and distribution in stores and offer the music digitally. He is not afraid of what people will think, his only concern is to make quality work."

In fact, Blades, whose long-standing relationship with Sony records ended in 2002, says his motivation for the online project was driven largely by his frustration with the major labels, which he sees as fixated on prefabricated pop acts and thus unable or unwilling to support quality artists who might not be suited for—or interested in—a mass audience. "Most record executives are narrow-minded," he explains. "If the record companies disappeared, then musicians would have to do what they always did: tour and play to get people to hear their music. Chopin and Bach didn't have any videos—they had to play live."

As a leader of the Nueva Canción ("New Song") movement and on records like the 1978 best-selling album, *Siembra* (*Seed*), Blades fused trenchant, politically conscious lyrics with smoldering tropical beats to give salsa an unprecedented element of social relevance. Later, as an established salsa superstar living in the United States, Blades blazed new musical trails with albums like 1984's *Buscando America* (*Searching for America*) and bilingual collaborations with Sting, Elvis Costello, and Lou Reed. At the same time, Blades, who took time out during the early 1980s to earn a master's degree in international law from Harvard University, was branching out into acting and politics. Early roles in films like 1985's *Crossover Dreams*, in which he plays a Latin American boxer and would-be salsa singer who craves success in the United States, led to acting work with a constantly expanding A-list of actors and directors that includes Robert Redford, Spike Lee, and Jack Nicholson. "He's a director's dream," says Elizabeth Avellán, a producer of *Once upon a Time in Mexico*, in which Blades plays a retired FBI agent in pursuit of a character played by Willem Dafoe. Avellán, the wife of Robert Rodriguez, who directed the film, attributes Blades's success as an actor to the aura of intelligence and humanity that he brings to the screen. "He's a very generous actor," she said. "He is consistently honest and humble. He respects and is interested in people, no matter who they are, and that sincerity comes across in his work."

Blades traces his abiding respect and concern for others back to his upbringing in Panama City, where standing up for friends and family who needed his help was part of a neighborhood code of honor. It was that same sense of duty that impelled Blades to run for the presidency of Panama in 1994. Blades lost the election, but not his conviction that the strong have a responsibility to help the weak and less fortunate. He still plans to return to his native country and play a part in its political future. "I came from a working-class neighborhood, but there were standards— the standard was how well you execute, how well you act under pressure," he said. "The streets are totally different from when I grew up, but the essentials have not changed. The unwritten rules are the same. They continue to exist and apply."

Blades's unique blend of authenticity and barrier-breaking innovation has inspired a whole new generation of admirers, some of whom were barely born when he was recording his first salsa hits. Among his many fans is the Mexican rock group Mana, who recorded a version of Blades's song "Desapariciones" ("Disappearances") on their popular MTV *Unplugged* album. The band also invited him to sing on a track for their 1993 hit record, "Revolución de Amor." "He's a humanitarian person who's in touch with reality, and it comes across in his music and as a person," explained Alex Gonzalez, Mana's drummer. "For us—and I think for all Latinos—he's an example that Latinos can achieve greatness in their lives." Blades, for his part, feels more affinity these days with the social consciousness expressed by "rock *en Español*" artists like Mana, Juanes, and La Ley than the dance-oriented confections of Jennifer Lopez or Ricky Martin. "The so-called salsa revival has become pop with a salsa beat," he observes. "The true spirit of the lyrics I was doing in 1969 is not to be seen in salsa today, but it's there in Latin rock. If I were to be born today, I'd be playing rock, not salsa."

Some Like It Hot

Eating is primal, social, and sensual. It stimulates the senses and creates a warm glow of satisfaction and well-being. Its communal nature is inherently inclusive and open. The gathering of people around food is one of the oldest human rituals; its appeal is primordial, tribal, and emotional. Throughout history, from the Last Supper to the first Thanksgiving, the breaking of bread has served as a symbol of communion and cultural encounter. Americans have always invented themselves through food, and vice versa. The cooking traditions of early English, Dutch, and German settlers evolved into hot dogs, hamburgers, and apple pie. As America's population has become increasingly diverse, so has its palate. Since World War II, successive waves of culinary influence from France and Italy, as well as Northern and Southern Europe, Asia and Latin America, have transformed the nation's eating habits. At a time when the world's most celebrated chefs are not French but Spanish, Americans are developing a taste for flavors and textures that were once considered esoteric, if not

wnright inedible. Today's cosmopolitan diners are almost blasé about
dering entrées like Oaxacan mole, a complex Mexican sauce made from
ilies and chocolate; kimchi, a spicy pickled cabbage from Korea; or fugu,
highly prized and potentially toxic Japanese dish made from blowfish.
lobal-minded innovators like Douglas Rodriguez, Nobu Matsuhisa,
bert del Grande, Sue Torres, and Ming Tsai have turned the dinner
ble into the new Ellis Island, a place where fresh ingredients are wel-
med and embraced, where regional differences are appreciated and
ized, and where the "melting pot" not only exists but can actually be
sted.

The new fusion chefs are historically aware and culturally omnivorous.
mpson Wong, a Malaysian of Chinese descent, learned to cook by help-
g his mother serve meals in the rain forest to employees of his father's
mber company. He worked as a banker in Kuala Lumpur and as a shiatsu
asseur in New York before opening Café Asean, a Manhattan eatery spe-
alizing in Thai, Vietnamese, and Malaysian dishes. It's hardly accidental
at Wong's new restaurant, Jefferson, is named after the U.S. president
sponsible for repealing the Alien and Sedition Acts, a set of laws that
ade it more difficult for immigrants to become citizens and that allowed
e government to deport or imprison foreigners who were considered a
reat to the United States. Wong's "New American" menu is an equal
portunity salute to gastronomic diversity, with dishes like ravioli made
om edamame, with gingko nuts and mascarpone cheese; snapper with
ramelized persimmon, baby leeks, and enoki mushrooms with coconut-
ndlenut foam; and scallops crusted in rice shavings with white miso tan-
rine scallops.

Adventurous eating is changing the business of food, the effects of
hich ripple out to every sector of the American economy. Ethnic food—
d its subliminal ability to open the mouth and mind to new cultures—is
coming ubiquitous and indispensable to the American way of life. If we
ally are what we eat, then the blue plate special now comes in every pos-
ble color and flavor, including some that never existed before. Serge
cker, a Swiss-born entrepreneur and designer of cutting-edge night-
ubs, restaurants, and hotels, has long reveled in the multicultural attrac-
ons of Los Angeles and New York. Now he hopes to meld the two with his

latest cross-cultural concept: a Mexican dim sum restaurant and tequ[i]
bar in Manhattan. "Mexican food is already sold off carts and ha[nd]
trucks," Becker explains, "so to bring them indoors and create a fun d[im]
sum atmosphere in a large room full of tasty food and great tequilas seem[s]
natural. The demographic shift is so powerful and swift, I don't think [we]
can fully grasp it yet."

New Mainstream fare of one sort or another is available in every sta[te]
in all price ranges, to stay or to go. National Mexican and Japanese chai[ns]
like Taco Bell and Teriyaki Stix vie with KFC on the fast-food front, wh[ile]
peasant staples from Oaxaca, Galicia, and Sichuan grace the menus of u[p-]
scale eateries. The boom in exotic eating was abundantly apparent at t[he]
National Association for the Specialty Food Trade annual Fancy Fo[od]
Show in New York City, where attendees sampled new flavors from mc[re]
than five thousand booths hawking everything from *lucama*, a fruit fr[om]
the Andes mountains that makes a luscious ice cream, to argan oil, [a]
cholesterol-free, vitamin E–rich oil that is harvested by tree-climbi[ng]
goats. Award winners included an intense ginger wasabi sauce, chipo[tle]
chili double fudge chunk cookies, a teriyaki vinaigrette, and caram[el]
made with sea-salt crystals.

As the once exotic flavors of New Mainstream cuisine filter down [to]
the local mall, even midrange chains and so-called casual restaurants a[re]
going gourmet. At Chipotle Grill, a chain owned by McDonald's th[at]
takes its name from smoked jalapeño peppers, customers dine on fre[e-]
range pork garnished with juniper berries. Darden Restaurants, whi[ch]
owns Olive Garden, Bahama Breeze, and Red Lobster, has launched Se[a-]
son 52, which advertises a trendy menu based on local seasonal ingre[di-]
ents. Even national supermarkets are jumping on the trend. In an effort [to]
fend off a groceries and produce push by a rival Wal-Mart supercenter, t[he]
Kroger company in Dallas, Texas, is expanding its upscale offerings to i[n-]
clude fresh handmade corn tortillas. In Clarksdale, Mississippi, Gilr[oy]
Chow and his family are famous for their Cantonese-style stir-fried cra[b,]
fish and collards, which they cook in a wok brought to the United States [as]
an heirloom from China. The Chinese community in the American Sou[th]
dates back to the Reconstruction era, when plantation owners lured Ch[i-]
nese immigrants with jobs in the hopes of using them to replace recent[ly]

freed black slaves. The fusion food revolution also spawned thousands of immigrant-owned restaurants, delis, and specialty markets. Otto Gonzales, who recently emigrated from Peru, teamed up with his brother to pioneer the importation of Peruvian crab to American restaurants and seafood outlets. And in Bernardsville, New Jersey, Arvind and Bhagwati Amin have started a booming family business selling vegetarian specialties derived from their native India. Their company makes sixty-five different snack foods, ice creams, and frozen entrées, which they ship across the United States.

Younger Americans, who grew up gorging on pan-ethnic flavors and tend to be more culturally open-minded, take their multiethnic palate for granted. At colleges like the University of Washington, undergrads demanding sushi and *pho*, a Vietnamese noodle soup, in their dormitory cafeteria offerings have forced campus food service companies to upgrade and expand their selections to include organic-ingredient Asian and Latin American dishes. Yale University has hired nouvelle cuisine legend Alice Waters to help it devise a dining hall menu that includes locally grown vegetables and entrées like Japanese eggplant parmesan. Dave Leiberman, a Yale senior and the star of the student-oriented public access show *Campus Cuisine*, epitomizes the gourmand generation, an army of embryonic epicureans who see chicken kebabs marinated in garlic, ginger, and hoisin sauce as an essential ingredient of their education and future lifestyle and are willing to fight for their right to kimchi.[9]

The rising domestic appetite for sushi and other ethnic traditions is launching new industries and transforming old ones. In California, evolving eating habits have revitalized the state's rice industry and turned it onto an Asian specialty powerhouse, with ripple effects across the U.S. economy. The Sacramento Valley, located in the northern half of the state, is one of only three places in world (the others are Japan and Australia) ideally suited to growing japonica rice, a short- and medium-grain variety that is prized in Japan and elsewhere for having the perfect flavor and stickiness for sushi. Since the early 1990s, thanks to a lowering of trade barriers with Japan and a growing Asian American population, the California rice industry has grown from almost nothing into a $500 million-a-year business.[10]

Rice, which has been cultivated for at least five thousand years, originated in China and was carried to ancient Greece, Persia, and the Nile delta before spreading to Europe and the Americas. Long associated with prosperity and plenty, rice is thrown at newlywed couples to bestow good luck and lack of want. In Asia and other parts of the world, rice remains a token of a life of "plenty." Rice has been a United States staple since 1685, when a storm-battered ship from Madagascar stopped in Charleston harbor for repairs and bestowed some rice plants as a parting gift to their hosts. The low-lying tidal marshes and flooding river deltas of the South Carolina and Georgia coastline proved a hospitable habitat for rice production, and by 1700, rice had become an important cash crop for the South. The same year, three hundred tons of rice—called "Carolina Golde"—were shipped to England from the flourishing antebellum plantations that rose along the Cooper and Ashley rivers, which provided irrigation and easy transportation to Charleston harbor. During the eighteenth century, rice cultivation, made feasible by slave labor, was a pillar of the southern economy and a major colonial export. "The rice dance" and other agriculturally inspired songs, dances, and games that reflect the tribal origins of African slaves are still performed today by the Georgia Sea Island Singers, a group of African Americans who trace their ancestors to slaves who came to the United States from the kingdom of Messina on the Niger River. The Civil War, hurricanes, and competition from other crops eventually pushed rice cultivation westward to the Gulf Coast states, where mechanized harvesting methods helped establish major rice holdings in Arkansas, Louisiana, Mississippi, Missouri, and Texas.[11]

Rice cultivation in California commenced in the mid-1800s, after the Gold Rush of 1849 attracted an estimated forty thousand Chinese immigrants who were accustomed to rice-based diets. Still, California did not become a major rice producer until farmers began planting varieties of short-grain rice favored by Japanese consumers, such as Akita Komachi and Koshihikari. Rice cognoscenti claim that the new varieties produce a cleaner, sweeter flavor in addition to a satisfying propensity to clump that is ideal for eating with chopsticks. Unlike the long-grain rice still produced in the American South, Japanese varieties are also favored for marketing as "new crop," meaning that it has been stored less than a month. "New crop" rice has been a delicacy in Japan since World War II, when food shortages made the superior flavor and texture of fresh rice a status symbol for the wealthy. While traditional rice-growing states still lead the United States in overall production, California dominates the fast-growing and more lucrative specialty rice segment. In 2002, the United States was the world's third largest rice exporter, after Thailand and India, with 2,950,000 metric tons. Japan is the third largest importer of American rice (after Central America and Mexico and before Europe), most of it from California. Ideal soil and climate conditions, as well as new Japanese-style mills that prevent cracking, have allowed California to produce harvests that are second to none. "We learned to evaluate rice quality by a world-class standard," said Tim Johnson, president of the California Rice Commission. "As a result, all of our rice is better—the rice we send to Kellogg's, the rice we send to breweries. The entire industry bumped itself up a notch."[12] And the resulting economic gains sent ripples across the state's economy, creating jobs and new business opportunities for immigrants and nonimmigrants alike.

Not all the flavors of the new American cuisine are transplants, of course. Some of the most interesting—and popular—foods being served today were being savored in North America long before the first white settlers arrived from Europe. A new wave of Mexican, Tex-Mex, and regional styles of cooking take their inspiration from indigenous and pre-Columbian cultures. Native Americans were cultivating corn, tomatoes, and tobacco long before the arrival of Columbus. During the fifteenth and sixteenth centuries, the tomato, botanically classified as a member of the nightshade family, was regarded with suspicion in Europe, where it was denounced as evil, sinful, and poisonous. Other foods native to the Americas include beans, pumpkin, squash, avocados, peanuts, potatoes, coffee, and chocolate.

Vanilla, which in America has become a synonym for ordinary, bland, and white, was initially enjoyed and cultivated by the hemisphere's brown inhabitants and comes from a tropical vine that is related to the orchid, the largest family of flowering plants in the world. Indigenous to the rain forests of the Caribbean, Central America, the southeastern coast of Mexico, and the northern parts of South America, vanilla orchids are now grown in most of the world's tropical regions. The harvesting and fermenting of vanilla pods was developed more than a thousand years ago by the Totonac people, who lived on the Gulf Coast of Mexico near the present-day city of Veracruz. According the Totonac origin myth, a beautiful young goddess named Xanath fell in love with a young Totonac. Forbidden to marry a mortal, Xanath turned herself into a vanilla vine so that the flowers and pods of the plant could serve the Totonacs as an eternal source of happiness. The Totonacs used vanilla as a perfume, as a flavoring for food and drink, and as a medicine, aphrodisiac, and insect repellent.[13]

Chili peppers, whose tongue-searing bite is anything but bland, took much less time to conquer most of the world.[14] Some botanists and anthropologists say that chili peppers originated in the semiarid regions of Bolivia; others contend that they first emerged from the leafy labyrinth of the Amazon rain forest. All agree that they are an ancient crop cultivated and prized by most of the indigenous cultures of Mexico, the Caribbean, and South America, including the Olmecs, Toltecs, Maya, and Aztecs, who called them by their Nahuatl name, *chilli*. Archaeological evidence suggests that chilies were used as a food ingredient at least since 6200 B.C., and evidence that they were included in burial sites from the same period has been found in Peru. At least three varieties of the capsicum plants, which evolved into the types now known as bell peppers, jalapeños, and cayenne, were first carried back to the Iberian Peninsula by Columbus, who mistook the pods for a variation of the black pepper he was seeking on the Pacific route to India. Their speedy dispersal was largely dictated by the trading empires of Spain and Portugal, which divided the world between them just a few years after the discovery of America. During the sixteenth century, Portuguese traders introduced the peppers to Africa and India, where they were quickly adopted as an important part the local cuisine. The Indians then exported new homegrown varieties to other parts of Asia, the Middle East, and Europe. The Spanish, meanwhile, took the piquant pods to the Philippines and other islands in the Pacific. By the time the first English and Dutch settlers arrived in the Americas in the early seventeenth century, chili peppers were well established in the cooking traditions of Africa, Asia, and the Middle East. Ironically, peppers did not take hold in on-Spanish North America until there were reintroduced by African and Caribbean slaves, who had long incorporated them into their native cuisines, and the Latin communities of Texas and the southwestern United States. During the twentieth century, the country's growing Hispanic population, along with successive waves of immigrants from Italy, Indonesia, Vietnam, India, and China, brought chili peppers into the American mainstream. Although the mild-mannered bell pepper is still the best-selling pepper in the United States, hotter varieties are gaining ground as American cuisine becomes increasingly diverse. Among the best known are the habanero, a Caribbean variety named after the Cuban city of Havana, believed by many to be the world's hottest; the jalapeño, named after the town of Jalapa in the Mexican state of Veracruz, a thick-fleshed pepper commonly added to nachos and salsa; the poblano, a chili often used for roasted chile rellenos; and the red and green Anaheim, a slender, mild-flavored pepper produced in New Mexico.

Today, hundreds of different varieties of chilies are grown in most countries, with Asia leading the world in production and consumption. The Thais consume more hot peppers per capita than any other people, eating an average of five grams of peppers per person per day. Other cultures with a hankering for hot foods are the Indians, who use peppers in spicy curries and other dishes, and the Koreans, who use powdered chili on kimchi. Peppers are a key ingredient in the cooking of China's Sichuan province, where it is used in fish sauces, sliced pork, chicken, and bean curd. In Senegal, chilies are added to the traditional *thiebou dieune,* or rice and fish. Most Senegalese meals are accompanied by a locally developed chili called *safi,* which is derived from *saf,* which means "pungent" in Wolof, the traditional Senegalese language.

Peppers are grown in most countries of the world, with more than 7.5 million acres dedicated to cultivation of the plant. In the United States, New Mexico is the leading state for chili production, with more than twenty-one thousand acres under cultivation in 1998. Nowhere is the cult of chilies stronger than New Mexico, where new age bohemians mingle with Native Americans and fifth-generation Spanish descendants. Chilies infuse the history, food, and commercial underpinnings of tourist centers like Santa Fe and Taos, where *ristras,* or garlands of dried red chilies, adorn businesses, homes, and public areas. At the annual Santa Fe Win and Chile Fiesta, several thousand self-described "chiliheads" dressed pepper-print shirts, skirts, and ties spend several days sampling chili dish and taking "chili tours" of the New Mexican countryside, with visits places like Embudo Station, a smokehouse and chili beer brewery locate on the site of a historic 1880s narrow-gauge railroad station. Every ye about twelve-thousand pepper lovers sporting chili pepper headgear an T-shirts with mottos like "Proud Sponsor of Global Warming," atten Albuquerque's Annual Fiery Foods & Barbeque Show, which feature more than two hundred exhibitors of chili-flavored beers, desserts, soup meats, toys, jewelry, Christmas ornaments, and other "pepperphernalia."

The heady rise of the once humble pepper has been fueled by a proli eration of Mexican and nouvelle Tex-Mex cuisine and a growing main stream appetite for endless incarnations of the fiery fruit. In 1991, sales salsa overtook ketchup, making it the country's most popular condimen and peppers are turning up the heat in mass-market products like Big Re cinnamon chewing gum, Le Menu Santa Fe–style frozen dinners, an Cineplex jalapeño nachos. Manufacturers are packaging chili pastas, chi jams and jellies, chili ketchup, and chili-spiced mustards, peanuts, potat chips, and pickles. Online merchants, like the Bozeman, Montana, Co mic Chile catalog, feature a veritable Dante's inferno of pepper-base condiments with fancifully fearsome names like Salsa de la Muerte, Mea Devil Woman, Burned at the Stake, Tibetan Fire, Tejas Tears, Lawyer Breath, Iguana Atomic, Chipotle Slam, Sharkbite, and Pure Hell.

Hot food was not always cool. If there is a single time and place whe chilies made the jump from hot to haute in the mainstream, it can b traced to Santa Fe, New Mexico, and the 1987 opening of Mark Miller Coyote Café. Dubbed "the Godfather of Southwestern Cuisine," he one of the nation's most successful—and knowledgeable—purveyors c neo-American cuisine. In 1996, he won the James Beard Award for Bes American Chef: Southwest. Miller's cooking, which he calls "moder western," ranges from nouvelle versions of Mexican dishes like "Canela scented Double-cut Pork Chop with Parsnip and Almond Puree, Oaxaca mole, and Fruit Preserves" and "Wild Boar Tamale with Huitlacoch Sauce" to authentic western fare like fresh-baked buckwheat cinnamo bread, smoked duck, and buffalo jerkey. "Smoking is a natural by-product of heat," Miller says. "There's an intensity of wildness, of untamed flavor. It's loaded symbolically with a primordial sense of fire. I read a lot of meaning into food. I think it's one of the last experimental frontiers."

Miller's passion for untamed flavor began in his native Massachusetts, where Mexican and Indian friends of his French Canadian family introduced him to the spicy pleasures of non-European cooking. Travels in Latin America, Africa, and Asia prompted him to experiment with ethnic accents, first as an assistant chef for Alice Waters at Chez Panisse in Berkeley and later in the same city at his own Fourth Street Grill, where he was one of the first chefs in the country to use mesquite wood for grilling. In 1987, Miller opened the Coyote Café in Santa Fe, New Mexico, specializing in a sophisticated fusion of nouvelle and traditional New Mexican fare. The restaurant was an instant hit that put both haute southwestern cuisine and Miller on the culinary front burner. In 1991, Miller launched Red Sage, a restaurant designed to "evoke the spirit of the West," in Washington, D.C., and he opened a version of Coyote Café in Las Vegas the following year. His books include *The Coyote Café Cookbook* (1990), *The Great Chile Book* (1991), and *Indian Market* (1997). Miller, who has often cooked with seasoning and textures derived from Plains Indian and Aztec recipes, remains dedicated to expanding the traditional limits of American cooking by incorporating native and Latin elements and to using flavor, history, and heat to open the mouths and minds of the people who enjoy his food. For the new breed of American chefs, food, and the flavors that go into it, is an expression of their own identity and a reflection of the world around them. Taste, in ways cerebral and visceral, is the flavor of human evolution with an added dash of destiny. "There were people in America before the arrival of Europeans," says Miller. "We are enriched as a culture by including, not by pushing them aside. The West has all these elements in its past, but it's still in the process of becoming. It's not just about looking back. It's about bringing it forward."

11. Beyond the New Mainstream

On a humid, rainy night in the summer of 2003, the sky over Central Park came alive in a cosmic display of explosions and blinding flashes of light. As thousands of New Yorkers watched in amazement from inside the park and the buildings that surround it, six massive towers of hissing sparks shot up above the trees. Next came a series of thudding reports and strobelike flashes merged in a pulsing nebula above the reservoir. Some said they saw the ring of fire, hanging in the air like a giant garland. Others were too overwhelmed by the blinding pyrotechnics and gusts of concussed air buffeting their bodies to be sure. Finally, garlands of white flares and spidery streamers etched luminous patterns against the clouds just before a cloudburst sent spectators running for cover. For some, Cai Guo-Qiang's *Light Cycle* was a monumental artwork that used the heavens as a giant canvas and gunpowder as paint. For others it was a momentary—albeit clamorous—distraction that evoked disturbing memories of 9/11. But anyone who witnessed Cai's cathartic computer-controlled tribute, which was commissioned by sev-

ral civic arts groups to mark the 150th anniversary of Central Park, knew
hey had experienced an epic act of creativity.

The artist, who had spent months planning the five-minute-long dis-
-lay, watched his brainchild from a building on the northwest corner of
he park. As the computer-fired shells clustered and rose in the air to com-
-lete a pulsating garland of condensed explosions, he was excited and en-
rgized to see how technology could enable him to mold burning matter
n ways that had never previously been possible. "Gunpowder is some-
hing you can never control," Cai observed a few days later in quiet, care-
ully worded Chinese. "I think it's a metaphor for mankind—and how as
oon as we discover or invent something, there's always a backlash or a
onsequence that is unexpected, that might mess things up, and so it's a
ery potent metaphor for humanity and its inventions."

Gunpowder—and its innate ability to illuminate the human
ondition—runs in Cai's blood. Born in 1957 in Quanzhou City, Fujian
province, China, a town known for firecracker manufacturing, he studied
tage design and began experimenting with gunpowder as a way to incor-
-orate spontaneity into his classically inspired drawings. After moving to
apan in 1986, he began using explosives on a large scale, which led to a se-
ies of works called *Projects for Extraterrestrials*, so named because the
vorks were meant to be seen best from outer space. Cai's use of explosives
is a creative medium draws on the visceral qualities of gunpowder, as well
is its origins in China as a by-product of the alchemical search for immorality. In the centuries since, gunpowder has been used to make weapons,
o entertain, and to embellish and punctuate cultural celebrations. Fire-
vorks stimulate the senses of sight, hearing, and smell; they defy gravity
ind tap the primal fascination with fire. By using fire to link earth and sky,
gunpowder can signify the collision of East and West and how the mixing
of cultures and races reflects the future of America.

Asked if the United States in the twenty-first century is a bit like
gunpowder—a volatile mix of elements that are potentially explosive but
ilso capable, if handled correctly, of being a beneficial and creative
force—Cai points out that gunpowder is made of three materials, gener-
illy speaking—sulfur, charcoal, and potassium nitrate—the colors of

which happen to correspond to the great races of mankind. "The yellow sulfur brings ignition, the white powder is extremely explosive, and the black charcoal slows it down a bit," he explains. "You have to have a perfect balance in order to get the desired result. If you have just the white it's hard to ignite, if you just have the black, it's too smoky, and with the sulfur alone you'll have the ignition, but nothing to burn. So it has to be very scientific and well-balanced formula in order to work. It's also a creative experiment."

Cai's pyrotechnic works are part of the growing visibility and viability of transcultural themes in American fine arts, music, movies, theater, and dance. By drawing on the ancient traditions and rituals of their own and other cultures, immigrant and American-born artists enhance their creative palettes and create a bridge between people of different races and nationalities. American art is increasingly transglobal and reflective of the myriad ethnic and cultural ingredients of the New Mainstream; the cathartic, transformative power of art is a reflection and expression of the dreams and yearnings of the society that spawns it. By connecting past and present and tapping the collective unconscious, art can amuse, instruct, and empower. And by reaffirming the universality of the human condition and transcending divisions among nations and individuals, it can also help to codify and shape a common culture. "It's about a meeting of worlds," says Rachel Cooper, director of performing arts and public programs at the Asia Society. "It's intuitive and immediate—you have to give a part of yourself in order to experience art, so the boundaries between nationalities become irrelevant. And because it's visceral it transcends politics—it's a reality that you have to respond to, not react to."

Founded in 1956 by John D. Rockefeller III, the Asia Society is a non profit institution dedicated to fostering understanding and communication between Americans and the peoples of Asia, which it broadly defines as the Asia Pacific region, an area encompassing more than thirty countries and extending from Japan to Iran and from Central Asia to New Zealand Australia, and the Pacific Islands. In recent years, the burgeoning Asian community in the United States has prompted the organization to rethink its mission. With Asians in the United States numbering 12 mil-on, or 4.2 percent of the population, the society's slate of exhibits, performances, and lectures has shifted toward an exploration of Asian identity and community in an increasingly multicultural and globalized society.

Vishakha Desai, the Asia Society's president, agrees that the evolving and increasingly global landscape of Asian arts and culture has led the society to rethink its mission and role in the "postmodern" Asian community. "We are very aware that because of the demographic shift we can't talk about Asia just as geography," says Desai. "It is as much about connecting Asians and Americans of all stripes everywhere. So you have to recognize it's as much about Asian*ness* as it is about Asia per se. And that has to do with how the diaspora community in America as well as in England and elsewhere is reacting to the country of origin as well as its country of domicile. And therefore we're very aware that you can't just conflate everything, either. So what you present from Asia is not necessarily the same as when you might do something with Asian America. At the very least, it's become much more complex and interesting—three-dimensional, if you will. There's less of an import-export model."

The cultivation of culture pays off in other ways. Museums, galleries, and institutions in the United States are also realizing that ethnically diverse exhibitions and shows are critical for attracting a new, increasingly multiethnic generation of collectors, ticket buyers, and art lovers. In New York City, ethnic-oriented museums and institutions like El Museo del Barrio, which focuses on Hispanic art, and Harlem's Studio Museum, which showcases African American artists, have seen attendance rise along with their clout in the New York arts community. Between 2001 and 2003 alone, the Studio Museum saw its attendance swell from 80,000 to 130,000 annual visitors.[1] On Broadway, *Russell Simmons' Def Poetry Jam on Broadway*, a musical produced by the leading hip-hop media mogul, won a 2003 Tony. El Museo's 2002 show on the art of Mexican painter and feminist icon Frida Kahlo was so successful that it planned a follow-up exhibit on Latin American artists in conjunction with the New York Museum of Modern Art for the following year. According to El Museo's chairman, Tony Bechara, 52 percent of the museum's attendees are now non-Latino New Yorkers and tourists. Founded in 1969 by a group of

Puerto Rican artists and educators, El Museo has become the leading New York art institution dedicated to Hispanic art and culture. The Apollo Theater, the most famous venue in Harlem and a mecca of black culture and performance, is also riding a new wave of artistic and commercial success with shows like George C. Wolfe's *Harlem Song* and a Royal Shakespeare Company theatrical adaptation of Salman Rushdie's novel *Midnight's Children*. *!Cantinflas!*, the eponymous one-man show about the legendary Mexican actor and comedian, has helped reverse the fortunes of Houston's Alley Theater, which found itself in dire financial straits after the bankruptcy of the Enron Corporation, one of the theater's biggest benefactors, during the late 1990s. By tapping nostalgia among Houston's Latino community for Cantinflas, who lived in Houston during the 1970s and 1980s, the theater reported more than 75 percent occupancy for the show's 2003 run.[2]

Urban planners and local civic groups are also waking up to the role art can play in revitalizing metropolitan areas and contributing to social prosperity. Governments throughout the world are hoping to re-create the success of Frank Gehry's Guggenheim Museum in Bilbao, Spain, the Imperial War Museum in North Liverpool, England, and the Rosenthal Center for Contemporary Art in Cincinnati, all of which contributed to the general welfare by raising cultural awareness, increasing tourism, and generating millions of dollars in incremental revenue for local economies. The Lower Manhattan Development Corporation, which oversees the rebuilding of New York City's World Trade Center, has already determined that cultural institutions will be an integral part of the new design for lower Manhattan.[3]

New York City's status as the nation's number one domestic tourist destination has made tourism the second largest contributor to the city's economy, second only to Wall Street. Rockefeller Center, a tourist destination in its own right as one of the world's most impressive art deco urban spaces, has attracted even more attention by turning its teeming central plaza into an open-air exhibition space. In 2000, it became the setting for *Puppy*, a forty-three-foot-tall topiarylike sculpture of a dog created by artist Jeff Koons. Two years later, it was the site for *Reversed Double Helix* by Takashi Murakami, a Japanese-born artist and designer who immigrated to New York in the 1990s. The installation included flags, mushroom-shaped benches, a thirty-foot-tall painted fiberglass Buddha-like figure named Tongari-Kun ("Mr. Pointy"), and twin thirty-foot-in-diameter balloons painted to resemble giant eyeballs that floated sixty feet above the ice rink. The work, at once whimsical and vaguely ominous, drew on Murakami's fascination with Japanese *okatu*, which roughly translates into "computer geek culture" and in turn takes its highly stylized, surreal images from Japanese *manga* cartoon books and animated films. Even before its month-long run had begun, Tongari-Kun and several smaller figures were sold to an investor for $1.5 million.[4]

The juxtaposition of American architecture and Japanese-inspired art reflects the cosmopolitan nature of the modern megalopolis and reinforces New York City's status as a creative mecca. Large-scale urban projects take advantage of the scale and mythic status of major cities and encourage other artists to use the cityscape as their canvas. In 2003, Mayor Bloomberg gave a green light to *The Gates*, an epic installation of 7,500 sixteen-foot-tall curtains draped over pedestrian walkways in Central Park by the artist Christo. The project, which is planned to extend for sixteen days during February 2005, will generate thousands of jobs and millions of dollars. But if all goes well, its true value will be in how it transforms the city's central garden into something magical and mythic—and produces indelible images of New York City that will linger in human minds for decades.

Public art can also instruct and empower. In California, where popular and Mexican culture have historical ties, murals have proliferated as an expression of social reality, merging the style and social consciousness of early-twentieth-century Mexican masters like Diego Rivera, José Clemente Orozco, and David Alfaro Siqueiros with the street-spawned graffiti art of the Chicano barrio. More than three thousand murals have been cataloged in Los Angeles, where the paintings have become tourist attractions and a source of civic and ethnic pride. One of the most famous is *The Great Wall of Los Angeles*, a thirteen-foot-tall, half-mile-long mural that is located in the Tujunga Flood Control Channel in West Hollywood. The *Great Wall* spans the entire history of Southern California, from prehistoric times to the post–World War II era. Commissioned by the U.S.

Army Corps of Engineers, who also built the channel, the mural was begun in 1976 by Los Angeles artist Judy Baca, a Mexican American, who led a team of four hundred underprivileged, mostly Hispanic teenagers in the initial design. By the time the mural was completed seven years later, it had evolved through consultations and contributions from hundreds of artists, historians, and academic experts and featured sections devoted to Jewish refugees, California's mountains and beaches, the zoot suit riots, Charlie Chaplin, Thomas Edison, and dust bowl migrant workers.[5]

Since the 1970s, California's murals have become less political and more ethnically diverse. The murals of Los Angeles, many of which have been painted by African American, Asian, and white artists, are considered the greatest creation of public art in the United States since the Works Progress Administration. Hundreds of new murals have been commissioned by city and state agencies, and with the help of private and corporate donations, including forty-seven murals that were commissioned by then mayor Tom Bradley to be painted along the Los Angeles freeways for the 1984 Olympics. The murals, which can easily be seen from the freeway, combine the city's car culture with a public display of shared cultural icons and historical events, not unlike the creation myths depicted in Aztec codices and totems, which were designed to create a communal sense of identity and historical continuity.

It's no accident that the spirit of syncretism that characterized the Aztec empire is taking hold in contemporary Los Angeles and other large cities. The Aztec capital, Tenochtitlán, located in the heart of present-day Mexico City, was founded in 1325 by a tribe called the Mexicas, who had migrated to central Mexico from Aztlán, an Edenic city in the north that was their primordial birthplace.[6] At the height of their civilization, during the fifteenth and early sixteenth centuries, the Aztecs were avid anthropologists who infused their own artworks and murals with the symbols and deities of the ancient cultures that preceded them, as well as those they encountered or conquered as their empire expanded to take up most of what is now modern-day Mexico.[7]

The Los Angeles County Museum of Art mounted a massive exhibition in 2001 called *The Road to Aztlán: Art from a Mythic Homeland*.[8] The show took five years to organize and included more than 250 pieces of pre-Columbian, Spanish colonial period, and contemporary art and artifacts from the southwest United States and Mexico. As Hispano-Asian creation myths and historical yearnings—both overt and subliminal, ancient and modern—seep into the mainstream, the notion of Los Angeles as a nexus for cutting-edge art and culture that reflects its geographic destiny as a Pacific Rim metropolis is only growing stronger. Not unlike its celebrated Asian-Latin-French fusion cuisine, Los Angeles is a jalapeño-wasabi-infused puree of new performance venues dedicated to presenting edgy music, theater, and art. A thriving and diverse student population, the creative energy of Hollywood, and a supportive critical establishment have merged with the city's expanding ethnic base to nurture a large and open-minded audience for unconventional art and performance events. The annual Performing Arts Series by the University of California at Los Angeles has led the way with an array of concerts and programs that spotlight nontraditional works and performances by European, Asian, Latin American, and local artists.

In affluent and increasingly multicultural Orange County, the Electric Orange Festival, a fall series produced in conjunction with the Philharmonic Society of Orange County, has staged pioneering works by Hawaiian, Latin American, and European artists, including a Mexican program by the Kronos Quartet.[9] The new centerpiece of avant-garde Los Angeles is the Walt Disney Concert Hall, a futuristic Frank Gehry–designed steel structure signaling the city's mission as an epicenter of forward-looking creativity. The Disney Concert Hall's inauguration was marked by the world premiere of *Invention for Paper Instruments and Orchestra*, a piece by Chinese-born conductor-composer Tan Dun that uses paper to help retell the story of its invention. The work, which includes sheets of paper and paper-covered drums, as well as a large string section that is dispersed throughout the audience, comprises four movements: "Wind," a sonic rendering of paper's fibrous origins; "Birds," an aural moment in the bamboo forest as animals witness the soaking of leaves and bark; "Storm," which uses paper to make the sound of clapping thunder; and "Paper Drums," an exploration of sounds made by taut surfaces and vibrating columns of air. "Paper is the most effective and portable means where ideas and images are captured and communicated afar," Dun said before the concert. "We are surrounded by paper in our lives. Paper not only communicates, but can transmit creativity in an acoustic way by blowing, rubbing, cracking, shaking, crumbling, tearing, popping, puckering, fingering, hitting, waving, slapping, plucking, whistling, swinging, and singing through the paper." [10]

Dun has built a world-class oeuvre from fearless sonic invention and an ability to reconcile ancient and modern, East and West, and classical and experimental modes of expression. His investigations into the origins and meaning of music and sound are oblivious to the borders between pop and classical contexts. Dun won a Grammy Award for his music in the film *Crouching Tiger, Hidden Dragon* and has conducted at major classical music festivals in New York City, Munich, Paris, Vienna, London, and Rome. By incorporating shamanistic and animistic traditions into avant-garde forms, he is both cataloging the world's new cultural realities and composing the sound track of its future. Dun's symphony *Heaven Earth Mankind*, which was commissioned by the government of Hong Kong to mark its unification with China on July 1, 1997, took its musical inspiration from the archaeological discovery in 1978 of sixty-five bronze bells that had been buried since 433 B.C. The bells, known collectively as *bianzhong*, could generate a nearly perfect fixed twelve-note chromatic scale, an evolutionary milestone previously believed not to have come until hundreds of years later. The *bianzhong* were played during the premiere performance of *Heaven Earth Mankind*, which also featured cellist Yo-Yo Ma, and is regarded by Dun as an invocation of a new global community that transcends national and cultural boundaries.

Cave Dwellers

As hybrid culture becomes the creative norm, mutation and mixture are reformulating the pop mainstream. In blockbuster films like *X-Men* and *Spider-Man*, mutants with strange powers are the misunderstood saviors of an intolerant world that persecutes them for being different. The epic *Lord of the Rings* trilogy hinges on a military alliance between men, elves, and dwarfs. In *Charlie's Angels*, *Laura Croft: Tomb Raider*, and Quentin

Tarantino's *Kill Bill Vol. 1* and *Vol. 2*, women are full-throttle action heroes who shoot guns, wield samurai swords, and otherwise dispatch their enemies with ruthless aplomb. Stories that traverse continents, races, and cultures are forging a shared global mythology—and driving the new economics of entertainment. Minorities and women have been granted superhuman strength; sex roles and genders are reversed, merged, and exchanged. Mysticism and magic flow freely across space and time, and the secrets of ancient cultures are precious and immutable. Reality and fantasy are interchangeable and fluid. The only absolutes are human emotion, sensuality, and love.

American culture continues to be the lingua franca of Western civilization, in no small part because it is the only truly multicultural industrial society. Despite the economic and political gains of the European Union, Europeans remain allergic to one another's national arts. With the exception of cultural imports from the United States, Italians, Germans, and Frenchmen prefer their own films, records, plays, and books to anyone else's. In 2002, 50 percent of the French film market went to American movies. Thirty-five percent went to homegrown French films, with only a fraction going to cinema from neighboring England (4.9 percent), Germany (0.8 percent), and Italy (0.2 percent). The same pattern holds for books, plays, and pop music, which means that for the foreseeable future, world culture will continue to become more American, but only if America continues to become more worldly.

In *The Matrix* and its sequels, Keanu Reeves—who was born in Beirut to an English-born mother and half-Hawaiian, half-Chinese father—leads a transethnic band of rebels against a computer-generated "reality" that can be defeated only by a potent mix of technology, Eastern mysticism, and a redemptive faith in the power of love. In Plato's *Republic*, a group of prisoners are chained facing a wall. Behind them is a fire, in front of which puppeteers manipulate objects, casting shadows on the wall, which is all that the prisoners are able to see. According to Plato, the prisoners, who represent human beings, mistakenly accept the shadows cast on the cave wall as reality, failing to understand the true nature of the objects they think they are seeing, and are in turn unable to advance to the stage of understanding the essential form of objects, which would ultimately reveal their meaning. In *The Matrix*, the world inhabited by humans is like Plato's Cave; people think they are experiencing reality, but it is actually a computer-generated illusion designed to keep them in blissful ignorance while machines use them as human batteries. When Neo is rescued from the Matrix by Morpheus, and he realizes the world he formerly lived in was made of shadows, the change is wrenching and painful. But for true understanding, he must the follow path out of the cave and into the sunlight, an act of faith and inner understanding that transcends reason. "I'm trying to free your mind, Neo," Morpheus tells him, "but all I can do is show you the door. You're the one that has to step through." When Neo is confronted with a chance to save his mentor, he risks his life against overwhelming odds. He dies, but his act of self-sacrifice redeems him, and he is resurrected as the One, the Messiah in the prophecy, the savior of the human race. The *Matrix* films, which are among the most popular and profitable movies ever made, blend technology with mythology, borrowing freely from Christianity, Buddhism, and metaphysical philosophy.

Since the advent of written language, when human events were cataloged in cave drawings and glyphs or preserved for future generations in tribal myths and stories, words were tools for remembering. Ethnic literature has traditionally staked out the margins of the mainstream, seeking to define a territory that confirms its own experience and existence. In the preface to the 1852 first edition of *Uncle Tom's Cabin*, Harriet Beecher Stowe, a white woman who wrote about black slavery, felt the need to explain: "The scenes of this story, as its title indicates, lie among a race hitherto ignored by the associations of polite and refined society; an exotic race, whose ancestors, born beneath a tropic sun, brought with them, and perpetuated to their descendants, a character so essentially unlike the hard and dominant Anglo-Saxon race, as for many years to have won from it only misunderstanding and contempt." Despite Beecher's success at depicting slavery with a veracity that white America had never before encountered, or perhaps because of it, the book aroused a backlash of skeptics and detractors who claimed that it had to be a fabrication. In order to refute her critics, Stowe published a companion book two years later, *The Key to Uncle Tom's Cabin*, which was subtitled *Presenting the Original Facts and Documents upon Which the Story Is Founded*.

Almost 150 years later, the discovery by Henry Louis Gates Jr. of *The Bondwoman's Narrative*, believed to be the earliest known work of fiction by an African American, would prove that black slaves were perfectly capable of speaking—and writing—for themselves. Meanwhile, African Americans and other ethnic writers managed to establish their credibility as artists and continued to extend the boundaries of racially and culturally specific fiction. While the majority of minority writers remained marginalized or unpublished, a handful broke into the mainstream and became best-sellers. James Baldwin's *Go Tell It on the Mountain*, Ralph Ellison's *The Invisible Man*, and Richard Wright's *Native Son* explored racial, political, and existential themes in the African American experience; Rudolfo Anaya, considered to be the founder of Chicano fiction, used a bicultural prism to depict the lives of Hispanic Americans in the southwestern United States in *Bless Me, Ultima*; Louise Erdrich, Tony Hillerman, and Gerald Vizenor grafted Native American myths and the subversive humor of the trickster onto postmodern literary forms; Amy Tan brought an epic scope to her tale of several generations of Asian women; Cristina Garcia and Oscar Hijuelos found lyricism and magic in the nationalist nostalgia of Cuban Americans; Toni Morrison, Rita Mae Brown, and Alice Walker injected feminism and sexuality into African American fiction. Philip Roth brought the Jewish-American experience into sharp comedic relief with *Portnoy's Complaint*, and journalist-novelist Pete Hamill put a multicultural stamp on the story of the Irish in America with novels like *Snow in August* and *Forever*, which meld Irish, Jewish, and African history with folkloric fantasy in New York City.

By the end of the twentieth century, the defiant, assertive posture of early ethnic fiction began to shift toward a more eclectic, reflective stance that took transnational realities for granted. It was no longer unusual for a Latino author to write in English or for a writer of color to snag a major advance from a mainstream publisher. Pioneers like Arte Publico Press, which had nurtured the Latino market since the 1970s, suddenly found themselves competing with mainstream houses like Farrar, Straus & Giroux, Doubleday, and Knopf. Convinced that ethnic fiction was commercially viable, and betting that minority readership would inevitably follow demographic trends, mainstream publishers launched boutique imprints that could better focus on ethnic authors, audiences, and marketing opportunities. The writing was changing, too. Books like Alisa Valdes-Rodriguez's *Dirty Girls Social Club*, which follows the lives of six Latina women of an assortment of Latin American nationalities and sexual orientations, and Cristina Garcia's *Monkey Hunting*, about a Chinese man who travels to Cuba in the mid–nineteenth century and is forced to become a slave, reflect the fast-forward blur of cultures, borders, and races that their authors were born into. Susan Choi, a Korean American, examines the frayed edges of the radical Left through the eyes of a Japanese American terrorist in her novel *American Woman*. And Colson Whitehead, an African American, examines the kaleidoscopic ecosystem of his hometown in *The Colossus of New York: A City in 13 Parts*. The book, whose title refers to the "The New Colossus," a poem by Emma Lazarus that is inscribed at the base of the Statue of Liberty, is a meditation on urban life that ponders the psychosocial intersection of identity, place, and belonging. "Part of writing is trying to make sense of the world," Whitehead said to *The New York Times*. "With a personal book like 'Colossus' I was trying to find out what discrete moments meant to me, to other people. Is there a community? How do we create community?"[11]

For Chilean author Alberto Fuguet, community transcends borders, cultures, and—most of all—history. Fuguet is the instigator and ideological leader of the McOndo movement, a pan-Latino literary posse that rejects the legacy of "El Boom," the Latin American literary phenomenon of the 1960s led by García Márquez, Mario Vargas Llosa, and Julio Cortázar that established magical realism as the trademark literary style of Latin America. The term *McOndo*, which wryly alludes to both McDonald's and Macondo, the fictional setting of García Márquez's masterpiece *One Hundred Years of Solitude*, is also the title of a fiction anthology edited by Fuguet that showcases a younger generation of Latin American writers who openly identify with American mainstream culture and a pan-regional sense of self.

Fuguet's 2003 novel, *The Movies of My Life*, is about a seismologist who measures temblors in his professional work, even as his psyche is rattled by the cultural tectonics shifting beneath his feet. The book is organized around flight itineraries and the titles of Hollywood movies—*Born*

Free, Woodstock, Lost Horizon—literal and allegorical references that trigger flashbacks of life that straddles countries, cities, and languages: Allende and Nixon, Santiago and Encino, Jordache and the Jetsons. In *Grand Prix*—a film the narrator watches at age two with his father and uncles at a drive-in theater "under the stars"—Fuguet describes America's lure as a land of reinvention, an almost mythical country where the two branches of his family attempt to escape the past and start over.

In Fuguet's Osterized ontology, movies loom bigger than life—not reality itself, but a projection of it—we are strangers in a dark room facing a wall of moving shadows. Subtitles appear at the bottom of the screen, translating the subtext of illuminated dreams; memories that can be replayed, rewound, fast-forwarded. The films in *The Movies of My Life* shape the protagonist's reality but are also anchored to the time and place where he watched them. By personalizing the images on the screen, and grafting their own fantasies and desire onto them, viewers transform American cinema into something universal and culturally relevant. "All the movies in my book, or on anybody's hard drive, I really consider to be Chilean," he says. "For me, *Jaws* is a Chilean movie, because I will always watch it in the context of where I was and who I was with when I saw it. *Brazil* is a movie about a futuristic, Orwellian world. It's a kind of social science fiction set in the future, but when it played in South America we all became convinced it was about Chile. For us, it had to be a metaphor about Pinochet—we saw the movie and made it ours. In the end, for me, *Brazil* is a local film. That's the way culture works; we appropriate it."

The McOndos, who grew up surfing the Net and watching American TV and movies, are forging a new Latin American literature that reflects their own experience and ignores linguistic and national boundaries. Like Fuguet, who grew up in Southern California and moved back to Chile when he was eleven, members of the McOndo generation are as much at home in Los Angeles, Miami, and New York City as they are in Santiago, Buenos Aires, and Mexico City. Among the new crop of Latin American intellectuals who reflect the trend are Ernestro Mestre-Reed, who was born in Cuba and attended Tulane University, and Anna Kuzami Stahl, a Louisiana native who emigrated to Argentina and writes in Spanish. It's worth noting that Mexico's Carlos Fuentes, a founding member of El

Boom, spent part of his childhood in Washington, D.C., and was deeply influenced by William Faulkner, which helps to explain why he has publicly applauded their cause. Not unlike the new wave of ethnic writers in the United States or, for that matter, the El Boomers who preceded them, the McOndos are breaking with tradition, but not with art; their rejection of the status quo is a by-product of their need to describe the world as they see it and experience it. They are telling their stories, and just like their counterparts to the north, they are keeping what is useful and discarding the rest. The metacultural visions of U.S. and Latin American writers overlap and interconnect; their voices harmonize and mirror each other, offering up myriad reflections of a mutually imagined America.

12. How Soon Is Now?

The multicultural consumer and the American consumer are one and the same. Americans come in every color and socioeconomic stratum; they are U.S. born and foreign-born, speak dozens of languages, yet are united by shared aspirations and a common capacity for transformation, evolution, and growth. As georelational databases, psychographic profiles, and behavioral models slice and dice the mind and heart of the American buyer, the images and messages of the media are reflecting and projecting thousands of different Americas, each one of which is a piece of a larger picture that is only beginning to come into focus. The "experiential economy," in which consumers place a greater value on things that they can experience, is evolving into the "transformational economy," which is the products, services, and experiences that will make each consumer a different, better person. Only by being transformed together—a mutual recognition of our common destiny as a people of many peoples, a race of many races, a nation of many nations—can we attain and complete the apex of the unfinished pyramid on the one-dollar bill.

The New Mainstream *is* America. The myth of "America = white" is slowly but surely being debunked by scientific, demographic, and economic forces that cannot be turned back or ignored. What will rise in its place is a rejuvenated, postethnic definition of America in which race and ethnicity are simply ingredients in the complex alloy of American identity.

The multicultural economy *is* the American economy, because the economics of diversity affect every American and every industry. The transformation of the consumer economy is driven by profits and magnified in the media. The growing buying power of ethnic groups will continue to transform how products and services are marketed and developed. The confluence of the creative class, the transethnic youth culture, and economically empowered minorities is molding the New Mainstream, which is by definition fluid, dynamic, and multifaceted.

The multicultural economy *is* the global economy because market trends in the United States drive—and are in turn determined by—market trends throughout the world. America is a global society because its media shapes the dreams of millions and because the issues and opportunities of the domestic ethnic market are a microcosm of America's relationship with the rest of the world.

The multicultural identity *is* the American identity, because no single culture or nationality owns the right to define a nation that is so diverse and dynamic and incomplete. The issues and conflicts that divide us also unite us, because they are the problems and issues of all Americans. Exclusion is by its very nature anti-American, just as separatism is inherently self-defeating. The majority on the margins has moved to the center and is already transforming the cultural, social, and economic destiny of the United States. As the New Mainstream flows across borders and races, the failure of America to appreciate the diversity and validity of other cultures and nations is a failure to recognize itself.

Five hundred years after Columbus reached the coast of America, a New World once again looms on the horizon, changed but still teeming with potential and possibility. The natives have even more colors to choose from, more gifts to offer, more tribes to which they can belong. They speak more languages and have more money, their houses are bigger, their armies stronger. The heirs of Columbus now stand among them, but they are still young, still eager to learn, still willing to accept others, still able to change.

In the loosely woven yet constantly expanding fabric of the New Mainstream, this tumultuous tangle of creatives and Cantonese, Latinas and Lebanese, geeks, gays, and ghetto boyz, there are endlessly new ways to dress and love, eat and work, pray and play, buy and die. The New Mainstream is international and the new kid on the block, overwhelmingly diverse and tolerant, but not radical or antiestablishmentarian. The New Mainstream does not seek to overthrow the existing order, it *is* the new order. These assimilating awakeners of the American dream, these de facto defenders of the founding faith, this race-bending, world-mending tribe, may in the end be the legitimate custodians and inheritors not only of our country's future, but also of its heart and soul.

Inner Visions

On the clear, crisp morning of September 11, 2003, I joined a few hundred people at the Asia Society in Manhattan for an opening ceremony and blessing of a mandala sand painting by the Tibetan monks from Drepung Loseling Monastery in south India. Dressed in crimson and saffron robes, with a framed photograph of the Dalai Lama behind them, the monks began the ceremony with a raucous fanfare of horns, cymbals, and bells. Then a single monk began to chant, emitting a long, guttural growl. The other monks and various instruments joined in, and the sound grew in complexity and volume until it had an almost elemental power. More fanfares followed, each one evoking the chaos and clamor of destruction and rebirth, giving way to a progression of overlapping chants that seemed to spiral up through the roof of the auditorium. As the music reached its crescendo, I noticed that the nicely dressed Anglo woman seated next to me was praying silently, her eyes closed in a kind of private rapture. Was she praying for the victims of 9/11? I wondered. Or for New York City? Or for world peace? Most of all I wondered how the mood of quiet catharsis and introspection, more hopeful than vengeful, could spread beyond the room and push back the shadows of paranoia and despair that still seemed to grip the nation, if not the whole world, two years after a band of Muslim terrorists armed with box knives inflicted a permanent wound on the earth's only superpower.

The singing stopped. In the silence that followed, the monks stood respectfully motionless for several minutes while the audience filed out. Then the monks shuffled offstage and retreated upstairs to a cool, dimly lighted room where they would spend the next ten days painstakingly creating the mandala—an intricately patterned representation of the cosmos—a few grains of colored sand at a time. The mandala was being created by the monks as a special gift and an invocation of healing energy and peace for New York City on the second anniversary of the World Trade Center attacks. The ritual of sand painting originated from Tantric Buddhism in India at least two thousand years ago and was introduced into Tibet around the seventh century.

The tradition of sand painting developed as a way of initiating monks into specific meditations and mental visualizations. The mandala is understood as a divine world consisting of a central deity, its residence, and its environment. The symbols in the mandala include the "seed" syllable, which represents the deity at the center of the painting, such as the *vajra*, drawn for the deity of Akshobaya. The Akshobaya Buddha is translated to mean "an unshakable victor" and "an enlightened quality of resolve" in the midst of crisis and negativity. *Vayra* is the enlightened mind, which is in an indivisible state of bliss and the wisdom of emptiness. Other mandala symbols include a lotus flower or ring of flames, which represents the fundamental steps for inner transformation. The lotus signifies the mind of renunciation, while the ring of flames symbolizes wisdom that cuts through ignorance.

The monks' conviction that their rituals can have a healing and transformative effect on America was explained by Geshe Lobsong Tenzin, a graduate of Drepung Loseling Monastery who teaches Tibetan studies at Emory University and serves as the director of the Drepung Loseling Institute in Atlanta. "It is a gift for New Yorkers, but also for all Americans on behalf of Tibetans," he said. "Our purpose is to create this mandala with the prayers for peace and protection. In Buddhism there is an idea, a concept, that says without difficulties there is no transformation. If we can recognize the difficulty, and instead of reacting with hatred and aversion, look into why such difficulties unfold, and look into the sources of that, then there is a unique opportunity to address those issues. And I think that in some ways that's what's happening."

Geshe Lobsong talked about the growing popularity of yoga and meditation in the United States and the increasing awareness of its health-enhancing powers. He also noted the growing hunger for a spiritual dimension in American life and a void that is left unfulfilled by traditional organized religions. He encouraged his listeners to attend the free "tech-in" that the Dalai Lama would be giving in Central Park the following Sunday and reported that the Dalai Lama had remarked on the difference in the way New Yorkers had behaved during the recent blackout. "This time there was no looting of supermarkets and the people were so helpful," Geshe Lobsong said, recalling the Dalai Lama's words. "And he remarked that this was something that he had seen: that America, and New Yorkers, have evolved and learned from this tragedy to help one another, to love one another. In Buddhism there is an idea about conducting adverse conditions into the path of transformation. So although what happened is horrific, and should never happen anywhere, it is to the credit of New Yorkers and Americans that they turned it into something good."

In a quiet, measured voice, Geshe Lobsong explained that in his view the United States, having achieved unparalleled progress in the material world, was in a unique position to recognize that materialism also has limitations. Geshe Lobsong is also sure that the United States has a very special role to play in the world and that it has reached a critical juncture in its historical and spiritual evolution, a fork in the road where it could take two very different paths. "America is going through a major change," he said. "Whenever difficulties like the attacks of September 11 happen, it gives in some ways an opportunity for a collective transformation as well. And I think in some ways that is happening. We realize how vulnerable we are in spite of the incredible technology and weaponry that we have. In some ways it forces us to think: What is lasting security? Is it by stopping production of weapons? Or is it the greater peace and security brought about by inner transformation?"

At a time of global turmoil and national doubt, more and more Americans seem to be asking the same question. Even before 9/11, non-Western spirituality was on the upswing in America. In 1989, when the Dalai Llama spoke in Central Park, five thousand people showed up. Ten years later, the crowd had swelled to nearly forty thousand. With seven out of ten Americans saying they are religious and consider spirituality to be an important part of their lives, a growing percentage are looking to Eastern and nontraditional forms of spirituality for inner peace and enlightenment. The quest for a deeper meaning in life runs across all ethnic, political, and economic groups. Between April 2001 and August 2003, *Time* magazine devoted no fewer than three of its covers to the phenomenon of yoga. "A path to enlightenment that winds back 5,000 years in its native India has suddenly become so hot, so cool, so suddenly of this minute," *Time* effused. "It's the exercise cum meditation for the new millennium, one that doesn't so much pump you up as bliss you out."

The media mantra has only become louder. An estimated 18 million Americans practice yoga, and the number is growing exponentially. Meditation is also starting to mean big money. *Yoga Journal* estimates that the annual expenditure on yoga-related instructional materials, clothing, weekend workshops, CDs, books, and videos is at least $1,500 per person, which translates into a $27 billion industry. "To put this into perspective," Russell Wild wrote in *Yoga Journal*, "if the yoga business were consolidated, the resulting corporation (Yoga-Mart?) would be slightly larger than DOW chemical, slightly smaller than Microsoft."[1]

In their desire to tap this lucrative niche, advertisers are becoming more enlightened. As yoga and Eastern spirituality enter the American mainstream, they are being used to sell everything from Apple computers to Hyundai automobiles to Tylenol PM and Playtex bras. Affluent professionals looking for a break from their hectic schedules are swapping reservations in the Bahamas to check in at no-frills ashrams that forbid talking, serve low-calorie vegan grub, and offer a purifying regimen of meditation, exercise, and self-deprivation. In Manhattan, a new thirty-five-thousand-square-foot dance club called Spirit will cater to new agers with a nocturnal bent. The club is divided into three areas: Body, a dance area; Mind, a spa offering aromatherapy and massage; and Soul, an organic raw-food restaurant.

Not everyone is comfortable with the commodification of higher consciousness. Critics worry that the fashion focus on expensive yoga clothing and gear, yoga-inspired ads for liquor and cars, and an erroneous assumption that nirvana is just a few group sessions away is cheapening, if not completely undermining, the discipline's essential message. Others contend that the Zenification of America, with its emphasis on health benefits and image-enhancing effects, is merely another form of narcissism masquerading as enlightenment. The online auction craze took a sacrilegious turn when a man from Des Moines, Iowa, offered his soul for sale on eBay. Bidding rose from $1 to $400 before the item was banished from the site.

But to dismiss America's fascination with Eastern traditions as a superficial fad is to overlook a genuine sense of spiritual crisis. The rational certainties of science that served as the gospel of the modern mind no longer inspire the same measure of confidence and awe. Technology, which once promised to deliver mankind into a future free from poverty and disease, has revealed a darker, less utopian side. The euphoria of sending men to the moon has given way to images of exploding space shuttles. The miraculous eradication of smallpox is overshadowed by the grim realities of AIDS and biological warfare. Airplanes have become flying bombs. Global warming and nuclear proliferation only add to the anxious air of impending apocalypse. The percentage of Americans who see scientists as having "very great prestige" has declined nine percentage points in the last quarter century, dropping from 66 percent to 57 percent. Another poll found that most Americans believe in miracles while half believe in ghosts and another third put their faith in astrology.[2]

Americans are also showing a renewed interest in homeopathic medicines and nontraditional cures. Felipe Korzenny has built a career out of designing ethnographic research and marketing methodologies for Fortune 500 companies. As the principal and cofounder of Cheskin, a marketing research firm based in Redwood Shores, California, Korzenny has helped businesses position their brands and services for the multicultural marketplace by linking them to archetypal sources and traditions. For example, a Spanish-language ad he helped develop for Toyota with the tag line *"El viaje de tu vida"* ("The journey of your life") imbues the Toyota brand with an expansive, almost philosophical message that transcends the practical functionality of a car as a vehicle to get from point A to point B. Instead, the ad reflects Korzenny's contention that "Hispanic consumers see themselves as a continuation of a historical and cultural tradition."

That tradition is characterized by a deeply spiritual dimension. Latin Americans are less materialistic because money—*dinero*—has no value in heaven. For them, heaven is not a distant place from which no one ever returns, but merely another version of reality from which spirits can return from time to time if they so choose. In the case of health products and services, Korzenny sees value in using anthropological and even cosmological filters to determine, say, the most effective way to market health insurance or an HMO medical center to a person with a Latin or Afro-Caribbean background. In Mexico and Latin America, for example, doctors have a social and cultural significance that goes far beyond the scientific and professional associations that most Anglo-Americans have of physicians. In Latin America, doctors are pillars of the community, whose judgment and advice go far beyond health matters to include economic, political, and interpersonal decisions. At the same time, doctors descend from a tradition of shamans, or *curanderos*, who were believed to be in touch with the supernatural. In Mexico, where Aztecs used more than three thousand herbs for medicinal purposes and a deep Catholic tradition fostered a fatalistic view of disease and death, homeopathic medicine and herbal remedies are considered valid forms of treatment. In Puerto Rico, foods, diseases, and remedies are divided into "hot" and "cold," which are categories that relate more to anthropophysiological associations than to temperature. Bananas, sugarcane, and coconut are "cold," whereas chocolate, garlic, alcoholic beverages, and cornmeal are "hot." Maladies that are "cold"—arthritis, colds, and gastrointestinal complaints—should be treated with "hot" foods and remedies, while "hot" illnesses—constipation, diarrhea, and stomach cramps—are treated with "cold" substances." An informed doctor can use this information to increase the cooperation and trust of patients when prescribing medicines to Puerto Rican patients. Hispanic women, according to Korzenny, because of a legacy of Catholic guilt and superstition, are more inclined to feel guilt, a personal affliction, as opposed to the Asian concept of shame, which is shared by the entire family.

Yet as the cultural divide between Latins and non-Latins continues to narrow, such distinctions may become harder and harder to quantify. Homeopathy, also referred to in the United States as "alternative medicine," is widespread in China, India, South America, and Europe. In recent years, its popularity has exploded in the United States as well.

In another sign of the mutual transformation of periphery and core, homeopathic treatments are becoming increasingly accepted by the American medical profession and the general public. GNC stores are the new apothecary, and herbs such as echinacea and Saint-John's-wort are no longer outside the mainstream. According to *The Washington Post*, the number of physicians in the United States who specialized in homeopathic medicine doubled from 1980 to 1982.[3] Americans are also more likely than ever to try alternative therapies such as acupuncture and practice meditation or yoga. Recent studies involving Tibetan monks at the University of Wisconsin have produced evidence that certain types of Buddhist-style meditation not only reduce psychological stress in otherwise ordinary office workers, but also boost the human body's immune response systems. And Dr. Jon Kabat-Zinn, founder of the Stress Reduction Clinic at the University of Massachusetts Medical School, has conducted research suggesting that "mindful meditation" techniques, which the monks use to separate themselves from negative thoughts, can accelerate the treatment of psoriasis, relieve symptoms for patients suffering from anxiety and chronic pain, and improve the mental condition of cancer patients. Kabat-Zinn is working with CIGNA HealthCare to determine if meditation can reduce health care costs for chronic fatigue syndrome, fibromyalgia, and irritable bowel syndrome. In coming years, that could mean the distinction between traditional and alternative medicine will all but vanish as Puerto Rican doctors dispense a mix of pharmaceutical drugs and homeopathic cures to multiethnic patients who regard meditation and chakra alignment essential parts of a healthy lifestyle regimen.

Spacious Skies

The spiritual vacuity of contemporary life is visible even in the modern urban skyline. For most of the history of human civilization, the tallest, most important structures in any community were those devoted to worship—all churches, mosques, and temples were built with peaked roofs, spires, domes, and minarets that pointed upward. Even as late as the early twentieth century, after science had supplanted metaphysics as the dominant philosophy of the West, skyscrapers like the Empire State and Chrysler buildings showed that steel and concrete could soar. But most buildings built since 1950—when the functional glass boxes of modernism became the new cathedrals of the postindustrial era—have flat, inexpressive tops. Architecturally, our connection to the heavens—and our spatial link to the sacred—has been symbolically severed.

"The whole idea of a piece of architecture mediating between heaven and earth is gone—it's lost," agrees Ron Pompei, a New York–based architect and designer who perceives cultural significance in public space. Pompei is best known for the pan-cultural retail environments he has created for clients like Urban Outfitters, Anthropologie, Levi's, MTV, and Sony. Pompei's design philosophy is centered on what he calls "C3"—the intersection between commerce, culture, and community. Together they constitute a "third place" outside the home and work where social interaction is facilitated and where the New Mainstream can take a physical shape. "The early ziggurats were all about making a sacred mountain," he says. "Our mission is to create the new sacred spaces for the new global America."

Pompei believes that American culture and architecture are on the brink of a transformation of public spaces into multidimensional areas where people can shop, learn, and socialize and where multicultural divides are nonexistent. These areas are de facto realms of the young and the young at heart. The future, Pompei believes, is already evident in the merged ethnic and social identities of urban and suburban American youths known as the "echo boomers," or Generation Y. Born between 1977 and 1994, they are 75 million strong and will make up 41 percent of the population by 2013. Pompei has found them intuitively receptive to the idea of space as a sacred representation of the world that can resonate with multiple meanings gleaned from different cultural traditions. "Kids are looking for the real purpose of their life, a confirmation of their uniqueness," Pompei observes. "Yet in that diversity is their unity. We see it in nature: we are all sons and daughters of humanity."

According to a study by Harris Interactive entitled "Youth Pulse," members of Generation Y have annual incomes that total $211 billion.[4] Spending levels rise with age, along with the ability of teens and young adults to earn extra income through part- and full-time jobs. Per capita spending is lowest for preteens (ages eight to twelve), followed by teens (ages thirteen to nineteen) and young adults (ages twenty to twenty-one). Echo boomers are significantly more numerous than the Gen X–ers who preceded them and are generally considered less cynical and more optimistic than their older brothers and sisters. For advertisers and the entertainment industry, teens and young adults have a value that goes far beyond their actual spending power as tastemakers and style setters. This is also the age when young consumers are forming brand loyalties than can last the rest of their lives.

Urban ethnic youths are considered by many to be the key to Generation Y, not just because of their disproportionate numbers, but because they tend to skew younger and be concentrated in the major cities where fashion, music, and other cultural expressions are forged and transmitted to the rest of the population and around the world. In 2000, Hispanics made up 12.5 percent of the U.S. population, but Hispanics under eighteen years old made up 17.1 percent. And since the number of Hispanic teens is growing faster than that of non-Hispanic whites by a margin of 34 percent to 6 percent, respectively, the Latino proportion of the population will only increase as they get older.

Roger Selbert, vice president of strategic planning for LatinWorks, a multicultural advertising and marketing agency based in Austin, Texas, found that 74 percent of the Hispanic teens it surveyed in Los Angeles said that they spoke Spanglish. "It's the voice of a new generation," Selbert predicts. "Spanglish will enter the mainstream." Common examples of English and Spanish grafted together include "parkiar *el carro*" ("park the car") and editorial copy from *Latina* magazine, which enjoins women to have "gorgeous *ojos*" ("gorgeous eyes"). A growing number of books are being written in Spanglish, and there's even a Spanglish translation of Cervantes's classic novel, *Don Quixote*. David Perez, the chairman of Cultural Access Group, a Hispanic consumer insight and marketing firm based in New York City, has identified a "multicultural commonality" among U.S. Latino youth, a third of whom live in either Los Angeles, New York City, or Miami. In a study that included 250 telephone surveys and 50 qualitative interviews with fourteen- to twenty-four-year-old Hispanics living in Los Angeles and New York City, Perez found that a solid majority expressed a preference for English, but more than 70 percent said they also spoke Spanglish, mainly at home or when with friends. Perez also found that rather than fitting into any existing demographic or language-based segmentation scheme, Latino urban youths identified with lifestyle "tribes" that revolved around a particular music style and the fashion, attitudes, and other social cues that went with it. From his surveys in Los Angeles and New York City, Perez was able to identify five major tribes: hip-hoppers, roqueros, traditionalists, popsters, and trailblazers.

The urban youth market that emerges from Perez's research is less a demographic segment than a constellation of interconnected networks and subcultures that construct their identity from a variety of sources and media. In Los Angeles, New York City, and Miami, they are already the numerical majority, and most of the rest of the country is not far behind. The cultural fusion they represent is both local and international, and the reverberations of that mix amplify and echo signals that are being picked up in Des Moines and New Delhi, as well Caracas, São Paulo, and Mexico City. As they fearlessly combine cultural ingredients, stitching together new ways of sounding, looking, and being from everything and anything in their reach, they are turning the urban youth market into a plugged-in global bazaar where a hot new idea or trend can zip across town—or the world—in the time it takes to type an instant message. Instinctively testing and reformulating the social glue that holds their tribe together, they are the de facto vanguard of the American present and the owners of its destiny.

Awakenings

In a fast-food, fast-forward society where traditional social bonds are being replaced by truncated forms of human communication and community, there is a new urgency in attending to the benefits of an "inner life." Americans have more demands on their time than ever and have replaced the Japanese as the world's most notorious workaholics. E-mail, instant messages, cell phones, and pagers are accelerating and enhancing our ability to receive information even as we have a diminished opportunity to digest its meaning. New Mainstreamers share a sense of optimism based on the conviction that society's problems can be solved and that all human beings share a responsibility to make their world better.

In earlier eras of American history, periods of accelerated social dislocation brought on by a combination of technological, political, economic, and demographic change have sparked religious movements that sought to heal those rifts and create a new sense of community. In his book *Bowling Alone: The Collapse and Revival of American Community*, Robert Putnam counts three great religious "awakenings." The first, from 1730 to 1760, was stoked by traveling preachers who held massive and continuous revival meetings. The second, from 1800 to 1830, was characterized by "circuit riders" who carried the gospel from one churchless frontier outpost to the next and by the founding of Sunday school, a movement that mixed revivalism with a mission to teach literacy to those who were excluded from regular schools, including women, factory children, and immigrant frontiersmen.[5]

The third awakening, which began around the end of the nineteenth century, is associated with drum-banging, soul-stirring exhortations of the Salvation Army. In the three decades between 1870 and 1900, which came to be known as the Gilded Age, the Industrial Revolution transformed the United States from an agrarian, rural country into an urban, modern nation. Huge fortunes were made, the railroads were built, and the first department stores planted the seeds of the modern consumer economy. During the same period, more than 12 million immigrants entered the

United States, more than the total number of people who had entered the country in the previous 250 years. It was also a time marked by xenophobia and cultural nativism, a yawning disparity between the rich and poor, and a widespread conviction that ordinary Americans were being exploited by powerful, profit-hungry "special interests" whose main goal was to satisfy their own greed at the expense of the common good.

"Americans at the end of the nineteenth century were divided by class, ethnicity and race, much as we are today, although today's dividing lines differ in detail from those of a century ago (as Asians and Hispanics, for example, have replaced Jews and Italians as targets of discrimination)," Putnam points out. "Equally evocative of our own social dilemmas were debates about the effects of the transportation and communications revolutions on traditional community bonds. The railroad and rural free delivery, mail-order firms and (somewhat later) chain stores, and the automobile disrupted local commerce and threatened place-based social connections. Sears, Roebuck, Montgomery Ward, the A&P, and Woolworth's were the counterparts to today's Wal-Mart and Amazon.com."[6]

The Progressive movement was a civic communitarian and political philosophy that sought to check or reverse the corruption and excess of the Gilded Age, which had embraced social Darwinism as its abiding rationale. In addition to pressing for economic and political reforms, the Progressives revived the legitimacy and importance of "social capital," or the organizations, institutions, and informal clubs that bond and unite people into communities of common purpose and identity. The Sierra Club, the American Red Cross, the 4-H Club, the YWCA, the United Way, the Boy Scouts, and dozens of other community groups were founded in the Progressive zeal to connect people in a way that they could know and help one another. Inclusiveness and compassion were regarded not as a weakness, but as critical ingredients in building a strong and cohesive democratic society.

Is America poised for another Great Awakening? "Americans cherish the First Amendment strictures that have enabled us to combine unparalleled religiosity and denominational pluralism with a minimum of religious warfare," writes Putnam. "On the other hand, it is undeniable that religion has played a major role in every period of civic revival in American history. So I challenge America's clergy, lay leaders, theologians, and ordinary worshippers: *Let us spur a new, pluralistic, socially responsible 'great awakening,' so that by 2010 Americans will be more deeply engaged than we are today in one or another spiritual community of meaning, while at the same time becoming more tolerant of the faiths and practices of other Americans.*"

Of course, the "spiritual community of meaning" that Putnam envisions was already part of America when the Pilgrims arrived. It would be more than a little ironic if the spiritual blueprint for America's postmodern future was borrowed from the native people whom the first white settlers dismissed as savages. But that's precisely what was suggested in an anonymous posting on the Native American Web site, Indiancountry.com.

"Increasingly American Indians and many within American society are questioning whether the connection between money and patronage has taken over American politics," the author observed. "Indian Country, for all its problems and contradictions, is still the soul of America. It contains and sustains primordial human values that can cut through the veils of confusion, and which could yet guide a much-needed reawakening in humanity. A recovering Indian country, growing stronger each generation, might need to contribute, in healing its own peoples, a healing for the heart of America itself."

If there is another Great Awakening, it will by definition be respectful of—if not emanating from—a medley of religious and cultural sources, including the Native American respect for nature and the sacred bonds of community. It will also be a movement led by globally savvy youths who embrace and embody a new philosophy that blends technology and optimism with conscience and mysticism. In fact, there are signs that Americans of all ages are reevaluating the imperatives of social responsibility and civic conscience. Like the founding fathers, who saw divinity in the communitarian compact that formed the United States and purposely separated the roles of church and state, America's multicultural neomystics are finding ways to bring a dimension of rapture into their lives without necessarily resorting to organized religion.

In the Black Rock desert of Nevada, about thirty thousand artists, actors, musicians, and other nonconformists gather every spring for the

Burning Man Festival, a freewheeling countercultural extravaganza that culminates in the burning of a seventy-seven-foot-high wooden effigy. Burners, as the attendees are called, can roam five square miles of themed camps, art installations, musical and theatrical performances, and other assorted manifestations of unfettered self-expression. Like the harvest rituals of long ago, the ensuing collective consciousness—and occasional loss of it—provides a sense of communion and primordial connection that is difficult if not impossible to conjure in the carefully modulated developments of suburbia, although it does surface from time to time at political rallies, sports events, and rock concerts.

Burning Man and other events like it fill a void brought about at least in part by the instant commoditization of any form of artistic expression that shows the least sign of turning a profit. In music, the transformative effects of alternative and non-Western traditions can offer a compelling alternative to the comparatively homogenized offerings of commercial pop. When Derek Bares, a descendant of Hungarian Polish immigrants who grew up in a mostly white town near Brunswick, New Jersey, entered Rutgers University in 1993, he knew nothing about yoga or ragas. But by the time he graduated, his exploration of South Asian devotional song forms had started him on a path of scholarship and personal discovery that led to a career as a journalist and musician in New York City.

Bares soon discovered that, at its best, digitally mixed hybrids of electronic and non-Western music can deliver the same ecstatic release as the ancient tribal rituals of so-called primitive societies. "While it is certain many create this music out of the love of the 'cool sounds,' others know this is modern ritual," he says. "Whereas a shaman would drink *ahayuasca* and trip out to drums all night, today's visionaries swallow a hit of Ecstasy and submerge themselves into digital pulsations. I've been fortunate enough to experience both worlds and have also led the ceremonies. It is an amazing experience on every end, as what is most important—the exchange of human energy—is still abundant." In his book in progress, *Global Beat Fusion*, Bares describes how his exposure to world music, particularly modern mixes that incorporate religious elements of Hindu Urdu lyrics, filled a spiritual void that extends far beyond the crass superficiality of most top 10 hits. Under the right conditions, the primordial impact of amplified sound along with the communal aspects of dancing and live performance can be physically and emotionally transporting. For Bares, the fusion of technology and non-Western ritual, and the reconciliation of mind, body, and spirit that electronic world music represents, is not just the cutting edge of modern entertainment, but the early stages of a numinous revolution in American culture.

"This music is the new religion," writes Bares. "America has so little by way of ritual and so much stress. We have little faith because there's nothing real from a God circulating in the sky, judging our every action. But when a few hundred souls gather in a room and share the experience of music, there's something eternal in the process. We live transiently to touch this, if but for a moment. The history of the future of music is being written as we speak, and the language all the world is speaking can be heard on the dance floor."

Dancing to "the history of the future" includes a new sense of community and brotherhood on local and global levels. Ignorance of the implications of one's actions is no longer acceptable; for the multicultural consumer, it matters if their favorite sneaker company exploits workers in Asia, or if their bank does business with oppressive regimes, or if their lipstick was tested in a way that tortured innocent animals. According to a 2002 Cone Corporate Citizenship Study, 89 percent of Americans say that in light of the Enron collapse and other examples of corporate corruption, it is "more important than ever for companies to be socially responsible." Consumers also say they are willing to back up their feelings with action, saying they would punish irresponsible firms by switching to another company's products or services (91 percent), speaking out against the company to family and friends (85 percent), refusing to invest in the company's stock (83 percent), and boycotting its product's and services (68 percent).

The multicultural consumer understands that the act of buying is not just an expression—but also an extension—of self. "Brands as identity reflectors need to somehow recognize the need that people have for deeper spiritual meaning in their lives," writes Marc Gobé in his book, *Emotional Branding: The New Paradigm for Connecting Brands to People.* "From an Emotional Branding aspect, this means approaching this need with respect, as an open-ended dialogue. . . . It is about recognizing who your consumers are and that their personal aspirations extend far beyond the world of commercialism."

In the New Mainstream, the mysticism and meaning printed on the dollar bill and the social and spiritual values of the people who spend it are one and the same. New Mainstream consumers seek out brands that speak to their definition of self and reflect their worldview and aspirations. They expect the companies they work for and buy from to share their values, but they are also willing to learn, to evolve, and to become better citizens, parents, and lovers. They realize that the true value of any product or service is determined by its ability to have meaning, to make sense, to matter. In other words, for the new multicultural consumer, making and spending money is nothing less than a sacred, life-affirming act.

Notes

INTRODUCTION

1. Christopher Columbus, October 11, 1492, Internet Medieval Sourcebook, For-dam University Center for Medieval Studies.
2. Jeffrey M. Humphreys, "The Multicultural Economy 2003: America's Minority Buying Power," Selig Center for Economic Growth, University of Georgia. Jeffrey M. Humphreys, "The Multicultural Economy 2003: America's Minority Buying Power," Selig Center for Economic Growth, University of Georgia.
3. Richard Florida, *The Rise of the Creative Class: And How It's Transforming Work, Leisure, Community, and Everyday Life* (Basic Books, 2002), pp. 1–11.
4. Ibid.
5. Ibid.

CHAPTER 1: ETHNICITY INC.

1. Jeffrey M. Humphreys, "The Multicultural Economy 2003: America's Minority Buying Power," Selig Center for Economic Growth, University of Georgia.
2. ———, "The Multicultural Economy 2002: Minority Buying Power in the New Century, Selig Center for Economic Growth, University of Georgia.
3. "The Gay & Lesbian Market: New Trends, New Opportunities" Witeck-Combs Communications, DiversityInc.com, December 10, 2002.

4. Jeffrey M. Humphreys, "The Multicultural Economy 2003: America's Minority Buying Power," pp. 1–2.

5. Target Market News, "The Buying Power of Black America—2003," October 6, 2003.

6. Karen J. Bannan, *The New York Times*, December 2, 2002, p. C12.

7. Leon Wynter, *American Skin: Pop Culture, Big Business and the End of White America* (Crown, 2002).

8. "Moving to America—Moving to Home Ownership," United States Department of Commerce News, Economics and Statistics Administration, Bureau of the Census.

9. Mike Mrkvicka, "Home Ownership Jumps 27.7%," *The El Paso Times*, elpaso times.com.

10. Alex Berenson, "What's the Story Between the Lines at Fannie Mae?" *New York Times*; Franklin D. Raines, "American Dream Commitment," Fannie May, 2001.

11. Yoji Cole, Diversityinc.com, September 22, 2003.

12. Ron Winslow, "Aetna Is Collecting Racial Data to Monitor Racial Disparities," *The Wall Street Journal.*

13. David Firestone, "Frist Points to Racial Inequities in Health Care," *The New York Times*, January 8, 2004.

14. Ron Winslow, "Aetna Is Collecting Racial Data to Monitor Racial Disparities."

15. Tim Weiner, "Bank Calls Purchase Way to Woo Hispanics," *The New York Times*, December 11, 2002.

16. Jeffrey Bierer, "Bank of America Taps into Unbanked Market," SRI conference, Miami, Florida, January 30, 2003.

17. Sandra Block, "Poll: Blacks Less Likely to Invest in Stocks," *USA Today*, June 25, 2003.

18. Christine Dugas, "Banks Pay Attention to Rising Wealth of Hispanics," Hispanic Business.com, July 21, 2003.

19. Ibid.

20. Elena Maria Lopez, "The Business Case for Diversity," *DiversityInc*, June/July 2003, p. 18.

21. Yoji Cole, "This Year's Top Company for Diversity," *DiversityInc*, June/July 2003, p. 34.

22. Tyco and the LaGrant Foundation Launch Intern Program for Students of Color, www.diversityonline.com, April 21, 2004.

23. Gary Strauss, "Good Old Boys' Network Still Rules Corporate Boards," *USA Today*, November 1, 2002, p. B1.

24. Ibid.

25. U.S. Hispanic Chamber of Commerce press release, September 12, 2003, CSR Wire.

26. Angela D. Johnson, "Congressional Hispanic Caucus Takes Corporate America to Task," DiversityInc.com, September 16, 2003.

27. Ibid.
28. Gary Strauss, "Good Old Boys' Network Still Rules Corporate Boards."

CHAPTER 2: THE TIGER EFFECT

1. Jason Rodriguez, *All Hip-Hop News*, June 12, 2003.
2. Minya Oh, MTV News, April 30, 2003.
3. Super Bowl Survey, Cliff Freeman & Partners, January 29, 2004.
4. www.rolemodel.net/tiger/tiger.htm; Michael McCarthy and Teresa Howard, "Super Bowl Advertisers Want Viewers to 'Be Like Mike,' Again," *USA Today*, January 8, 2003.
5. "New World Order," SI.com, May 2, 2003.
6. Ibid.
7. Maureen Tkacik, "Hoops Phenom Nets $90 Million Deal With Nike," *The Wall Street Journal*, May 23, 2003, p. B5.
8. C. Stone Brown, "The Next Superstar: Freddy Adu Helps Soccer Go Mainstream," DiversityInc.com, April 8, 2004.
9. Angela D. Johnson, "Are You Spending Enough on the Latino Market?" Diversity Inc.com, April 22, 2004.
10. "Hispanic-Oriented Ads Have Crossover Potential for Mainstream Market," HispanicBusiness.com, June 30, 2003; *Austin American-Statesman*, 2003; Knight Ridder/Tribune Business News.
11. Laurel Wentz, "Puncturing the Advertising Language Barrier," AdAge.com, October 6, 2003.
12. ———, "Hispanic Marketing Magic Found in Spanglish Language Mix," AdAge.com, July 7, 2003.
13. Ibid.
14. Ibid.
15. Arlene Davila, *Latinos, Inc: The Marketing and Making of a People* (University of California Press, 2001.
16. www.sitv.com, October 2003; www.quote.com, July 21, 2003.
17. Laurel Wentz, "Media Diversity: Ethnic Buying Breaks Out," AdAge.com, March 2003.
18. ———, "Hispanic Marketing Magic Found in Spanglish Language Mix."
19. Ibid; Andrew Wallenstein, *Spanix*, Latin Film Network, January 29, 2003.
20. Courtney Kane, "Marketers Extend Their Holiday Efforts to a Mexican Celebration and Even to Lent," *The New York Times*, May 2, 2003, p. C2.
21. Vanessa Colon, "America Drinks Up All Things Hispanic," *Fresno Bee*, May 5, 2004.
22. Ibid.
23. www.cuervonation.com/cn_home.html.
24. Vanessa Colon, "America Drinks Up All Things Hispanic."
25. Michael Lafleur, *Arizona Daily Wildcat*, October 20, 1998.

26. Joseph Berger, "Of Milk and Cookies, or How Orthodox Jews Saved an Italian Recipe," *The New York Times*, January 12, 2003.

27. Jim Fusilli, "In the Fray," *The Wall Street Journal*, February 11, 2003, p. D8; Minya Oh and Jon Wiederhorn, VH1.com, September 6, 2002.

28. Ibid.

29. Yoji Cole, "More Rush Fallout: Eagles Owner Slams Disney, ABC, ESPN for 'Institutionalized Racism,'" DiversityInc.com, October 4, 2003.

30. Elena Maria Lopez, "Golfer Who Wants Asian Quota Apologizes," DiversityInc .com, October 13, 2003; Michael Arkush, "Asian Golfers at Home in L.P.G.A.," *The New York Times*, September 1, 2003.

CHAPTER 3: EYE OF THE BEHOLDER

1. David Carr, "On Covers of Many Magazines, a Full Racial Palette Is Still Rare," *The New York Times*, November 18, 2002, p. C1.

2. Ibid.

3. Ruth La Ferla, "Generation E.A.: Ethnically Ambiguous," *The New York Times*, December 28, 2003, Section 9, p. 1.

4. Yoji Cole, "Miss America Tells DiversityInc Her Story, Plans to Reach Corporate America," DiversityInc, November 13, 2003.

5. Jay Krall, "The Ethnically Correct Nose Job," *The Wall Street Journal*, July 29, 2003; Kimberly Palmer, "Ads for Ethnic Hair Care Show a New Face," *The Wall Street Journal*, Sept. 1, 2003.

6. Ibid.

7. Kimberly Palmer, "Ads for Ethnic Hair Care Show a New Face."

8. Shelly Branch, "If You Don't Have a 'Do,' Why Wear a Doo-Rag?" *The Wall Street Journal*, September 12, 2003.

9. Tracie Rozhon, "Can Urban Fashion Be Def in Des Moines?" *The New York Times*, August 24, 2003, p. 9.

10. Ibid.

11. Michael Quintanilla, "Of Culture and Commodity," *Los Angeles Times*, June 4, 2003, p. E1.

12. Ibid.

13. Ruth La Ferla, "First Hip-Hop, Now Cholo Style," *The New York Times*, November 30, 2003; Seth Kugel, "And Bloomingdale's Returns His Calls," *The New York Times*, October 5, 2003.

14. The Official Homesite of the Homies, www.homies.com, Gonzales Graphics. Also, Aurelio Sanchez, "David Gonzales' Barrio Figurines Cause Tiny Sensation," *Albuquerque Journal*, July 6, 2003; Jo Napolitano, "Two Inch Latino Role Models for Good or Ill," *The New York Times*, April 31, 2003.

15. Queena Sook Kim, "Mijos Figures Make Leap to Mass-Market Toy Shelves," *The Wall Street Journal*.

16. www.mijos.com.

17. Maureen Tkacik, "Mattel Turns to the Hip Hop Crowd," *The Wall Street Journal*, 2003.

18. Guy Trebay, "Memo to Barbie: You Aren't the Only Model Ken Knows," *The New York Times*, June 1, 2003.

19. Gary Levin, "Hispanics Finally Break the TV Barrier," *USA Today*, September 9, 2003.

20. Stuart Elliott, "Prime Time Differences," *The New York Times*, April 21, 2003.

21. Ibid.

22. Raymond Hernandez and Stuart Elliot, "Nielsen Delays New Method of Tracking in New York," *The New York Times*, April 7, 2004.

23. Alessandra Stanley, "Check In, Get a Free Civics Lesson," *The New York Times*, September 9, 2003.

24. Samuel G. Freedman, "Mr. Freeman, You Look Divine," *The New York Times*, June 11, 2003.

25. Michael D. Roberts, "Was Jesus Christ Black?" www.caribvoice.org, March 2002.

26. C. Stone Brown, "Was Jesus African? Biblical Scholars Challenge Mel Gibson's *Passion of Christ*," DiversityInc.com, March 1, 2004.

27. Jamie Malanowski, "Colorblind Buddies in Black and White," *The New York Times*, November 10, 2002.

28. Melanie Austria Farmer, *DiversityInc*, June/July 2003, p. 74.

29. 2002–2003 Hispanic Opinion Tracker, AOL Time-Warner Foundation, *People en Español*, the Cheskin Group.

30. Ibid.

31. Ibid.

32. New California Media, 2002, Bendixon & Associates.

33. Frank Ahrens and Krissah Williams, "Spanish-Language Media Expand," *The Washington Post*, August 11, 2003; HispanicBusiness.com, "Dallas Morning News Set to Launch Spanish-Language Daily Paper," June 30, 2003, Cox News Service.

34. "New Spanish-Language Paper to Challenge 'La Opinión,'" Associated Press, March 3, 2004.

35. Jacques Steinberg, "New Publisher Enters Race to Reach Hispanic Readers," *The New York Times*, April 12, 2004.

36. Sarah Rodman, "TV Most Fowl? 'Sawn' Creator Claims FOX's Ads Don't Reveal Show's True Beauty," BostonHerald.com, April 6, 2004.

37. Fernando Espuelas, VOY press release, 2003.

CHAPTER 4: DIVERSITY.COM

1. Nicholas Negroponte, *Being Digital* (Alfred A. Knopf, 1995).

2. Internet Software Consortium, Biannual Strategic Note, March 15, 2001; August 12, 1999.

3. Nielsen/NetRatings Inc., December 29, 2003.

4. Global Reach, www.glreach.com/globstats.

5. Jennifer L. Schenker, "Nations Chafe at U.S. Influence over the Internet," *The New York Times*, December 8, 2003.

6. Brian Knowlton, "Blackboard Expands Reach in Deal to Set Up Chinese Colleges with Its Software," *The New York Times*, August 2003.

7. Geoffrey A. Fowler, "Target: Expats," *The Wall Street Journal*, June 16, 2003.

8. Bob Tedeschi, "E-Commerce Report: To Reach Internet Users Overseas, More American Web Sites Are Speaking Their Language, Even Mandarin," *The New York Times*, January 12, 2004.

9. Ibid.

10. George Gilder, *Microcosm* (Touchstone Books, 1991).

11. Lisa Guernsey, "A Dissent on the Digital Divide," *The New York Times*, September 18, 2003.

12. HispanicBusiness.com, "Latinos Are the Fastest Growing Internet Users," HispanicBusiness.com, August 4, 2003; Brian Morrissey, "U.S. Hispanics Are Biggest Share of Spanish Speakers Online," Internetnews.com, March 17, 2003.

13. comScore Media Metrix, comScore Networks, March 17, 2003.

14. AOL/Roper CyberStudy, "U.S. Hispanic Online Consumer Population Survey," 2003.

15. Harris Interactive/Witeck Combs, Washington, D.C., April 27, 2000.

16. The Insight Research Corporation, www.insight-corp.com.

17. Lynda Richardson, "Entrepreneur Takes Black-Oriented Site Out of Red," *The New York Times*, November 27, 2002.

18. A gigabyte is a unit of information equal to 1 billion (1,000,000,000) bytes or 1,000 megabytes. The mp3 standard takes large digital music files and compresses them into smaller files (approximately 3 to 4 megabytes per song). Storage on commercial mp3 players ranges from a few hundred megabytes to 40 or more gigabytes.

19. Seth Kugel, "Tough Times at Columbia: One Latina's Tale on the Web," *The New York Times*, October 27, 2002.

20. Jonathan Dee, "Playing Mogul," *The New York Times Sunday Magazine*, December 21, 2003.

21. David Gelernter, *Mirror Worlds: Or, The Day Softward Puts the Universe in a Shoebox,* (Oxford University Press, 1993).

22. Robin Dunbar, *Grooming, Gossip, and the Evolution of Language* (Harvard University Press, 1996).

23. Ibid.

24. Ibid.

25. Ibid.

CHAPTER 5: MELTING POTS AND SALAD BOWLS

1. Robert Ryal Miller, *Shamrock and Sword: The St. Patrick's Battalion in the U.S.-Mexican War* (University of Oklahoma Press, 1989).

2. Ibid., pp. 161–62.

3. Richard Alba and Victor Nee, *Remaking the American Mainstream: Assimilation and Contemporary Immigration* (Harvard University Press, 2003), p. 51.

4. Jim Zwick, ed., *Mark Twain's Weapons of Satire: Anti-Imperialist Writings on the Philippine-American War* (Syracuse University Press, 1992).

5. Gary Y. Okihiro, *Margins and Mainstreams: Asians in American History and Culture* (University of Washington Press, 1994).

6. Jim Zwick, *The Profits of Racism: The Campaign Against Philippine Independence,* 2003; Jim Zwick, ed., *Anti-Imperialism in the United States, 1898–1935.*

7. Richard Alba and Victor Nee, *Remaking the American Mainstream,* p. 171.

8. Ibid., pp. 172–73.

9. Sethard Fisher, *From Margin to Mainstream: The Social Progress of Black Americans* (Rowman & Littlefield, 1992), p. 195.

10. Arthur M. Schlesinger Jr., *The Disuniting of America: Reflections on a Multicultural Society* (W. W. Norton & Company, 1998), p. 150.

11. Richard Alba and Victor Nee, *Remaking the American Mainstream,* p. 17.

12. David Horowitz, Salon.com, May 21, 2001.

13. Nathan Glazer, *We Are All Multiculturalists Now* (Harvard University Press, 1997), p. 20.

14. The plaintiff in the case, Barbara Grutter, applied to the university's law school in 1996 but was rejected. When Grutter, who is white, found out that African Americans and other minorities had been admitted despite having lower overall admission scores, she sued the university on the grounds that she had been a victim of illegal discrimination because of her race. Grutter's lawyers, citing the landmark 1978 Supreme Court decision in *Regents of the University of California v. Bakke,* which outlawed admissions quotas based on race, argued that the university's admissions policy was unconstitutional. Grutter won the first round in U.S. District Court but took her case to the Supreme Court after losing in a close decision in the Sixth Circuit Court of Appeals.

15. Thomas A. Gottschalk, Kenneth S. Geller, Francis S. Jaworski, Eileen Penner, Elizabeth G. Taylor, Supreme Court of the United States, Nos. 02-241 and 02-516, Brief of Amici Curiae Media Companies in Support of Respondents; *Barbara Grutter v. Lee Bollinger, James J. Duderstadt, and the Board of Regents of the University of Michigan,* February 18, 2003.

16. Howard W. French, "Insular Japan Needs, But Resists, Immigration," *The New York Times,* July 24, 2003; Richard Bernstein, "An Aging Europe May Find Itself on the Sidelines," *The New York Times,* June 29, 2003.

17. William H. Frey, "Census 2000 Reveals New Native-Born and Foreign-Born Shifts Across U.S.," Population Studies Center at the Institute for Social Research, University of Michigan, Report No. 02-520, August 2002. Also, Joel Garreau, *The Nine Nations of North America* (Houghton Mifflin, 1981).

18. U.S. Census 2000; Social Science Data Analysis Network, CensusScope, www.censusscope.org.

19. A Social Science Data Analysis Network, analysis of 2000 U.S. census data that vi-

sually maps demographic trends reveals a high concentration of Americans sixty-five and over running through the Great Plains as well as in the retirement hot spots of the Southwest and Florida. When presented in the horizontal bars of a "population pyramid," the chart hints at patterns of future growth. A normal population pyramid, which shows horizontal bars representing percentages of men and women in different age groups in a vertical stack, would look roughly square, with the top (oldest) and bottom (youngest) bars of nearly equal length. A topheavy pyramid, like the one for Grant County, North Dakota—with bars representing men and women between the ages of forty and eighty-five-plus extending out farther than bars for men and women between the ages of twenty and thirty-nine, indicates negative population growth that can be attributable to a number of factors, including high death rates, low birth rates, and increased emigration from the area. By contrast, the population pyramid for Orange County, Florida, suggests high birthrates, falling or stable death rates, and the potential for rapid population growth. When the two counties are compared on the basis of race and ethnicity and nativity and citizenship, the disparities are equally striking. While Hispanics and blacks make up a combined 18.76 percent of the population of Orange County, they make up only 0.32 percent of Grant County's population. And the total foreign-born percentage of the population in Orange County is 7.95 percent versus 1.66 percent for Grant County. Finally, a comparison of the two counties in terms of household income showed that the percentage of families that earned $150,000 or more in 1999 in Orange County (3.99) was more than double the percentage for Grant County (1.50). In the same year, the percentage of families in Grant County that earned $9,999 or less in Grant County (21.10) was about three times that of Orange County (7.74). Comparisons between the two counties between 1989 and 1999, showed incomes increasing for both over the ten-year period, but the growth in the percentage of $150,000-plus households for Orange County grew from 1.33 percent to 3.99 percent, while the percentage of Grant County households earning $150,000 or more increased over the same period by less than 1 percent, from 0.57 percent to 1.50 percent.

While comparing two counties in different parts of the country is anecdotal at best, the data does suggest a correlation among diversity, population, immigration, and economic vitality. And while there are without a doubt tolerant, highly skilled, and well-educated people in Grant County (and, conversely, intolerant, lower-wage earners in Orange County), it's not a giant leap to speculate which county had a higher percentage of viewers tuned in to the 2003 Latin Grammys. As Richard Florida puts it, "I fear we may well be splitting into two distinct societies with different institutions, different economies, different incomes, ethnic and social makeups, social organizations, religious orientations and politics. One is creative and diverse—a cosmopolitan admixture of high-tech people, bohemians, scientists and engineers, the media and the professions. The other is a more close-knit, church-based, older civic society of working people and rural dwellers. The former is ascendant and likely to dominate the nation's economic future."

20. William H. Frey, "Census 2000 Reveals New Native-Born and Foreign-Born Shifts Across U.S."

21. Ibid.

22. Patrick J. Buchanan, *The Death of the West: How Dying Populations and Immigrant Invasions Imperil Our Country and Civilization* (St. Martin's Press, 2002).

23. Simon Romero and Janet Elder, "Hispanics in U.S. Report Optimism," *The New York Times*, August 6, 2003.

24. Lynette Clemetson, "For Schooling, a Reverse Emigration to Africa," *The New York Times*, September 4, 2003.

25. Elena Maria Lopez, Melanie Austria Farmer, C. Stone Brown, "Power of the Communities: 3 Case Studies Prove Emerging Markets' Economic Clout," *Diversity Inc*, August/September 2003, pp 30–50.

26. Hector V. Barreto, Knight Ridder/Tribune Information Services, August 2003. Also, Roger Harris, "Barreto: Small Business Will Lead U.S. Economy," harris @insidevc.com, HispanicBusiness.com., August 8, 2003.

27. Robert D. Putnam, *Bowling Alone: The Collapse and Revival of American Community* (Simon & Schuster, 2000), p. 390.

28. Gary Y. Okihiro, *Margins and Mainstreams: Asians in American History and Culture* (University of Washington Press, 1994), p. 175.

29. Richard Alba and Victor Nee, *Remaking the American Mainstream*, pp. 313–32.

30. Samuel P. Huntington, "The Hispanic Challenge," *Foreign Policy* (March/April 2004).

31. Richard Alba and Victor Nee, *Remaking the American Mainstream*, pp. 286–86.

CHAPTER 6: COWBOYS AND INDIANS

1. "Vaqueros: The First Cowboys," Texas Parks and Wildlife, State Parks and Historic Sites, www.tpwd.state.tx.us/park/jose/vaquero.htm.

2. Ibid.

3. Juan Gonzalez, *Harvest of Empire* (Viking Penguin, 2000) pp. 42–43.

4. Ronald Takaki, *A Different Mirror: A History of Multicultural America* (Little, Brown & Company, 1993), p. 175.

5. Juan Gonzalez, *Harvest of Empire*, p. 44.

6. Joel H. Silbey, Cornell University, *The American Presidency* (Grolier Interactive Products, Grolier, Inc.).

7. Jose Antonio Navarro: "A Bicentennial Tribute, 1795–1995," Texas Parks and Wildlife, State Parks and Historic Sites, www.tpwd.state.tx.us/park/jose/ book .htm.

8. Ibid.

9. Kenneth Carley, *The Sioux Uprising of 1862* (Publications of the Minnesota Historical Society, St. Paul, Minnesota, Historical Society, 1961); Scott Tubbs, *Annals of Wyoming, 1923–1994* 54, no. 1:36–50.

10. Ibid.

11. Francis Amasa Walker, "The Indian Question," *North American Review* 116, no. 239 (April 1873): 487–95.

12. Ibid.

13. Ibid.

14. Ibid.

15. The Dawes Act reflected a general view among whites that the social insularity and cultural backwardness that typified reservation life was holding Indians back by encouraging bad habits and isolating them from the assimilating influences of modern American society. To be eligible to register for the Dawes Act grants, Indians were required to anglicize their names, which made it possible for unscrupulous government agents to add friends and family members to the land registration rolls, resulting in the wholesale robbery of millions of acres of Indian land. When the pattern of massive fraud and corruption by government agents and others was finally revealed in the Miriam Report of 1928, Congress launched an investigation. What the government found was that by 1933, almost half of the Indians livings on reservations that had been subject to the allotment policy had lost the title to their land, representing about 60 percent of the 138 million acres owned by Native Americans when the Dawes Act went into effect. A year later, the Dawes Act was repealed.

16. Ronald Takaki, *A Different Mirror: A History of Multicultural America*, pp. 228–31.

17. Ibid.

18. Stanley Vestal, *Sitting Bull: Champion of the Sioux* (University of Oklahoma Press, 1989); "The Ghost Dance Religion and the Sioux Outbreak of 1890," Report of the Bureau of Ethnology, 1892–1893, Part II, Washington, D.C.

19. Fredrick Jackson Turner, *The Significance of the Frontier in American History*, 1893.

20. Ibid.

21. Ibid.

22. Gerald Vizenor, *Earthdivers: Tribal Narratives on Mixed Descent* (University of Minnesota Press, 1981).

23. Ibid.

24. Ibid.

CHAPTER 7: AMEXICA

1. Carlos Fuentes, *The Buried Mirror: Reflections of Spain and the New World* (Houghton Mifflin, 1982), p. 342.

2. "Welcome to Amexica," *Time*, June 2001, pp. 46–47.

3. *Ethnic Diversity Survey: Portrait of a Multicultural Society*, Statistics Canada, www.statcan.ca/english/sdds/4508.htm.

4. Clifford Krauss, "Canada's View on Social Issues Is Opening Rifts with the U.S.," *New York Times*, December 2, 2003.

5. Pico Iyer, The Global Soul: Jet Lag, Shopping Malls, and the Search for Home (Alfred A. Knopf, 2000), pp. 123–24.

6. Pew Research Center for the People and the Press, June 2003; Environics 2002; Princeton Data Source, 2002.

7. Tim Weiner, "Americans Stake Claim in Baja Land Rush," The New York Times, October 26, 2003.

8. Simon Romero, "Shaking Up Journalism in El Paso," The New York Times, May 27, 2003.

9. ———, "Dallas–Fort Worth Papers Fight It Out in Spanish," The New York Times, August 4, 2003.

10. Ibid.

11. Tino Villaneuva, Scene from the Movie Giant (Curbstone Press, 1993).

12. Oscar Casares, "Crossing the Border Without Losing Your Past," The New York Times, September 16, 2003.

13. Ibid.

14. Octavio Paz, The Labyrinth of Solitude.

15. Geraldine Brooks, "The Painted Desert," The New Yorker, July 28, 2003.

16. Tripti Lahiri, "In Death, Homeward Bound," The New York Times, June 26, 2003.

17. Elena Maria Lopez, "Culturally Competent Grieveing: Recognizing Community Rituals," DiversityInc.com, September 23, 2003.

18. David W. Chen, "Displaced Chinese Ancestors Reburied in U.S.," The New York Times, August 10, 2003.

19. Ibid.

CHAPTER 8: DESTINATIONS

1. The New Neighbors: A User's Guide to Data on Immigrants in U.S. Communities, (The Urban Institute, Washington, D.C.), 2003.

2. Nancy Foner, From Ellis Island to JFK: New York's Two Great Waves of Immigration (Yale University Press, 2000).

3. The New York Times Guide for Immigrants in New York City (St. Martin's Press, 2004).

4. Nancy Foner, From Ellis Island to JFK.

5. Ibid.

6. The New Neighbors: A User's Guide to Data on Immigrants in U.S. Communities.

7. According to the U.S. census, between 1990 and 2000, the Atlanta metro area experienced a 264.2 percent increase in the immigrant population, or a rise from 3.7 percent of the population to 10.3 percent, a total of 423,105 foreign-born residents. In a study released by the Center for Immigration Studies in 2001, the top ten countries of origin for legal immigrants admitted to the United States between 1991 and 1998 who indicated they intended to settle in the Atlanta area were Vietnam (11,245 immigrants), India (4,410), the Soviet Union (3,991),

China (3,516), Mexico (3,422), Korea (2,130), the United Kingdom (2,075), Ethiopia (1,931), Canada (1,918), and Nigeria (1,885).

8. Federation for American Immigration Reform, Metro Area Factsheet: Atlanta, Georgia MSA, www.fairus.org.

9. New Nation News, Online Athens, "The Occupied South: Athens, Georgia."

10. Rural Migration News, "Southeast: Vidalia Onions," migration.ucdavis.edu; *The Washington Post*, July 5, 1998; *Chicago Tribune*, May 28, 1998.

11. Ronald Takaki, *A Different Mirror: A History of Multicultural America* (Little, Brown & Company, 1993, pp. 12–13).

12. Joseph Berger, "From Philippines, with Scrubs," *New York Times*, November 24, 2003.

13. *The New Neighbors: A User's Guide to Data on Immigrants in U.S. Communities.*

14. The status of admission for immigrants is critical since it can make a huge difference in the kinds of federal services and support that are made available to them. Refugees who are admitted for humanitarian reasons because they are fleeing persecution in their home countries are prescreened overseas. After admission, they are usually resettled by family members or resettlement services, which are often religious organizations supported by federal funds. Refugees who fled persecution without advance authorization are allowed to apply for asylum but generally have to prove their case in court before they are granted permanent residence and asylum privileges. In 2000, there were about 2.5 million immigrants who had entered the United States since 1980 as refugees, or about 8 percent of the total immigrant population.

15. *The New Neighbors: A User's Guide to Data on Immigrants in U.S. Communities.*

16. Phil Meyer and Paul Overberg, "Updating the USA *Today* Diversity Index," January 2001.

17. Graham Gori, "A Card Allows U.S. Banks to Aid Mexican Immigrants," *The New York Times*, July 6, 2002; Ginger Thompson, "Migrants to U.S. Are a Major Resource for Mexico," *The New York Times*, March 25, 2002; "New ID Helps Mexicans Come Out of the Shadows," *El Diario*, March 20, 2002.

18. Ibid.

19. Mary Anastasia O'Grady, "At Last, a Bill for Treating Immigrants Humanely," *The Wall Street Journal*, August 29, 2003.

20. Ibid.

21. Ibid.

22. Philp Shenon, "Ridge Favors a Status Short of Citizenship for Illegal Immigrants," *The New York Times*, December 11, 2003.

23. Ibid.

24. Frank Herbert, "Jailing Immigrants: Some Strange Goings-On in America," *The New York Times*, August 4, 2003.

25. Rachel L. Swarns, "Allowing Those Who Fight for Their Country to Be Part of It," *The New York Times*, May 7, 2003.

26. Pew Hispanic Center Fact Sheet, "Hispanics in the Military," March 2003; Tom Infield, "Today's Army: A Mixed Group, Ready to Serve," Knight Ridder News Service, February 2, 2003.

27. Ibid.

CHAPTER 9: LIQUID ASSETS

1. The U.S. One Dollar Bill, www.enchantedlearning.com.

2. David Ovason, *The Secret Symbols of the Dollar Bill* (HarperCollins, 2004); "The Great Seal and National Mottos of the United States of America," U.S. Scouting Service Project, www.usscouts.org.

3. Ibid.

4. Joseph Campbell, with Bill Moyers, *The Power of Myth* (Anchor Books, 1991).

5. Thomas Paine, *Common Sense* (Dover, unabridged, 1997).

6. Joseph Campbell, *The Power of Myth.*

7. The Great Seal, www.GreatSeal.com.

8. Ibid.

9. George Mallis, Walt Whitman Birthplace Association; Walt Whitman, Academy of American Poets, www.poets.org.

10. Linda Bean, "Lack of Diversity at Root of FBI's Failure to Assess Terror Threat," DiversityInc.com, June 10, 2002.

11. Richard Florida, "Creative Class War: How the GOP's Anti-elitism Could Ruin America's Economy," *Washington Monthly*, January/February 2004.

12. Ibid.

13. Barry Newman, "For Asians in U.S., Mini-Chinatowns Sprout in Suburbia," *The Wall Street Journal*, April 28, 2004.

14. The International Organization for Migration, June 2003.

15. Ruth Zeilberger, "Changing Faces: How Immigrants Impact U.S. Businesses," *DiversityInc*, October/November 2003.

16. Octavio Paz, *The Labyrinth of Solitude* (Grove Press, 1985).

CHAPTER 10: CREATIVE CONSUMPTION

1. Yankelovich MONITOR Multicultural Study, 2003.

2. John Frank, "One Nation, Indescribable," *Roanoke Times*, July 4, 2002.

3. Jim Cullen, *American Dream* (Oxford University Press, 2003).

4. Ibid.

5. The "Hierarchy of Needs," a graphical representation of human motives and desires developed by the psychologist Abraham Maslow in the 1970s, is often visualized as a pyramid with ascending levels of achievement. At the base of the pyramid are basic physiological needs, such as shelter, food, and clean water. Those needs must be met before one can ascend to the next level of needs—local

law and order, protection of predators, employment, and national defense. Next are needs of love, social acceptance, friendship, and community, followed by success, respect, and status. At the top of the pyramid is self-actualization, the acme of professional accomplishment and personal achievement. Before one can climb the pyramid of needs, the lower levels must be satisfied. When too many people in any social system are prevented from satisfying the basic needs at the base of the pyramid, law and order become harder to maintain, which in turn erodes the ability of others to enjoy fulfillment at the apex. If the base of the pyramid becomes too large, everybody gets pulled toward the bottom. But if some of those at the base are allowed to climb and give hope to those below, then the lucky few at the top can keep their position.

6. Tricia Rose, *Black Noise: Black Music and Rap Culture in Contemporary America* (Wesleyan University Press, 1994).

7. John McWhorter, *Losing the Race: Self-Sabotage in Black America* (Perennial, 2001).

8. www.rubenblades.com.

9. Amanda Hesser, "Dude, Where's My Spice Grinder?" *The New York Times*, April 23, 2003.

10. Kay Rentschler, "California's New Gold Rush," *The New York Times*, October 8, 2003.

11. Ibid.

12. The Totonacs dutifully delivered a portion of their vanilla harvest to their new masters but after the arrival in the New World of the Spanish explorer Hernán Cortés, they helped Cortés overthrow the Aztecs. By 1571, vanilla was being used as a flavoring in Europe, although it was so rare and expensive that only royalty and the richest classes could afford it. Despite attempts to harvest vanilla in the Old World, a lack of natural pollinators allowed the Totonacs to control the global market for the pods until 1841, when a pollinating technique using a bamboo stylus made vanilla a viable commodity for the rest of the world.

13. Chili gets its heat from capsaicin, a chemical that is usually concentrated in the seeds and veins of the chili pod. When capsaicin comes into contact with the taste glands on the tongue and mouth, the burning sensation sends signals to the brain that trigger the production of endorphins, natural painkillers that produce a sensation of well-being and stimulation. This is the source of the legendary "chili high" that pepper aficionados celebrate and crave. While nonaddictive in any physical sense, peppers, which belong to the nightshade family, contain alkaloids that are chemically related to the active ingredients in caffeine, morphine, quinine, strychnine, and nicotine. The physiological effects of peppers bypass the conscious appreciation of food and tap a primordial response that is instinctual and cathartic. No wonder that the Aztecs attributed mystical powers to chilies and used them in ritual foods and as a medicinal treatment for arthritis, bronchitis, epilepsy, malaria, and toothaches. Peppers are also low in calories and sodium. They are cholesterol-free and high in vitamin A and C and are good sources of

potassium, folic acid, and vitamin E. Studies have shown that they increase the metabolic rate and may help to avert heart disease and blood clots. The first scientific measurement of chili heat was devised in 1912 by a Detroit pharmacist named Wilbur L. Scoville, who devised a scale that ranges from the bell pepper (0) to the Mexican habañero (350,000). Falling between those two extremes are the Anaheim green (250–1,400), the poblano (about 3,000), the jalapeño (3,500–4,500), the serrano (7,000–25,000), cayenne (100,000–105,000), and the Japanese kumataka (125,000–150,000).

CHAPTER 11: BEYOND THE NEW MAINSTREAM

1. Miriam Kreinin Souccar, Crain.com, 2003.
2. Ibid.
3. Julie Salamon, "Following a Trend, Downtown Looks to the Arts," *The New York Times*, September 15, 2003.
4. Marion Maneker, "The Giant Cartoon Landing at Rockefeller Center," *The New York Times*, August 24, 2003; Carol Vogel, "A New Friend for Mr. Pointy," *The New York Times*, September 12, 2003.
5. Barbara Tannenbaum, "Where Miles of Murals Preach a People's Gospel," *The New York Times*, May 26, 2002; Robin J. Donitz, "Street Gallery—A Guide to 1000 Los Angeles Murals," RJD Enterprises, Los Angeles, 1993.
6. Eduardo Matos Moctezuma, *The Great Temple of the Aztecs* (Thames & Hudson, 1988); Johanna Broda, David Carrasco, and Eduardo Matos Moctezuma, *The Great Temple of Tenochtitlán* (University of California Press, 1987).
7. Not only did they adopt and worship Toltec gods like Quetzalcoatl, the Plumed Serpent, but they also revered the ruins of older civilizations like Teotihuacan and Tula and made special pilgrimages there to pray and consult with oracles. The Aztecs built their capital around the sacred complex of Templo Mayor, which was dominated by twin pyramids dedicated to Huitzilopochtli, the god of war, and Tlaloc, the god of water. Templo Mayor was constructed in seven overlapping layers, each one representing a new stage of conquest and power. As the empire's new shrines were built, statues, gold, jewels, conch shells, and other sacred artifacts from their defeated enemies were encased within the walls of the rising pyramids, literally incorporating them into the Aztec cosmology and political structure. After the Aztecs were defeated by the Spanish conquistador Hernán Cortés in 1521, the surviving Indian masons were forced to use the stones of their dismantled pyramids to build the first Spanish cathedrals, which were often placed directly atop the foundations of the razed Aztec shrines. The Spaniards, hearing stories of a golden paradise that lay to the north, sent exploratory parties into modern-day California, New Mexico, and Colorado to find Aztlán's lost treasures. The Spanish explorers were followed by Catholic missionaries, who eventually settled in the region and colonized it as a territory of New Spain. Like the mythical city of Atlantis, the exact location of Aztlán has never been determined, but its

symbolic power as a lost paradise and place of origin was invoked during the 1960s and 1970s by Chicano civil rights activists, who used it as a metaphor to represent their moral and ancestral claim to lands that were now part of the United States.

8. Richard Chang, "Part 1: The Allure of Aztlán Visual Art: An Old Myth Is Emerging as a New Reality for Multicultural California," Asian American Journalists Association, May 31, 2001, www.aaja-la.org.

9. John Rockwell, "Los Angeles Becomes a Base for Cutting-Edge Performance," *New York Times*, January 12, 2003.

10. Inventions for Paper, Schirmer News, October 2003; "Tan Dun's Background and Development," Tan Dun-Composer Essay, September 16, 1998, www.schirmer.com/composers/tan_essay.html.

11. Felicia R. Lee, "Singing the City Evanescent," *The New York Times*, October 20, 2003.

CHAPTER 12: HOW SOON IS NOW?

1. Russell Wild, "Yoga, Inc.," *Yoga Journal* 170 (November 2002).

2. William J. Broad and James Glanz, "Does Science Matter?" *The New York Times*, November 11, 2003.

3. Ann Chase, "Options: Homeopathy," *The Washington Post*, April 28, 1983.

4. Dawn Anfuso, "Study Shows Buying Power of Youth," imediaconnection.com, September 8, 2003.

5. Robert D. Putnam, *Bowling Alone: The Collapse and Revival of American Community* (Simon & Schuster, 2000).

6. Ibid.

Acknowledgments

The New Mainstream was not born in a vacuum, and it was not written alone. In the course of researching and describing the mutual transformation of margins and mainstream, of consumerism and culture, of ethnicity and identity, I myself was transformed. The trajectory that took me from beginning to end, from the first page to the last, was also a journey of self-discovery and an exploration and appreciation of community in the broadest and most personal sense. I owe a deep debt to the hundreds of entrepreneurs, writers, scholars, researchers, historians, sociologists, and visionaries whose ideas and words preceded mine and whose works provided the foundation and building blocks for my own.

While there is no way to thank everyone who helped and inspired me, certain individuals deserve to be singled out. I offer my thanks and gratitude to Carlos Fuentes, Rubén Blades, Pete Hamill, Gerald Vizenor, Alberto Fuguet, Abel Quesada, Louis Valdez, Julie Taymor, and Elliot Goldenthal, who opened my eyes to new ways of seeing, hearing, and feeling; to Bob Pittman, Ted Leonsis, Michael Lynton, Lisa Hook, Kevin Conroy, Kimberly Till, and my former colleagues at AOL; to Charles

Herington, Gustavo Cisneros, Ricardo Cisneros, Eduardo Cisneros, Peter Blacker, Eduardo Hauser, Hugh Stockton, John Gardiner, and my former colleagues at AOL Latin America; to John Borthwick, Ted Werth, Adeo Ressi, Carter Adamson, Janice Gjertsen, and my fellow cybernauts at Total New York; to Strategic Research Institute's Rupa Ranganathan, for indulging me; to Henry Cisneros, Nely Galán, Christy Haubegger, and Gabriel Reyes for "getting it"; to Mark Miller, Douglas Rodriguez, and Simpson Wong for letting me taste it.

Thanks also to Dr. Mahzarin Banaji at Harvard University; to Mara Manus and George C. Wolfe at the Joseph Papp Public Theater; William H. Frey at the Brookings Institution; Rachel Cooper and Vishakha Desai at the Asia Society; Daniel Shapiro at the Americas Society; Bob Goldhammer and Michael Becker at Broadsword Partners; Craig Hagen and José Martin at Electronic Arts; Jackie Hernandez Fallous, Richard Perez-Feria, Carmen Lopez, Joaquim Ribiero, and Lou Lopez at *People en Español*; Ben Sun and Omar Wasow at Community Connect; Shari Grossman and Luisa Fairborne at Planet Sur; Daisy Esposito and Yehudit Mam at the Bravo Group; Manny Vidal at Vidal Partnership; Givi Topchishvili and Vica Vinogradova at Global Advertising Strategies; Steve Drimmer, Anthony James, and Derrick Gold at Veritalk; and Steve Pena at Montebello Entertainment.

I owe a special debt to Lisa Quiroz, Michael Andrews, Kenneth Willardt, Serge Becker, Bill Bragin, Derek Bares, Fabian Alsultany, Cai Guo-Qiang, John Perry Barlow, Mario Bosquez, Jesus Trevino, Sandra Gibson, Anna Liza Bella, Ron Pompei, Luis Gonzalez, Vijay Iyer, Ravish Momin, Geshe Lobsang Tenzin, Eduardo Verastegui, Sergio Aguero, Laura Muller White, and Leon Wynter for generously contributing their time and thoughts; and to Barbara Howard, Brian Siberell, Patty Dryden, Rob Bragin, Elizabeth Stewart, Peter and Ashley Christus, Michael and Nancy Carmody, Will and Suzanne Schutte, Richard and Lori Stoney, Lucy Kaylin and Kimball Driggs, Natasha Von Blumencron, Mark Uttecht, Colin Bill, John Merz, Jennifer Fiore, Dori Rubin, Tarquin Cardona, Ruth Infarinato, Anthony James, Darrin Hong, Margaret Trujillo, and all my friends and family for their patience and understanding; to David Kuhn and Michael Carlisle for their early encouragement; to my agent, Wes Neff, for his sage advice; to my editor, Rene Alegria, for his acumen and unerring instincts; to my parents, Dan and Charlotte Garcia, for their unconditional support; to Cathleen Carmody, for being there before the New Mainstream, and to William Garcia, who will be there after it.

Index

Lopez, Lou, 66
Lord of the Rings (films), 209, 258
Los Angeles, California, 125, 134–35, 175, 187, 255–56, 276
Los Angeles County Museum of Art, 256–57
Los Angeles Police Department, 52
Lott, Trent, 15
Lotus (New York City club), 226
Louisiana, 244
Love, Courtney, 238
Lower East Side Tenement Museum (New York City), 182
Lower Manhattan Development Corporation, 254
Lowrider magazine, 51
Lozano, Monica, 68–69
Lucas Arts, 96
Lucas, Gary, 227
Ludacris, 38, 96, 231
Ludlow, Peter, 98
Lugar, Richard G., 189–90
Luis (TV), 55
Luna, Diego, 59
Lund, Daniel, 11

Ma, Yo-Yo, 258
Madden, Steve, 96
Madonna, 27
magazines, 42, 43–44, 46, 62–65. *See also specific magazine*
Malcolm & Eddie (TV), 35
Malcolm X, 60
Mamacita, 49
Mana (rock group), 240
mandala, 268
Mandoki, Luis, 58
manifest destiny, 143, 147, 156, 160
mankind: "universal history" of, 155
marginalization, 168, 180–81
Marin, Cheech, 35
marketing/advertising: acculturating effect of, 221; and categorization of consumers, 224; celebrities and public figures in, 27–30, 32, 39–40; change in strategy for, 19–25, 31, 32–34; and ethnicity, 35, 67; and Generation Y, 275; IAT as tool for, 220; increase in budgets for, 6; and language, 31–34; of Latin American brands, 172–74; in magazines, 63–64; mixed race models in, 43; at MTV Movie Awards, 26–28; in newspapers, 68; pitfalls in, 37–41; and professional athletics, 28–41; and self-image of consumers, 30; on television, 55; transnational, 214;

to urban youth, 275–76; and yoga, 270, 271
Markvukaj, Elizabeta, 192–93
Márquez, García, 262
Martin, José, 96
Martin, Ricky, 46, 240
Martinez, Ruben, 83
Martinez, Zarela, 34
Mason, Luba, 237
Massive Attack (trip-hop band), 228
Mastermind Group, 29–30
materialism, 206, 269, 272
matricula consular, 188–89
The Matrix (films), 43, 259, 260
Matsuhisa, Nobu, 241
Mattel, 53–54
Maxim magazine, 43–44, 46
Maya people, 246
MC Hammer, 230
McCain, John, 190
McCarran-Walter Immigration Act (1952), 118
McDonald's, 31, 173, 242, 262
McGente, 92
McIntosh, Shawn, 188
McNabb, Donovan, 40
McOndo movement, 262–64
McWhorter, John H., 231–33
media, 221, 266. *See also type of media or specific organization*
Media Economics Group, 6
medicine, 15–16, 271–73
meditation, 269, 270, 273
melting pot, 121, 125, 128, 137, 138, 154, 183, 184, 206
"memes," 103–4
men: beauty products for, 46–47; on magazine covers, 46
Men in Black series, 61
Men's Health magazine, 65
Merchant, Ismail, 226–27
Mestre-Reed, Ernestro, 263
Method Man, 96, 231
Me'tis, 158–61
metrosexuals, 46–47, 54
Mexican-American War (1846–48), 114–16, 143–45
Mexican Fine Arts Center Museum (Chicago), 175
Mexico/Mexicans, 118, 162–79; activism of, 119; Anglo resentment of, 145; Aztecs in, 256–57, 272; border between U.S. and, 162–63, 164–67; as cowboys, 142; entrepreneurial energy of, 131; food of, 242, 245–46, 248–49; as immigrants,

COLLECTION FOLIO

Herta Müller

L'homme est un grand faisan sur terre

Traduit de l'allemand
par Nicole Bary

Maren Sell

Titre original :

DER MENSCH IST EIN GROSSER FASAN AUF DER WELT

© *Rotbuch-Verlag, Berlin, 1986.*
© *Éditions Maren Sell, 1988, pour la traduction française.*

Herta Müller est née en 1953 dans la province de Banat en Roumanie, au sein de la minorité allemande des Souabes. Persécutée par le régime de Ceaucescu, elle émigre en 1987 en Allemagne de l'Ouest, à Berlin où elle vit encore. Elle reçoit en 2009 le Prix Nobel de Littérature, récompensée pour avoir, « avec la densité de la poésie et la franchise de la prose, dépeint l'univers des déshérités ».

Entre les paupières d'est en ouest,
l'œil est blanc, la pupille est invisible.

Ingeborg Bachmann

L'ornière

Des roses poussent autour du monument aux morts. Un buisson de roses. Si folles qu'elles étouffent l'herbe. Les fleurs sont blanches, rabougries, serrées comme des fleurs en papier. Elles froufroutent. C'est l'aube. Il fera bientôt jour.

Chaque matin, quand Windisch fait tout seul la route qui le mène au moulin, il compte : quel jour sommes-nous? Arrivé devant le monument aux morts, il compte les années. Plus loin, près du premier peuplier, à l'endroit où le vélo s'enfonce toujours dans la même ornière, il compte les jours. Et le soir, quand Windisch ferme le moulin, il compte encore une fois les années et les jours.

De loin, il voit les petites roses blanches, le monument aux morts et le peuplier. Lorsque, par temps de brouillard, Windisch passe à bicyclette, il a le blanc des roses et le blanc de la pierre juste sous les yeux. Windisch passe au travers. Il a le visage humide et va jusqu'au moulin. Deux fois déjà le buisson de roses n'a eu que des épines et les mauvaises herbes dessous étaient roussies. A deux reprises le peuplier a perdu tant de feuilles que le bois a failli éclater. Deux fois la neige a recouvert les routes.

Devant le monument aux morts, Windisch compte deux années et, dans l'ornière près du peuplier, deux cent vingt et un jours.

Tous les matins, quand Windisch roule dans l'ornière en cahotant, il se dit : « Ça va être la fin. » Depuis que Windisch veut émigrer, il voit la fin partout dans le village. Le temps s'arrête pour ceux qui veulent rester. Que le veilleur de nuit reste, c'est pour Windisch au-delà de la fin.

Et quand Windisch a compté deux cent vingt et un jours et qu'il est passé en brinquebalant dans l'ornière, il pose pied à terre pour la première fois. Il met la bicyclette contre le peuplier. On entend ses pas. Des tourterelles sauvages s'envolent des cerisiers. Elles sont grises comme la lumière. Seul le froissement de leurs ailes permet de les percevoir.

Windisch se signe. La poignée de la porte est mouillée. Elle lui reste collée à la main. La porte de l'église est fermée à clé. Saint Antoine est enfermé derrière le mur. Il a à la main un lis blanc et un livre marron.

Windisch a froid. Il regarde la route. Elle s'arrête là où les herbes envahissent le village. Tout là-bas au bout de la route un homme marche. Ligne noire dans les champs. La houle herbeuse le soulève au-dessus de la terre.

La grenouille rousse

Le moulin est muet. Muets les murs et le toit.
Les roues aussi. Windisch a appuyé sur l'interrupteur et éteint la lumière. Il fait nuit entre les roues
du moulin. L'obscurité a englouti la poussière de
farine, les mouches et les sacs.

Le veilleur de nuit est assis sur le banc. Il dort.
La bouche ouverte. Les yeux du chien brillent
sous le banc.

Windisch s'aide des mains et des genoux pour
porter le sac. Il l'appuie contre le mur du moulin.
Le chien regarde et bâille. Ses dents blanches
dessinent une morsure.

La clé tourne dans la serrure du moulin. La
serrure craque sous les doigts de Windisch. Il
compte. Il sent battre ses tempes et il se dit : « Ma
tête est une pendule. » Il met la clé dans sa poche.
Le chien aboie. « Je vais la remonter jusqu'à ce
que le ressort se casse », dit-il à haute voix.

Le veilleur de nuit enfonce son chapeau sur son
crâne. Il ouvre les yeux, bâille. « Soldat, montons
la garde », dit-il.

Windisch va jusqu'à l'étang près du moulin. Sur
la rive il y a une meule de paille. Tache noire à la
surface, elle s'enfonce dans l'eau comme un
entonnoir. Windisch dégage son vélo de la paille.

« Il y a un rat dans la paille », dit le veilleur de

nuit. Windisch cueille les brindilles égarées sur la selle. Il les jette dans l'eau. « Je l'ai vu, dit-il, il a sauté dans l'eau. » Les brins de paille flottent comme des cheveux. L'eau frissonne et les retourne. La masse sombre de l'entonnoir flotte. Windisch regarde son image qui elle aussi se trouble.

Le veilleur donne un coup de pied dans le ventre du chien qui glapit. Windisch regarde l'entonnoir et entend les glapissements au fond de l'eau. « Les nuits sont longues », dit le veilleur. Windisch recule d'un pas. S'éloigne du bord. Il regarde la meule de paille. Elle se dresse immobile, le dos à la rive. Elle ne bouge pas. Elle n'a rien à voir avec l'entonnoir. Elle est claire, plus claire que la nuit.

On entend le frémissement du journal. « Mon estomac est vide », dit le veilleur. Il déballe le lard et le pain. Le couteau brille dans sa main. Il mâche. Il se gratte le poignet avec la lame du couteau.

Windisch marche en poussant son vélo. Il regarde la lune. Le veilleur dit à voix basse, tout en mastiquant : « L'homme est un grand faisan sur terre. » Windisch soulève le sac et le pose sur son vélo. « L'homme est fort, dit-il, plus fort que les bêtes. »

Un coin du journal s'agite dans la main du vent. Le veilleur pose le couteau sur le banc. « J'ai un peu dormi », dit-il. Windisch est penché sur le vélo. Il relève la tête. « Et je t'ai réveillé ?

— Non, ce n'est pas toi, c'est ma femme qui m'a réveillé. »

12

Le veilleur enlève les miettes de sa veste. « Je savais bien que je ne pourrais pas dormir, reprend-il. La lune est grosse. J'ai rêvé de la grenouille desséchée. J'étais épuisé, incapable d'aller me coucher. La grenouille rousse était dans mon lit. J'ai parlé à ma femme et c'est la grenouille qui m'a regardé avec les yeux de ma femme. Comme elle, elle avait une tresse. Elle portait sa chemise de nuit retroussée jusqu'au ventre. Je lui ai dit : " Couvre-toi, tes cuisses sont flétries. " Voilà ce que j'ai dit à ma femme. La grenouille a tiré sur sa chemise de nuit pour cacher ses cuisses. Je me suis assis sur la chaise à côté du lit. La grenouille m'a souri avec la bouche de ma femme. " La chaise couine ", a-t-elle dit. Mais la chaise ne couinait pas. La grenouille s'est mis la tresse de ma femme sur l'épaule. Elle était aussi longue que la chemise de nuit. Je lui ai dit que ses cheveux avaient poussé. La grenouille m'a crié, en levant la tête : " Tu es ivre, tu vas finir par tomber de la chaise! " »

La lune est tachée de nuages rouges. Windisch s'est adossé au mur du moulin. « L'homme est bête, dit le veilleur, il est toujours prêt à pardonner. »

Le chien mange une couenne de lard. « Je lui ai tout pardonné, dit-il, je lui ai pardonné le boulanger, je lui ai pardonné de s'être fait soigner à la ville. » Il caresse du bout des doigts la lame du couteau. « Tout le village s'est moqué de moi », poursuit-il. Windisch soupire. « Je ne pouvais plus la regarder dans les yeux, dit le veilleur. Seule cette mort si rapide, comme si elle n'avait pas eu de famille, ça je n'ai pas pu lui pardonner.

– Dieu seul sait pour quelles raisons elles existent, les femmes », dit Windisch. Le veilleur hausse les épaules. « Pas pour nous, ni pour toi ni pour moi. » Le veilleur caresse le chien. « Et nos filles, grands dieux, dit Windisch, elles aussi, elles deviendront des femmes. »

Sur le vélo une ombre, dans l'herbe aussi. « Ma fille, continue Windisch en pesant les mots dans sa tête, mon Amélie, elle non plus elle n'est plus vierge. » Le veilleur de nuit regarde la tache rouge des nuages. « Elle a des mollets comme des melons, Amélie. Comme tu dis, je ne peux plus la regarder dans les yeux. Il y a une ombre dans ses yeux. »

Le chien tourne la tête. « Les yeux mentent, dit le veilleur, les mollets ne mentent pas. » Il écarte les pieds. « Regarde ta fille. Si elle écarte les pieds en marchant, alors c'est fait. »

Le veilleur tourne son chapeau dans sa main. Le chien est couché, il regarde. Windisch se tait. « Il y a de la rosée, la farine va être humide, dit le veilleur, et le maire ne sera pas content. »

Un oiseau vole au-dessus de l'étang. Lentement et sans dévier comme sur un fil. Au ras de l'eau. Comme si c'était la terre. Windisch le suit des yeux. « On dirait un chat, dit-il.

– Une chouette », dit le veilleur. Il met la main devant sa bouche. « Depuis trois nuits la lumière brûle chez la vieille Kroner. » Windisch pousse son vélo. « Elle ne peut pas mourir, la chouette ne s'est pas encore posée sur un toit. »

Windisch marche dans l'herbe et regarde la lune. « Je te le dis, Windisch, lui crie le veilleur, les femmes nous trompent! »

L'aiguille

La lumière brille encore dans la maison du menuisier. Windisch s'arrête. La vitre brille. Elle renvoie l'image de la rue. Des arbres. Leur image traverse le rideau, les guirlandes de bouquets de fleurs en dentelle. Pénètre dans la pièce. Contre le mur à côté du poêle de faïence le couvercle d'un cercueil. Il attend la mort de la vieille Kroner. Son nom est gravé dessus. Malgré les meubles, la pièce semble vide, tant elle est éclairée.

Le menuisier assis sur une chaise tourne le dos à la table. Sa femme, en face de lui, porte une chemise de nuit à rayures. Elle tient une aiguille à la main, avec du fil gris. Le menuisier lui tend l'index. De la pointe de l'aiguille, elle lui enlève une écharde du doigt. Il saigne. Le menuisier retire son doigt. Sa femme laisse tomber l'aiguille. Elle baisse les yeux et rit. Le menuisier passe la main sous la chemise de nuit. La retrousse. Les rayures se tordent. Le menuisier lui touche les seins de son doigt plein de sang. Elle a de gros seins. Qui frémissent. Le fil gris est accroché au pied de la chaise. L'aiguille, la pointe en bas, se balance.

A côté du couvercle du cercueil, il y a le lit. Le

damas de l'oreiller est parsemé de motifs, des petits et des grands. Le lit est ouvert. Le drap est blanc, la couverture aussi.

La chouette passe devant la fenêtre. Vol étiré comme une aile dans la vitre. La chouette tressaille en volant. Dans la lumière oblique, elle est deux fois plus grande.

La femme courbée va et vient devant la table. Le menuisier lui met la main entre les cuisses. La femme voit l'aiguille qui pend. Elle l'attrape. Le fil se balance. La femme laisse tomber les bras le long du corps, elle ferme les yeux. Ouvre la bouche. Le menuisier la saisit par le poignet et l'attire vers le lit. Il jette son pantalon sur la chaise. Son caleçon reste coincé dans une jambe de pantalon. Comme un chiffon blanc. La femme lève les cuisses et plie les genoux. Son ventre est mou comme de la pâte. Ses jambes dessinent une embrasure blanche sur le drap.

Au-dessus du lit il y a un tableau dans un cadre noir. La mère du menuisier touche de son fichu le bord du chapeau de son mari. Il y a une tache sur le verre. Sur le menton de la femme. Du cadre elle sourit. A l'approche de la mort elle sourit. Dans un an tout juste. Son sourire va vers la chambre d'à côté.

A la fontaine, la roue tourne parce que la lune est ronde et qu'elle boit. Parce que le vent est accroché dans les rayons de la roue. Le sac est humide. Masse endormie, il pend au-dessus de la roue arrière. « Le sac pend derrière moi comme un mort », pense Windisch.

Windisch sent le long de sa cuisse son sexe dur

et buté. « La mère du menuisier est refroidie », se dit Windisch.

Le dahlia blanc

En pleine canicule, au mois d'août, la mère du menuisier a plongé une grosse pastèque dans le puits. L'eau a formé des vagues autour du seau. Elle glougloutait autour de la peau verte. Elle refroidissait la pastèque.

Munie de son grand couteau, la mère du menuisier est allée au jardin. Le chemin était un sillon. Les salades étaient montées, les feuilles gluantes du lait blanc qui parcourt les côtes. La mère du menuisier a traversé le sillon avec son couteau. Entre clôture et jardin fleurissait un dahlia qui lui arrivait à l'épaule. La mère du menuisier a respiré le parfum du dahlia. Elle a humé très longuement l'odeur des pétales blancs. Elle a inhalé leurs senteurs. Elle s'est frotté le front. Elle a regardé dans la cour. La mère du menuisier a coupé le dahlia blanc avec son grand couteau.

« La pastèque n'était qu'un prétexte, a expliqué le menuisier après l'enterrement. Le dahlia lui a été fatal. » Et la voisine du menuisier ajouta : « Le dahlia, c'était une vision.

– L'été a été tellement sec, dit la femme du menuisier, que le dahlia était couvert de pétales blancs tout recroquevillés. Il avait fait une grosse fleur comme jamais un dahlia n'en fait. Il n'y avait pas de vent, la fleur n'est pas tombée. Il y a longtemps que le dahlia était sans vie, mais il n'arrivait pas à se faner.

– Ça, c'est insupportable, dit le menuisier, personne ne peut supporter cela. »

Personne ne sait ce que la mère du menuisier a fait du dahlia qu'elle a coupé. Elle ne l'a pas rapporté à la maison. Elle ne l'a pas mis dans sa chambre. On ne l'a pas retrouvé non plus au jardin.

« Elle est sortie du jardin, le grand couteau à la main, dit le menuisier. Dans ses yeux il y avait un reste de dahlia. Le blanc de son œil était sec.

« Peut-être, poursuivit-il, qu'en attendant la pastèque, elle a effeuillé le dahlia. Dans sa main. Elle n'a pas laissé tomber un seul pétale par terre. Comme si le jardin avait été une chambre.

« Je crois, dit le menuisier, qu'elle a creusé un trou dans la terre avec son grand couteau et qu'elle y a enterré le dahlia. »

En fin d'après-midi, la mère du menuisier a remonté le seau du puits. Elle a porté la pastèque sur la table de la cuisine. De la pointe du couteau elle a percé la peau verte. D'un geste circulaire elle a fendu la pastèque en deux avec son grand couteau. Un grondement s'en est échappé. Un râle. La pastèque était encore vivante dans le puits et sur la table de la cuisine jusqu'à ce que les deux moitiés se détachent.

La mère du menuisier a écarquillé les yeux, mais comme ils étaient aussi secs que le dahlia, ils sont restés tout petits. Le jus dégoulinait de la lame du couteau. Ses petits yeux fixaient la chair rouge avec haine. Comme les dents d'un peigne, les pépins noirs se recouvraient les uns les autres.

La mère du menuisier n'a pas coupé la pastèque en tranches. Elle a placé les deux moitiés devant elle. De la pointe du couteau, elle a creusé la chair rouge. « Elle avait des yeux avides, comme je ne lui en ai jamais vu », a dit le menuisier.

Le jus rouge a coulé sur la table. Il lui dégoulinait de la bouche. Jusqu'au coude. Le jus rouge de la pastèque collait par terre.

« Les dents de ma mère n'ont jamais été aussi blanches, ni aussi froides. Elle mangeait et elle m'a dit : " Ne me regarde pas ainsi, ne regarde pas ma bouche. " Elle crachait les pépins noirs sur la table.

« J'ai détourné les yeux. Je ne suis pas sorti de la cuisine. J'ai eu peur de la pastèque. J'ai regardé par la fenêtre. Un inconnu est passé. A la hâte. Il parlait tout seul. Derrière mon dos, j'ai entendu ma mère creuser avec son couteau. Mâcher. Avaler. " Mère, ai-je dit, sans la regarder, cesse de manger. " »

La mère du menuisier a alors levé la main. « Elle a crié et je l'ai regardée tant elle avait crié fort. Elle m'a menacé avec le couteau. " C'est un été qui n'en est pas un et toi, tu es un monstre, s'est-elle écriée, ma tête éclate! Les tripes me brûlent. C'est un été qui crache le feu des années passées. Seule la pastèque me rafraîchit. " »

La machine à coudre

Le pavé est inégal et étroit. La chouette hulule derrière les arbres. Elle cherche un toit. Les maisons sont blanches, figées dans la chaux.

Windisch sent sous son nombril son sexe buté. Le vent frappe contre le bois. Il coud. Le vent coud un sac dans la terre.

Windisch entend la voix de sa femme. « Monstre », dit-elle. Tous les soirs, au lit, quand il tourne sa respiration vers elle, elle le traite de monstre. Depuis deux ans son ventre n'a plus d'utérus. « Le médecin me l'a interdit, je ne me laisserai pas crever la vessie pour ton bon plaisir. »

Chaque fois qu'elle dit cela, Windisch sent une colère froide monter en elle et s'installer entre leurs deux visages. Elle prend Windisch par l'épaule. Parfois cela prend du temps avant qu'elle trouve son épaule. Lorsqu'elle l'a trouvée, elle lui dit à l'oreille dans le noir : « Tu pourrais déjà être grand-père. Ce n'est plus de notre âge. »

L'été dernier, Windisch, chargé de deux sacs de farine, était sur le chemin du retour.

Il a frappé à une fenêtre. Le maire a éclairé avec la lampe électrique à travers le rideau. « Tu n'as pas besoin de frapper, a-t-il dit. Pose la farine dans la cour. Le portail est ouvert. » Sa voix était endormie. C'était une nuit d'orage. Un éclair est passé devant la fenêtre, il est tombé dans l'herbe. Le maire a éteint sa lampe. Sa voix s'est réveillée, il a parlé plus fort. « Encore cinq livraisons, Windisch, au jour de l'an tu me donnes l'argent. Et à Pâques, tu auras ton passeport. »

Un coup de tonnerre a retenti et le maire a regardé la vitre. « Mets la farine à l'abri, il va pleuvoir. »

« Et voilà, se dit Windisch, c'est la douzième livraison, je lui ai donné dix mille lei, et Pâques est passé depuis belle lurette. » Il y a longtemps qu'il ne toque plus au carreau. Il ouvre le portail. Appuie le sac contre son ventre et le pose dans la cour. Même quand il ne pleut pas, il met la farine à l'abri.

Le vélo est léger. Il roule et Windisch marche à côté. Lorsque le vélo roule dans l'herbe, Windisch ne s'entend pas marcher.

En cette nuit d'orage toutes les fenêtres étaient noires. Windisch s'est arrêté dans le long couloir. La foudre a déchiré la terre. Un coup de tonnerre a précipité la cour dans la crevasse. La femme de Windisch n'a pas entendu la clé tourner dans la serrure.

Windisch s'est arrêté dans le vestibule. Le tonnerre est tombé si loin par-delà le village, derrière les jardins, si loin qu'un silence glacé a empli la nuit. Windisch avait l'impression que la nuit allait se briser et que d'un seul coup une clarté éblouissante recouvrirait le village. Il était dans le vestibule et il savait que s'il n'était pas rentré dans la maison, il aurait vu, dans tous les jardins, de part en part, la fin étroite de toutes choses et sa propre fin.

Derrière la porte de la chambre, Windisch a entendu le gémissement obstiné et régulier de sa femme. On aurait dit une machine à coudre.

D'un coup sec, Windisch a ouvert la porte de la chambre, allumé la lumière. Les jambes de sa femme dessinaient sur le drap blanc les battants d'une fenêtre ouverte. Les jambes frémissaient dans la lumière. La femme de Windisch ouvrit grand les yeux sans être éblouie. Elle avait simplement le regard fixe.

Windisch se pencha. Il délaça ses souliers. Pardessous son bras, il regarda les cuisses de sa femme. Il la vit retirer de sa toison un doigt visqueux. Elle ne savait pas où poser le doigt, la main. Elle la mit sur son ventre nu.

Windisch regarda son soulier.

« C'est donc ça. C'est ça, cette histoire de vessie, chère madame. »

De la même main, la femme de Windisch se cacha le visage. Elle fit glisser ses jambes vers le fond du lit. Elle les serra de plus en plus fort, l'une contre l'autre, jusqu'à ce que Windisch ne voie plus qu'une seule jambe avec deux plantes de pieds.

La femme de Windisch tourna le visage vers le mur et pleura bruyamment. Longs sanglots de jeune fille. Sanglots brefs et étouffés d'une femme de son âge. Trois fois, on l'entendit geindre d'une voix étrangère. Puis plus rien.

Windisch éteignit la lumière. Il se glissa dans le

lit chaud. Il sentit la vase de sa femme comme si elle avait vidé son ventre dans le lit.

Windisch l'entendit s'enfoncer dans le sommeil sous cette vase. Elle ronflait et sa respiration était fatiguée et vide. Et loin de tout. Elle ronflait comme si c'était la fin de toutes choses et sa propre fin à lui aussi.

Cette nuit-là, le sommeil l'avait emportée si loin qu'aucun rêve ne pouvait la trouver.

Les taches noires

Derrière le pommier il y a les fenêtres du mégissier. Toutes illuminées. « Lui, il a son passe-port », se dit Windisch. Les fenêtres ont une lumière crue et les vitres sont nues. Le mégissier a tout vendu. Les pièces sont vides. « Ils ont même vendu les rideaux », pense Windisch.

Le mégissier est adossé au poêle de faïence. Sur le sol des assiettes blanches. Sur le rebord de la fenêtre les couverts. A la poignée de la porte le manteau noir du mégissier. La femme du mégissier passe devant les grosses valises en se penchant. Windisch voit ses mains. Elles projettent leur ombre sur les murs nus de la pièce. Elles s'allongent et se tordent. Les bras ondoient comme des branches à la surface de l'eau. Le mégissier compte son argent. Il met la liasse de billets dans le tuyau du poêle de faïence.

L'armoire est un carré blanc, les lits des cadres

blancs. Entre eux les murs forment des taches noires. Le plancher est de travers. Il se soulève. Remonte le long du mur. Se poste devant la porte. Le mégissier compte une seconde liasse. Le plancher va cacher le mégissier. La femme du mégissier souffle sur sa cape de fourrure grise pour enlever la poussière. Le plancher va la soulever jusqu'au plafond. A côté du poêle de faïence la pendule a sonné une longue tache blanche. A côté du poêle de faïence le temps est resté accroché. Windisch ferme les yeux. « Il est temps », pense-t-il. Il entend le tic-tac de la tache blanche et il voit le cadran au milieu des taches noires. Le temps n'a plus d'aiguilles. Seules les taches noires tournent. Elles se bousculent. S'extraient de cette tache blanche. Tombent le long du mur. Elles ne font qu'un avec le plancher. Les taches noires sont le plancher dans l'autre pièce.

Rudi est agenouillé par terre dans la pièce vide. Devant lui en longues rangées des objets de verre de toutes les couleurs. Ou en cercle. A côté de Rudi la valise vide. Il y a encore un tableau au mur. Ce n'est pas un tableau. Le cadre est tout de verre émeraude. A l'intérieur, du verre dépoli avec des vagues rouges.

La chouette vole au-dessus des jardins. Son cri est aigu, son vol bas. Tout chargé de nuit. « Un chat, se dit Windisch, un chat volant. »

Rudi tient une cuillère en verre bleu devant son œil. Son cristallin s'agrandit. Sa pupille est une boule humide, brillante dans la cuillère. Le plancher reflue les couleurs vers le seuil de la pièce. Le temps de la pièce voisine roule des vagues. Les

taches noires se laissent emporter par les flots.
L'ampoule électrique tressaille. La lumière est
déchirée. Les deux fenêtres voguent l'une vers
l'autre. Les deux planchers poussent les murs
devant eux. Windisch se tient la tête dans les
mains. Son pouls bat dans sa tête. Sa tempe bat à
son poignet. Les planchers se soulèvent. Ils se
rapprochent. Se touchent. Retombent le long de
leur étroite fissure. Ils sont lourds. La terre va se
briser. Le verre brillera, ce sera une tumeur trem-
blante dans la valise.

Windisch ouvre la bouche. Il les sent grandir
sur son visage, les taches noires.

La boîte

Rudi est ingénieur. Il a travaillé pendant trois
ans dans une verrerie. L'usine est située dans une
région de montagnes.

Au cours de ces trois années, le mégissier a
rendu visite une fois à son fils. « Je vais une
semaine à la montagne chez Rudi », a-t-il dit à
Windisch.

Trois jours après, le mégissier était déjà de
retour. L'air de la montagne lui avait donné des
joues rouge vif et l'insomnie avait blessé ses yeux.
« Là-bas je ne pouvais pas dormir. Je n'ai pas
fermé l'œil. La nuit je sentais les montagnes dans
ma tête.

« Où que l'on regarde, continua-t-il, il n'y a

que des montagnes. Pour se rendre là-bas, on traverse des tunnels. Qui sont aussi des montagnes. Noires comme la nuit. Le train traverse les tunnels. La montagne tout entière pétarade dans le train. Les oreilles bourdonnent, la tête est prise dans un étau. Tantôt il fait nuit noire, tantôt la lumière du jour éblouit. Cela change sans arrêt. C'est insupportable. Tout le monde est assis et personne ne regarde. Quand il fait jour, ils lisent des livres. Ils prennent tous garde de ne pas faire tomber les livres qui sont sur leurs genoux. Il a fallu que je fasse attention de ne pas les toucher du coude. Quand il fait nuit, ils laissent les livres ouverts. J'ai écouté. J'ai écouté quand on traverse les tunnels pour savoir s'ils ferment les livres. Je n'ai rien entendu. Quand il a fait jour à nouveau, j'ai tout de suite regardé les livres et ensuite leurs yeux. Les livres étaient ouverts, les yeux fermés. Ils n'ont rouvert les yeux que plus tard. Tu sais, Windisch, que j'étais fier d'avoir ouvert les yeux avant eux. Je sens quand la fin du tunnel arrive. Depuis que j'ai été en Russie, dit le mégissier qui se prend le front dans les mains. Toutes ces nuits qui pétaradent, tous ces jours qui éblouissent, je n'avais jamais connu ça. La nuit dans mon lit, j'entendais encore le bruit des tunnels. Ils étaient assourdissants, assourdissants comme les bennes dans l'Oural. »

Le mégissier hoche la tête. Son visage s'illumine. Par-dessus son épaule il regarde en direction de la table. Il regarde si sa femme écoute. Puis il ajoute à voix basse : « Mais alors, les femmes là-bas, Windisch, je peux te dire qu'il y a des sacrées femmes là-bas. Elles ont un de ces rythmes. Elles fauchent plus vite que les hommes. » Il rit.

« Hélas, mon Dieu, ce sont des Valaques, ajoute-t-il. Elles sont bonnes au lit, mais elles ne savent pas faire la cuisine comme nos femmes. »

Sur la table il y a un saladier en fer-blanc. La femme du mégissier est en train de monter des blancs en neige. « J'ai lavé deux chemises. Il en est sorti une eau toute noire. Il y a une de ces saletés là-bas. On ne s'en aperçoit pas à cause des forêts. »

Le mégissier regarde le saladier. « Tout en haut, sur la montagne la plus haute, il y a une clinique. Pour les fous. Ils se promènent derrière une clôture, portent des caleçons bleus et des manteaux épais. Il y en a un qui cherche toute la journée des pommes de pin dans l'herbe. Il parle tout seul. Rudi dit que c'est un mineur et qu'une fois il a fait grève. »

La femme du mégissier trempe son doigt dans les blancs battus. « Et voilà le résultat », dit-elle en se léchant le bout du doigt.

« Un autre, poursuit le mégissier, n'est resté qu'une semaine à la clinique. Il est retourné à la mine. Il s'est fait écraser par une voiture. »

La femme du mégissier soulève le saladier. « Les œufs sont vieux, dit-elle, la neige est aigre. » Le mégissier approuve d'un signe de tête. « De là-haut on voit des cimetières qui pendent de guingois aux flancs des montagnes. »

Windisch pose les mains à plat sur la table à

côté du saladier. « En tout cas, ce n'est pas là-haut que je voudrais être enterré. »

La femme de Windisch regarde sans les voir les mains de Windisch. « Oui, ce doit être beau la montagne, dit-elle. Seulement, c'est loin d'ici. On ne peut pas y aller et Rudi ne revient plus à la maison. »

« Voilà qu'elle recommence à faire des gâteaux que Rudi ne mangera pas », dit le mégissier. Windisch retire ses mains de la table. « Des lambeaux de nuages traînent sur la ville, dit le mégissier. Les gens vont et viennent au milieu des nuages. Tous les jours il y a un orage. Chaque fois que les gens sont aux champs, ils sont tués par la foudre. »

Windisch met les mains dans la poche de son pantalon. Il se lève, se dirige vers la porte.

« J'ai rapporté quelque chose, dit le mégissier. Rudi m'a donné une petite boîte pour Amélie. » Le mégissier ouvre un tiroir. Le referme. Regarde dans une valise vide. Sa femme fouille dans les poches de la veste de son mari. Qui ouvre l'armoire.

La femme du mégissier lève les bras au ciel avec un air de lassitude. « Il faut que nous retrouvions cette boîte. » Le mégissier explore aussi les poches de son pantalon. « Ce matin je l'avais encore dans la main », dit-il.

Le rasoir

Windisch est assis dans la cuisine devant la fenêtre. Il se rase. Il badigeonne la mousse blanche sur son visage. Elle crisse sur ses joues. Du bout du doigt, Windisch répartit la neige autour de sa bouche. Il regarde dans le miroir. Il voit la porte de la cuisine. Et son visage.

Windisch voit qu'il s'est badigeonné trop de neige sur le visage. Il voit sa bouche au milieu de la neige. Il sent que la neige, dans ses narines et sur son menton, l'empêche de parler.

Il déplie son rasoir. Vérifie la lame sur la peau de son doigt. La place sous son œil. Sa pommette ne bouge plus. De l'autre main, Windisch lisse la peau sous son œil. Il regarde par la fenêtre. Il voit l'herbe verte.

Tressaillement du rasoir. Brûlure de la lame.

Pendant plusieurs semaines Windisch a une blessure sous l'œil. Elle est rouge. Le bord est mou et infecté. Chaque soir il y a beaucoup de poussière de farine dedans.

Depuis quelques jours, une croûte s'est formée sous l'œil.

Quand Windisch sort de la maison le matin, la croûte est encore sur sa joue. Après avoir ouvert la porte du moulin et mis la clé dans sa poche,

Windisch porte la main à sa joue. La croûte n'y est plus.

« Elle est peut-être dans l'ornière », se dit Windisch.

Lorsqu'il commence à faire jour dehors, Windisch va jusqu'à l'étang près du moulin. Il s'agenouille dans l'herbe. Regarde son visage dans l'eau. Des petits cercles battent son oreille. Ses cheveux rendent l'image floue.

Sous l'œil Windisch a une cicatrice blanche, irrégulière.

Une feuille de roseau est cassée. Elle s'ouvre et se ferme à côté de sa main. La feuille du roseau a le tranchant brun d'un couteau.

La larme

Amélie sort de la cour du mégissier. Elle marche dans l'herbe. Elle tient à la main une petite boîte. Hume ce qu'il y a dedans. Windisch regarde l'ourlet de la jupe d'Amélie jeter une ombre sur l'herbe. Ses mollets sont blancs. Windisch remarque qu'Amélie balance les hanches.

Une ficelle argentée est nouée autour de la boîte. Amélie se met devant le miroir. Elle se regarde. Elle cherche dans le miroir la ficelle argentée et tire dessus.

« La boîte était dans le chapeau du mégissier », dit-elle.

Le papier de soie blanc froufroute dans la boîte.

Sur le papier une larme en verre. Avec un trou dans la partie supérieure. Dans son ventre un sillon. Sous la larme un billet écrit par Rudi : « La larme est vide. Remplis-la avec de l'eau. De l'eau de pluie de préférence. »

Amélie ne peut pas remplir la larme. C'est l'été, le village est à sec. Et l'eau de la fontaine, ce n'est pas de l'eau de pluie. Amélie tient la larme devant la fenêtre, à la lumière. Extérieurement, elle est immobile. Mais à l'intérieur, le long du sillon, elle tremblote.

Le ciel s'est consumé pendant sept jours. Il s'est déplacé jusqu'à l'extrémité du village. Dans la vallée il a regardé le fleuve dont il a bu l'eau. Il a plu.

Dans la cour l'eau coule sur les pavés. Amélie est plantée sous la gouttière avec la larme. Elle regarde l'eau couler dans le ventre de la larme.

Dans l'eau de pluie il y a aussi du vent. Qui pousse des cloches de verre au travers des arbres. Elles sont opaques, des feuilles tourbillonnent à l'intérieur. La pluie chante. Elle a aussi du sable dans la voix et des morceaux d'écorce.

La larme est pleine. Amélie la rapporte dans sa chambre. Elle a les mains toutes mouillées, les pieds nus pleins de sable.

La femme de Windisch prend la larme dans sa main. L'eau brille à l'intérieur. Lumière dans le verre. L'eau de la larme lui coule entre les doigts.

Windisch étend la main. Il prend la larme. L'eau lui dégouline le long du coude. Sa femme lèche du bout de la langue ses doigts mouillés.

Windisch la regarde se lécher le doigt qu'elle a retiré tout visqueux de sa toison le soir de l'orage. Il regarde la pluie dehors. Dans sa bouche il sent la vase de sa femme. Sa gorge se serre. Il a envie de vomir.

Windisch pose la larme dans la main d'Amélie. Quelques gouttes tombent. Le niveau de l'eau dans la larme ne baisse pas. « L'eau est salée. Elle brûle les lèvres », dit la femme de Windisch.

Amélie lèche son poignet. « La pluie est douce. C'est la larme qui est salée. »

Le charnier

« Les écoles n'y changent rien », dit la femme de Windisch. Windisch regarde Amélie. « Rudi est ingénieur, mais l'école n'y change rien. » Amélie rit. « Rudi connaît la clinique, et pas seulement de l'extérieur. Il y a été interné, dit la femme de Windisch. C'est la postière qui me l'a dit. »

Windisch fait avancer et reculer son verre sur la table. Il regarde dans le verre et dit : « C'est de famille. Ils font des enfants qui sont fous, eux aussi. »

Au village on appelait l'arrière-grand-mère de Rudi « la larve ». Elle avait une tresse fine qu'elle laissait toujours pendre dans son dos. Elle ne pouvait pas supporter de peigne. Son mari était mort jeune, sans même avoir été malade.

Après l'enterrement la larve alla chercher son

mari au village. Elle se rendit à l'auberge. Elle se mit à dévisager tous les hommes.

« Ce n'est pas toi », disait-elle en allant d'une table à l'autre. L'aubergiste vint vers elle et lui dit : « Tu sais bien que ton mari est mort. » Elle prit sa petite tresse dans sa main. Elle se mit à pleurer et s'enfuit en courant dans la rue.

Tous les jours la larve allait à la recherche de son mari. Elle entrait dans les maisons et demandait si on l'avait vu.

Un jour d'hiver où le brouillard avait étendu sur le village des voiles blancs, la larve est partie aux champs. Elle portait une robe d'été et elle n'avait pas de bas. Seules ses mains étaient habillées pour la neige. Elle portait d'épais gants de laine. Elle marcha dans des fourrés dénudés. C'était l'après-midi. Le garde forestier la vit. Il la renvoya au village.

Le lendemain le garde forestier vint au bourg. La larve gisait dans les prunelliers. Elle était morte de froid. Il la rapporta au village sur son épaule. Elle était raide comme une planche. « Complètement irresponsable, dit la femme de Windisch, elle a laissé un petit enfant de trois ans tout seul au monde. »

L'enfant de trois ans, c'était le grand-père de Rudi. Il était menuisier. Il ne savait absolument pas travailler un champ. « Sur une bonne terre il a laissé pousser des teignes », dit Windisch.

Le grand-père de Rudi ne pensait qu'au bois. Il dépensait tout son argent à acheter du bois. « Il en faisait des personnages, dit la femme de Windisch. Dans chaque morceau de bois il a sculpté un visage, une vraie horreur. »

« Puis le temps des expropriations est venu », dit Windisch. Amélie est en train de se mettre du vernis rouge sur les ongles. « Tous les paysans ont tremblé. Des hommes sont venus de la ville. Ils ont mesuré les champs. Ils ont noté les noms des gens et ils ont dit : " Tous ceux qui ne signeront pas iront en prison. " Toutes les portes d'entrée étaient verrouillées. Le vieux mégissier n'a pas verrouillé sa porte. Il l'a ouverte en grand. Lorsque les hommes sont venus, il leur a dit : " C'est bien que vous preniez mon champ. Prenez aussi les chevaux. Que j'en sois débarrassé. " »

La femme de Windisch arrache le flacon de vernis des mains d'Amélie. « Il est le seul à avoir dit ça! »

Dans sa colère, elle a crié si fort qu'elle a fait gonfler une petite veine bleue derrière l'oreille. « Tu écoutes, oui! » crie-t-elle.

Avec sa hache le vieux mégissier a taillé dans le tilleul une femme nue. Il l'a placée devant la fenêtre de la chambre dans la cour. Sa femme s'est mise à pleurer. Elle a pris son enfant, l'a posé dans un couffin. « Elle est partie s'installer dans une maison vide à la lisière du village avec l'enfant et les quelques affaires qu'elle a pu emporter », dit Windisch.

« L'enfant a hérité de tout ce bois un trou de mélancolie dans la tête », dit la femme de Windisch.

L'enfant, c'est le mégissier. Dès qu'il a su marcher, il est allé tous les jours aux champs.

Pour y attraper des lézards et des crapauds. Quand il a été plus grand, il s'est glissé la nuit dans le clocher. Il a pris dans leur nid les chouettes qui ne savaient pas voler. Il les a rapportées sous sa chemise à la maison. Il leur a donné à manger les lézards et les crapauds. Quand les chouettes ont été adultes, il les a tuées. Vidées. Plongées dans la chaux. Et bourrées de paille.

« Avant la guerre, raconte Windisch, le mégissier a gagné le vieux bouc en jouant aux quilles. En plein milieu du village, il l'a écorché vif. Les gens se sont enfuis. Les femmes se sont trouvées mal. »

« A l'endroit où il a saigné le vieux bouc, ajoute la femme de Windisch, l'herbe ne repousse toujours pas. »

Windisch est appuyé contre l'armoire.

« Il n'a jamais été un héros, poursuit-il dans un soupir, un bourreau, c'est tout ce qu'il était. A la guerre on ne se bat pas contre des chouettes et des crapauds. »

Devant le miroir Amélie se coiffe. « Il n'a jamais été dans les SS, dit la femme de Windisch, il n'était que dans la Wehrmacht. Après la guerre il a continué à chasser et à empailler les chouettes, les cigognes et les merles. Il a abattu tous les moutons et les lièvres des environs qui étaient malades. Et tanné leurs peaux. Son grenier tout entier n'est qu'un charnier. »

Amélie attrape le petit flacon de vernis à ongles. Windisch sent le grain de sable sous son crâne. Il le fait passer d'une tempe à l'autre. Du flacon une goutte rouge tombe sur la nappe.

« En Russie tu as fait la putain », dit Amélie à sa mère en se regardant les ongles.

La pierre dans la chaux

En volant, la chouette trace un cercle au-dessus du pommier. Windisch regarde la lune. Il regarde où vont les taches noires. La chouette n'achève jamais son cercle.

Il y a deux ans le mégissier a empaillé la dernière chouette qu'il avait attrapée dans le clocher et il l'a offerte au curé. « Cette chouette vient d'un autre village », se dit Windisch.

C'est toujours ici, au village, que la nuit surprend la chouette venue d'ailleurs. Personne ne sait où elle repose ses ailes pendant la journée.

Personne ne sait où elle ferme son bec ni où elle dort.

Windisch, lui, sait que la chouette venue d'ailleurs sent les animaux empaillés qui sont dans le grenier du mégissier.

Le mégissier a donné les animaux empaillés à un musée de la ville. Il n'a pas reçu d'argent en échange. Deux hommes sont venus. Leur auto est restée toute une journée devant la porte du mégissier. L'auto était blanche et fermée comme une maison.

Les hommes ont dit que les animaux empaillés provenaient des réserves de chasse. Ils ont enfermé tous les oiseaux dans des boîtes. Ils ont menacé le mégissier d'une forte amende. Il leur a donné toutes les peaux de mouton qu'il avait. Alors ils ont dit que ça allait bien comme cela.

L'auto blanche est sortie lentement du village, comme une maison. La femme du mégissier a eu un sourire d'angoisse et elle a agité la main pour dire au revoir.

Windisch est assis sous la véranda. Il pense au mégissier : « Il a déposé sa demande de visa d'émigration après nous et il a donné de l'argent en ville. »

Windisch entend le bruit d'une feuille sur le carrelage du couloir. Elle racle les pierres. Le mur est long et blanc. Windisch ferme les yeux. Il sent le mur monter jusqu'à son visage. La chaux brûle son front. Une pierre prise dans la chaux ouvre la gueule. Le pommier tremble. Ses feuilles sont des oreilles. Elles épient. Le pommier nourrit ses pommes vertes.

Le pommier

Avant la guerre il y avait un pommier derrière l'église. C'était un pommier qui dévorait ses propres pommes.

Le père du veilleur de nuit était lui aussi veilleur. Une nuit d'été, alors qu'il était derrière la haie de buis, il vit le pommier ouvrir la gueule à l'extrémité du tronc, à l'endroit où les branches se séparent. Le pommier dévorait ses pommes.

Au matin le veilleur n'alla pas se coucher. Il se rendit chez le juge de paix. Il lui raconta que le pommier, derrière l'église, dévorait ses propres pommes. Le juge éclata de rire. Il en avait les paupières qui tremblaient. Mais pour le veilleur ce rire trahissait la peur du juge dont les tempes retentissaient des petits coups de marteau de la vie.

Le veilleur rentra chez lui. Il se mit au lit tout habillé. Il dormit baigné de sueur.

Pendant que le veilleur dormait, le pommier frotta les tempes du juge jusqu'au sang. Ses yeux étaient tout rouges, sa bouche était sèche. Après le déjeuner le juge battit sa femme. Dans la soupe il avait vu nager des pommes. Il les avait avalées.

Après manger le juge ne put dormir. Il ferma les yeux et il entendit les écorces d'arbres derrière le mur. Elles étaient pendues les unes derrière les autres, elles se balançaient au bout d'une corde et elles engloutissaient des pommes.

Le soir le juge de paix organisa une réunion. Les gens y vinrent. Le juge créa une commission chargée de surveiller le pommier. Faisaient partie de la commission quatre grands propriétaires terriens, le curé, l'instituteur et le juge lui-même.

L'instituteur fit un discours. Il donna à la commission le nom de « Commission d'une nuit d'été ». Le curé refusa de surveiller le pommier derrière l'église. Il se signa trois fois, s'excusa en implorant le Seigneur pour qu'Il pardonne aux pécheurs. Il menaça d'aller en ville le lendemain matin et de mettre l'évêque au courant de ce blasphème.

Ce soir-là, la nuit vint très tard. Le soleil était tellement chaud qu'il ne pouvait trouver la fin du jour. La nuit jaillit de la terre et s'étendit sur le village.

La Commission d'une nuit d'été se faufila dans l'obscurité le long de la haie de buis. Elle s'allongea sous le pommier. Elle fixa la voûte des branches.

Le juge avait une hache. Les paysans posèrent leurs fourches dans l'herbe. L'instituteur était assis sous un sac, une lampe tempête, un crayon et un cahier à côté de lui. D'un œil, il regardait par un trou gros comme le pouce ménagé dans le sac. Il écrivait le procès-verbal.

La nuit était à son apogée. Elle poussait le ciel hors du village. Il était minuit. La Commission d'une nuit d'été fixait le ciel qui était déjà à demi vide. Sous le sac l'instituteur regarda l'heure. Il était minuit passé. L'horloge du clocher n'avait pas sonné.

Le curé avait arrêté l'horloge. Ses roues édentées ne devaient pas mesurer le temps du péché. Le silence devait accuser le village.

Au bourg personne ne dormait. Les chiens étaient dans la rue. Ils n'aboyaient pas. Les chats étaient dans les arbres. Ils regardaient, eux aussi, avec leurs yeux de vers luisants.

Les gens étaient restés chez eux. Les mères faisaient les cent pas, leurs enfants dans les bras. Elles avaient allumé des chandelles, les enfants ne pleuraient pas.

Windisch était assis avec Barbara sous le pont.

L'instituteur avait vu à sa montre que l'on avait dépassé le milieu de la nuit. Il sortit la main du sac et fit signe à la Commission d'une nuit d'été.

Le pommier ne bougeait toujours pas. Le juge de paix se racla la gorge. Il était resté trop longtemps silencieux. Une toux de fumeur secoua l'un des paysans. Il cueillit une poignée d'herbe, se la mit dans la bouche. Il enterra sa toux.

A deux heures du matin le pommier commença à trembler. Tout en haut, là où les branches se séparent, la gueule s'ouvrit. Elle engloutit les pommes.

La Commission d'une nuit d'été entendait le bruit glouton de la gueule. Derrière le mur, dans l'église, les grillons chantaient.

La gueule en était à sa sixième pomme. Le juge courut jusqu'au pommier. Il lui donna un coup de hache sur la gueule. Les paysans brandirent leurs fourches. Et s'avancèrent derrière le juge.

Un morceau d'écorce, avec un peu de bois jaune et humide, tomba dans l'herbe.

Le pommier referma la gueule.

Aucun des membres de la Commission d'une nuit d'été n'avait vu quand et comment le pommier avait refermé la gueule.

L'instituteur rampa hors du sac. C'était lui, l'instituteur, dit le juge, qui aurait dû repérer le moment.

A quatre heures du matin, le curé, dans sa longue soutane noire, sous son grand chapeau noir, sa serviette noire à côté de lui, se rendit à la gare. Il marchait vite. Il avait les yeux fixés sur les pavés. L'aube s'étalait sur les murs des maisons. La chaux était claire.

Trois jours après, l'évêque arriva au village. L'église était pleine. Les gens le virent passer parmi les bancs pour se rendre à l'autel. Il monta en chaire.

L'évêque ne pria pas. Il dit qu'il avait lu le rapport de l'instituteur. Qu'il avait conféré avec Dieu.

« Dieu sait tout cela depuis longtemps! s'écria-t-il. Dieu m'a rappelé Adam et Eve. Dieu, dit doucement l'évêque, Dieu m'a dit que le diable était dans le pommier. »

L'évêque avait écrit une lettre au curé. En latin. Le curé du haut de la chaire lut la lettre. A cause du latin, la chaire semblait très haute.

Le père du veilleur dit qu'il n'avait pas entendu la voix du curé.

Lorsqu'il eut fini de lire la lettre, le curé ferma les yeux. Joignit les mains et pria en latin. Il descendit de la chaire. Il semblait tout petit. Son visage était fatigué. Il se tourna vers l'autel. « Il ne faut pas abattre le pommier, dit-il. Il faut le brûler vivant. »

Le vieux mégissier aurait bien acheté le pommier au curé. Mais celui-ci lui dit : « La parole de Dieu est sacrée. L'évêque sait de quoi il parle. »

Le soir les hommes apportèrent une botte de paille. Les quatre paysans en enveloppèrent le tronc. Le maire, du haut de l'échelle, répandit la paille sur la cime.

Le curé, lui, se tenait derrière l'arbre et priait à haute voix. Le long de la haie de buis il y avait la chorale de l'église qui chantait de longs cantiques. Il faisait froid et le souffle des chants montait jusqu'au ciel. Les hommes et les enfants priaient en silence.

L'instituteur mit le feu à la paille avec un morceau de bois enflammé. La flamme dévora la paille. Elle grossit. Engloutit l'écorce de l'arbre. Le feu craqua dans le bois. La couronne de l'arbre lécha le ciel. La lune se voila.

Les pommes gonflèrent. Eclatèrent. Le jus geignit. Le jus hurla dans le feu comme une chair vivante. La fumée empestait. Elle brûlait les yeux. Les cantiques furent déchirés par des quintes de toux.

Le village resta dans la fumée jusqu'à ce que vînt la première pluie. L'instituteur écrivit dans son cahier. Il appela la fumée « brouillard de pomme ».

Le bras de bois

Une souche noire et tordue resta longtemps encore derrière l'église.

Les gens disaient que derrière l'église il y avait un homme. Il ressemblait au curé, mais sans chapeau.

Le matin il y avait de la gelée blanche. Le buis était saupoudré de blanc. La souche était noire.

Le sacristain emporta derrière l'église les roses fanées qui étaient sur les autels. Il passa devant la souche. Elle était le bras en bois de sa femme.

Des feuilles noircies tourbillonnaient dans l'air. Il n'y avait pas de vent. Les feuilles n'avaient plus de poids. Elles se soulevèrent jusqu'à ses genoux. Elles tombèrent devant ses pieds. Elles tombèrent en poussière. Elles n'étaient que suie.

Le sacristain arracha la souche à coups de hache. Qui ne firent aucun bruit. Il versa une bouteille de pétrole sur la souche. Il mit le feu. La souche brûla. Il ne resta plus sur le sol qu'une poignée de cendres.

Le sacristain mit les cendres dans une boîte. Il alla jusqu'à l'extrémité du village. Il gratta le sol de ses mains et fit un trou. Devant son front il y avait une branche tordue. C'était un bras de bois qui voulait l'attraper.

Le sacristain recouvrit la boîte de terre. Par des chemins poussiéreux il gagna les champs. De loin il entendait les arbres. Le maïs était sec. Les feuilles se cassaient partout où il passait. Il sentait la solitude de toutes ces années. Sa vie était transparente. Vide.

Les corneilles passèrent au-dessus du maïs. Elles se posèrent sur leurs tiges. Elles étaient charbonneuses. Lourdes. Les tiges de maïs se balancèrent. Les corneilles s'envolèrent.

Lorsque le sacristain fut de retour au village, il sentit son cœur nu et figé entre ses côtes. Les cendres dans la boîte reposaient près de la haie de buis.

La chanson

Les porcs tachetés du voisin grognent bruyamment. Un troupeau dans les nuages. Ils traversent la cour. Les feuilles ont tissé une toile qui enserre la véranda. Chaque feuille a une ombre.

Une voix d'homme chante dans une rue voisine. La chanson ondoie à travers les feuilles. « La nuit, le village est très grand, se dit Windisch, et le bout du village est partout. »

Windisch connaît cette chanson.

> *J'allais un jour en ville*
> *J'allais donc à Berlin*
> *Tirila-la-la, tirila-la-la, tirila-la-la-lin*

La véranda devient plus haute quand il fait aussi sombre. Quand les feuilles ont de l'ombre. Poussée tellurique sous le carrelage. Vers le haut. Sur une tige. Arrivée à une certaine hauteur, elle se casse. La véranda s'effondre. Sur place. Quand le jour revient, on ne voit pas que la véranda a poussé et qu'elle est retombée.

Windisch sent la poussée sur les pierres. Devant lui, il y a une table vide. Sur la table, la frayeur. La frayeur est dans la poitrine de Windisch. Il la sent comme une pierre dans la poche de son vêtement.

La chanson enlace le pommier.

> *Faut qu' tu m'envoies ta fille*
> *Que j' la lutine un brin*
> *Tirila-la-la, tirila-la-la, tirila-la-la-lin*

Windisch met sa main froide dans sa poche. Dedans il n'y a pas de pierre. La chanson est dans ses doigts. Windisch chantonne doucement.

> *T'auras pas ma fille*
> *Vu qu' c'est pas la catin*
> *Tirila-la-la, tirila-la-la, tirila-la-la-lin*

Il est grand le troupeau de porcs là-haut dans les nuages. Ils se traînent au-dessus du village. Les porcs se taisent. Il n'y a plus que la chanson.

> *Laisse-moi donc faire Maman*
> *Je n'ai pas peur du loup*
> *Tirila-la-la, tirila-la-la, tirila-la-la-lou*

Il est long le chemin de la maison. L'homme avance dans l'obscurité.
La chanson reprend.

> *Prête-moi ton trou, Maman,*
> *Le mien est tout petiout*
> *Tirila-la-la, tirila-la-la, tirila-la-la-lou*

La chanson est pesante. La voix est profonde. Il y a une pierre dans la chanson. De l'eau froide ruisselle sur la pierre.

Ah, ma fille, l'en a besoin
Ton père demain, de mon trou
Tirila-la-lin, tirila-la-lan, tirila-la-lin-lan-lou

Windisch retire la main de sa poche. Il perd la pierre. Il perd la chanson. « Amélie, se dit Windisch, elle marche en écartant les pieds. »

Le lait

Lorsque Amélie eut sept ans, Rudi l'entraîna dans le champ de maïs. Au bout du jardin. « Le maïs est une forêt », dit Rudi. Il entra avec Amélie dans la grange. « La grange est un château », ajouta-t-il.

Dans la grange il y avait un vieux tonneau. Rudi et Amélie se glissèrent dedans. « Ce sera ton lit », dit encore Rudi. Il disposa dans les cheveux d'Amélie des teignes séchées. « Tu portes une couronne d'épines. Tu es maudite. Je t'aime. Il faut que tu souffres. »

Rudi avait les poches pleines de morceaux de verre de toutes les couleurs. Il les aligna au bord du tonneau. Ils scintillaient. Amélie s'assit dans le tonneau. Rudi s'agenouilla devant elle. Il lui retroussa sa robe. « Je bois ton lait », dit Rudi. Il téta les seins d'Amélie. Elle ferma les yeux. Rudi lui mordit ses petits tétons marron.

Les mamelons d'Amélie étaient tout enflés. Elle

pleurait. Rudi s'enfuit dans les champs par le bout du jardin. Amélie courut à la maison.

Les teignes collaient à ses cheveux. Ils étaient tout enchevêtrés. La femme de Windisch coupa les nœuds avec des ciseaux. Elle lava les seins d'Amélie avec de la camomille. « Il ne faut plus que tu joues avec lui. Le fils du mégissier est fou. Il a hérité de toutes ces bêtes empaillées un trou de mélancolie dans la tête. »

Windisch hocha la tête.

« Amélie jettera la honte sur nous. »

Le loriot

Fentes grises dans les volets. Amélie a de la fièvre. Windisch n'a pas sommeil. Il pense aux morsures sur les seins d'Amélie.

La femme de Windisch s'assoit au bord du lit. « J'ai fait un rêve, dit-elle, je suis montée au grenier. J'avais un tamis à la main. Sur l'escalier qui conduit au grenier, il y avait un oiseau mort. C'était un loriot. Je l'ai attrapé par les pattes et je l'ai soulevé. Il y avait un tas de grosses mouches noires à la place. Un essaim s'est envolé. Les mouches se sont posées sur le tamis. Je l'ai secoué. Les mouches ne sont pas parties. J'ai alors ouvert la porte. J'ai couru dans la cour. J'ai jeté le tamis et les mouches dans la neige. »

L'horloge

Les fenêtres du mégissier se sont évanouies dans la nuit. Rudi est allongé sur son manteau. Il dort. Le mégissier et sa femme sont allongés sur leurs manteaux. Ils dorment également.

Windisch voit sur la table nue la tache blanche de la pendule. Un coucou habite dans la pendule. Il devine les aiguilles. Il chante. Le mégissier a offert la pendule au milicien.

Il y a deux semaines, le mégissier a montré à Windisch une lettre. En provenance de Munich. « Mon beau-frère vit là-bas », lui a-t-il dit. Il a posé la lettre sur la table et du bout des doigts il a cherché les lignes qu'il voulait lire à Windisch. « " Apportez votre vaisselle et vos couverts. Les lunettes sont très chères ici. Et les fourrures hors de prix. " » Le mégissier a tourné les pages.

Windisch entend le coucou chanter. A travers le plafond, l'odeur des animaux empaillés vient jusqu'à lui. Le coucou est le seul oiseau en vie dans la maison. Son chant déchire le temps. Les oiseaux empaillés empestent.

Tout à coup le mégissier rit. Il a fait glisser son doigt sous une phrase au bout de la lettre. « " Ici les femmes ne valent rien, lit-il, elles ne savent pas faire la cuisine. C'est ma femme qui doit tuer les poules pour la propriétaire de notre maison. Cette dame refuse de manger le foie et le sang. Elle jette le gésier et la rate. Sans compter qu'elle fume toute la journée et qu'elle se fait sauter par n'importe quel type. "

« La pire de nos Souabes vaut encore mieux que la meilleure de leurs Allemandes », conclut le mégissier.

Le réveille-matin

La chouette ne hulule plus. Elle s'est posée sur un toit. « La vieille Kroner est certainement morte », se dit Windisch.

L'été passé, la vieille Kroner a cueilli les fleurs du tilleul du tonnelier. L'arbre se trouve à gauche dans le cimetière. A cet endroit, dans l'herbe, des narcisses fleurissent. Il y a aussi une mare. Tout autour, les Roumains sont enterrés. Leurs tombes sont plates. L'eau les attire sous la terre.

Le tilleul du tonnelier a une odeur douceâtre. Le curé dit que les tombes des Roumains ne font pas partie du cimetière. Que les tombes des Roumains ont une autre odeur que celles des Allemands.

Le tonnelier allait de maison en maison. Il portait un sac plein de petits marteaux. Il fixait les cercles autour des tonneaux. Pour ce travail il recevait, en échange, le couvert. Et le gîte dans la grange.

C'était en automne. Derrière les nuages, on

devinait déjà le froid de l'hiver. Un matin, le tonnelier ne s'est pas réveillé. Personne ne savait qui il était. D'où il venait. « Quelqu'un comme lui est toujours par monts et par vaux », se sont dit les gens.

Les branches du tilleul descendaient jusqu'à la tombe. « On n'a pas besoin d'échelle, disait la vieille Kroner. On n'a pas le vertige. » Elle était assise dans l'herbe et elle cueillait le tilleul dont elle remplissait une corbeille.

Tout l'hiver la vieille Kroner but du tilleul qu'elle ingurgitait tasse après tasse. Elle était droguée au tilleul. La mort était au fond de la tasse.

Le visage de la vieille Kroner resplendissait. Les gens disaient que le visage de la vieille Kroner fleurissait. Son visage était jeune. D'une jeunesse qui était une faiblesse. Son visage exprimait la jeunesse qui précède la mort. Quand on redevient de plus en plus jeune, et même si jeune que le corps meurt. Et retourne en deçà de la naissance.

La vieille Kroner ne chantait qu'une chanson et toujours la même : *Près de la fontaine devant la porte il y a un tilleul.* Elle y ajoutait de nouvelles strophes. Des strophes de feuilles de tilleul.

Lorsque la vieille buvait sa tisane sans sucre, sa chanson devenait triste. En chantant elle se regardait dans un miroir. Sur son visage elle voyait les feuilles du tilleul. Ses plaies au ventre et aux jambes se réveillaient.

La vieille alla cueillir du réveille-matin. Elle le fit infuser. Elle frotta ses plaies de ce liquide brunâtre. Elles s'agrandirent. Elles avaient une odeur de plus en plus douceâtre.

La vieille avait cueilli tout le réveille-matin qui poussait dans les champs. Elle se prépara de plus en plus de tisane de tilleul et de décoction de réveille-matin.

Les boutons de manchette

Rudi était le seul Allemand de toute la verrerie. « Il est le seul Allemand de toute la région », racontait le mégissier. Au début les Roumains se sont étonnés qu'après Hitler il y eût encore des Allemands. « Il y a encore des Allemands, avait dit la secrétaire, il y en a encore. Même en Roumanie. »

« Ça peut être un avantage, pensait le mégissier, Rudi gagne beaucoup d'argent à l'usine. Il a de bonnes relations avec l'agent de la police secrète. C'est un grand blond aux yeux bleus qui a l'air d'un Allemand. Rudi dit qu'il est très capable. Il connaît toutes les sortes de verre. Rudi lui a offert une épingle de cravate et des boutons de manchette en verre. Ça a payé. Cet homme nous a beaucoup aidés à obtenir le passeport. »

Rudi a offert à cet homme des services secrets tous les objets en verre qui étaient dans son appartement. Des vases à fleurs. Des peignes. Une chaise à bascule en verre bleu. Des tasses et leurs soucoupes en verre. Des tableaux en verre. Une lampe de chevet en verre avec un abat-jour rouge.

Les oreilles, les lèvres, les yeux, les doigts, les orteils en verre, Rudi a rapporté tout cela dans sa valise à la maison. Il a tout posé sur le plancher. En rangées ou en cercles. Sous son regard.

La potiche

Amélie est jardinière d'enfants à la ville. Elle revient chaque samedi à la maison. La femme de Windisch va l'attendre à la gare. Elle l'aide à porter ses lourds bagages. Chaque samedi Amélie rapporte un sac rempli de provisions et un sac plein de verre. « Du cristal », dit-elle.

Les armoires regorgent de cristaux. Ils sont rangés par taille et par couleur. Des verres à vin rouges, des verres à vin bleus, des verres à eau-de-vie blancs. Sur la table des compotiers, des vases, des corbeilles en verre.

« Cadeaux des enfants », répond Amélie quand Windisch lui demande d'où viennent tous ces objets en verre.

Depuis un mois Amélie parle d'une potiche en cristal. D'un signe, elle indique qu'elle lui arrive à la taille. « Haute comme ça, dit-elle. Elle est rouge foncé. Sur le vase il y a une danseuse vêtue d'une robe en dentelle blanche. »

La femme de Windisch ouvre de grands yeux quand elle entend parler de la potiche. Chaque samedi elle dit à Amélie que son père ne comprendra jamais la valeur d'une potiche.

« Autrefois les vases suffisaient, dit Windisch, aujourd'hui les gens ont besoin de potiches. »

Pendant qu'Amélie est en ville, la femme de Windisch parle de la potiche. Son visage sourit. Ses mains se font douces. Elle lève les doigts comme pour caresser une joue. Windisch sait que pour avoir une potiche, elle écarterait les cuisses. Elle les écarterait comme elle bouge les doigts, avec douceur.

Windisch s'entête quand elle parle de la potiche. Il se souvient du temps qui a suivi la guerre : « En Russie, elle a écarté les cuisses pour un morceau de pain, ont raconté les gens après la guerre. »

« Elle est belle et la faim fait mal », s'était dit Windisch à cette époque.

Au milieu des tombes

De retour de captivité, Windisch s'était réinstallé au village. Qui portait encore les blessures de nombreux morts et disparus.

Barbara était morte en Russie.

Katharina était revenue de Russie. Elle voulait épouser Joseph. Il était mort à la guerre. Katharina avait un visage très pâle, les yeux creux.

Comme Windisch, Katharina avait vu la mort. Comme Windisch, Katharina avait rapporté sa vie. Windisch attacha rapidement la sienne à celle de Katharina.

Le premier samedi, Windisch l'avait embrassée dans le village blessé. Il l'avait adossée à un arbre. Il sentait la jeunesse de son ventre et la rondeur de ses seins. Windisch se promena avec elle le long des jardins.

Les pierres tombales traçaient des lignes blanches. Le portail de fer grinça. Katharina se signa. Elle pleurait. Windisch savait qu'elle pleurait Joseph. Windisch ferma le portail. Il pleurait. Katharina savait qu'il pleurait Barbara.

Katharina s'assit dans l'herbe derrière la chapelle. Windisch se pencha vers elle. Elle le saisit par les cheveux, le sourire aux lèvres. Il lui retroussa sa jupe. Déboutonna son pantalon. S'allongea sur elle. Elle enfonça ses doigts dans l'herbe. Elle haletait. Windisch regardait par-delà les cheveux de Katharina. Les pierres tombales brillaient. Elle tremblait.

Puis Katharina s'assit. Lissa sa jupe sur ses genoux. Windisch était debout devant elle. Il reboutonnait son pantalon. Le cimetière était grand. Windisch savait qu'il n'était pas mort. Qu'il était chez lui. Que ce pantalon l'avait attendu ici, au village, dans l'armoire. Qu'il avait oublié quand il était à la guerre, et ensuite prisonnier, où se trouvait son village et combien de temps il existerait encore.

Katharina avait un brin d'herbe à la bouche. Windisch la prit par la main. « Partons d'ici », dit-il.

Les coqs

Les cloches de l'église sonnent cinq coups. Windisch sent que ses jambes sont froides et enflées. Il va dans la cour. Il voit passer au-dessus de la clôture le chapeau du veilleur.

Windisch s'approche du portail. Le veilleur se tient au poteau télégraphique. Il parle tout seul : « Où est-elle donc, où se cache-t-elle la plus belle de toutes les roses ? » Son chien est assis par terre. Il mange un ver.

« Konrad », dit Windisch. Le veilleur le regarde. « La chouette s'est posée derrière la meule de paille dans les prés. La vieille Kroner est morte. » Il bâille. Son haleine sent l'alcool.

Dans le village, les coqs chantent. Ils ont encore la nuit dans le gosier.

Le veilleur se tient à la clôture. Ses mains sont sales. Ses doigts sont recroquevillés.

La marque de la mort

Pieds nus sur les dalles, la femme de Windisch est dans le couloir. Elle a les cheveux hirsutes comme s'il y avait du vent dans la maison. A ses mollets, Windisch voit qu'elle a la chair de poule. La peau de ses chevilles est rêche.

Windisch sent l'odeur de sa chemise de nuit. Elle est chaude. Ses pommettes ont une expression dure. Elles tressaillent. Sa bouche se déchire. « C'est à cette heure que tu rentres à la maison! crie-t-elle. J'ai regardé l'heure quand il était trois heures, et maintenant cinq heures viennent de sonner. » Ses mains papillonnent dans l'air. Windisch regarde son doigt. Il n'est pas visqueux.

Windisch écrase dans sa main une feuille sèche de pommier. Il entend sa femme crier dans le vestibule. Elle claque les portes. Elle va dans la cuisine en hurlant. Il écoute le cliquetis des cuillères qui tombent sur le fourneau.

Windisch se tient dans l'encadrement de la porte de la cuisine. Sa femme brandit une cuillère. « Tu n'es qu'un enfileur de putes! hurle-t-elle. Je vais dire à ta fille ce que tu fais! »

Au-dessus de la théière il y a une bulle verte. Au-dessus de la bulle son visage. Windisch s'approche d'elle. Il la gifle. Elle se tait. Elle baisse la tête. Elle pose la théière sur la table en pleurant.

Windisch est assis devant son bol. La vapeur dévore son visage. La vapeur de menthe se répand dans toute la cuisine. Windisch voit son œil dans la tisane. Le sucre se détache de la cuillère et tombe dans l'œil. La cuillère est dans la tisane.

Windisch boit une gorgée. « La vieille Kroner est morte. »

Sa femme souffle sur la tasse. Ses petits yeux sont rouges. « Le glas sonne », dit-elle.

Sur sa joue il y a une marque rouge. C'est la marque qu'a laissée la main de Windisch. La marque de la vapeur de tisane. De la mort de la vieille Kroner.

Le son du glas passe au travers des murs. La lampe sonne. Le plafond aussi.

Windisch respire profondément. Il trouve son souffle au fond du bol.

« Qui sait où et quand nous mourrons! » dit la femme de Windisch. Elle se passe la main dans les cheveux. Elle est complètement échevelée. Une goutte de tisane lui coule du menton.

Dans la rue, c'est l'aube grise. Les fenêtres du mégissier sont éclairées.

« L'enterrement a lieu cet après-midi », dit Windisch.

Les lettres noyées dans l'alcool

Windisch se rend au moulin. Les pneus de son vélo crissent dans l'herbe. Il regarde la roue tourner entre ses genoux. Les clôtures filent sous la pluie. Les jardins murmurent. Des gouttes tombent des arbres.

Le monument aux morts est drapé de gris. Les petites roses ont un liséré marron.

L'ornière est pleine d'eau. Le pneu du vélo s'y noie. L'eau éclabousse les jambes du pantalon de Windisch. Sur les pavés, les vers de terre se tortillent.

La fenêtre du menuisier est ouverte. Le lit est fait. Il est recouvert d'un dessus-de-lit en peluche rouge. La femme du menuisier est assise à la table, seule. Devant elle un tas de haricots verts.

Le couvercle du cercueil de la vieille Kroner n'est plus à sa place contre le mur de la pièce. De son cadre, au-dessus du lit, la mère du menuisier sourit. Son sourire a quitté la mort du dahlia blanc pour la mort de la vieille Kroner.

Le plancher est nu. Le menuisier a vendu les tapis rouges. Il a maintenant les grands formulaires. Il attend son passeport.

La pluie tombe sur la nuque de Windisch. Ses épaules sont mouillées.

La femme du menuisier est convoquée tantôt par le curé pour le certificat de baptême, tantôt par le policier pour le passeport.

Le veilleur a raconté à Windisch que le curé a, dans la sacristie, un lit en fer. C'est là qu'il cherche avec les femmes les certificats de baptême. « Si tout va bien, a raconté le veilleur, il les cherche cinq fois. Mais s'il faut un travail plus approfondi, c'est dix fois. Quant au policier, il perd les demandes de passeport et les timbres fiscaux de certaines familles et recommence jusqu'à sept fois. Il les cherche avec les femmes qui veulent émigrer sur un matelas qui est dans l'entrepôt de la poste. »

Le veilleur a ajouté en riant : « Ta femme est trop vieille pour lui. Il lui fichera la paix, à ta Kathi. Mais ta fille y passera elle aussi. Le curé en fera une catholique et le policier une apatride.

C'est la postière qui donne la clé au policier quand il a un travail à faire dans l'entrepôt. »

Windisch donne un coup de pied dans la porte du moulin. « Qu'il essaye. Il aura toute la farine qu'il veut, mais il n'aura pas ma fille.

– C'est pour cela que nos lettres n'arrivent pas, dit le veilleur. La postière prend notre courrier. Et l'argent pour les timbres. Avec l'argent des timbres, elle achète de l'eau-de-vie. Et les lettres, elle les lit, puis elle les jette à la corbeille. Et si le policier n'a rien à faire dans l'entrepôt, il reste assis à côté de la postière au guichet et se soûle au schnaps. Car, pour ce qui est du lit, la postière est trop vieille pour lui. »

Le veilleur se met à caresser son chien. « La postière a déjà bu des centaines de lettres, des centaines de lettres ont déjà été répétées mot pour mot au policier. »

Windisch ouvre la porte avec la grande clé. Il compte deux ans. Il tourne la petite clé dans la serrure. Il compte les jours. Windisch va à l'étang près du moulin.

L'étang est sens dessus dessous. Des vagues frappent les bords. Les saules sont emmitouflés dans les feuilles et le vent. La meule de paille qui se reflète dans l'étang ondoie sans jamais disparaître. Des grenouilles rampent autour de la meule. Elles traînent leurs ventres blancs dans l'herbe.

Le veilleur est assis au bord de l'étang. Il a le hoquet. Sa pomme d'Adam bondit hors de sa veste. « C'est à cause des oignons violets. Les Russes font de fines incisions sur le dessus de l'oignon et mettent du sel. Les oignons s'ouvrent alors comme des roses. Ils dégorgent une eau claire et transparente. Ils ressemblent à des nénuphars. Les Russes les écrasent à coups de poing. J'en ai vu qui les ont écrasés à coups de pied. Ils ont dansé dessus. Les femmes ont relevé leurs jupes et elles se sont agenouillées sur les oignons. Elles les ont écrasés. Avec leurs genoux. Nous, les soldats, nous avons pris les femmes par les hanches et nous avons tourné avec elles. »

Le veilleur a les yeux humides. « J'ai mangé des oignons doux et tendres comme du beurre d'avoir été foulés par des genoux de femmes russes. » Ses joues sont fanées. Ses yeux retrouvent leur jeunesse comme l'éclat de l'oignon.

Windisch porte deux sacs jusqu'à la rive. Il les couvre d'une bâche. Cette nuit le veilleur les portera au policier.

Les roseaux se balancent. De l'écume blanche s'est déposée sur leurs tiges. « Voilà comment doit être la robe de dentelle de la danseuse, se dit-il, mais cette potiche n'entrera pas chez moi. »

« Les femmes sont partout. Dans l'étang aussi », dit le veilleur. Windisch voit leurs dessous dans les roseaux. Il retourne au moulin.

La mouche

Vêtue de noir, la vieille Kroner repose dans son cercueil. Ses mains sont attachées avec des ficelles blanches pour qu'elles restent sur son ventre. Pour qu'elles prient quand elles arriveront là-haut à la porte du ciel.

« Qu'elle est belle, on dirait qu'elle dort », dit la voisine, Wilma-la-Maigre. Une mouche se pose sur sa main. Wilma-la-Maigre remue les doigts. La mouche se pose sur une petite main près d'elle.

La femme de Windisch secoue les gouttes de pluie de son fichu. Des fils transparents tombent sur ses chaussures. A côté des femmes en prière, il y a des parapluies. Sous les chaises, des rigoles d'eau vont à la dérive. Elles serpentent. Elles brillent au milieu des chaussures.

La femme de Windisch s'assied sur une chaise libre à côté de la porte. Elle laisse tomber de chaque œil une grosse larme. La mouche se pose sur sa joue. La larme roule jusqu'à la mouche. Le bord des ailes humides, elle s'envole dans la pièce. Elle revient. Se pose sur la femme de Windisch. Sur son index flétri.

La femme de Windisch prie et regarde la mouche. Qui lui chatouille la peau autour de l'ongle. « C'est la mouche qui était sous le loriot, se dit-elle, c'est la mouche qui s'est posée sur le tamis. »

La femme de Windisch s'attendrit dans sa prière. Qui lui arrache un soupir. Si fort que ses mains en tremblent. Que la mouche sur l'ongle de son doigt sent le soupir. S'envole au-dessus de sa joue.

Avec un léger murmure des lèvres, la femme de Windisch dit une prière de supplication.

La mouche vole sous le plafond. Elle bourdonne une longue chanson pour la veillée mortuaire. Une chanson d'eau de pluie. De terre. Comme une tombe.

En murmurant sa prière, la femme de Windisch, tourmentée, laisse encore tomber quelques petites larmes. Elles roulent sur sa joue. Elles ont un goût de sel autour de sa bouche.

Wilma-la-Maigre cherche son mouchoir sous les chaises. Elle le cherche entre les chaussures. Entre les rigoles qui s'épanchent sous les parapluies noirs.

Wilma-la-Maigre trouve un chapelet entre les chaussures. Son petit visage est pointu. « A qui appartient ce chapelet? » demande-t-elle. Personne ne la regarde. Tout le monde se tait. « Va savoir! soupire-t-elle. Il y a tellement de gens qui sont déjà venus ici! » Elle fourre le chapelet dans la poche de sa longue jupe noire.

La mouche se pose sur la joue de la vieille Kroner. Elle est la vie sur la peau morte. La mouche bourdonne au coin de sa bouche. La mouche danse sur son menton raidi.

La pluie crépite derrière la fenêtre. La diseuse de prières bat des cils comme si la pluie lui tombait sur le visage. Comme si elle lui lavait les cils, ses cils brisés à force de prier.

« Il tombe une pluie diluvienne sur tout le pays », dit-elle. En parlant elle ferme la bouche comme si la pluie lui coulait dans le cou.

Wilma-la-Maigre regarde la morte. « Il ne pleut que dans le Banat. Le temps ici nous vient d'Autriche, pas de Bucarest. »

L'eau prie dans la rue. La femme de Windisch

renifle en versant une dernière petite larme. « Les anciens disaient : si la pluie tombe dans le cercueil, on enterre un honnête homme », dit-elle à haute voix dans la pièce.

Sur le cercueil de la vieille Kroner il y a des bouquets d'hortensias. Ils se fanent rapidement et deviennent violets. La mort qui est dans le cercueil, dans cette peau, dans ces os, les emporte. Et la prière de la pluie aussi.

La mouche furète dans les boules d'hortensias qui n'ont pas d'odeur.

Le curé apparaît sur le seuil de la porte. Son pas est pesant comme si son cœur était plein d'eau. Le curé donne à l'enfant de chœur son parapluie noir en disant : « Loué soit Jésus-Christ. » Les femmes murmurent, la mouche aussi.

Le menuisier apporte le couvercle du cercueil.

Une feuille d'hortensia tressaille. A demi violette, à demi morte, elle tombe sur les mains qui sont retenues par la ficelle blanche et qui prient. Le menuisier pose le couvercle sur le cercueil. Quelques brefs coups de marteau sur des petits clous noirs et le cercueil est fermé.

Le corbillard brille. Le cheval regarde les arbres. Le cocher met une couverture grise sur le dos du cheval. « Il va prendre froid », dit-il au menuisier.

L'enfant de chœur tient le grand parapluie noir au-dessus de la tête du curé. Qui n'a pas de jambes. L'ourlet de la soutane traîne dans la boue.

Windisch sent l'eau glousser dans ses chaussures. Il connaît le clou dans la sacristie. Il connaît le long clou auquel la soutane est accrochée. Le menuisier marche dans une flaque d'eau. Windisch voit les lacets tremper dans l'eau.

« La soutane noire en a déjà vu pas mal, se dit-il. Elle a vu le curé chercher avec les femmes les certificats de baptême dans le lit de fer. » Le menuisier pose une question. Windisch entend sa voix. Il ne comprend pas ce qu'il dit. Il entend la clarinette et le gros tambour derrière lui.

Le veilleur porte en couronne autour de son chapeau une frange de fils de pluie. Sur le corbillard le drap noir claque au vent. Les bouquets d'hortensias frémissent dans les trous du chemin. Ils sèment leurs feuilles dans la boue. La boue scintille sous les roues. Le corbillard tourne sur le verre des flaques.

Les instruments à vent sont froids. Le gros tambour donne un son étouffé et mouillé. Au-dessus du village, les toits penchent dans le sens de l'eau.

Le cimetière et ses croix de marbre blanc luisent. La cloche avec sa langue balbutiante domine le village. Windisch voit son chapeau traverser une flaque. « L'eau va monter dans l'étang, pense-t-il, et la pluie va entraîner dans l'eau les sacs destinés au policier. »

Dans la tombe, il y a de l'eau. Jaune comme de la tisane. « La vieille Kroner va pouvoir boire, maintenant », chuchote Wilma-la-Maigre.

Sur le chemin entre les tombes, la diseuse de prières met le pied sur une marguerite. L'enfant de chœur tient le parapluie de travers. La fumée de l'encens pénètre dans la terre.

Le curé laisse tomber lentement une poignée de terre boueuse sur le cercueil. « Prends cette terre qui est la tienne. Que le Seigneur reprenne ce qui Lui appartient », dit-il. D'une voix mouillée l'enfant de chœur chante un « Amen » qui n'en finit plus. Windisch voit ses molaires dans sa bouche.

L'eau du sol lèche le drap mortuaire. Le veilleur tient son chapeau sur sa poitrine. Il en écrase le bord de la main. Le chapeau est plié. Il est recroquevillé comme une rose noire.

Le curé ferme son livre de prières. « Nous nous reverrons dans l'au-delà », dit-il.

Le fossoyeur est roumain. Il appuie la pelle sur son ventre. Il se signe. Il crache dans ses mains. A grandes pelletées il recouvre la tombe.

La fanfare joue une musique funèbre. Froide et informe. L'apprenti tailleur souffle dans le cor de chasse. Ses doigts bleuis ont des taches blanches. Il se glisse dans la musique. Le grand cornet jaune est juste à côté de son oreille. Il brille comme le pavillon d'un gramophone. La musique funèbre explose en sortant de l'instrument.

Le gros tambour bourdonne. La pomme d'Adam de la diseuse de prières apparaît entre les pointes de son fichu. La tombe se remplit de terre.

Windisch ferme les yeux. Les croix de marbre, blanches et mouillées, leur font mal. La pluie leur fait mal.

Wilma-la-Maigre se dirige vers le portail du cimetière et sort. Sur la tombe de la vieille Kroner, il reste des monticules d'hortensias déchirés. Le menuisier est devant la tombe de sa mère. Il pleure.

La femme de Windisch a les deux pieds sur la marguerite. « Viens, allons-nous-en », dit-elle. Windisch marche à côté d'elle sous le parapluie noir. C'est un grand chapeau noir. La femme de Windisch porte un chapeau au bout d'une tige.

Le fossoyeur est tout seul, pieds nus dans le cimetière. Avec la pelle il nettoie ses bottes en caoutchouc.

Le roi dort

Avant la guerre la fanfare du village en grand uniforme rouge foncé s'était un jour rassemblée à la gare. Le fronton de la gare était décoré de guirlandes de lis, d'asters et de feuilles d'acacias. Les gens avaient mis leurs habits du dimanche. Les enfants avaient des chaussettes blanches. Leurs visages étaient cachés derrière de lourds bouquets de fleurs.

Lorsque le train est entré en gare, la fanfare a joué une marche. Les gens ont applaudi. Les enfants ont jeté des fleurs.

Le train est entré lentement en gare. Un jeune homme a tendu un long bras par la fenêtre. D'un geste de la main, il a réclamé le silence.

« Taisez-vous, Sa Majesté le roi dort. »

Après le départ du train, un troupeau de chèvres blanches arriva des champs. Elles suivirent la voie ferrée et mangèrent les fleurs. Interrompue la musique.

Les musiciens sont rentrés chez eux. Interrompu également le geste de bienvenue des hommes et des femmes. Ils sont retournés à la maison. Et les enfants aussi, les mains vides.

Une fillette qui, après la musique et les applaudissements, devait réciter un poème devant le roi resta assise, seule, dans la salle d'attente, jusqu'à ce que les chèvres aient mangé tous les bouquets de fleurs. Et elle pleura.

Une grande maison

La femme de ménage enlève la poussière des escaliers. Elle a une tache noire sur la joue et la paupière violette. Elle pleure. « Il m'a encore battue », dit-elle.

Les portemanteaux vides brillent sur les murs du vestibule. Comme une couronne d'épines. Les petites savates éculées sont en rang d'oignons sous les portemanteaux.

Chaque enfant est venu au jardin d'enfants avec une décalcomanie. Amélie a collé les petites images sous les patères.

Tous les matins, les enfants cherchent leur auto, leur chien, leur poupée, leur fleur ou leur ballon.

Udo entre. Il cherche son drapeau. Il est noir,

rouge et or. Udo accroche son manteau au porte-
manteau au-dessus du drapeau. Il quitte ses
chaussures. Enfile ses savates rouges. Met ses
chaussures sous le manteau.

La mère d'Udo travaille dans une chocolaterie.
Chaque mardi elle apporte à Amélie du sucre, du
beurre, du cacao et du chocolat. « Udo viendra
encore trois semaines, a-t-elle dit hier à Amélie,
notre demande de passeport a été acceptée. »

La dentiste pousse sa fille dans l'entrebâille-
ment de la porte. La fillette a un béret blanc sur
les cheveux comme une tache de neige. Elle cherche son chien. La dentiste donne à Amélie un
bouquet d'œillets et une petite boîte. « Anca a pris
froid. Donnez-lui, s'il vous plaît, ces cachets à dix
heures. »

La femme de ménage secoue son chiffon à
poussière par la fenêtre. L'acacia est jaune. Le
vieil homme, comme tous les matins, balaie le
trottoir devant sa maison. L'acacia disperse ses
feuilles au vent.

Les enfants portent l'uniforme des Faucons :
chemise jaune et pantalon, ou jupe plissée, bleu
marine. « Aujourd'hui, nous sommes mercredi,
pense Amélie, c'est le jour des Faucons. »

On entend le bruit des jeux de construction, le
bourdonnement des grues. Des Indiens défilent,
en colonne, devant les petites mains. Udo construit une usine. Les doigts des petites filles don-
nent du lait à boire aux poupées.

Le front d'Anca est chaud.

A travers le plafond de la classe on entend

l'hymne national. A l'étage supérieur les grands chantent.

Les cubes sont les uns sur les autres. Les grues se taisent. La colonne d'Indiens s'arrête au bord de la table. L'usine n'a pas de toit. La poupée dans sa longue robe de soie est couchée sur une chaise. Elle dort. Elle a les joues roses.

Rangés par ordre de taille, les enfants sont en demi-cercle devant le bureau. Ils ont les mains sur les hanches. Ils lèvent le menton. Leurs yeux humides sont écarquillés. Ils chantent à haute voix.

Les garçons et les filles sont de petits soldats. L'hymne a sept strophes.

Amélie accroche une carte de Roumanie au mur.

« Tous les enfants habitent dans des immeubles ou dans des maisons. Chaque maison est composée de pièces. Ensemble, toutes les maisons forment une grande maison. Cette maison est notre pays. Notre patrie. »

Du doigt Amélie montre la carte. « Voilà notre patrie. » Du bout du doigt, elle cherche des points noirs sur la carte. « Voici les villes de notre patrie. Les villes sont des pièces de cette grande maison qui est notre pays. Dans nos maisons habitent nos pères et nos mères. Ce sont nos parents. Chaque enfant a des parents. De la même façon que chacun de nos pères est le père dans la maison où nous habitons, le camarade Nicolae Ceausescu est le père de notre pays. Et de la même façon que chacune de nos mères est la mère dans la maison où nous habitons, la camarade Hélène Ceausescu est la mère de notre pays. Tous les enfants aiment les camarades Ceausescu parce qu'ils sont leurs parents. »

La femme de ménage place une corbeille à papier vide près de la porte.

« Notre pays s'appelle la République socialiste de Roumanie, poursuit Amélie. Le camarade Ceausescu est le Secrétaire général de notre pays, la République socialiste de Roumanie. »

Un petit garçon se lève. « A la maison mon père a une mappemonde. » D'un geste de la main il dessine la sphère. Il heurte le vase de fleurs. Les œillets baignent dans l'eau. La chemise d'uniforme est mouillée.

Sur la petite table, devant lui, il y a des morceaux de verre. Il pleure. Amélie pousse la table. Il ne faut pas qu'elle se mette en colère. Le père de Claudius est le gérant de la boucherie au coin de la rue.

Anca pose la tête sur la table. « Quand est-ce qu'on rentre à la maison? » demande-t-elle en roumain. L'allemand lui échappe et la fatigue.

Udo construit un toit. « Mon père est le Secrétaire général de notre maison », dit-il.

Amélie regarde les feuilles jaunes de l'acacia. Le vieil homme, comme d'habitude, est à la fenêtre. « Dietmar a acheté des billets pour le cinéma », se dit-il.

Les Indiens défilent sur le plancher. Anca avale ses cachets. Amélie est adossée à la fenêtre. « Qui est-ce qui récite un poème? » demande-t-elle.

70

Au pied d'une montagne,
Je connais un pays
Rouge au soleil levant.

Dans les grands bois mugit,
Comme la vague en mer,
Le souffle du printemps.

Claudius parle bien l'allemand. Il lève le menton. Il parle allemand avec une voix d'adulte, modèle réduit.

Dix lei

La petite Tsigane du village voisin tord son tablier vert. L'eau dégouline de sa main. Du sommet du crâne, la tresse lui tombe sur l'épaule. Pris dans les cheveux, un ruban rouge. Langue pendante au bout de la tresse. Pieds nus, pieds boueux, la petite Tsigane est plantée devant les conducteurs de tracteurs.

Ils ont des petits chapeaux tout trempés. Leurs mains noires sont à plat sur la table. « Fais voir, dit l'un d'eux, je te donnerai dix lei. » Il pose les dix lei sur la table. Les autres rient. Leurs yeux brillent, leurs visages sont rouges. Leurs regards s'agrippent à la longue jupe à fleurs. La Tsigane retrousse sa jupe. Le conducteur de tracteur vide son verre. La Tsigane prend le billet sur la table.

Elle entortille sa tresse autour de son doigt. Elle rit.

Windisch sent les odeurs d'alcool et de sueur qui viennent de la table voisine. « Ils ne quittent pas leurs petits gilets de fourrure de tout l'été », dit le menuisier. La bière a laissé de la mousse sur son pouce. Il trempe le doigt dans le verre.

« Ce salaud, à côté, me souffle la cendre dans le verre », dit-il. Il regarde le Roumain debout derrière lui. Le Roumain, une cigarette tout imbibée de salive au coin de la bouche, rit. « Vous plus parler allemand. » Puis il ajoute en roumain : « Ici on est en Roumanie. »

Le menuisier a un regard gourmand. Il lève son verre, le vide. « Vous serez bientôt débarrassés de nous! » hurle-t-il. Il fait signe au patron qui est debout à la table des conducteurs. « Une autre bière. »

Il s'essuie la bouche du revers de la main. « Tu es déjà allé voir le jardinier? demande-t-il à Windisch.

– Non.

– Tu sais où il habite? »

Windisch fait signe que oui. « En banlieue.

– A Fratella, rue Enescu », ajoute le menuisier.

La petite Tsigane tire sur la langue rouge de sa tresse. Elle rit, se retourne. Windisch regarde ses mollets. « Combien? demande-t-il.

– Quinze mille par personne », répond le menuisier. Il prend le verre de bière des mains du patron. « Une maison à un étage. A gauche il y a les serres. Si la voiture rouge est dans la cour, cela veut dire que c'est ouvert. Dans la cour il y a quelqu'un qui coupe du bois. C'est lui qui te conduira à l'intérieur de la maison. Surtout ne sonne pas. Si tu sonnes, il se sauvera. Et il ne t'ouvrira plus la porte. »

Les hommes et les femmes, debout dans un coin de la salle, boivent à la bouteille. Un homme qui porte un chapeau de velours noir tout chiffonné tient un enfant dans les bras. Windisch voit la plante de ses pieds nus. L'enfant attrape la bouteille. L'homme lui met le goulot à la bouche. L'enfant ferme les yeux et boit. « Ivrogne », dit l'homme.

Il retire la bouteille, il rit. La femme à côté de lui mange une croûte de pain. Elle mâche, elle boit. Flocons blancs dans la bouteille.

« Ils puent tous l'étable », dit le menuisier. Un long cheveu brun pend à son doigt. « Ce sont des vachers », dit Windisch. Les femmes chantent, l'enfant titube devant elles et les tire par leurs jupes.

« Aujourd'hui, c'est le jour de la paye, dit Windisch. Ils vont boire pendant trois jours. Ensuite ils n'auront plus rien.

« La vachère au fichu bleu habite derrière le moulin », dit Windisch.

La petite Tsigane retrousse sa jupe. Le fossoyeur debout à côté de sa pelle fouille dans sa poche. Lui donne dix lei.

La vachère au fichu bleu chante, puis elle vomit contre le mur.

Le coup de feu

La receveuse du tramway a les manches retroussées. Elle mange une pomme. Sur le cadran de sa montre, la trotteuse tremblote. Il est l'heure passée de cinq minutes. Le tramway grince.

Un enfant bouscule Amélie qui heurte la valise d'une vieille femme. Amélie avance.

Dietmar est à l'entrée du parking. Sa bouche est chaude sur la joue d'Amélie. « Nous avons le temps, dit-il. Les billets sont pour sept heures. Pour cinq heures il n'y en avait plus. »

Le banc est froid. Des petits hommes marchent dans la prairie en portant des corbeilles d'osier pleines de feuilles mortes.

Dietmar a une langue chaude. Elle brûle l'oreille d'Amélie. Qui ferme les yeux. Le souffle de Dietmar est plus grand que les arbres dans la tête d'Amélie. Sa main, sous son corsage, est froide.

Dietmar parle : « J'ai reçu ma convocation pour l'armée. Mon père a apporté ma valise. »

Amélie éloigne la bouche de Dietmar de son oreille. Elle lui met la main sur la bouche. « Viens, allons en ville, j'ai froid », dit-elle.

Amélie s'appuie contre Dietmar. Elle le sent marcher. Elle est blottie contre lui sous sa veste.

Dans la vitrine il y a un chat. Il dort. Dietmar

tape à la vitre. « Il faut encore que je m'achète des chaussettes de laine », dit-il.

Amélie mange un petit gâteau. Dietmar lui envoie un nuage de fumée dans la figure. « Viens, dit Amélie, je vais te montrer la potiche. »

La danseuse lève le bras au-dessus de la tête. La robe en dentelle blanche est figée derrière la vitre.

Dietmar ouvre la porte en bois à côté de la vitrine. Derrière la porte il y a un couloir sombre. De l'obscurité s'élève une odeur d'oignons pourris. Trois poubelles sont alignées contre le mur. Comme trois boîtes de conserve géantes.

Dietmar presse Amélie contre une poubelle. Le couvercle grince. Amélie sent le sexe de Dietmar lui marteler le ventre. Elle le tient par les épaules. Dans l'arrière-cour, un enfant parle.

Dietmar reboutonne son pantalon. Par une fenêtre, au fond de la cour, on entend de la musique.

Amélie voit les chaussures de Dietmar avancer dans la file d'attente. Une main déchire les billets par le milieu. L'ouvreuse a un fichu noir sur la tête et une robe noire. Elle éteint sa lampe de poche.

Les épis de maïs coulent le long du cou élancé de la moissonneuse jusqu'à la remorque du tracteur. Le documentaire est fini.

La tête de Dietmar repose sur l'épaule d'Amélie. Sur l'écran des lettres rouges s'inscrivent : *Pirates du XXe siècle*. Amélie pose la main sur le genou de Dietmar. « Encore un film russe », chuchote-t-elle. Dietmar relève la tête. « Au moins un film en couleurs », lui glisse-t-il à l'oreille.

De l'eau verte tremble. Des forêts vertes projettent leur image de l'autre côté de la rive. Le pont du bateau est large. Une belle femme a les mains posées sur le bastingage. Ses cheveux claquent au vent comme du feuillage.

Dietmar presse les doigts d'Amélie dans sa main. Il regarde l'écran. La femme parle.

« Nous ne nous reverrons plus, dit-il. Moi, je vais au service militaire, et toi, tu vas émigrer. » Amélie regarde la joue de Dietmar. Elle bouge. Elle parle. « Il paraît que Rudi t'attend », dit Dietmar.

Sur l'écran une main s'ouvre. Elle saisit quelque chose dans la poche d'un vêtement. Sur l'écran un pouce et un index. Entre eux un revolver.

Dietmar parle. En même temps que sa voix, Amélie entend un coup de feu.

L'eau ne connaît pas le repos

« La chouette est paralysée, dit le veilleur. Une journée de deuil et une pluie torrentielle, c'est trop pour elle. Si cette nuit elle ne voit pas la lune, elle ne volera plus jamais. Si elle crève, l'eau sentira mauvais.

– Les chouettes ne connaissent pas le repos, dit Windisch, et l'eau non plus. Si elle crève, une autre chouette viendra au village. Une chouette jeune et bête, qui n'y connaîtra rien. Elle se posera sur n'importe quel toit. »

Le veilleur regarde la lune. « Alors ce seront à nouveau des jeunes gens qui mourront. » Windisch sent que l'air devant son visage appartient au veilleur. Il a encore juste assez de force pour dire d'une voix lasse : « Ce sera à nouveau comme pendant la guerre.

– Les grenouilles coassent à l'intérieur du moulin », dit le veilleur.

Elles rendent le chien fou.

Le coq aveugle

La femme de Windisch est assise au bord du lit. « Deux hommes sont venus aujourd'hui. Ils ont compté les poules et noté leur nombre. Ils en ont attrapé huit et ils les ont emportées. Ils les ont enfermées dans des cages. La remorque du tracteur était pleine de poules. » La femme de Windisch soupire.

« J'ai signé. J'ai signé aussi pour quatre cents kilos de maïs et cent de pommes de terre. Ils viendront les chercher plus tard, c'est ce qu'ils ont dit. Les cinquante œufs, je les leur ai déjà donnés. Ils sont allés dans le jardin avec leurs bottes de caoutchouc. Devant la grange ils ont vu le trèfle. Ils ont dit que, l'année prochaine, il faudra planter de la betterave à sucre à cet endroit-là. »

Windisch soulève le couvercle de la marmite.
« Et les voisins?

– Ils ne sont pas allés chez eux. Ils ont dit que les voisins ont huit enfants en bas âge et que nous, nous n'en avons qu'un, et qui gagne sa vie. »

La marmite est pleine de sang et de foie. « J'ai été obligée de tuer le gros coq blanc, dit la femme de Windisch. Les deux hommes ont couru partout dans la cour. Le coq a pris peur. Il est allé se prendre les ailes dans la clôture et il s'est cogné la tête dedans. Après leur départ, il était aveugle. »

Dans la marmite, des rondelles d'oignons flottent parmi les yeux de graisse. « Et tu avais pourtant dit que nous garderions le gros coq blanc pour avoir l'an prochain de belles poules blanches, dit Windisch.

– Et toi, tu as dit que tout ce qui est blanc est fragile. Tu avais raison. »

L'armoire grince.

« Lorsque je suis allé au moulin, je me suis arrêté devant le monument aux morts, dit Windisch dans l'obscurité. Je voulais aller à l'église et prier. Mais l'église était fermée. Il m'a semblé que c'était mauvais signe. Saint Antoine est juste derrière la porte. Son livre épais est marron. Il ressemble à un passeport. »

Dans l'atmosphère chaude et obscure de la chambre, Windisch rêve que le ciel s'ouvre. Les nuages se dissipent au-dessus du village. Un coq blanc vole dans le ciel dégagé. Il se fracasse la tête contre un peuplier mort dans la prairie. Il n'y voit plus. Il est aveugle. Windisch est à la lisière d'un champ de tournesols. Il crie : « L'oiseau est aveugle ! » L'écho lui renvoie la voix de sa femme. Windisch entre dans le champ de tournesols et crie : « Je ne te cherche pas, je sais que tu n'es pas là. »

La voiture rouge

La baraque en bois est un cube noir. D'un tuyau en fer-blanc s'échappe de la fumée qui pénètre dans la terre mouillée. La porte de la baraque est ouverte. A l'intérieur un homme en bleu de travail est assis sur un banc de bois. Sur la table un récipient en fer-blanc. D'où monte de la vapeur. L'homme regarde Windisch.

On a repoussé les tôles qui étaient sur le canal. Dans le canal, il y a un homme. Au ras du sol, Windisch voit une tête couverte d'un casque jaune. Windisch passe devant le menton de l'homme. Qui le suit des yeux.

Windisch a les mains dans les poches de son manteau. Il sent les liasses de billets dans la poche intérieure de sa veste.

Les serres sont à gauche dans la cour. Il y a de la buée sur les vitres. Elle estompe le feuillage. Seules les roses lancent des flammes rouges dans la brume. Au milieu de la cour, une voiture rouge. A côté, des bûches. Contre la maison, une pile de bois. La hache est près de la voiture.

Windisch avance lentement. Dans la poche de son manteau, il fait des boulettes avec son billet de tram. A travers ses chaussures, il sent l'humidité de l'asphalte.

Windisch regarde autour de lui. Le bûcheron n'est pas dans la cour. La tête au casque jaune suit Windisch du regard.

Il n'y a plus de clôture, Windisch entend des voix dans la maison d'à côté. Un nain en porcelaine traîne un buisson d'hortensias. Il a une casquette rouge. Un chien, tout blanc, aboie en courant tout autour. Windisch regarde la rue en contrebas. Les rails du tram avancent dans le vide. Entre les rails, de l'herbe noircie par l'huile, rabougrie et toute cassée à cause des trams qui crissent et des rails qui hurlent.

Windisch revient sur ses pas. La tête au casque jaune plonge dans le canal. L'homme en bleu de travail pose un balai contre le mur de la baraque. Le nain a un tablier vert. Le buisson d'hortensias tremble. Le chien blanc, devant la clôture, se tait. Il suit Windisch des yeux.

Du tuyau en fer-blanc de la baraque jaillit de la fumée. L'homme en bleu de travail balaie la boue autour de la baraque. Il suit Windisch du regard.

Les fenêtres de la maison sont fermées. Les rideaux blancs rendent la maison aveugle. Au-dessus de la clôture, on a tendu deux rangées de fil de fer barbelé entre des crochets rouillés. L'extrémité des bûches empilées est blanche. Le bois a été coupé récemment. La lame de la hache brille. La voiture rouge est au milieu de la cour. Les roses fleurissent dans la brume.

Windisch passe encore une fois devant le menton de l'homme au casque jaune.

Il n'y a plus de fil de fer barbelé. L'homme en bleu de travail est assis dans la baraque. Il suit Windisch des yeux.

Windisch revient sur ses pas. Il est devant le portail.

Windisch ouvre la bouche. La tête au casque jaune dépasse du sol.

Windisch a froid. Sa voix s'éteint dans sa bouche.

On entend le tram. Il y a de la buée sur les vitres. Le contrôleur suit Windisch du regard.

Au montant de la porte il y a une cloche. Elle a un bout de doigt blanc. Windisch appuie dessus. Sonnerie dans son doigt. Sonnerie dans la cour. Sonnerie au loin dans la maison. Le son de la cloche s'éteint derrière les murs. Il est enterré.

Windisch sonne quinze fois. Il compte. Les sons aigus sous ses doigts, les sons qui retentissent dans la cour, les sons enterrés dans la maison s'entrechoquent.

Le jardinier est enterré dans les vitres, dans la clôture, dans les murs.

L'homme en bleu de travail lave son récipient en fer-blanc. Il regarde. Windisch passe devant le menton de l'homme au casque jaune. Il marche le long des rails du tram. Il a toujours l'argent dans sa poche.

Les pieds de Windisch ont mal sur l'asphalte.

Le message secret

Du moulin Windisch rentre au village. Le village est un point minuscule dans le soleil de midi. Le soleil brûle tout sur son passage. L'ornière est à sec et lézardée.

La femme de Windisch balaie la cour. Autour de ses orteils il y a du sable comme si c'était de l'eau. En rond, autour du balai, des vagues immobiles.

« C'est encore l'été, mais les acacias jaunissent déjà », dit la femme de Windisch.

Windisch déboutonne sa chemise. « On aura un hiver rude si les arbres sont déjà secs en été. »

Les poules mettent la tête sous les ailes. Leurs becs cherchent leur propre ombre qui ne les rafraîchit pas. Derrière la clôture les porcs tachetés du voisin creusent dans les carottes sauvages aux fleurs blanches.

Windisch regarde à travers le grillage. « Ils ne nourrissent pas leurs porcs. Quelle racaille ces Valaques! Ils ne savent même pas nourrir leurs porcs. »

La femme de Windisch tient le balai contre son ventre. « Il leur faudrait des anneaux dans les naseaux, dit-elle, sinon, avant l'hiver, ils auront mis la maison à sac. »

Elle porte le balai dans la remise. « La postière

est venue, dit-elle, elle a roté, elle sentait l'alcool. Le policier te remercie pour la farine et il attend Amélie à l'audience dimanche matin. C'est ce qu'elle a dit. Amélie doit apporter une demande écrite et soixante lei pour les timbres. »

Windisch se mord les lèvres. Sa bouche envahit son visage tout entier, jusqu'au front. « A quoi bon ses remerciements! »

La femme de Windisch lève la tête. « J'en étais sûre que tu n'irais pas bien loin avec ta farine.

— Assez loin pour que ma fille serve de matelas! » crie Windisch. Il crache dans le sable. « Nom de Dieu, quelle honte! » Un filet de salive est resté accroché à son menton.

« Tu n'iras pas bien loin non plus avec tes jurons. »

Les pommettes de la femme de Windisch sont deux briques incandescentes. « L'important c'est notre passeport, ce n'est pas la honte. »

D'un coup de poing, Windisch ferme la porte de la remise. « Tu es bien placée pour le savoir, crie-t-il, depuis la Russie, tu es bien placée pour le savoir! Là-bas non plus, il n'était pas question de honte pour toi.

— Tu n'es qu'un salaud! »

La porte de la remise bat comme si le vent s'était engouffré dans le bois. Du bout des doigts, la femme de Windisch cherche sa bouche à tâtons.

« Lorsque le policier verra que notre Amélie est encore vierge, l'envie lui passera. »

Windisch rit. « Vierge! Vierge comme tu l'étais autrefois dans le cimetière après la guerre, dit-il.

En Russie les autres sont mortes de faim, et toi, tu as survécu en te prostituant. Tu aurais continué après la guerre si je ne t'avais pas épousée. »

La femme de Windisch reste bouche bée. Elle lève la main, elle tend l'index. « Avec toi, tout le monde est mauvais, parce que tu es toi-même mauvais et que ça ne va pas très bien dans ta tête. » Les talons écorchés, elle marche dans le sable.

Windisch la poursuit. Elle s'arrête dans la véranda. Elle relève un pan de son tablier pour essuyer la table vide. « Chez le jardinier aussi, tu t'es mal débrouillé. Ils arrivent tous à entrer. Ils s'occupent tous de leur passeport. Il n'y a que toi, toi qui es si avisé et si honnête. »

Windisch va dans le vestibule. Le réfrigérateur ronronne. « Toute la matinée, on a été privés de courant, dit sa femme. Le réfrigérateur a dégivré. La viande va pourrir si ça continue. »

Sur le réfrigérateur il y a une enveloppe. « La postière a apporté une lettre, dit-elle. Le mégissier a écrit. »

Windisch lit la lettre. « Il n'est pas question de Rudi dans la lettre. Il doit être de nouveau en clinique. »

La femme de Windisch regarde dans la cour. « Il envoie ses amitiés à Amélie. Pourquoi ne lui écrit-il pas lui-même?

– C'est la seule phrase qu'il ait écrite, dit Windisch, la phrase précédée de *P.S.* » Il remet la lettre sur le réfrigérateur.

« Qu'est-ce que ça veut dire, *P.S.*? »

Windisch hausse les épaules. « Autrefois ça

voulait dire pur-sang. Ça doit être un message secret. »

La femme de Windisch est sur le pas de la porte. « Voilà ce que c'est quand les enfants vont aux écoles », soupire-t-elle.

Windisch est dans la cour. Le chat est couché sur les pierres. Il dort. Sous une couverture de soleil. Son visage est mort. Son ventre respire doucement sous la fourrure.

Windisch voit, en face, la maison du mégissier dans le soleil de la mi-journée. Le soleil lui donne un éclat doré.

La maison du culte

Devant le moulin, le veilleur dit à Windisch : « Sûr que les baptistes valaques vont faire de la maison du mégissier un lieu de culte. Ceux qui portent des petits chapeaux, ce sont des baptistes. Ils miaulent quand ils prient. Et quand leurs femmes chantent des cantiques, elles gémissent comme si elles étaient au lit. Elles ont les yeux tout écarquillés, comme mon chien. »

Le veilleur parle à voix basse bien qu'il soit tout seul, avec Windisch et son chien, près de l'étang. Il scrute la nuit pour voir si une ombre ne les espionne pas.

« Chez eux il n'y a que des frères et des sœurs. Les jours de fête, ils s'accouplent. Chacun avec ce qu'il attrape dans l'obscurité. »

Le veilleur observe un rat d'eau. Le rat crie comme un enfant et se jette dans les roseaux. Le chien n'écoute pas ce que chuchote le veilleur. Il est au bord de l'eau et aboie après le rat. « Ils font l'amour sur le tapis dans la maison du culte, voilà pourquoi ils ont tant d'enfants. »

L'eau de l'étang et le chuchotement de la voix du veilleur déclenchent dans le nez et dans la tête de Windisch un rhume brûlant et salé. L'étonnement et le silence trouent sa langue.

« Cette religion vient d'Amérique », dit le veilleur. Windisch essaie de respirer malgré le rhume salé. « C'est de l'autre côté de l'eau.

– Le diable aussi sait traverser l'eau, dit le veilleur. Les baptistes ont le diable dans la peau. Même mon chien ne peut pas les sentir. Il aboie quand il les voit. Les chiens savent reconnaître le diable. »

Le trou dans la langue de Windisch se comble lentement. « Le mégissier a toujours dit qu'en Amérique, ce sont les Juifs qui sont à la barre.

– Oui, dit le veilleur, les Juifs pourrissent le monde. Les Juifs et les femmes. »

Windisch acquiesce. Il pense à Amélie. « Chaque samedi, quand elle revient à la maison, pense-t-il, elle écarte les pieds en marchant. »

Le veilleur mange une pomme verte. Il en est déjà à la troisième. La poche de sa veste en est remplie. « Ce que tu dis des femmes en Allemagne, dit Windisch, c'est vrai. Le mégissier l'a écrit. La pire chez nous vaut mieux que la meilleure des leurs. »

Windisch regarde les nuages. « Les femmes

s'habillent à la dernière mode. Même que ça ne leur déplairait pas de s'exhiber toutes nues. Déjà à l'école, dit le mégissier dans sa lettre, les enfants lisent des magazines avec des femmes nues. »

Le veilleur triture les pommes vertes dans la poche de sa veste. Il crache une bouchée. « Depuis qu'il y a eu cette pluie diluvienne, les vers sont dans les fruits. » Le chien lèche le morceau de pomme qu'il a craché. Il mange le ver.

« Il y a quelque chose qui cloche depuis le début de l'été, dit Windisch. Ma femme balaie tous les jours la cour. Les acacias sont déjà jaunes. Dans notre cour il n'y en a pas. Mais dans la cour des Valaques il y en a trois qui sont loin d'avoir perdu toutes leurs feuilles. Et tous les jours dans notre cour il y a des feuilles mortes d'au moins dix arbres. Ma femme ne sait pas d'où peuvent bien venir toutes ces feuilles mortes. Nous n'en avons jamais eu autant dans notre cour.

– C'est le vent qui les apporte », dit le veilleur.

Windisch ferme la porte du moulin à clé. « Il n'y a pas de vent », dit-il.

Le veilleur tend la main, les doigts écartés. « Il y a toujours du vent, dit-il, même quand on ne le sent pas.

– En Allemagne aussi les forêts jaunissent au milieu de l'année, dit Windisch. Le mégissier l'a écrit », ajoute-t-il. Il regarde le ciel large et bas. « Ils se sont installés à Stuttgart. Rudi habite dans une autre ville. Le mégissier ne dit pas où. On a attribué au mégissier et à sa femme un logement social de trois pièces. Ils ont une cuisine avec un coin salle à manger et une salle de bains avec des glaces aux murs. »

Le veilleur rit. « A son âge, on a encore envie de se regarder tout nu dans une glace, dit-il.

– Des voisins riches leur ont donné des meubles, dit Windisch, et un téléviseur aussi. Une femme seule habite à côté de chez eux. La vieille est une mijaurée qui ne mange pas de viande, écrit de mégissier. Elle en mourrait, dit-elle.

– Ces gens-là ont la vie trop belle, dit le veilleur. Ils devraient venir en Roumanie, ils apprendraient à manger de tout.

– Le mégissier a une bonne pension, dit Windisch. Sa femme est fille de salle dans un hospice où la cuisine est bonne. Et quand un vieux fête son anniversaire, on danse. »

Le veilleur rit. « Ce serait bien pour moi. Bonne chère et jeunes femmes. » Il mord dans le trognon de la pomme. Des pépins blancs tombent sur sa veste. « Je ne sais pas, dit-il, j'ai du mal à me décider et à demander un passeport. »

Windisch voit le temps qui s'arrête sur le visage du veilleur. La fin sur ses joues. Il le voit rester au-delà de la fin.

Windisch regarde dans l'herbe. Ses chaussures sont blanchies par la farine. « Une fois qu'on a fait le premier pas, le reste suit », dit-il.

Le veilleur soupire. « Quand on est tout seul, c'est difficile, dit-il, il faut attendre longtemps, et on vieillit, on ne rajeunit pas. »

Windisch pose sa main sur sa cuisse. Elle est chaude, mais sa main, elle, est froide. « Ici, c'est de pire en pire, dit-il. Il nous prennent nos poules, nos œufs. Ils nous prennent même le maïs avant qu'il ait poussé. Ils finiront par te prendre aussi la maison et la cour. »

La lune est grosse. Windisch entend les rats dans l'eau. « Je sens le vent, dit-il, j'ai les articulations des jambes qui me font mal. Il va bientôt pleuvoir. »

Le chien est devant la meule de paille et aboie. « Le vent qui vient de la vallée n'apporte pas la pluie, dit le veilleur, seulement des nuages et de la poussière.

– On aura peut-être de la tempête, dit Windisch, ça va encore faire tomber les fruits des arbres. »

La lune s'est drapée de rouge.

« Et Rudi? demande le veilleur.

– Lui, il se repose, dit Windisch qui sent le mensonge rougir ses joues. En Allemagne, ça ne marche pas comme ici avec le verre. Le mégissier nous dit d'apporter nos verres en cristal, nos porcelaines aussi et le duvet pour les coussins. Le linge de maison et les sous-vêtements, ce n'est pas la peine. Là-bas il y en a à foison. Les fourrures coûtent cher. Les fourrures et les lunettes. »

Windisch mâchonne un brin d'herbe. « Au début, ce n'est jamais simple », dit-il.

Le veilleur se cure une molaire du bout du doigt. « N'importe où que l'on soit, il faut toujours travailler », dit-il.

Windisch attache le brin d'herbe autour de son doigt. « Il y a une chose très dure, dit le mégissier dans sa lettre. C'est un mal que nous connaissons depuis la guerre. Le mal du pays. »

Le veilleur tient une pomme dans sa main. « Je n'aurai pas le mal du pays, dit-il, là-bas on est entre Allemands. »

Windisch fait des nœuds avec le brin d'herbe. « Là-bas, il y a plus d'étrangers qu'ici, écrit le mégissier, il y a des Turcs et des nègres. Ils se multiplient rapidement. »

Windisch passe le brin d'herbe entre ses dents. Il est froid. Sa gencive aussi est froide. La bouche de Windisch avale le ciel entier. Le vent et le ciel de la nuit. Le brin d'herbe se casse entre ses dents.

La piéride du chou

Amélie est devant son miroir. En combinaison rose. Sous son nombril, de la dentelle blanche. Au-dessus du genou, Windisch voit la peau d'Amélie à travers les trous de la dentelle. Son genou est recouvert d'un léger duvet. Il est blanc et rond. Windisch regarde encore une fois le genou d'Amélie dans la glace. Il voit les trous de la dentelle se fondre les uns dans les autres.

Dans la glace il voit aussi les yeux de sa femme. Windisch cligne ses paupières, chassant les dentelles de l'œil vers la tempe. Une veine rouge a jailli dans le coin de son œil. Elle déchire les dentelles.

L'œil de Windisch fait tourner l'accroc dans la pupille.

La fenêtre est ouverte. Sur les vitres on voit les feuilles du pommier.

Les lèvres de Windisch brûlent. Elles disent quelque chose qui, dans la pièce, ne s'adresse qu'à lui. Qui va dans son crâne.

« Il parle tout seul », dit sa femme en regardant le miroir.

Par la fenêtre une piéride du chou entre dans la chambre. Windisch la regarde. Vol de farine et de vent.

La femme de Windisch esquisse un geste dans le miroir. De ses doigts fanés elle remet en place les bretelles de la combinaison sur les épaules d'Amélie.

La piéride volette au-dessus du peigne d'Amélie. Celle-ci passe le peigne dans ses cheveux d'un geste du bras beaucoup plus ample. Elle souffle sur le papillon pour le faire partir, lui et sa farine. Il se pose, il zigzague sur le miroir au-dessus du ventre d'Amélie.

La femme de Windisch presse ses doigts sur la glace. Elle écrase le papillon sur le miroir.

Amélie se vaporise deux grands nuages sous les aisselles. Nuages qui ruissellent sous ses bras jusqu'à la combinaison. Le flacon de spray est noir. Avec des lettres vert vif : « Printemps irlandais ».

La femme de Windisch pose sur le dossier de la chaise une robe rouge. Sous la chaise, elle place des sandales blanches à talons hauts et à fines lanières. Amélie ouvre son sac à main. Du bout du doigt, elle farde ses paupières. « N'en mets pas trop, dit la femme de Windisch, sinon les gens vont jaser. » Son oreille est contre le miroir. Elle est grande et grise. Les paupières d'Amélie sont turquoise. « Ça suffit », dit la femme de Windisch. Le mascara d'Amélie est noir comme de la suie. Amélie approche son visage tout près du miroir. Son regard est en verre.

Du sac d'Amélie une bande de papier d'étain tombe sur le tapis. Elle est pleine de petites verrues blanches. « Qu'est-ce que c'est? » demande la femme de Windisch. Amélie se penche et remet la plaquette dans son sac. « La pilule », dit-elle. Elle sort son rouge à lèvres de son étui noir.

Les pommettes de la femme de Windisch apparaissent dans le miroir. « Tu as besoin de pilules, tu n'es pourtant pas malade? »

Amélie enfile la robe rouge par la tête. Son front apparaît hors du col blanc. Les yeux encore sous la robe, Amélie répond : « Je la prends, on ne sait jamais. »

Windisch se prend la tête dans les mains. Il sort de la pièce. S'assied sous la véranda, devant la table vide. Il fait sombre. C'est un coin d'ombre dans le mur. Le soleil crépite dans les arbres. Seul le miroir brille. Dans le miroir, la bouche rouge d'Amélie.

Devant la maison du mégissier, des petites vieilles marchent. L'ombre des fichus noirs qui leur couvrent la tête les précède. L'ombre sera dans l'église avant les petites vieilles.

Les talons blancs d'Amélie avancent sur les

pavés. A la main, la demande de passeport pliée en quatre comme un portefeuille blanc. La robe rouge se balance sur les mollets. La cour embaume le Printemps irlandais. Sous le pommier, la robe d'Amélie est plus foncée que dans la lumière du soleil.

Windisch voit Amélie marcher en écartant les pieds.

Une mèche de ses cheveux s'envole au-dessus du portail. Claquement du portail que l'on ferme.

La grand-messe

La femme de Windisch est dans la cour derrière les raisins noirs. « Tu ne vas pas à la grand-messe? » demande-t-elle. Les grains de raisin jaillissent de ses yeux, les feuilles de son menton.

« Je reste à la maison, dit Windisch, je n'ai pas envie d'entendre les gens dire que c'est le tour de ma fille maintenant. »

Windisch met le coude sur la table. Ses mains sont lourdes. Il appuie son visage sur ses mains lourdes. La véranda ne grandit pas. Il fait plein jour. Un court instant la véranda sombre dans une position qu'elle n'a jamais eue jusque-là. Windisch sent le coup. Il a une pierre dans la poitrine.

Windisch ferme les yeux. Il sent la courbe de ses

yeux entre ses mains. Ses yeux qui n'ont pas de visage.

Avec ses seuls yeux et sa pierre dans la poitrine, Windisch dit à haute voix : « L'homme est un grand faisan sur terre. »

Ce que Windisch entend, ce n'est pas sa voix. Il sent que sa bouche est nue. Ce sont les murs qui ont parlé.

La boule de feu

Les porcs tachetés du voisin sont couchés dans les carottes sauvages et dorment. Les femmes en noir reviennent de l'église. Le soleil brille. Il les soulève au-dessus du trottoir avec leurs petits souliers noirs. Elles ont les mains blettes d'avoir égrené leur chapelet. Leur regard est encore transfiguré par la prière.

Au-dessus du toit de la maison du mégissier, la cloche de l'église sonne le milieu de la journée. Le soleil est une grande horloge au-dessus des cloches de midi. La grand-messe est finie. Le ciel est brûlant.

Derrière les petites vieilles le trottoir est vide. Windisch regarde la rangée de maisons. Il voit le bout de la rue. « Amélie devrait arriver », pense-t-il. Dans l'herbe il y a des oies. Elles sont blanches, comme les chaussures à talons d'Amélie.

La larme est dans le placard. « Amélie ne l'a

pas remplie, se dit-il, Amélie n'est jamais à la maison quand il pleut. Elle est toujours en ville. »

Le trottoir tremble dans le soleil. Les oies déploient leurs voiles. Leurs ailes sont de longs fichus blancs. Les chaussures d'Amélie, blanches comme la neige, ne traversent toujours pas le village.

La porte de l'armoire grince. La bouteille glouglloute. Dans la bouche de Windisch, une boule de liquide et de feu. Elle roule dans son gosier. Ses tempes s'embrasent. La boule se désagrège. Des flammes lui lèchent encore le front. La boule trace dans ses cheveux des raies zigzagantes.

La casquette du policier tourne tout autour du miroir. Ses épaulettes sont étincelantes. Les boutons de son uniforme bleu s'imposent au centre du miroir. Au-dessus de la veste du policier le visage de Windisch.

Une seule fois le visage de Windisch est imposant au-dessus de l'uniforme. A deux reprises Windisch appuie son petit visage abattu sur les épaulettes. Sourire du policier sur les joues de Windisch, sur son visage imposant. Ses lèvres humides répètent : « Tu n'iras pas loin avec ta farine. »

Windisch lève le poing. L'uniforme du policier vole en éclats. Le visage imposant et supérieur de Windisch a une tache de sang. Windisch donne un coup mortel aux deux petits visages découragés au-dessus des épaulettes.

Sans un mot, la femme de Windisch balaie les débris du miroir.

Le suçon

Amélie est sur le seuil de la porte. Sur les éclats de verre il y a des taches de sang. Le sang de Windisch est encore plus rouge que la robe d'Amélie.

Un reste de Printemps irlandais monte des mollets d'Amélie. Sur son cou un suçon plus rouge que sa robe. Amélie quitte ses chaussures blanches. « A table », dit la femme de Windisch.

La soupe fume. Amélie est assise dans le brouillard. Du bout de ses doigts rouges, elle tient la cuillère. Elle regarde la soupe. La fumée fait bouger ses lèvres. Elle souffle. La femme de Windisch s'assied en soupirant dans le grand nuage gris devant son assiette.

Le murmure des feuilles pénètre par la fenêtre. « Elles volent jusqu'à notre cour, se dit Windisch. Il y a autant de feuilles que s'il y avait dix arbres dans la cour. »

Le regard de Windisch glisse sur l'oreille d'Amélie. Elle n'est qu'une petite partie de ce qu'il voit. Rougie et plissée comme une paupière.

Windisch avale une nouille blanche et molle. Elle se coince dans sa gorge. Windisch pose sa cuillère sur la table et tousse. Ses yeux se remplissent de larmes.

Windisch vomit dans son assiette la soupe qu'il

vient de manger. Il a la bouche amère. Elle
envahit toute sa tête. Dans l'assiette la soupe est
souillée de vomissures.

Dans l'assiette de soupe, Windisch voit une
grande cour. Un soir d'été.

L'araignée

Windisch avait dansé le samedi soir, avec Barbara, devant le grand pavillon du gramophone,
jusqu'aux premières heures du dimanche. Ils
avaient parlé de la guerre. Sur un rythme de
valse.

La lueur de la lampe à pétrole posée sur une
chaise sous un cognassier vacillait.

Barbara avait un cou mince. Windisch dansait
avec son cou mince. Barbara avait une bouche
pâle. Windisch était suspendu à son souffle. Il
chavirait. Au rythme de la danse.

Du cognassier une araignée est tombée dans les
cheveux de Barbara. Windisch n'a pas vu l'araignée. Son visage touchait l'oreille de Barbara. Il
entendait la musique qui sortait du pavillon à
travers sa lourde tresse noire. Il sentait la dureté
du peigne.

Sous la lampe à pétrole deux trèfles verts
brillaient aux oreilles de Barbara. Barbara tour-
nait. Au rythme de la danse.

Barbara sentit l'araignée dans son oreille. Elle
eut peur et s'écria : « Je vais mourir! »

Le mégissier dansait sur le sable. Il passa en dansant. Rit. Enleva l'araignée de l'oreille de Barbara. La jeta dans le sable. L'écrasa de son soulier. Au rythme de la danse.

Barbara s'était adossée au cognassier. Windisch lui tenait le front.

Barbara mit la main à l'oreille. Le trèfle vert n'y était plus. Barbara ne le chercha pas. Elle ne dansa plus. Se mit à pleurer. « Je ne pleure pas à cause de la boucle d'oreille », dit-elle.

Plus tard, bien plus tard, Barbara et Windisch étaient assis sur un banc dans le village. Le cou de Barbara était mince. Un trèfle vert brillait. L'autre oreille était sombre dans la nuit.

Timidement, Windisch lui demanda où était la deuxième boucle d'oreille. Barbara le regarda. « Où aurais-je pu la chercher, dit-elle, l'araignée l'a emportée à la guerre. Les araignées mangent l'or. »

Barbara a suivi l'araignée après la guerre. En Russie, la neige, en fondant pour la seconde fois, l'a emportée.

La feuille de salade

Amélie ronge un os de poulet. Dans sa bouche la salade craque. La femme de Windisch tient une aile de poulet devant sa bouche.

« Il s'est envoyé toute une bouteille de

schnaps », dit-elle. Elle suçote la peau jaune. « De désespoir. »

Amélie pique une feuille de salade avec les dents de la fourchette. Elle la porte à sa bouche. Elle fait trembler la feuille en parlant. « Avec ta farine, tu n'iras pas loin », dit-elle. Ses lèvres se collent l'une à l'autre comme une limace à une feuille de salade.

« Les hommes ont besoin de boire quand ils souffrent », dit la femme de Windisch en souriant. L'ombre à paupières d'Amélie forme un pli bleu au-dessus de ses cils. « Et ils souffrent parce qu'ils boivent », ricane-t-elle. La femme de Windisch regarde au travers d'une feuille de salade.

Le suçon s'épanouit sur le cou d'Amélie. Il vire au bleu, et il se déplace quand elle avale. Elle lèche les petites vertèbres blanches. Elle avale les petits morceaux du cou du poulet. « Quand tu te marieras, aie l'œil, dit-elle. La boisson est un mal terrible. » Amélie lèche les pointes rouges de ses doigts. « Et ce n'est pas sain », dit-elle.

Windisch regarde l'araignée noire. « Faire la pute, c'est plus sain », dit-il.

La femme de Windisch tape sur la table de la paume de la main.

La soupe aux herbes

La femme de Windisch est restée cinq ans en Russie. Elle dormait dans une baraque où il y avait des lits en fer-blanc. Au coin des lits on entendait les poux. On l'avait tondue. Son visage était gris. Les morsures des poux avaient laissé des marques rouges sur la peau de son crâne.

Au-dessus des montagnes on voyait une autre chaîne de nuages et de poussière de neige. Sur le camion la morsure du gel brûlait. Tout le monde ne descendait pas devant la mine. Chaque matin, des hommes et des femmes restaient assis sur les bancs, les yeux grands ouverts. Ils laissaient passer les autres devant eux. Ils étaient morts de froid. Ils étaient dans l'au-delà.

La mine était noire. La pelle froide. Le charbon lourd.

Lorsque la neige eut fondu pour la première fois, l'herbe pointue et maigre poussa entre les rochers. Katharina vendit son manteau d'hiver pour deux tranches de pain. Son estomac était un vrai hérisson. Katharina cueillait chaque jour une poignée d'herbes. La soupe aux herbes était chaude et bonne. Pendant quelques heures le hérisson rentrait ses piquants.

Mais la neige tomba pour la seconde fois. Katharina avait une couverture de laine. Le jour, elle lui servait de manteau. Le hérisson avait de nouveau sorti ses piquants.

Lorsqu'il fit nuit, Katharina s'en alla à la lueur de la neige. Elle s'accroupit, rampa devant le gardien. Elle alla retrouver un homme dans son lit de fer. C'était le cuisinier. Il l'appela Käthe. Il la réchauffa et lui donna des pommes de terre. Elles étaient chaudes et douces. Pour quelques heures, le hérisson rentra ses piquants.

Lorsque la neige eut fondu pour la seconde fois, la soupe aux herbes poussait sous les souliers. Katharina vendit sa couverture de laine pour dix tranches de pain. Pour quelques heures, le hérisson rentra ses piquants.

La neige tomba pour la troisième fois. Katharina avait, pour seul manteau, un gilet de fourrure.

Après la mort du cuisinier, l'éclat de la neige l'attira vers une autre baraque. Katharina passa en rampant devant l'ombre d'un nouveau gardien. Elle monta dans le lit de fer d'un autre homme. Il était médecin. Il l'appela Katiouchka. La réchauffa et lui donna une feuille de papier blanc. Une maladie y était inscrite. Trois jours de suite Katharina fut dispensée d'aller à la mine.

Lorsque la neige eut fondu pour la troisième fois, Katharina vendit son petit gilet de fourrure pour un bol de sucre. Katharina mangea du pain trempé et le saupoudra de sucre. Le hérisson rentra ses piquants pour quelques jours encore.

Vint la quatrième neige. Les socquettes de laine grise étaient le manteau de Katharina.

Après la mort du médecin, la clarté de la neige éclaira la cour du camp. Katharina passa en rampant devant le chien endormi. Elle monta dans le lit de fer d'un homme. C'était le fossoyeur. Il enterrait aussi les Russes au village. Il l'appela Katia. La réchauffa. Lui donna un morceau de viande qu'il avait rapporté d'un repas de funérailles au village.

Lorsque la neige fondit pour la quatrième fois, Katharina vendit ses socquettes de laine pour une assiette de farine de maïs. La bouillie de maïs était brûlante et bien gonflée. Pour quelques jours le hérisson rentra ses piquants.

Puis vint la neige pour la cinquième fois. La robe de drap brun servit de manteau à Katharina.

Après la mort du fossoyeur, Katharina enfila le manteau de celui-ci. Elle traversa la clôture en rampant dans la neige. Elle se rendit au village, chez une vieille Russe. Elle était seule. Le fossoyeur avait enterré son mari. La vieille reconnut le manteau de Katharina, il avait appartenu à son mari. Katharina se réchauffa dans cette maison. Elle se mit à traire la chèvre. La vieille l'appela Devotchka. Elle lui donna du lait.

Lorsque la neige fondit pour la cinquième fois, des panicules jaunes fleurirent dans l'herbe.

Dans la soupe aux herbes flottait une poudre jaune. Une poudre sucrée.

Un après-midi, des voitures vertes entrèrent dans la cour du camp. Elles écrasèrent l'herbe. Katharina était assise devant la baraque, sur une pierre. Elle vit les traces boueuses des pneus. Elle vit des gardiens qu'elle ne connaissait pas.

Les femmes montèrent sur les voitures vertes. Les traces boueuses des pneus ne conduisaient pas à la mine. Les voitures vertes s'arrêtèrent devant la petite gare.

Katharina monta dans le train. Elle pleurait de joie.

Quand Katharina apprit que le train la ramenait à la maison, de la soupe aux herbes lui collait encore aux mains.

La mouette

La femme de Windisch allume la télévision. La chanteuse est appuyée à un parapet devant la mer. L'ourlet de sa jupe s'envole. Les dentelles de son jupon recouvrent son genou.

Une mouette survole l'eau. Elle passe, en volant, juste au bord de l'écran. Du bout des ailes, elle pénètre dans la pièce. « Je ne suis encore jamais allée à la mer, dit la femme de Windisch. Si la mer n'était pas aussi loin, les mouettes viendraient jusqu'au village. » La mouette plonge dans l'eau. Elle avale un poisson.

La chanteuse sourit. Elle a un visage de mouette. Elle ouvre et ferme les yeux aussi souvent que la bouche. Elle chante une chanson qui parle des filles de Roumanie. Ses cheveux ondulent. Des petites vagues frisottent sur son front.

« Les filles de Roumanie, chante-t-elle, sont tendres comme les fleurs des prés au mois de mai. » Ses mains montrent la mer. Sur le sable de la rive, des buissons tremblotent.

Dans l'eau, un homme nage en suivant ses mains. Il va très loin vers le large. Il est seul et on ne voit plus le ciel. Sa tête dérive. Les vagues ont une couleur sombre. La mouette est blanche.

Le visage de la chanteuse est doux. Le vent montre la bordure de son jupon en dentelle.

La femme de Windisch est devant l'écran. Elle montre du doigt le genou de la chanteuse. « C'est une belle dentelle, dit-elle, elle ne vient sûrement pas de Roumanie. »

Amélie se plante devant l'écran. « Elle est exactement comme la dentelle de la robe de la danseuse qui est sur la potiche. »

La femme de Windisch pose sur la table des petits sablés. Sous la table il y a une gamelle en fer-blanc. Le chat lape les vomissures de soupe.

La chanteuse sourit. Elle ferme la bouche. Derrière la chanson, la mer bat le rivage. « Il faut que ton père te donne l'argent pour acheter la potiche, dit la femme de Windisch.

– Non, dit Amélie, j'ai fait des économies. Je me la paierai moi-même. »

La jeune chouette

Depuis une semaine, la jeune chouette reste dans la vallée. Les gens la voient tous les soirs quand ils rentrent de la ville. La voie du chemin de fer baigne dans la grisaille du crépuscule. A droite et à gauche du train, un maïs qu'ils ne connaissent pas, noir, agité par le vent. La jeune chouette est là, au milieu des chardons fanés, comme posée sur de la neige.

Les voyageurs descendent à la gare. Ils se taisent. Depuis une semaine, le train ne siffle plus. Les gens serrent leurs sacs contre eux et rentrent à la maison. Lorsqu'ils se rencontrent sur le chemin du retour, ils se disent : « C'est le dernier répit. Demain la chouette sera là, et la mort avec elle. »

Le curé envoie l'enfant de chœur dans le clocher. Sonner la cloche. Lorsqu'il redescend, il est tout pâle. « Ce n'est pas moi qui ai tiré la cloche, c'est elle qui m'a tiré. Si je ne m'étais pas tenu aux poutres, je me serais envolé dans le ciel depuis longtemps. »

Les cloches ont rendu la jeune chouette comme folle. Elle est repartie. Elle a repris son vol vers l'intérieur du pays. Elle est descendue vers le sud en suivant le Danube. Elle a volé jusqu'aux eaux maléfiques, là où il y a les soldats.

Dans la plaine du Sud, il n'y a pas un seul arbre. Il fait chaud. La campagne est brûlante. La jeune chouette allume ses yeux à un buisson d'églantine pourpre. Les ailes au-dessus des fils de fer barbelés, elle souhaite une mort.

Les soldats sont allongés dans le petit matin gris. Au milieu des fourrés. Ils font des manœuvres. Leurs mains, leurs yeux, leurs fronts sont en guerre.

L'officier crie un ordre.

Un soldat voit la jeune chouette dans le fourré. Il pose son fusil dans l'herbe. Se lève. La balle part. Elle atteint sa cible.

Le mort est le fils du tailleur. C'est Dietmar.

« La jeune chouette s'est posée au bord du Danube et elle a pensé à notre village », dit le curé.

Windisch regarde son vélo. De retour du village, il rapporte chez lui la nouvelle de la balle qui a tué. « Ça recommence comme pendant la guerre », dit-il.

La femme de Windisch fronce les sourcils. « La chouette n'y est pour rien, dit-elle, c'est un accident. » Elle arrache une feuille de pommier jaunie. Elle regarde Windisch des pieds à la tête. Regarde longuement la poche de sa veste, sur la poitrine, là où bat le cœur.

Windisch sent le feu dévorer sa bouche. « Tu as le cerveau tellement petit, hurle-t-il, qu'il n'est pas capable de commander à ta bouche! »

La femme de Windisch pleure et écrase la feuille jaunie.

Windisch sent un grain de sable se coincer dans sa tête. « Elle pleure sur elle-même, pense-t-il, les femmes pleurent toujours sur elles-mêmes. »

La cuisine d'été

Le veilleur de nuit dort sur le banc devant le moulin. Le chapeau noir rend son sommeil doux et lourd, comme du velours. Son front n'est qu'un trait pâle. « Il rêve encore à la grenouille », se dit Windisch qui voit sur les joues du veilleur le temps arrêté.

Du fond de son rêve, le veilleur parle. Il bouge les jambes. Le chien aboie. Le veilleur se réveille. Effrayé, il enlève le chapeau de sa tête. Son front est mouillé. « Elle va me tuer », dit-il. Sa voix est profonde. Elle replonge dans le rêve.

« Ma femme était allongée, nue et recroquevillée sur la planche à nouilles, dit le veilleur. Son corps n'était pas plus grand que celui d'un enfant. De la planche dégoulinait un liquide jaunâtre qui inondait le sol. Des vieilles femmes étaient assises autour de la table. Elles étaient habillées de noir. Leurs chignons étaient ébouriffés. Elles n'avaient pas coiffé leurs cheveux depuis longtemps. Wilma-la-Maigre était aussi petite que ma femme. Elle avait un gant noir à la main. Ses pieds ne touchaient pas le sol. Un bref instant elle a regardé par la fenêtre, et elle a laissé tomber le gant. Elle a regardé sous la chaise. Le gant n'y était pas. Il n'y avait rien par terre. Ses pieds étaient si loin du sol qu'elle s'est mise à pleurer. Son visage ridé s'est renfrogné et elle a dit que c'était une honte de laisser les morts dans la cuisine d'été. J'ai répondu que je ne savais pas que nous avions une cuisine d'été. Ma femme a soulevé la tête de la planche à nouilles sur laquelle elle gisait et a souri. Wilma-la-Maigre l'a regardée. " Ne t'en fais pas ", lui a-t-elle dit, et elle a ajouté à mon intention : " Elle se vide et elle pue. " »

Le veilleur reste la bouche ouverte. Des larmes coulent sur ses joues.

Windisch le prend par l'épaule. « Tu perds la tête », lui dit-il. On entend le bruit des clés dans la poche de Windisch.

Il appuie la pointe de son soulier contre la porte du moulin.

Le veilleur regarde dans son chapeau noir. Windisch pousse son vélo jusqu'au banc. « Je vais avoir mon passeport », dit-il.

La garde d'honneur

Le policier est dans la cour du tailleur. Il sert du schnaps aux officiers. Il en offre aussi aux soldats qui ont apporté le cercueil à la maison. Windisch voit leurs épaulettes avec les étoiles.

Le veilleur tourne la tête vers Windisch. « Le policier est heureux d'avoir de la compagnie », dit-il.

Le maire est sous le prunier aux feuilles déjà jaunies. Il transpire. Il regarde une feuille de papier. « Il n'arrive pas à lire l'éloge funèbre, dit Windisch. C'est l'institutrice qui l'a écrit. »

« Il veut deux sacs de farine pour demain soir », dit le veilleur. Qui sent l'alcool.

Le curé entre dans la cour. Sa traîne noire glisse sur le sol. Les officiers ferment prestement la bouche. Le policier cache la bouteille de schnaps derrière l'arbre.

Le cercueil est en métal. Il est soudé. Il brille dans la cour comme une énorme boîte à tabac. La garde d'honneur sort de la cour, au pas, en portant le cercueil. Les bottes scandent le rythme de la marche. La voiture démarre.

Elle a un drapeau rouge.

Les chapeaux noirs des hommes avancent d'un

pas rapide. Les fichus noirs des femmes, à l'arrière, se déplacent plus lentement. Elles zigzaguent en suivant les boules noires de leurs rosaires. Le cocher du corbillard avance à pied. Il parle à haute voix.

La garde d'honneur, dans la voiture, est ballottée. Lorsque la chaussée est défoncée, elle se cramponne aux fusils. Elle est trop haut au-dessus de la terre, trop haut au-dessus du cercueil.

La tombe de la vieille Kroner est encore noire et haute. « La terre ne s'est pas tassée parce qu'il n'a pas plu », dit Wilma-la-Maigre. Les boules d'hortensias, en se fanant, tombent en poussière.

La postière vient se mettre à côté de Windisch. « Comme ce serait bien, dit-elle, si les jeunes, eux aussi, assistaient à l'enterrement. Il y a des années qu'ils ne le font plus. Quand quelqu'un meurt au village, les jeunes ne viennent pas. » Une larme tombe sur sa main. « Dimanche matin, Amélie doit venir à l'audience », poursuit-elle.

La diseuse de prières chante dans l'oreille du curé. L'encens lui écrase la bouche. Béate, elle met tant d'obstination à chanter que le blanc de son œil s'agrandit démesurément et ruisselle lentement sur ses pupilles.

La postière sanglote. Elle prend Windisch par le coude. « Et deux sacs de farine », ajoute-t-elle.

La cloche sonne à s'en blesser la langue. Une salve d'honneur s'élève au-dessus des tombes. Les lourdes mottes de terre s'écrasent sur le métal du cercueil.

La diseuse de prières reste près du monument aux morts. Du coin de l'œil, elle repère l'endroit où elle veut aller. Elle regarde Windisch. Elle tousse. Windisch entend des glaires se déchirer dans sa gorge vide d'avoir trop chanté.

« Amélie doit venir voir le curé samedi après-midi, dit-elle. Il cherchera dans les registres son extrait de baptême. »

La femme de Windisch achève sa prière. Elle fait deux pas en avant. Elle se plante devant le visage de la diseuse de prières. « Cette histoire de certificat de baptême ne doit pas être aussi urgente que cela, dit-elle.

– Très urgente, répond la diseuse de prières. Le policier a dit au curé que vos passeports étaient prêts à la mairie. »

La femme de Windisch roule son mouchoir en boule. « Amélie doit rapporter samedi une potiche, dit-elle, elle est très fragile.

– Amélie ne peut pas aller directement de la gare chez le curé », ajoute Windisch.

De la pointe de son soulier, la diseuse de prières fait des dessins dans le sable. « Dans ce cas, qu'elle aille d'abord à la maison, elle ira ensuite chez le curé. Les jours sont encore longs. »

Les Tsiganes portent bonheur

Le buffet de la cuisine est vide. La femme de Windisch claque les portes. Pieds nus, la petite Tsigane du village voisin est plantée au milieu de la cuisine, là où il y avait la table. Elle fourre les casseroles dans son grand sac. Elle défait le nœud de son mouchoir. Elle donne à la femme de Windisch vingt-cinq lei. « C'est tout ce que j'ai », dit-elle. La langue rouge dépasse de la tresse. « Donne-moi encore une robe. Les Tsiganes portent bonheur. »

La femme de Windisch lui donne la robe rouge d'Amélie. « Va-t'en maintenant. »

La petite Tsigane montre la théière. « La théière aussi, je te porterai bonheur. »

La vachère au fichu bleu franchit le portail avec les planches du lit qu'elle a mises sur une brouette. Elle s'est attaché les vieux coussins sur le dos.

Windisch montre le téléviseur à l'homme au petit chapeau. Il le met en marche. De l'écran monte un murmure. L'homme emporte le téléviseur. Il le pose sur la table de la véranda. Windisch prend les billets de la main de l'homme.

Devant la maison il y a une voiture à cheval. Le vacher et la vachère sont devant la tache blanche, là où se trouvait le lit. Ils regardent l'armoire et la coiffeuse. « Le miroir est cassé », dit la femme de Windisch. La vachère soulève une chaise et examine le dessous du siège. Le vacher frappe du doigt sur la table. « C'est du bon bois, dit Windisch. De nos jours, on ne trouve plus de meubles de cette qualité dans le commerce. »

La pièce est vide. L'armoire avance dans la rue, sur une voiture tirée par des chevaux. Les pieds de chaises sont à côté de l'armoire. Ils brinquebalent comme les roues. La coiffeuse et la table sont restées dans l'herbe devant la maison. La vachère, assise à côté, regarde la voiture s'éloigner.

La postière enveloppe les rideaux dans un journal. Elle lorgne le réfrigérateur. « Il est vendu, dit la femme de Windisch. Le conducteur de tracteur vient le chercher ce soir. »

Les poules sont couchées, la tête dans le sable, les pattes attachées. Wilma-la-Maigre les met dans un panier en osier. « Le coq était aveugle, dit la femme de Windisch. J'ai dû le tuer. » Wilma-la-Maigre compte les billets. La femme de Windisch tend la main.

Le tailleur a un large crêpe à son revers. Il roule le tapis. La femme de Windisch regarde ses mains. « On n'échappe pas à son destin », soupire-t-elle.

Par la fenêtre, Amélie regarde le pommier. « Je ne sais pas, dit le tailleur. Il n'a rien fait de mal en ce monde. » Amélie sent les larmes monter dans sa gorge. Elle s'appuie à la balustrade. Penche la tête par la fenêtre. Elle entend le coup de feu.

Windisch est dehors avec le veilleur. « Il y a un nouveau meunier au village, dit ce dernier. Un Valaque qui porte un petit chapeau et qui vient d'un coin où il y a encore des moulins à eau. » Le veilleur accroche des chemises, des vestes, des pantalons au porte-bagages de son vélo. Il fouille dans sa poche. « J'ai dit que je te l'offrais », dit Windisch. La femme de Windisch tiraille son tablier. « Prends, dit-elle, il te les donne de bon cœur. Il y a encore un tas de vieux vêtements pour les Tsiganes. » Elle se touche la joue. « Les Tsiganes portent bonheur », ajoute-t-elle.

La bergerie

Le nouveau meunier est dans la véranda. « C'est le maire qui m'envoie, dit-il, je vais habiter ici. »

Son minuscule chapeau est de travers sur sa tête. Il a un petit gilet en fourrure tout neuf. Il regarde la table qui est sur la véranda. « Je peux avoir besoin de cette table », dit-il.

Il visite la maison. Windisch le suit. Derrière eux, pieds nus, la femme de Windisch.

Le nouveau meunier regarde la porte du vestibule. Il appuie sur la clenche. Il examine les murs et le plafond. Il frappe sur la porte de la chambre. « La porte est vieille », dit-il. Il s'adosse au chambranle et regarde la chambre vide. « On m'a dit que la maison était meublée.

– Comment meublée? dit Windisch. J'ai vendu les meubles. »

La femme de Windisch sort de la pièce d'un pas saccadé. Windisch sent battre ses tempes.

Le nouveau meunier regarde les murs de la pièce et le plafond. Il ouvre et referme la fenêtre. De la pointe de son soulier, il appuie sur les lames de parquet. « Bon, alors je vais téléphoner à ma femme qu'elle apporte les meubles. »

Le meunier va dans la cour. Il examine les clôtures. Il aperçoit les porcs tachetés du voisin.

« J'ai dix porcs et vingt-six moutons. Où est la bergerie? »

Windisch voit les feuilles mortes sur le sable. « Nous n'avons jamais eu de moutons », dit-il.

La femme de Windisch vient dans la cour avec un balai. « Les Allemands n'ont jamais de moutons », dit-elle. Le balai crisse sur le sable.

« La remise peut servir de garage, dit le meunier. Je vais me procurer des planches pour construire une bergerie. »

Il serre la main de Windisch. « Le moulin est beau. »

En balayant, la femme de Windisch dessine de larges vagues rondes sur le sable.

La croix d'argent

Amélie est assise par terre. Les verres à vin sont rangés les uns derrière les autres par ordre de grandeur. Les verres à liqueur brillent. Les fleurs laiteuses sur les courbes des coupes à fruits sont figées. Le long du mur les vases à fleurs. Dans un coin la potiche.

Amélie tient dans la main la petite boîte où se trouve la larme.

Amélie entend la voix du tailleur marteler ses tempes : « Il n'a rien fait de mal en ce monde. » Amélie a la tête en feu.

Elle sent la bouche du policier sur son cou. Son haleine empeste l'alcool. Il presse ses mains sur les genoux d'Amélie. « *Ce dulci esti*[1] », dit-il en lui relevant sa robe. La casquette du policier est posée à côté de sa chaussure. Les boutons de son uniforme brillent

Le policier déboutonne son uniforme. « Déshabille-toi », dit-il. Sous son uniforme bleu, il porte une croix d'argent. Le curé quitte sa soutane noire. Il arrange une mèche de cheveux qui pend sur la joue d'Amélie. « Enlève ton rouge à lèvres. » Le policier embrasse l'épaule d'Amélie. La croix d'argent lui tombe devant la bouche. Le curé lui caresse les cuisses. « Quitte ton jupon. » Amélie voit l'autel par la porte ouverte. Au milieu des roses il y a un téléphone noir. La croix d'argent pend entre les seins d'Amélie. Les mains du policier les pétrissent. « Tu as de belles pommes », dit le curé. Sa bouche est mouillée. Les cheveux d'Amélie, sur le bord du lit, se déploient jusqu'au sol. Sous la chaise, les chaussures blanches. Le policier murmure : « Tu sens bon. » Les mains du curé sont blanches. La robe rouge étincelle au bout du lit de fer. Le téléphone noir au milieu des roses sonne. « Je suis occupé pour le moment », gémit le policier. Les cuisses du curé sont lourdes. « Croise tes jambes dans mon dos », dit-il à voix basse. La croix d'argent s'enfonce dans l'épaule d'Amélie. Le policier a le front en sueur. « Retourne-toi », dit-il. La soutane noire est accrochée à un grand clou derrière la porte. Le nez du curé est froid. « Mon petit ange », dit-il d'une voix haletante.

1. « Que tu es mignonne. » En roumain dans le texte.

Amélie sent dans le ventre les talons de ses sandales blanches. La braise qui est dans sa tête lui brûle les yeux. La langue d'Amélie est lourde dans sa bouche. La croix d'argent brille sur le carreau de la fenêtre. Dans le pommier, il y a une ombre. Un trou noir. C'est une tombe.

Windisch paraît soudain dans l'encadrement de la porte. « Es-tu sourde? » Il tend à Amélie la grande valise. Amélie regarde vers la porte. Ses joues sont mouillées. « Je sais, dit Windisch. Les départs sont difficiles. » Il semble très grand dans la pièce vide. « Pour le moment, c'est comme à la guerre, dit-il. On s'en va et on ne sait ni quand ni comment on reviendra, on ne sait surtout pas si on reviendra. »

Une fois encore, Amélie remplit la larme. « L'eau de la fontaine ne l'humidifiera pas assez », dit-elle. La femme de Windisch met les assiettes dans la valise. Elle prend la larme dans sa main. Ses joues sont douces et ses lèvres humides. « Il est difficile de croire que de telles choses existent », dit-elle.

Sa voix résonne dans la tête de Windisch. Il jette son manteau dans la valise. « J'en ai assez d'elle! crie-t-il. Je ne veux plus la voir. » Il baisse la tête et ajoute à voix basse : « Donner le cafard, c'est tout ce qu'elle sait faire. »

La femme de Windisch essaie de caser les couverts entre les assiettes. « Ça, elle sait le faire », dit-il. Windisch regarde le doigt qu'elle a retiré tout visqueux de sa toison. Il contemple sa propre photo sur son passeport. Hoche la tête. « C'est un pas difficile », dit-il.

Les verres d'Amélie étincellent dans la valise. Les taches blanches sur les murs de la chambre grandissent. L'ampoule jette de longs rayons de lumière sur les valises.

Windisch met les passeports dans la poche de sa veste. « Qui sait ce que nous allons devenir... », soupire sa femme. Windisch regarde la lumière de la lampe qui le blesse. Sa femme et Amélie bouclent les valises.

La permanente

Un vélo en bois grince dans la clôture. Là-haut dans le ciel, une bicyclette sort tranquillement des nuages blancs. Les autres nuages alentour sont de l'eau. Gris et vides comme un étang. Autour de l'étang, des montagnes silencieuses. Des montagnes grises, pleines de mal du pays.

Windisch porte deux grandes valises. Sa femme aussi. Sa tête avance trop vite. Elle est trop petite. Les os de ses pommettes sont enfermés dans quelque chose de sombre. La femme de Windisch s'est fait couper les cheveux. Ses cheveux courts sont permanentés. Sa bouche est dure et étroite à cause du nouveau dentier. Elle parle fort.

Une mèche s'échappe de la coiffure d'Amélie, elle vole des cerisiers jusqu'au buis et revient au-dessus de son oreille.

L'ornière est grise, lézardée. Le peuplier ressemble à un balai dressé vers le ciel.

Jésus dort sur la croix à côté de la porte de l'église. Quand il se réveillera, il sera vieux. L'air dans le village sera plus clair que sa peau nue.

A la poste il y a un cadenas au bout d'une chaîne. La clé est chez la postière. La clé ouvre le cadenas. Elle ouvre le lit pour les audiences.

Amélie porte la lourde valise remplie d'objets de verre. Son sac en bandoulière. Dedans il y a la boîte avec la larme. De l'autre main, Amélie porte la potiche avec la danseuse.

Le village est petit. Dans les rues étroites il y a des gens. Ils sont loin. Ils s'éloignent. A l'extrémité de chaque rue, le maïs forme un mur noir.

Windisch voit autour du soubassement de la gare les flaques grises du temps arrêté. Une nappe de lait recouvre les rails. Jusqu'aux talons. Au-dessus, une peau glauque. Le temps qui s'arrête tisse une toile autour des bagages. Il tire sur les bras. Windisch avance à petits pas sur le ballast. Il s'enfonce.

Les marches du train sont hautes. Windisch décolle ses chaussures de la nappe de lait.

La femme de Windisch essuie la poussière des sièges avec son mouchoir. Amélie pose la potiche sur ses genoux. Windisch presse son visage contre la vitre. Au mur du compartiment une photo de la mer Noire. L'eau est calme. La photo se balance. Elle est du voyage.

« Dans l'avion, j'ai mal au cœur, dit Windisch. Je le sais depuis la guerre. » Sa femme rit. Son dentier, tout neuf, fait du bruit.

Le costume de Windisch est trop juste. Une

manche remonte. « Le tailleur te l'a mal coupé. Un tissu cher pour un costume loupé! »

Pendant le voyage Windisch sent son front se remplir de sable. Sa tête est lourde. Ses yeux sombrent dans le sommeil. Ses mains tremblent. Ses jambes sont sur le qui-vive. A travers la vitre Windisch voit à perte de vue les fourrés roussis. « Depuis que la chouette lui a pris son fils, le tailleur ne peut plus penser », dit Windisch. Sa femme tient son menton dans ses mains.

Amélie laisse aller sa tête sur son épaule. Ses cheveux cachent ses joues. Elle dort. « Elle a bien raison, dit la femme de Windisch. Depuis que je n'ai plus de chignon, je ne sais plus comment je dois tenir ma tête », poursuit-elle. Sa robe neuve au col de dentelle blanc a un reflet vert d'eau.

Dans un grand fracas le train roule sur le pont de fer. Au-dessus du fleuve, la mer, dans le compartiment, oscille de droite à gauche. Dans le fleuve, il y a peu d'eau et beaucoup de sable.

Des petits oiseaux passent à tire-d'aile. Windisch les regarde. Vols d'oiseaux qui se déchirent. Ils cherchent des forêts dans la prairie. Ils ne trouvent que taillis, sable et eau.

Le train roule lentement, parce que les voies s'emmêlent, parce que la ville commence. Dans les faubourgs, des vieilles ferrailles. Des petites maisons dans des jardins abandonnés. Windisch remarque que les rails se mélangent. Dans cet enchevêtrement, il voit des trains qu'il ne connaît pas.

Sur la robe verte, une croix d'or est suspendue à une chaîne. Prairie verte autour de la croix.

La femme de Windisch bouge le bras. La croix se balance au bout de la chaîne. Le train roule vite. Il a trouvé une voie libre au milieu des trains inconnus.

La femme de Windisch se lève. Elle a le regard fixe et décidé. Elle voit la gare. Sous ses cheveux permanentés, dans son crâne, la femme de Windisch s'est déjà organisé un monde nouveau dans lequel elle emmène ses grandes valises. Ses lèvres sont de la cendre froide. « Si le Seigneur le veut, dit-elle, l'été prochain nous reviendrons ici, en visite. »

Le trottoir est lézardé. Les flaques ont bu l'eau. Windisch ferme sa voiture à clé. Sur l'auto un cercle d'argent brille. Dedans trois petits bâtons comme trois doigts. Des cadavres de mouches jonchent le capot du moteur. Sur le pare-brise une crotte d'oiseau s'étale, sur le coffre une inscription : DIESEL. On entend une voiture à cheval. Les chevaux n'ont que la peau sur les os. La voiture n'est que poussière. Le cocher est un inconnu. Il a de grandes oreilles et un petit chapeau.

Windisch et sa femme marchent dans le même ballot d'étoffe. Lui, en costume gris. Elle, en tailleur gris.

La femme de Windisch a des chaussures noires à talons hauts.

Dans l'ornière Windisch sent, sous ses chaussures, des lézardes qui le déséquilibrent. Sa femme a des varices bleues sur ses mollets blancs.

La femme de Windisch regarde les toits rouges et pentus. « On dirait que je n'ai jamais habité ici », dit-elle. Elle dit cela comme si les toits étaient des cailloux rouges sous ses souliers. Un arbre lui fait de l'ombre sur le visage. Ses joues restent de pierre. L'ombre se retire dans l'arbre. Lui laisse quelques plis sur le menton. Sa croix en or brille. Le soleil l'attrape. Il pose des flammes sur la croix.

La postière est près de la haie de buis. Son sac verni est déchiré. Elle tend la joue pour recevoir un baiser. La femme de Windisch lui donne une tablette de chocolat Ritter-Sport. Le papier bleu ciel brille. La postière met les doigts sur le bord doré.

La femme de Windisch remue les pierres qui lui servent de joues. Le veilleur s'approche de Windisch. Il soulève son chapeau noir. Windisch reconnaît sa chemise et sa veste. Le vent pose une tache d'ombre sur le menton de la femme de Windisch. Elle détourne la tête. La tache tombe sur la veste de son tailleur. Elle porte cette tache comme un cœur mort, près de son col.

« J'ai pris femme, dit le veilleur. Elle est vachère dans la vallée. »

La femme de Windisch voit la vachère au fichu bleu qui attend devant l'auberge, à côté du vélo de Windisch. « Je la connais, dit-elle, c'est elle qui a acheté notre lit. »

La vachère regarde de l'autre côté de la rue, vers la place de l'église. Elle mange une pomme, elle attend.

« Alors, tu ne veux plus émigrer? » lui demande Windisch. Le veilleur écrase son chapeau dans sa main. Il regarde vers l'auberge. « Je reste ici », dit-il.

Windisch voit des traces de saleté sur la chemise

du veilleur. Une veine bat sur son cou. Elle marque l'arrêt du temps. « Ma femme m'attend », dit-il, et il fait un geste de la main en direction de l'auberge.

Le tailleur soulève son chapeau devant le monument aux morts. Il marche les yeux rivés sur la pointe de ses souliers. Il s'arrête devant la porte de l'église à côté de Wilma-la-Maigre.

Le veilleur lève sa bouche jusqu'à l'oreille de Windisch. « Il y a une jeune chouette au village, dit-il. Elle s'y connaît. Wilma-la-Maigre a déjà été malade à cause d'elle. » Le veilleur sourit. « Wilma-la-Maigre est maligne. Elle a fait peur à la chouette pour qu'elle s'en aille. » Il regarde l'auberge de l'autre côté de la rue. « Bon, il faut que j'y aille », dit-il.

Un papillon passe devant le front du tailleur. Ses joues sont pâles. On dirait qu'il y a un rideau sous ses yeux.

Le papillon traverse les joues du tailleur. Il baisse la tête. Le papillon ressort à l'arrière de son crâne, tout blanc et pas froissé du tout. Wilma-la-Maigre agite son mouchoir. Le papillon traverse sa tête de part en part.

Le veilleur marche sous les arbres. Il pousse le vieux vélo de Windisch. Le cercle d'argent de la voiture cliquette dans la poche de sa veste. La vachère marche à côté de la bicyclette, pieds nus dans l'herbe. Son fichu bleu est une tache d'eau. Les feuilles nagent dedans.

La diseuse de prières entre à pas lents dans l'église avec le gros livre de cantiques. Elle porte le livre de saint Antoine.

La cloche de l'église sonne. La femme de Windisch est devant la porte de l'église. Dans l'obscurité, l'orgue bourdonne dans les cheveux de Windisch. Dans l'allée vide bordée de bancs, Windisch avance à côté de sa femme. Ses talons claquent sur les dalles. Windisch serre ses mains jointes. Il est accroché à la croix en or de sa femme. Sur la joue de Windisch une larme de verre.

Wilma-la-Maigre ne le quitte pas des yeux. Elle penche la tête. « Il a un costume de la Wehrmacht, dit-elle au tailleur. Ils vont communier et ils ne sont même pas confessés. »

Impression CPI Bussière
à Saint-Amand (Cher),
le 12 octobre 2009.
Dépôt légal : octobre 2009.
Numéro d'imprimeur : 092882/1.
ISBN 978-2-07-038238-5./Imprimé en France.
(Précédemment publié aux Éditions Maren Sell
ISBN 2-87604-0190).